# Communications in Computer and Information Science 843

More information about this series at http://www.springer.com/series/7899

Simon K. S. Cheung · Jeanne Lam
Kam Cheong Li · Oliver Au
Will W. K. Ma · Wai Shing Ho (Eds.)

# Technology in Education

## Innovative Solutions and Practices

Third International Conference, ICTE 2018
Hong Kong, China, January 9–11, 2018
Revised Selected Papers

Springer

*Editors*
Simon K. S. Cheung
The Open University of Hong Kong
Hong Kong
China

Oliver Au
The Open University of Hong Kong
Hong Kong
Hong Kong

Jeanne Lam
HKU School of Professional and Continuing Education
Hong Kong
Hong Kong

Will W. K. Ma
Technological and Higher Education Institute
Hong Kong
Hong Kong

Kam Cheong Li
The Open University of Hong Kong
Kowloon
Hong Kong

Wai Shing Ho
Caritas Institute of Higher Education
Hong Kong
Hong Kong

ISSN 1865-0929 ISSN 1865-0937 (electronic)
Communications in Computer and Information Science
ISBN 978-981-13-0007-3 ISBN 978-981-13-0008-0 (eBook)
https://doi.org/10.1007/978-981-13-0008-0

Library of Congress Control Number: 2018940141



Printed on acid-free paper

This Springer imprint is published by the registered company Springer Nature Singapore Pte Ltd.
part of Springer Nature
The registered company address is: 152 Beach Road, #21-01/04 Gateway East, Singapore 189721, Singapore

# Preface

This edited volume consists of extended papers selected from the Third International Conference on Technology in Education (ICTE 2018), which was held at the Caritas Institute of Higher Education, Hong Kong, China, during January 9–11, 2018.

Technology has become an integral part in virtually all aspects of education, broadly covering curriculum planning, instructional design, content development and delivery, communication among learners, instructors, and institution, performance assessment, and program evaluation. New and innovative approaches, practices, methods, and tools are emerging. Taking "Innovative Solutions and Practices" as its main theme, ICTE 2018 provided a platform for knowledge exchange and experience sharing among researchers and practitioners in the field of technology in education.

After a careful paper review process, a total of 27 papers were selected for inclusion in this volume. These papers are organized in four groups, namely, new learning experience with technologies, mobile learning and flipped classrooms, instructional design and teaching practices, and learning administration with technologies.

Our sincere thanks go to the conference's Organizing Committee for their effective administration and unfailing support. Our thanks also go to the international Program Committee. The high quality of the papers could not have been maintained without their professional comments and advice during the paper review process.

February 2018

Simon K. S. Cheung
Jeanne Lam
Kam Cheong Li
Oliver Au
Will W. K. Ma
Wai Shing Ho

# Organization

## Organizing Committee

### Conference Chair

| | |
|---|---|
| Fu Lee Wang | The Open University of Hong Kong, SAR China |

### Program Chairs

| | |
|---|---|
| Jeanne Lam | HKU School of Professional and Continuing Education, Hong Kong, SAR China |
| Kam Cheong Li | The Open University of Hong Kong, SAR China |

### Organizing Chair

| | |
|---|---|
| Chung Keung Poon | Caritas Institute of Higher Education, Hong Kong, SAR China |

### Financial Chair

| | |
|---|---|
| Oliver Au | The Open University of Hong Kong, SAR China |

### Members

| | |
|---|---|
| Simon K. S. Cheung | The Open University of Hong Kong, SAR China |
| Wai Shing Ho | Caritas Institute of Higher Education, SAR China |
| Ivan Lai | City University of Macau, SAR China |
| Kat Leung | Caritas Institute of Higher Education, Hong Kong, SAR China |
| Louise Luk | Caritas Institute of Higher Education, Hong Kong, SAR China |
| Will Ma | Technological and Higher Education Institute of Hong Kong, SAR China |
| Steven Ng | University of Sunderland in Hong Kong, SAR China |

## International Program Committee

### Chairs

| | |
|---|---|
| Jeanne Lam | HKU School of Professional and Continuing Education, Hong Kong, SAR China |
| Kam Cheong Li | The Open University of Hong Kong, SAR China |

### Members

| | |
|---|---|
| Zoraini Wati Abas | Open University Malaysia, Malaysia |
| Oliver Au | The Open University of Hong Kong, SAR China |

| | |
|---|---|
| Ching Sing Chai | Nanyang Technological University, Singapore |
| Gary Cheng | Education University of Hong Kong, SAR China |
| Simon K. S. Cheung | The Open University of Hong Kong, SAR China |
| Wing Sum Cheung | Nanyang Technological University, Singapore |
| Daniel Churchill | The University of Hong Kong, SAR China |
| Khe Foon Hew | The University of Hong Kong, SAR China |
| Wai Shing Ho | Caritas Institute of Higher Education, Hong Kong, SAR China |
| Kian Sam Hong | University Malaysia Sarawak, Malaysia |
| Gwo Jen Hwang | National University of Tainan, Taiwan |
| Morris Siu Yung Jong | The Chinese University of Hong Kong, SAR China |
| Ivan Lai | City University of Macau, SAR China |
| Kwok Wing Lai | University of Otago, New Zealand |
| Chwee Beng Lee | University of Western Sydney, Australia |
| Ji Yeon Lee | Inha University, South Korea |
| Ping Li | Education University of Hong Kong, SAR China |
| Chiu Pin Lin | National Hsin Chu University of Education, Taiwan |
| Will Ma | Technology and Higher Education Institute of Hong Kong, SAR China |
| Kwan Keung Ng | University of Sunderland in Hong Kong, SAR China |
| Shaun Nykvist | Queensland University of Technology, Australia |
| Innwoo Park | Korea University, South Korea |
| Choon Lang Quek | Nanyang Technological University, Singapore |
| Ali Simsek | Anadolu University, Turkey |
| Yanjie Song | Education University of Hong Kong, SAR China |
| Vincent Tam | University of Hong Kong, SAR China |
| Jeff Tang | Caritas Institute of Higher Education, Hong Kong, SAR China |
| Fu Lee Wang | The Open University of Hong Kong, SAR China |
| Chun Wang Wei | Far East University, Taiwan |
| Tak Lam Wong | Douglas College, Canada |
| Su Luan Wong | University Putra Malaysia, Malaysia |
| Yau Yeun Yeung | Education University of Hong Kong, SAR China |
| Yuen Tak Yu | City University of Hong Kong, SAR China |

## Organizer

明愛專上學院
Caritas Institute of Higher Education

## Co-organizer

INTERNATIONAL
HYBRID LEARNING SOCIETY
LEARN EVERYWHERE, EVERY WAY

## Sponsors

香港培華教育基金會
Hong Kong Pei Hua Education Foundation

VPETCity
Funded by QESS, EDB, HKSAR

# Contents

## Learning Administration with Technologies

# New Learning Experience with Technologies

# Investigating the Effectiveness of Vocabulary Learning Tasks from the Perspective of the Technique Feature Analysis: The Effects of Pictorial Annotations

Di Zou[1], Fu Lee Wang[2], Reggie Kwan[3], and Haoran Xie[1(✉)]

[1] The Education University of Hong Kong, Tai Po, Hong Kong SAR, China
hxie@eduhk.hk
[2] Caritas Institute of Higher Education, Tseung Kwan O, Hong Kong SAR, China
[3] The Open University of Hong Kong, Ho Man Tin, Hong Kong SAR, China

**Abstract.** This research examines the effectiveness of vocabulary learning tasks from the perspective of Nation and Webb's (2011) technique feature analysis. Three frequently practiced word learning exercises (reading comprehension, cloze-exercises, and sentence writing), and two types of annotations for target words (pictorial annotations, and textual annotations) were investigated. One hundred and twenty undergraduate students participated in the study and were randomly assigned to four groups to complete four tasks: reading comprehension with pictorial annotations, cloze-exercises with textual annotations, cloze-exercises with pictorial annotations, and sentence-writing with textual annotations. The post-test scores showed that the tasks of reading comprehension with pictorial annotations and doing cloze-exercises with textual annotations were similarly effective; and cloze-exercises with pictorial annotations were similarly effective as sentence-writing with textual annotations. Such results are consistent with the checklist for technique feature analysis, indicating that this framework is reliable in evaluating and predicting task effectiveness. It also shows that the involvement of imaging in an activity is conducive to word learning, and pictorial annotations promote effective learning. More integration of pictorial annotations in language learning materials is therefore suggested.

**Keywords:** Vocabulary acquisition · Technique feature analysis
Pictorial annotations · Imaging

## 1 Introduction

The importance of word knowledge and vocabulary acquisition has been widely acknowledged among language learners, teachers, and researchers. Studies have shown that a learner's word knowledge is a basic indicator and determiner of his or her language proficiency levels (Nation 2001; Zou 2016). Research on effective word learning strategies has also been a keen area among linguistics and educators for quite a long time


S. K. S. Cheung et al. (Eds.): ICTE 2018, CCIS 843, pp. 3–15, 2018.
https://doi.org/10.1007/978-981-13-0008-0_1

(Zou 2017), and the question of what factors promote effective word learning has been the focus of numerous studies on vocabulary acquisition (Hu and Nassaji 2016).

Among various research areas related to vocabulary acquisition, the topic of annotations that accompany texts to explain meanings of target words has drawn much attention of researchers (Boers et al. 2017). Many researchers are interested in comparing the effectiveness of different types of glosses. There are two main streams of research in this specific field: comparing annotations in learners' first languages and annotations in target languages; and comparing textual annotations and multimedia annotations. The present research is of the second stream; it investigates the effectiveness of word learning tasks with different types of annotations from the perspective of Nation and Webb's (2011) technique feature analysis.

The following parts of this paper include a literature review on relevant studies in multimedia annotations and the technique feature analysis, a detailed explanation of the research methodology, a report and discussions of the results, as well as a conclusion of the study.

# 2 Literature Review

## 2.1 Effectiveness of Multimedia Annotations

Over the past decades, there has been a dramatic increase in studies and practices of multimedia learning. With the fast development of computer and mobile assisted language learning, integration of multimedia in word learning activities has been widely popularized (Mohsen and Balakumar 2011). Given the importance of word knowledge in language learning, there has been an increasing number of studies on effective word learning strategies and factors that facilitate word learning (Zou et al. 2015; Xie et al. 2016; Xie et al. 2017). Being an essential part of word learning in multimodality, multimedia annotations have been widely discussed in relevant literature (Chun 2006). Multimedia annotations are also often referred to as multimedia glosses; they are defined as short definitions or notes which involve various modalities and modes: "text, picture, video, and sound" (Chun and Plass 1996, p. 183).

Compared to traditional annotations which are mainly comprised of texts, multimedia annotations are easier to understand and hence better promote learning of target words (Jacobs et al. 1994; Chun and Plass 1996; Nation 2001; Ko 2005; Abraham 2008). This is probably because images are more likely to be remembered than words, so words that are strongly associated with images can be learnt better (Underwood 1989). Learners also report that multimedia annotations better meet their needs and preferences (Jacobs et al. 1994; Plass et al. 1998). Chun and Plass (1996), Al-Seghayer (2001), and Yoshii (2006) explained that multimedia annotations are conducive to retention as they provide learners with multiple access routes to the word and therefore strengthen a deeper memory trace. From the perspective of Schmidt's (1990) noticing hypothesis, multimedia annotations facilitate word learning in that words with multimedia annotations are better noticed and recognized (Yanguas 2009). Moreover, educators believe that multimedia annotation make better use of authentic materials (Jacobs et al. 1994).

## 2.2 Technique Feature Analysis

Nation and Webb (2011) proposed a checklist for technique feature analysis to better predict, evaluate and explain the effectiveness of diverse word-focused tasks. The TFA includes five main categories that are conducive to word learning, including motivation, noticing, retrieval, generation and retention. The importance of motivation for language learning has been acclaimed by a large number of researchers; three representatives are Bagnole (1993), Dornyei (1994), and Gardner (2007). Noticing is also believed to be an essential factor for successful word learning as learners ought to consciously pay attention to a particular aspect of word knowledge so as to retain this piece of information (Schmidt 2010). Retrieval is defined as the process of accessing stored information or recalling previously encountered information (Nation 2001). The act of recalling an item is more conducive to word learning than presenting it again, and the retrieval route to the target information can also be strengthened by being used successfully (Baddeley 1990), so retrieval is widely considered as a facilitative factor for word learning. The fourth factor, generation, plays an important role in effective word learning as many researchers noticed that tasks involving generative use of words lead to better learning than those without generative use (Joe 1998; Nation 2001). Additionally, retention promotes effective word learning as it involves successful linking of form and meaning, instantiation, imaging and elimination of interference (Nation and Webb 2011).

According to the technique feature analysis, the category motivation includes three questions asking whether the activity has a clear word learning goal, whether it motivates learning, and whether learners decide what words to learn (Nation and Webb 2011). The category noticing also includes three questions asking whether the activity focuses attention on target words, raises learners' awareness of the learning of the words, and induces negotiation of the words' meanings, forms or use. The four questions in the category retrieval include whether the activity involves retrieval of the word, whether the retrieval is productive and recall, whether there are multiple retrievals, and whether there is spacing between them. The category generation focuses on whether generative use is induced, whether it's productive, and whether a marked change involving use of other words is entailed. The last category retention checks whether the activity ensures form-meaning linking, involves instantiation and imaging, and avoids interference (Nation and Webb 2011). To sum up, there are eighteen questions in the checklist.

Based on this checklist for technique feature analysis, the effectiveness of a task can be evaluated by checking how many factors in the list are involved in the activity (Nation and Webb 2011). If the answer to a question is yes, one point is obtained; and if no, zero point is given (see Table 1). For example, the task doing a cloze-exercise with textual annotations has a score of 7 because (1) it involves a clear goal of matching the target words with appropriate contexts; (2) it motivates learning as meaningful contexts with semantic associations are given; (3) learners need to focus on the target words, understand them and fill them in the blanks; (4) learners are aware of the learning of the target words as the activity focuses on the words; (5) receptive generative use of the target words is induced since learners need to compare different words so as to select those that best suit the given contexts; (6) successful linking of form and meaning is ensured when learners write down the target words in the blanks where the contexts are appropriate; and (7) no inference is involved.

**Table 1.** The checklist for technique feature analysis (adopted from Nation and Webb 2011, p. 7)

| Criteria | Scores | |
|---|---|---|
| *Motivation* | | |
| Is there a clear vocabulary learning goal? | 0 | 1 |
| Does the activity motivate learning? | 0 | 1 |
| Do the learners select the words? | 0 | 1 |
| *Noticing* | | |
| Does the activity focus attention on the target words? | 0 | 1 |
| Does the activity raise awareness of new vocabulary learning? | 0 | 1 |
| Does the activity involve negotiation? | 0 | 1 |
| *Retrieval* | | |
| Does the activity involve retrieval of the word? | 0 | 1 |
| Is it productive retrieval? | 0 | 1 |
| Is it recall? | 0 | 1 |
| Are there multiple retrievals of each word? | 0 | 1 |
| Is there spacing between retrievals? | 0 | 1 |
| *Generation* | | |
| Does the activity involve generative use? | 0 | 1 |
| Is it productive? | 0 | 1 |
| Is there a marked change that involves the use of other words? | 0 | 1 |
| *Retention* | | |
| Does the activity ensure successful linking of form and meaning? | 0 | 1 |
| Does the activity involve instantiation? | 0 | 1 |
| Does the activity involve imaging? | 0 | 1 |
| Does the activity avoid interference? | 0 | 1 |
| *Maximum score* | 18 | |

## 2.3 Word Learning Tasks

Among various word learning tasks, three of them are frequently examined by researchers, for example reading comprehension, cloze exercises and sentence-writing, as they are three most commonly practiced word learning activities (Zou 2016, 2017). Results of previous studies have basically agreed that cloze exercises are more effective than reading comprehension, but less effective than sentence-writing (Kim 2008; Keating 2008; Zou 2012). According to Laufer and Hulstijn's (2001) involvement load hypothesis, the main differences among the three tasks include: (1) cloze exercises and sentence-writing involve evaluation of the meanings and use of target words as learners need to decide what contexts are appropriate for the words or create new contexts for the words, but reading comprehension does not; and (2) sentence-writing induces deeper levels of processing than cloze-exercises as it involves creating new contexts, while cloze-exercises do not.

However, much of the research up to now has been restricted to the investigation of these tasks with textual annotations, and little has been conducted to examine the effectiveness of these tasks when multimedia annotations are involved, although multimedia annotations can also be easily integrated in the three activities.

Inferred from the checklist of technique feature analysis, cloze-exercises with textual annotations may be similarly effective as reading comprehension with pictorial annotations as they both induce 7 scores. The difference between them is that cloze-exercises involves generative use, while reading comprehension does not; and reading comprehension with pictorial annotations involves imaging, but cloze-exercises with textual annotations does not (see Table 2).

**Table 2.** Differences among the four tasks

| | Generative use | Productive generative use | Imaging |
|---|---|---|---|
| Task 1: Reading comprehension with pictorial annotations | – | – | + |
| Task 2: Cloze-exercises with textual annotations | + | – | – |
| Task 3: Cloze-exercises with pictorial annotations | + | – | + |
| Task 4: Sentence-writing with textual annotations | + | + | - |

Also, the task cloze-exercises with pictorial annotations may be similarly effective as sentence-writing with textual annotations as they both have 8 scores according to the checklist for technique feature analysis. The difference between them is that cloze-exercises with pictorial annotations involve imaging, while sentence-writing with textual annotations does not; and sentence-writing involves productive generative use, but cloze-exercises does not.

## 3 Method

One hundred and twenty non-English-major-freshmen aged between 18 and 21 participated in the study. Their English proficiency levels were intermediate. These participants were asked to complete one of the four tasks randomly, as shown in Fig. 1.

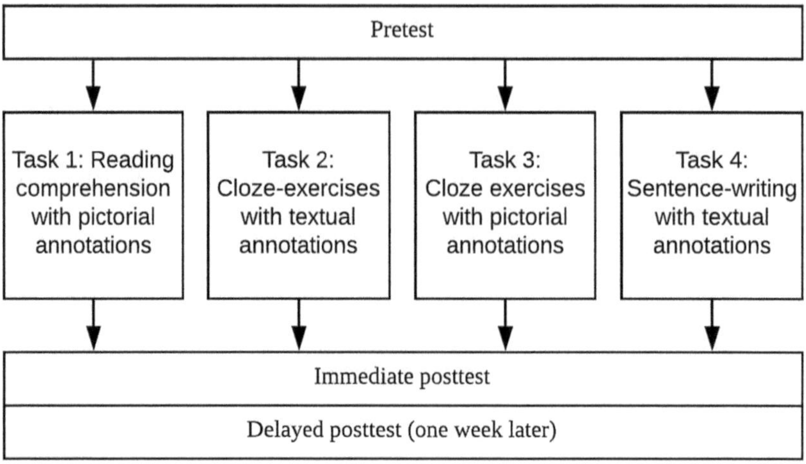


**Fig. 1.** Research design

To measure the effectiveness of these tasks, thirty participants from each group (see Table 3) were tested immediately after task completion and unexpectedly one week later. The two posttests were the same; the participants were asked to provide English synonyms or definitions of the target words and generate original sentences using them. The same procedure of Zou's (2016) study was applied in this project.

**Table 3.** Modified vocabulary knowledge scale

| | |
|---|---|
| 1. | I feel I have learnt this word before, but I do not know what it means |
| 2. | I think the word means_________ |
| 3. | I know this word means_________ |
| 4. | I do not know how to use this word in a sentence |
| 5. | I can use this word in a sentence:_________ |

## 3.1 Tasks

Task 1 provided the participants with a reading text and a list of ten target words with pictorial annotations. Task 2 provided the participants with the same reading text, but the ten target words were replaced by ten blanks, and the annotations for the target words were textual; the participants were asked to fill in the blanks with the most appropriate words. Task 3 also asked the participants to do cloze-exercises, but pictorial annotations were provided in this task. Task 4 provided the participants with textual annotations and asked them to write sentences using the target words. As illustrated in Fig. 2, Task 1 and 3 both involved pictorial annotations, and Task 2 and 4 involved textual annotations. Task 2 and 3 were similar in that they both were cloze-exercises but were different as Task 2 provided textual annotations while Task 3 pictorial annotations.

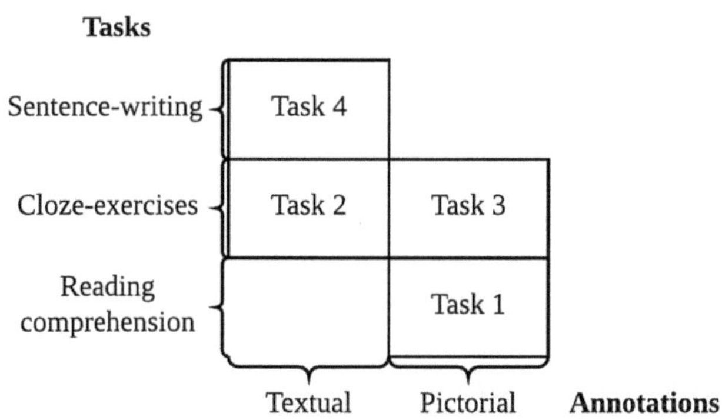


**Fig. 2.** Similarities and differences of the four tasks

The ten target words were *burglarize, dash, grin, inflammation, rake, scribble, shatter, shiver, tumble, and wrath.* These ten words were selected as they are all tangible to the senses and can be easily imagined, and they were likely to be unknown to the participants because they were out of the most frequently used 6000 words.

An excerpt of the reading text is shown as follows:

> "I have a test tomorrow. I need to read two chapters, but the pain caused by the inflammation of my neck makes it difficult to concentrate on the text. I can't pass the test. What do I do? Shall I keep studying? Can I take the test some other time? Shall I give up?"

## 3.2 Annotations

The textual annotations of the target words were developed from their definitions given by The Longman Dictionary of Contemporary English, Fifth Edition with Writing Assistant (2014). This dictionary was selected as it is one of the most commonly used dictionaries among English learners and the participants of this study were very familiar with it.

The pictorial annotations of the target words were developed by adding images that can depict the meanings of the target words well to the textual annotations. A pilot study was conducted among ten students and teachers, asking them whether the images could represent the meanings of the target words well. And very positive comments were received. An example of the pictorial annotation is given in Fig. 3 below. All images were from the internet.

Inflammation (n.) a red, painful, and often swollen area in or on a part of your body.

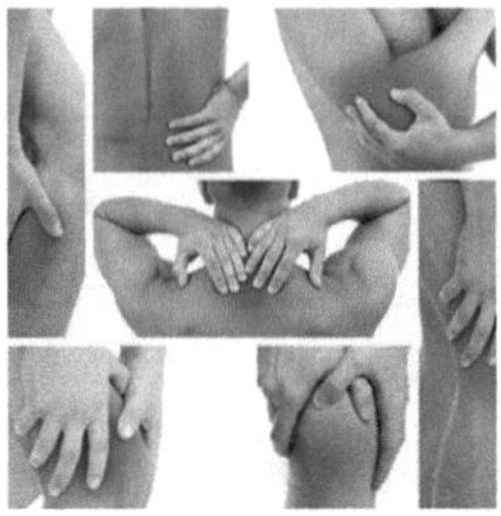

**Fig. 3.** An example pictorial annotation (Retrieved from https://www.google.com.hk/search?q=inflammation&rlz=1C1ASVB_enHK730HK730&source=lnms&tbm=isch&sa=X&ved=0ahUKEwj6-PrxwZ3ZAhXHfbwKHRkTDX0Q_AUICigB&biw=1862&bih=886#imgrc=B9–GkThq35XWM)

### 3.3 Pretest and Posttests

As demonstrated in Fig. 1, a pretest was conducted to measure the participants' initial knowledge of the target words. The format of the pretest is very simple; the participants were asked to indicate whether they knew the meanings of the target words before. The results showed that these participants had zero pre-knowledge of the words.

A modified version of Paribakht and Wesche's (1997) vocabulary knowledge scale (see Table 3) was used in the posttests to measure the participants' learning of the target words. This testing tool was used as the participants' initial development of word knowledge was the focus of this research (Zou et al. 2017a, b, c; Xie et al. 2016). Another advantage of this modified vocabulary knowledge scale is that it can measure even partial development of learners' word knowledge. This is very important as learners can hardly learn all aspects of knowledge of a word by encountering it once only (Nation 2001), so it is crucial to select a measurement that can evaluate even small developments of learners' word knowledge.

One posttest was conducted immediately after the participants completed the assigned tasks to measure their initial learning of the target words; and a delayed posttest was conducted one week after the experiment to evaluate the participants' retention of the target words.

Two researchers marked the participants' answers to the modified vocabulary knowledge scales independently. Their scores were analyzed later, and the inter-rater reliability was around .95. Such scores were then entered into SPSS. One-way ANOVA tests were run to check whether statistical significance existed among the four groups of participants' immediate and delayed posttest scores.

### 3.4 Interview

To further tap into the participants' thinking processes while doing the assigned tasks, ten participants were interviewed after task completion. The questions were basically open-ended questions, and the participants were encouraged to report whatever they think and feel during task completion. Some of the guided questions are: what do you think about the tasks? Do you feel the annotations helpful for your learning of the target words? What may be the possible effects of the annotations on your learning of the target words? What other factors do you feel important for word learning? Why do you think so?

The participants could speak either Chinese or English, as they preferred, during the interviews. This aimed to ensure that all participants were able to express themselves freely as some participants may feel difficult to convey their feelings or thoughts in English.

## 4 Results

The participants who did the tasks of reading comprehension with pictorial annotations and doing cloze-exercises with textual annotations had similar posttest scores. The immediate posttest scores of the participants who did these two tasks were respectively 6.16 and 6.32; and the delayed posttest scores were respectively 4.07 and 4.18. Cloze-exercises with pictorial annotations were similarly effective as sentence-writing with textual annotations. The immediate and delayed posttest scores of the cloze-exercises were 7.68 and 5.45, and those of the sentence-writing were 7.85 and 5.52 (Table 4).

**Table 4.** Participants' scores in the immediate and delayed posttests

| | Immediate posttest | | Delayed posttest | |
|---|---|---|---|---|
| | M. | SD | M. | SD |
| Task 1: Reading comprehension with pictorial annotations | 6.16 | 4.02 | 4.07 | 4.67 |
| Task 2: Cloze-exercises with textual annotations | 6.32 | 3.89 | 4.18 | 4.65 |
| Task 3: Cloze-exercises with pictorial annotations | 7.68 | 4.13 | 5.45 | 4.82 |
| Task 4: Sentence-writing with textual annotations | 7.85 | 4.11 | 5.52 | 4.70 |

Results of the ANOVA tests also showed that these four tasks can be grouped into two homogenous subsets. Cloze-exercises with pictorial annotations and sentence-writing with textual annotations were in one subset, and they led to significantly better word learning than reading comprehension with pictorial annotations and cloze-exercises with textual annotations, which were in the other subset.

Such results are consistent with the checklist for technique feature analysis. Pictorial annotations contribute one more score than textual annotations as the element imaging is involved. The task cloze-exercises has one more score than the task reading comprehension because of the element generative use. Moreover, the task sentence-writing has the highest score as it induces productive generative use. Therefore, the TFA scores of task 3 and 4 are the same, and those of task 1 and 2 are the same. Also, the scores of task 3 and 4 are higher than those of task 1 and 2. The empirical results indicate that the predictions of the technique feature analysis are correct.

## 5 Discussion

The results of this study provide supporting evidence for the checklist for technique feature analysis, indicating that this framework is reliable in evaluating and predicting task effectiveness. Moreover, it shows that the involvement of imaging in an activity is conducive to word learning, as cloze-exercises with pictorial annotations were more effective than cloze-exercises with textual annotations. Such results add further support to previous studies like Chun and Plass (1996), Yeh and Wang (2003), Yoshii and Flaitz (2002), Yoshii (2006), and Boers et al. (2017). That is, learners who were given annotations with pictures had better learning outcomes than those who were provided with text-only annotations. Different from the previous studies, the present research investigated annotations from the perspective of the technique feature analysis. This is one of the innovations of this research.

The interview scripts of the participants also showed that the participants believed that images could help them better understand the meanings of the target words. Some participants even noted that they had some difficulties in understanding the texts, and it were the images that facilitated their comprehension. They felt more confident about their understanding, and they also believed that the images contributed largely to their learning of the target words. Moreover, many participants who learned with the textual annotations stated that they believed they could learn better if images that depict the meanings of the target words could be given. Additionally, some participants pointed out that they often used visual aids to facilitate their word learning and they found visual aids very effective in facilitating their understanding of the words' meanings. Several participants reported that they liked using word learning APPs that integrated visual aids.

The checklist for technique feature analysis is an effective framework that can be used to predict or estimate the effectiveness of word learning tasks. It was developed by Nation and Webb in 2011, but only two studies (Hu and Nassaji 2016; Gohar et al. 2018) have investigated the reliability of this checklist so far as we know. This study further examined the technique feature analysis and highlighted the importance of imaging for word learning.

## 6 Conclusion

This research examines the effectiveness of four word-focused tasks from the perspective of Nation and Webb's (2011) technique feature analysis. One hundred and twenty undergraduate students participated in the study, the results of which showed that the tasks of reading comprehension with pictorial annotations and doing cloze-exercises with textual annotations were similarly effective, and that cloze-exercises with pictorial annotations were similarly effective as sentence-writing with textual annotations. Such results are consistent with the checklist for technique feature analysis, indicating that this framework is reliable in evaluating and predicting task effectiveness. It also shows that the involvement of imaging in an activity is conducive to word learning, more integration of pictorial annotations in language learning materials is therefore suggested.

This study is limited in terms of its scope and time span. Future research is therefore suggested to investigate more types of tasks and more types of annotations. Annotations in the formats of audios, GIFs, videos, etc. are of interest. It is also advised that two delayed posttests or a delayed posttest that is arranged two weeks after the treatment could be conducted so that the participants' retention of the target words can be better evaluated.

**Acknowledgement.** This study was fully supported by the Start-Up Research Grant (RG 54/2017-2018R) of The Education University of Hong Kong and a grant from Research Grants Council of Hong Kong Special Administrative Region, China (UGC/FDS11/E03/16).

## References

Abraham, L.: Computer-mediated glosses in second language reading comprehension and vocabulary learning: a meta-analysis. Comput. Assist. Lang. Learn. **12**(3), 199–226 (2008)

Al-Seghayer, K.: The effect of multimedia annotation modes on L2 vocabulary acquisition: a comparative study. Lang. Learn. Technol. **5**(1), 202–232 (2001)

Baddeley, A.D.: Human Memory. Lawrence Erlbaum Associates, London (1990)

Bagnole, J.W.: The magic and mystery of motivation in TEFL and language learning. TESOL Matters, February/March, 10–16 (1993)

Boers, F., Warren, P., He, L., Deconinck, J.: Does adding pictures to glosses enhance vocabulary uptake from reading? System **66**, 113–129 (2017)

Chun, D.: CALL technologies for L2 reading. In: Ducate, L., Arnold, N. (eds.) Calling on CALL: From Theory and Research to New Directions in Foreign Language Teaching, pp. 69–98. CALICO, San Marcos (2006)

Chun, D.M., Plass, J.L.: Effects of multimedia annotations on vocabulary acquisition. Modern Lang. J. **80**(2), 183–198 (1996)

Dornyei, Z.: Motivation and motivating in the foreign language classroom? Modern Lang. J. **78**, 273–284 (1994)

Gardner, R.C.: Motivation and second language acquisition. Porta Linguarum **8**, 9–20 (2007)

Gohar, M.J., Rahmanian, M., Soleimani, H.: Technique feature analysis or involvement load hypothesis: estimating their predictive power in vocabulary learning. J. Psycholinguist. Res. 1–11 (2018). https://doi.org/10.1007/s10936-018-9568-5

Hu, H.C.M., Nassaji, H.: Effective vocabulary learning tasks: involvement load hypothesis versus technique feature analysis. System **56**, 28–39 (2016)

Jacobs, G.M., Dufon, P., Fong, C.H.: L1 and L2 vocabulary glosses in L2 reading passages: their effectiveness for increasing comprehension and vocabulary knowledge. J. Res. Read. **17**(1), 19–28 (1994)

Joe, A.: What effects do text–based tasks promoting generation have on incidental vocabulary acquisition? Appl. Linguist. **19**, 357–377 (1998)

Keating, G.: Task effectiveness and word learning in a second language: the involvement load hypothesis on trial. Lang. Teach. Res. **12**(3), 365–386 (2008)

Kim, Y.: The role of task-induced involvement and learner proficiency in L2 vocabulary acquisition. Lang. Learn. **58**(2), 285–325 (2008)

Ko, M.: Glosses, comprehension, and strategy use. Read. Foreign Lang. **17**(2), 125–143 (2005)

Mohsen, M.A., Balakumar, M.: A review of multimedia glosses and their effects on L2 vocabulary acquisition in CALL literature. ReCALL **23**(02), 135–159 (2011)

Nation, I.S.P.: Learning Vocabulary in Another Language. Cambridge University Press, New York (2001)

Nation, P., Webb, A.: Researching and Analyzing Vocabulary. Cengage Learning, Heinle (2011)

Paribakht, T.S., Wesche, M.: Vocabulary enhancement activities and reading for meaning in second language vocabulary acquisition. In: Coady, J., Huckin, T. (eds.) Second Language Vocabulary Acquisition: A Rationale for Pedagogy, pp. 174–200. Cambridge University Press, New York (1997)

Plass, J.L., Chun, D.M., Mayer, R.E., Leutner, D.: Supporting visual and verbal learning preferences in a second-language multimedia learning environment. J. Educ. Psychol. **90**, 25–36 (1998)

Schmidt, R.: The role of consciousness in second language learning. Appl. Linguist. **11**, 129–158 (1990)

Schmidt, R.: Attention, awareness, and individual differences in language learning. In: Chan, W.M., Chi, S., Cin, K.N., Istanto, J., Nagami, M., Sew, J.W., Suthiwan, T., Walker, I. (eds.) Proceedings of CLaSIC 2010, pp. 721–737. Centre for Language Studies, National University of Singapore, Singapore (2010)

Underwood, J.: HyperCard and interactive video. CALICO **6**(3), 7–20 (1989)

Yanguas, I.: Multimedia glosses and their effect on L2 text comprehension and vocabulary learning. Lang. Learn. Technol. **13**(2), 48–76 (2009)

Yeh, Y., Wang, C.-W.: Effects of multimedia vocabulary annotations and learning styles on vocabulary learning. CALICO J. **21**, 131–144 (2003)

Yoshii, M.: L1 and L2 glosses: their effects on incidental vocabulary learning. Lang. Learn. Technol. **10**(3), 85–101 (2006)

Yoshii, M., Flaitz, J.: Second language incidental vocabulary retention: the effect of picture and annotation types. CALICO J. **20**, 33–58 (2002)

Xie, H.R., Zou, D., Lau, Y.K., Wang, F.L., Wong, T.L.: Generating incidental word-learning tasks via topic-based and load-based profiles. IEEE Multimedia **23**(1), 60–70 (2016)

Xie, H.R., Zou, D., Wang, F.L., Wong, T.-L.: A review on recent development of the involvement load hypothesis. In: Cheung, S.K.S., Kwok, L.-F., Ma, W.W.K., Lee, L.-K., Yang, H. (eds.) ICBL 2017. LNCS, vol. 10309, pp. 447–452. Springer, Cham (2017). https://doi.org/10.1007/978-3-319-59360-9_39

Zou, D.: A study of the components of the involvement load hypothesis: how involvement load should be allocated to "Search" and "Evaluation". Unpublished Ph.D. dissertation, City University of Hong Kong, Hong Kong (2012)

Zou, D.: Comparing dictionary-induced vocabulary learning and inferencing in the context of reading. Lexikos **26**, 372–390 (2016)

Zou, D.: Vocabulary acquisition through cloze exercises, sentence-writing and composition-writing: extending the evaluation component of the involvement load hypothesis. Lang. Teach. Res. **21**(1), 54–75 (2017)

Zou, D., Wang, F.L., Xie, H.R., Wong, T.L., Kwan, R.: A flexible graph-based model for facilitating digital learning activities. Int. J. Innov. Learn. (2017a, forthcoming)

Zou, D., Xie, H.R., Wang, F.L.: The use of monolingual mobile dictionaries in the context of reading by intermediate Cantonese EFL learners in Hong Kong. In: Helm, F., Bradley, L., Guarda, M., Thouesny, S. (eds.) Critical CALL, pp. 569–574. Researchpublishing.net (2015)

Zou, D., Xie, H.R., Wang, F.L., Wong, T.L.: Modeling second language learners for learning task recommendation. Int. J. Innov. Learn. (2017b, forthcoming)

Zou, D., Xie, H., Wong, T.-L., Wang, F.L., Kwan, R., Chan, W.H.: An Explicit Learner Profiling Model for Personalized Word Learning Recommendation. In: Huang, T.-C., Lau, R., Huang, Y.-M., Spaniol, M., Yuen, C.-H. (eds.) SETE 2017. LNCS, vol. 10676, pp. 495–499. Springer, Cham (2017c). https://doi.org/10.1007/978-3-319-71084-6_58

# A Virtual Clinical Learning Environment for Nurse Training

Sin-Chun Ng[1(✉)], Lap-Kei Lee[1], Andrew K. Lui[1], Ka-Fai Wong[2], Wan-Yee Chan[2], and Hiu-Hin Tam[1]

[1] School of Science and Technology, The Open University of Hong Kong, Ho Man Tin, Kowloon, Hong Kong SAR, China
{scng, lklee, alui, thhtam}@ouhk.edu.hk

[2] School of Nursing and Health Studies, The Open University of Hong Kong, Ho Man Tin, Kowloon, Hong Kong SAR, China
{kafwong, awychan}@ouhk.edu.hk

**Abstract.** Every nursing student is trained to possess certain skill set before they go for the clinical training in a hospital. This paper introduces the use of virtual reality to simulate a hospital ward for nurse training. The equipment in our virtual ward is carefully designed to simulate the equipment in Hong Kong hospital wards. Our virtual ward will provide several demonstrations on common ward operation tasks. Through the interactions provided in the virtual ward, nursing students can understand the ward operation routines in a better way. Our application is expected to reduce inexperienced nursing students' anxiety and make them more familiar with the ward environment, which can then minimize medical error in their real practicum.

**Keywords:** Virtual reality · Nurse training · Virtual ward environment

## 1 Introduction

Every nursing student is trained to possess the fundamental nursing skills, e.g., reporting vital signs of a patient, performing simple wound dressing, before they go for the clinical training in a hospital. Nursing students have also to be familiar with a general hospital ward environment. For junior nursing students who have no clear understanding on the ward environment, the most effective teaching way is to bring them to a real clinical ward. Ward orientation is the way to achieve this goal (Lee and French 1997). Yet in Hong Kong, it is hard to arrange the ward orientation visits due to the high nurse-to-patient ratio of the hospitals; the ward space is always filled with patients, medical staff and equipment. Traditionally, the nursing students are trained by videos, live demonstration and hands-on practices in the nursing laboratories. The effectiveness of these methods is not questioned as they have been adopted for many years. Medley and Horne (2005) showed that using simulation technology to provide more interactions in nursing education can enhance nursing students' learning experience and facilitate their understanding on the general ward environment. With the advancement in virtual reality (VR), it is now possible to offer an immersive learner experience to supplement the traditional ways for nursing education.


S. K. S. Cheung et al. (Eds.): ICTE 2018, CCIS 843, pp. 16–25, 2018.
https://doi.org/10.1007/978-981-13-0008-0_2

In this paper, we propose the use of virtual reality as a contemporary teaching and learning strategy for nursing students. Virtual reality is a computer technology that uses software to generate a 3D virtual environment and simulates a physical presence of the user in an imagined world. Most of the existing virtual ward simulators are designed based on non-local wards with a spacious environment or wards with specific use (see Sect. 2 for more details). These virtual wards are too different than the wards in Hong Kong and cannot help the local nursing students to get familiar with the hospital wards in Hong Kong. We therefore implemented a virtual ward environment using VR to simulate a general ward environment in Hong Kong. With that VR experience in ward environment, nursing students can be more familiar with real practicum settings. Their anxiety towards learning in practicum can be reduced effectively.

This paper focuses on the design of our virtual ward environment for nurse education in Hong Kong. The virtual ward is designed with high similarity to the real one in Hong Kong hospitals; we include characteristics of local ward, e.g., room design, floor plan, nurse station, treatment room, signage, posters and human characters. The equipment in our virtual ward is also carefully designed to simulate the equipment in Hong Kong hospital wards. This will help the nursing students to get familiar with the ward equipment and better understand how to select the correct equipment during ward operations.

Mastering common ward operations is an essential skill of nursing student for their future duties in hospital (McCaugherty 1991). More interaction between the nursing students and the virtual ward environment can enhance nursing students' understanding of the ward operation routines (Manias and Street 2001). We incorporated several interactive elements and features into the virtual ward. The interactions are designed for understanding the ward operation routines and recognizing the ward facilities and equipment. The virtual ward also provides several demonstrations on common ward operation. Our application is expected to reduce inexperienced nursing students' anxiety and make them more familiar with the ward environment, which can then minimize medical error in their real practicum.

## 2 Background in Nursing Education

### 2.1 Ward Orientation

In nursing education, the theories taught are much related in the real ward and clinical practices. Before the nursing students go for real training in a hospital as a practicum, they must be competent in the basic ward duty and operation, including patient cares and observation. It is essential for them to be familiar with a hospital ward environment to understand the setup of each room in ward (Papp et al. 2003). The acknowledgement of each equipment involved and its function are also important in their learning. A ward orientation is included in the syllabus of nursing education so as to prepare nursing students for their practicum in different Hong Kong hospitals.

It is becoming harder to arrange the ward orientation in Hong Kong hospitals. One reason is the high ward occupation rate, which was as high as 130% as of March 2016 (Tsang 2016). Another reason is the shortage of nursing trainer among all the Hong

Kong hospitals (Tsang 2017). These two limitations are long-term and is expected to worsen. A plausible solution to these limitations is using computational simulation and virtual reality in the nurse training, which has been already adopted in other parts of the nursing education for several years.

## 2.2 Applications of Computational Simulation and Virtual Reality

Traditionally, the nursing students are trained by videos, live demonstration and hands-on practices in the nursing laboratories. Yet nursing students often find difficulties to visualize a dummy model as a real patient and to make the transition from the learning laboratories to the real patient setting. Medley and Horne (2005) used simulation technology to provide experiential learning to the nursing students, which improve the learning experience and effectiveness of the nursing students. Besides, computational simulation does not make threats to safety of real patients and can simulate specific and unique patient situations. Computational simulation has also been applied to develop serious games for nursing education (see Skiba (2008) for some examples).

With the advancement on computer graphics techniques and tools, virtual reality (VR) is growing in popularity on various applications (see the survey by Zhao (2009) and references therein). VR is a new technology that offers much beyond the previous simple 2D and 3D display of computational simulation. With the use of VR technology, the user can enter the virtual world with the related VR headset to experience something that the user seldom has the chance to come across. The VR platform also allows us to create, modify and manipulate the 3D objects in the same way as we do on physical object without the existence of real-world limitations (Bricken 1991). In other words, VR is a platform of a high degree of realistic simulation for the freedom to create any scenario we would like to implement for.

Educational researchers are aware of the possibilities given by virtual reality (Christou 2010). VR is particularly suitable for nursing education, as it provides a safe learning environment without the risk of harming real patients and it provides a controlled environment for the instructors to interact and keep track of the performance of the students. Second Life (Skiba 2009) is a well-known web-based VR environment that provides clinical simulations of a number of scenarios where the students have to carry out some routine tasks (e.g. checking a patient's vital signs) in the ward. It mainly focuses on providing a social interaction platform with people and it works like playing a clinical game. de Freitas et al. (2009) proposed an evaluation methodology for learning activities in Second Life. Jenson and Forsyth (2012) implemented a virtual ward for teaching ward duty including patient care and clinical judgment in an entertaining and interactive way. Besides clinical simulation, a children hospital is also simulated for training nurses to get familiar with the real environment of Lurie Children's Hospital (Vila et al. 2003) with a focus on wayfinding and navigation. Lau (2009) also implemented a virtual psychiatric ward for psychiatric education.

# 3 Virtual Ward Environment

This section gives the detailed design of the virtual ward environment, which aims to simulate a typical medical ward in a Hong Kong hospital so that it can be used for ward orientation for junior nursing students. A nursing student can explore and "see" the virtual ward through the headset of the VR system, and interact with some items in the virtual ward by using wireless controller of the VR system.

The virtual ward environment is built with the VR development platform Unity3D and several software for building the 3D models of objects in the virtual ward including Autodesk Maya, Blender, MotionBuilder and Adobe Photoshop. The virtual ward can be run with a virtual reality system (e.g., HTC Vive) on a personal computer with at least 8 GB of main memory and a graphics card (GPU) (e.g., NVidia GeForce GTX 1050).

## 3.1 Overview of Design

To achieve a high degree of realism, our design references the features of wards in Hong Kong public hospitals. Yet there is no unified design of wards for different hospitals and a difficulty is to integrate this divergence of designs into the limited space of our virtual ward environment. We study and figure out some important common features of these designs (to be discussed in the subsequent subsections) so that the virtual ward is able to offer a similar appearance of a real ward environment in Hong Kong. Our design of the virtual ward also takes reference to the standard requirements of the Hospital Authority (HA) in Hong Kong.

## 3.2 Ward Setup

**Room Design.** A medical ward in Hong Kong typically includes plenty of beds for inpatient care services. These beds for patients are separately located in different rooms called *patient cubicles*. According to general ward layout of Hong Kong public hospitals, a general ward has the capacity of at least 60 patients normally. These 60 patients are allocated to several patient cubicles. Each patient cubicle is normally designed to accommodate 8 patient beds, as shown in Fig. 1. There may also be a small patient cubicle with only 4 patient beds. Our virtual ward has 7 normal patient cubicles and one small patient cubicle for patient allocation.

**Floor Plan.** The floor plan of the virtual ward is shown in Fig. 2. A T-shape corridor is commonly found at the floor plan of the real ward among all hospitals and this is thus included in the design of our floor plan. We also allocated 8 temporary patient beds in the corridor to reflect the common phenomenon in public hospitals in Hong Kong due to the high ward occupation rate.

**Nurse Station.** Nurse station is a basic ward facility where the on-duty nurses handle assembles and carry out administrative or other duties behind the patients. It is a semi-open area with a service counter. As a precaution measurement, patients in more serious condition are allocated to the patient cubicle directly opposite to the nurse

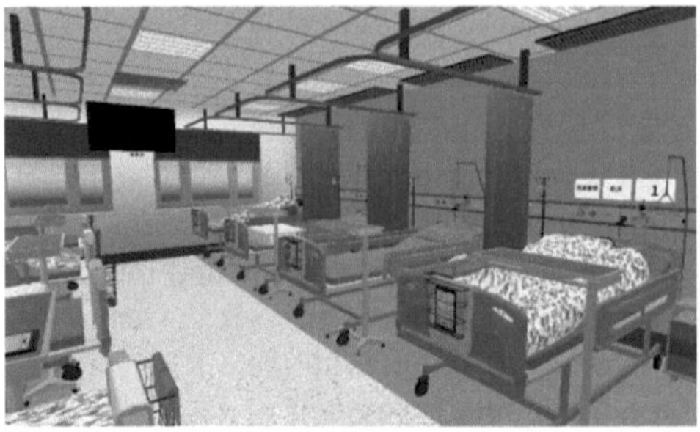

**Fig. 1.** A patient cubicle in our virtual ward.

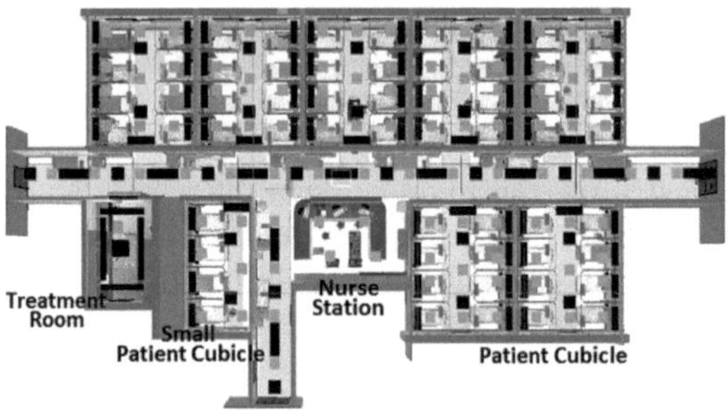


**Fig. 2.** Floor plan of our virtual ward.

station so that these patients can be observed by nurses in the nurse station directly and immediate action can be taken for urgent cases (as shown in Fig. 3). To facilitate patient observation, we replace the wall of that patient cubicle (which faces the nurse station) with a glass.

**Fig. 3.** The patient cubicle observable from the nurse station is for patients under special care.

**Treatment Room.** Treatment room is a special room for on-duty nurses to give a basic medical treatment to patients in need. Our treatment room (Fig. 4) follows the common design of Hong Kong public hospitals with limited space.

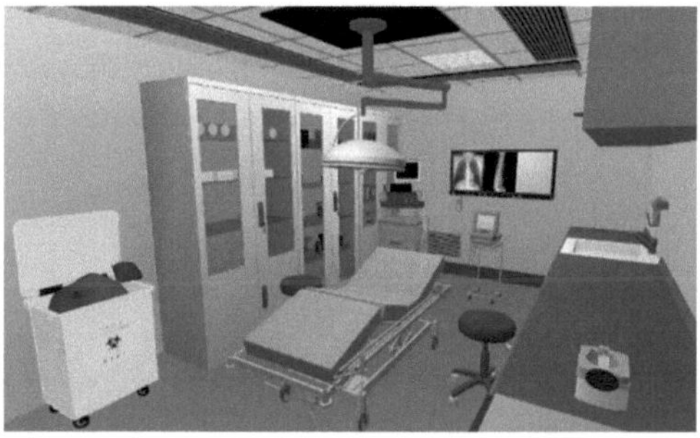

**Fig. 4.** The treatment room in our virtual ward. (Color figure online)

**Signage and Posters.** Signage and posters are included in the virtual ward, which are commonly found in the public hospitals in Hong Kong such that the nursing students can understand the location of each room and nurse station in an easy way (Fig. 5).

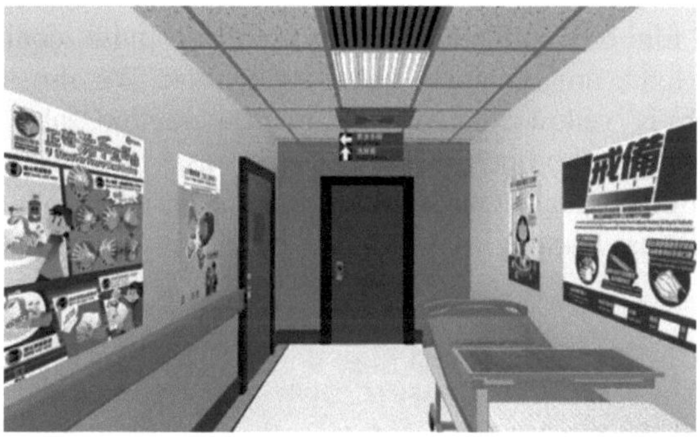

**Fig. 5.** Signage and posters in our virtual ward.

### 3.3 Equipment and Interactive Labels

Ward equipment is a crucial element in our virtual ward. A nursing student has to be able to recognize the equipment, memorize its name and acknowledge its location. To this end, we include interactive name labels for the important equipment in our virtual ward to enhance students' learning. These name labels are 3D text words hidden originally so that they do not obstruct the user's view. The labels are popped up when the user is walking nearby the target area of the equipment.

**Patient Bed.** Patient care is one of the normal ward duty which takes place at each patient cubicle. Patient bed is the basic unit of every patient cubicle, in which a bed table and a ring handrail are provided. There are also the patient care labels on the wall above the patient bed to indicate the health condition of the patient and the special needs for the patient. Some patients have extra equipment such as oxygen tube, intravenous drip and heart rate monitor, which are set up to simulate the situation that a patient is under a relatively serious condition (Fig. 6).

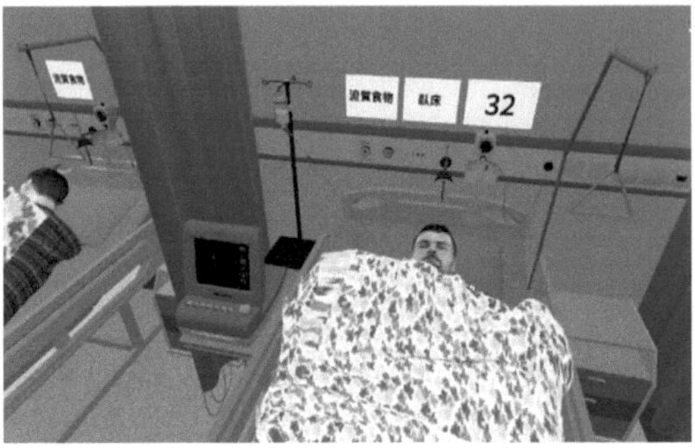


**Fig. 6.** Patient bed for a patient with a relatively serious condition.

**Equipment in Treatment Room.** We label several important equipment in the treatment room which should be recognized by the nursing students (Fig. 7). This includes an X-ray film box, a digital blood pressure and pulse monitor, an ultrasonic device, a surgical light, drug cabinets, and a sharps box. We also include a medical waste box, which is yellow-colored with a clear caution label and contains a red-colored waste bag tied properly (Fig. 4). Such waste bin is essential in the treatment rooms of public hospitals. Our treatment room is designed to highlight the above equipment for students' learning.

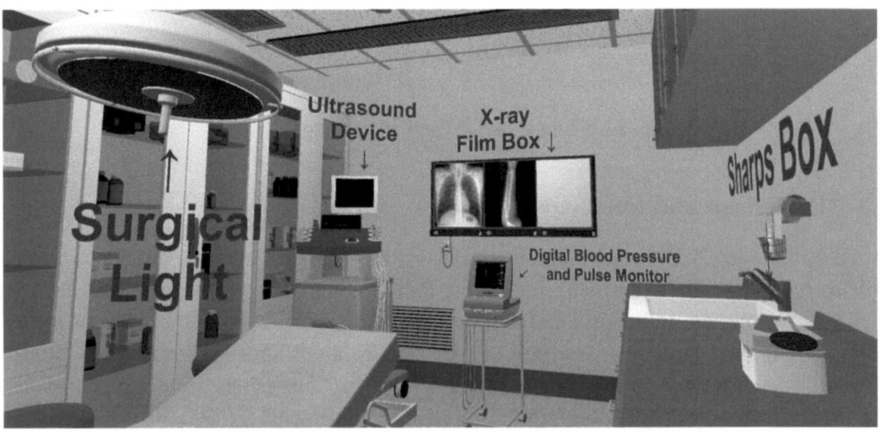


**Fig. 7.** Interactive labels for each critical item at the treatment room.

**Equipment in Emergency Trolley.** The *emergency trolley* is used for immediate treatment under urgent case and it is commonly found in the nurse station. The top of the emergency trolley is for rescue equipment including a defibrillator and a resuscitator (or *Ambu Bag*) inside a box. A sharps box is also presented here to collect used disposable materials like injection syringe and sterilized cotton. The sharps box in Hong Kong is yellow-colored with a caution label. The emergency trolley has a number of trays for specialized equipment. Interactive labels are included to annotate equipment types in each tray and the labels are triggered by opening the tray. Figure 8 shows that the interactive arrow and cross labels next to the tray for tray opening and closing.

**Fig. 8.** Interactive labels for equipment in the trays of the emergency trolley. (Color figure online)

## 3.4 Human Characters

Human characters, e.g., medical staff and patients, are crucial to make the ward look realistic. Our virtual ward has patients lying on their patient beds and nurses observing patients in some of the patient cubicles and nurse station. The clothes and uniform design of these human characters follows those commonly found in the Hong Kong public hospitals; the medical staff has their roles indicated by the uniform color, a clear label on the uniform and a staff card hanged in front (Fig. 9).

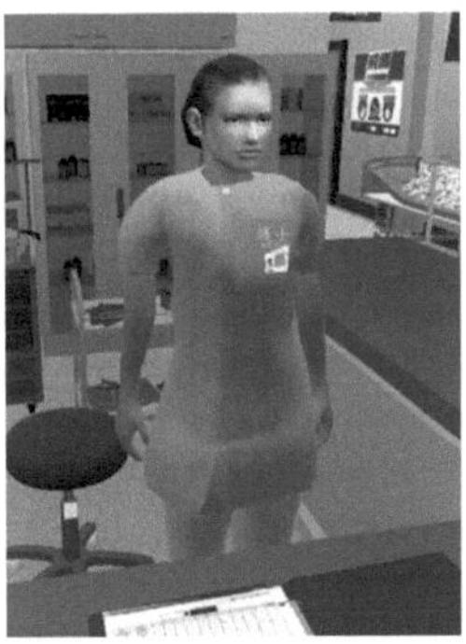

**Fig. 9.** Our nurse uniform.

**Fig. 10.** A scenario simulating the patient care procedure.

To demonstrate the ward duty, a simple scenario is set up at one of the patient cubicles where a nurse is examining a patient after his operation and a ward assistant is giving massage (a procedure of patient care) to him (Fig. 10).

## 4 Conclusion and Future Work

In this paper, an immersive reality of 3D scenarios and models has been implemented for nurse training. The virtual ward environment including patient cubicles, the nurse station and the treatment room are built with high similarity to actual ward settings of Hong Kong hospitals. The equipment for ward duty and operation in the virtual ward is also specially designed for their basic understanding. With the use of interactive labels for the ward equipment, it is expected that the nursing students will become more familiar with the ward environment and have a better understanding of their future tasks of the real practicum.

In order to evaluate the effectiveness of this application, we planned to go for empirical research to test whether the application meets the pedagogical outcomes in March 2018. We will invite some of the nursing students to use our virtual ward application for a period of time. Questionnaires will be collected for OUHK nursing students for their feedbacks on our virtual ward. The results of the questionnaires are used to analyze whether the end users are satisfied with our application. We believe our virtual ward will reduce inexperienced nursing students' anxiety and will arouse the students' interests in learning and visualizing the ward environment.

**Acknowledgment.** This research work was supported by OUHK Katie Shu Sui Pui Charitable Trust Research and Publication Fund (Applied Research) (KS 2016/2.6).

## References

Bricken, M.: Virtual reality learning environments: potentials and challenges. ACM SIGGRAPH Comput. Graph. **25**(3), 178–184 (1991)

Christou, C.: Virtual reality in education. In: Affective, Interactive and Cognitive Methods for E-Learning Design, pp. 228–243 (2010)

de Freitas, S., Rebolledo-Mendez, G., Liarokapis, F., Magoulas, G., Poulovassilis, A.: Developing an evaluation methodology for immersive learning experiences in a virtual world. In: The Conference in Games and Virtual Worlds for Serious Applications (VS-GAMES 2009), pp. 43–50. IEEE, March 2009

Jenson, C.E., Forsyth, D.M.: Virtual reality simulation: using three-dimensional technology to teach nursing students. CIN: Comput. Inf. Nurs. **30**(6), 312–318 (2012)

Lau, W.C.: Effectiveness of virtual reality orientation for patient first admitted into a psychiatric unit. Doctoral dissertation, School of Nursing, The Hong Kong Polytechnic University (2009)

Lee, C.H., French, P.: Education in the practicum: a study of the ward learning climate in Hong Kong. J. Adv. Nurs. **26**(3), 455–462 (1997)

Manias, E., Street, A.: Nurse-doctor interactions during critical care ward rounds. J. Clin. Nurs. **10**(4), 442–450 (2001)

McCaugherty, D.: The theory-practice gap in nurse education: its causes and possible solutions. Findings from an action research study. J. Adv. Nurs. **16**(9), 1055–1061 (1991)

Medley, C.F., Horne, C.: Using simulation technology for undergraduate nursing education. J. Nurs. Educ. **44**(1), 31 (2005)

Papp, I., Markkanen, M., von Bonsdorff, M.: Clinical environment as a learning environment: student nurses' perceptions concerning clinical learning experiences. Nurse Educ. Today **23** (4), 262–268 (2003)

Skiba, D.J.: Nursing education 2.0: games as pedagogical platforms. Nursing Educ. Perspect. **29** (3), 174–175 (2008)

Skiba, D.J.: Nursing education 2.0: a second look at second life. Nursing Educ. Perspect. **30**(2), 129–131 (2009)

Tsang, E.: Inside Hong Kong's public hospital crisis: temporary beds, angry patients, nurses and doctors stretched to breaking point. South China Morning Post, 27 March 2016. http://www.scmp.com/news/hong-kong/health-environment/article/1931049/inside-hong-kongs-public-hospital-crisis-temporary

Tsang, E.: Hong Kong faces medical manpower crisis, government study warns. South China Morning Post, 14 June 2017. http://www.scmp.com/news/hong-kong/health-environment/article/2098354/hong-kong-faces-medical-manpower-crisis-government

Vila, J., Beccue, B., Anandikar, S.: The gender factor in virtual reality navigation and wayfinding. In: The 36th Annual Hawaii International Conference on System Sciences (HICSS 2003). IEEE, January 2003

Zhao, Q.: A survey on virtual reality. Sci. China Ser. F: Inf. Sci. **52**(3), 348–400 (2009)

# Computer Game-Based Foreign Language Learning: Its Benefits and Limitations

Blanka Klimova(✉) and Jaroslav Kacetl

University of Hradec Kralove, Rokitanskeho 62, Hradec Kralove, Czech Republic
{blanka.klimova,jaroslav.kacetl}@uhk.cz

**Abstract.** The aim of this article is to discuss the effectiveness of computer games in foreign language learning and highlights its advantages and disadvantages. The authors searched for available studies on this topic in the world's databases Web of Science, Scopus, and Science Direct in the period of 2010–2017. The findings indicate that computer game-based foreign language learning seems to be especially effective in the vocabulary acquisition. They obviously generate a lot of advantages, for example, contact with foreign language environment, higher motivation for foreign language learning, or increased engagement in foreign language communication. On the other hand, there are also disadvantages of using technological devices in students' learning, for instance, a lack of students' concentration on the vocabulary acquisition and learning, inappropriate choice of the games which are not relevant for foreign language learning, unfamiliarity of computer games among teachers, or their unwillingness and anxiety to use them. Thus, in order to prove the effectiveness of the exploitation of computer games in foreign language learning, more research studies with larger subject samples should be conducted in this area.

**Keywords:** Games · Computers · Foreign language learning · Review
Effectiveness

## 1 Introduction

Currently, young people cannot imagine their life without exploiting information and communication technologies (ICT). Therefore it is no wonder that the exploitation of technological devices is becoming an indispensable part of their school learning. Prensky [1] claims that young people nowadays devote most of their time to playing computer games. He also reports that the American teenagers are able to spend one and half hour on the Internet. In addition, on average, they spend one and half hour by playing video games. Letchumanan and Bee Hoon [2] state that ICT and new technologies create non-threatening learning environment, learners feel safe to practise the target language without being embarrassed or even anxious. They add that computer games can be downloaded and used for free. Thus, it is no surprice that the exploitation of these computer games is becoming as common as the exploitation of traditional textbooks. Nevertheless, it is the didactics of the use of technological devices that matters [3]. In fact, one of the motivational strategies seems to be computer games. As Uzun [4] argues,


S. K. S. Cheung et al. (Eds.): ICTE 2018, CCIS 843, pp. 26–34, 2018.
https://doi.org/10.1007/978-981-13-0008-0_3

games can create an environment where education is mostly personalized and with a good opportunity for socialization. Klimova [5] further extends that game is a natural means for children to understand the world around them. Therefore, it should be part and parcel of their learning, including the learning of foreign languages.

Findley [6] explains that game-based learning is used to teach a specific skill or attain a specific study result. The main advantage of computer game-based learning lies in vocabulary learning. Vasileiadou and Makrina [7] ask whether computer game-based learning makes learning new vocabulary more enjoyable and effective and the data collected during their research seem to confirm the hypothesis that computer-based learning motivates learners and it is an effective means of improving their English vocabulary.

In fact, computer game-based learning is deemed to be one of the most preferred ways of vocabulary acquisition (e.g. [1, 7]). As Letchumanan and Bee Hoon [2] found out, most learners preferred learning vocabulary through computer games since playing games was interesting and fun. Moreover, authors like Ashraf et al. [8] maintain that computer games facilitate effective vocabulary acquisition and Calvo-Ferrer's [9] findings also support the view that computer game-based learning improves vocabulary acquisition in the short run.

As Vasileiadou and Makrina [7] maintain, drilling activities are often applied instead of teaching other vocabulary learning strategies. Yudintseva [10], among others, suggests that computer game-based learning provides learners with various vocabulary learning strategies, as well as opportunities to use the newly learned words in authentic contexts. Concerning the vocabulary learning strategies, Caro and Mendinueta [11] discern incidental learning suitable for proficient intermediate to advanced learners, explicit instruction used with beginners and intermediate learners and independent strategy where learners become autonomous.

Caro and Mendinueta [11] consider lexis as the most vital component of language and add that limited lexical knowledge may lead learners to frustration and demotivation. They even maintain that it is widely acknowledged that lexis is an essential component of language acquisition. Vasileiadou and Makrina [7] agree about the importance of vocabulary acquisition and divide factors affecting vocabulary acquisition into intra-lexical, which concerns e.g. pronunciation, morphology, register, or meaning, and extra-lexical, which are more personal like personal experience, motivation as well as learning environment. The authors view the latter ones as more important [7].

Franciosi [12] states that computer game-based learning belongs to mainstream foreign language teaching as it is based on meaning-focused activities that imply performing tasks in the target language and lead to better retention of learned vocabulary. Franciosi [12] distinguishes between output-oriented and input-oriented tasks and maintains that the former facilitate word retention more effectively. The latter tasks should require learners to do a task based on the input.

Alyaz and Genc [13] recommend implementing computer game-based learning as a part of foreign language training curriculum but emphasize that computer games should be divided into two categories. They distinguish commercial off-the-shelf adventure-entertainment games and educational (or serious) games and propose considering the latter ones for adult language learners as well as language teachers.

As far as the language teachers are concerned, Alyaz and Genc [13] also discuss the fact that whereas learners usually like game-based language learning, teachers' attitudes are considered not to be as positive as those of their students and neither are they widely explored. Consequently, there is a lack of game-based learning pedagogy for teachers. As Alyaz and Genc [13] conclude, should teachers experience playing computer games on their own, they will be more open to using them in their classes.

However, so far, there has not been any consensus if the computer games have a positive or negative impact on foreign language learning. In fact, research on the exploitation of computer games in learning is novel, but rising fast and many teachers attempt to introduce these games in their teaching since they feel that these computer games might be effective on their students' learning [14]. Another pitfall is the fact that there are also other barriers to implementing game-based learning, specifically technical, instructional, financial and sociological [13].

The aim of this article is to discuss the effectiveness of computer games in foreign language learning and highlights its advantages and disadvantages.

## 2 Methods

The authors searched for available studies on this topic in the world's data-bases Web of Science, Scopus, and Science Direct in the period of 2010–2017. In addition, they analyzed and evaluated the findings in order to perform comparison of the finding the research studies detected on the basis of the following keywords: *foreign language learning* AND *computer games, foreign language learning* AND *videogames.* Figure 1 below describes the selection criteria.

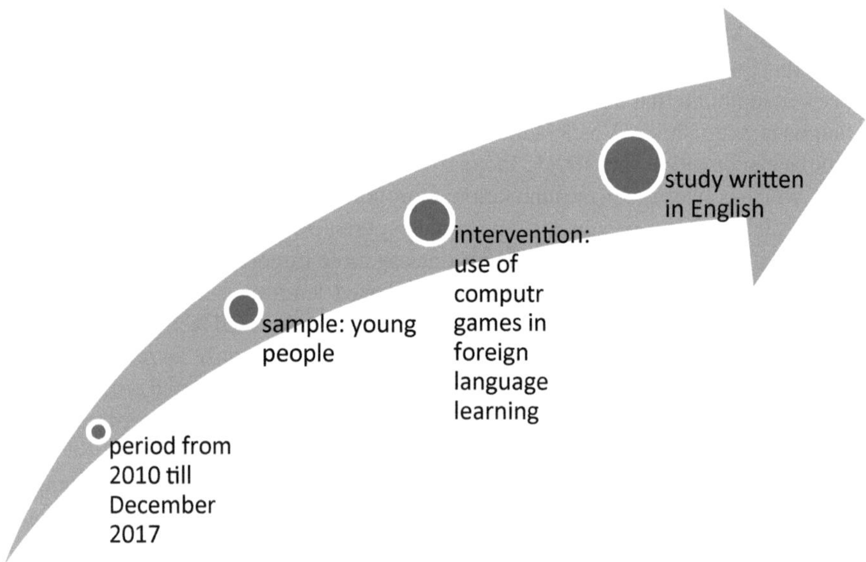


**Fig. 1.** Criteria of the selection procedure (authors' own processing)

The authors chose as the starting point of their search the year of 2010 because until then, already a few studies on the research topic had been published (e.g., [15, 16]).

## 3 Findings and Discussion

Based on the relevant reviewed studies, the findings [7–13] indicate that computer game-based foreign language learning seems to be especially effective in the vocabulary acquisition and learners find it motivating. Aghlahara and Tamjid [14] in their study with 40 subjects aged 6–7 years reveal that digital games have a positive effect on learning process since the mean score of English vocabulary test in the experimental group was significantly higher. In this study 20 pupils were taught English vocabulary with the help of digital computer game SHAIEx and the other half of pupils in a traditional, face-to-face method. During one week pupils had three 90-min sessions and this lasted for 45 days.

Furthermore, Smith et al. [17] argues that inference-based computer games result in better learning of new vocabulary than with traditional hardcopy lists of new words. Inferencing, i.e., determining the meaning of a new word from its context, is a key strategy for second- and foreign-language vocabulary learning. Bado and Franklin [18] in their study report that besides the improvement of the EFL vocabulary and knowledge, educational videogames also enhance the development of cooperation, scaffolding, and motivation.

However, there are also studies, which contradict with these positive results. For instance, deHaan et al. [19] show in their research study with eighty Japanese university students that videogames can have negative impact on students' acquisition of English language words. This might be caused by high interactivity of computer games, which seems to be less supportive for learning novel words in a foreign language. This fact has been also mentioned in the study by Yudintseva [10]. Another study by Letchumanan and Bee Hoon [2] compared learners' essays in terms of vocabulary richness after exposing them to two methods of vocabulary acquisition, specifically computer vocabulary games and traditional vocabulary strategies such as dictionary and contextual clues. The study did not find any significant difference between the essays written after the two strategies were respectively applied.

Obviously, there are certain problems with using computer games in language classrooms. As it has already been mentioned, there is not much on-going research on game-based foreign language learning and the same applies to evaluations of using these activities in language classrooms [19]. Moreover, as Ashraf et al. [8] claim, teachers cannot bring games into the class without having thoroughly planned how to use them. Aghlahara and Tamjid [14] warn teachers not to apply digital games for their own sake as they teach students from different backgrounds with various needs and expectations. deHaan et al. [19] maintain that not all video games are useful for language learning, and they also strongly recommend traditional techniques like pre-teaching vocabulary using drills and dictionary work. Even though playing video games may be a pleasant way to learn vocabulary, it is not the best one to retain vocabulary [19, 20]. Moreover, deHaan [20] emphasizes that effective game-based foreign language teaching and learning is more likely to occur if practical conclusions can be drawn from empirical evidence and adds that language teachers and institutions must know more about computer games to use them effectively.

In this respect, Alyaz and Genc [13] show that institutions should focus on addressing issues like the lack of game-based learning pedagogy for teachers and aim to remove technical, instructional, financial and sociological barriers to implementing game-based learning. Last but not least, teachers should be aware of the fact that computer games can be divided into off-the-shelf adventure-entertainment ones and educational ones.

Alyaz and Genc [13] turn their focus on teachers' views of computer game-based learning and the way how serious games may help develop their professional language skills. The sample group consisted of 60 second year pre-service teachers of German in Turkey. The study generated some interesting results. Most of the respondents (86.7%; n = 52) responded that they find digital games useful for learning a foreign language. Other findings show that the respondents' vocabulary expanded and other language skills were improved, too. The study also revealed that pre-service teachers older than 25 were more successful than their younger counterparts, which may be viewed as an unexpected result. On the other hand, the sample group consisted of mainly young people ranging between the ages of 19 and 35.

Other authors, like Letchumanan and Bee Hoon [2] claim that computer games can easily be adapted to various age groups. Khaksari and Javanmard [21] emphasize the need for efficient utilization of computer games and add that learners themselves regard video games as an opportunity for facilitation of their learning skills, their sense of curiosity, discovery, pleasure.

All in all, Alyaz and Genc [13] suggest that teachers should not be overlooked. On the contrary, pre-service as well as practising teachers ought to be provided with opportunities to experience computer games. It is vital for spreading the implementation of computer game-based learning at schools.

Another author whose ideas implicitly suggest that teachers should be able to include video games in their lessons is Gee [22]. He maintains that good video games are beneficial in and out of classrooms not because they are games but due to the learning principles built into them. He adds that different games exercise different skills and result in different effects. Some of them may teach facts in a funny way whereas others exercise recognition capacities but they do not do this all by themselves. It is important how they are used and what sorts of wider learning activities they involve. It is therefore essential to realize the potential of a particular game for learning and implement good games into good learning systems in and out of classrooms.

In fact, teachers face four pedagogical challenges when using computer educational games in their classrooms, which are as follows [23]:

- they have to direct pupils' attention to the potential of the games and to what has to be learnt in them;
- they have to make learners aware of the relevant contents and their learning accomplishments;
- they have to establish the missing connection between the real world and the simulated game;

- they have to encourage learners to be critical of what has to be learnt while playing the computer game.

There were limitations of the reviewed studies in the sense that these studies involved a small scale samples of subjects and they did not last long. Thus, their effectiveness is slightly questionable. Furthermore, the tests conducted shortly after the interventions generate short-term effects in terms of students' short-term knowledge retention [24].

Furthermore, recently more and more students have been going mobile. Thus, the computer-based language learning is shifting from the desktop computers to the mobile devices such as smartphones, laptops, or tablets [25]. Therefore, there is an increasing number of games which can be played both on desktops and mobile devices. One of such popular game sis called KAHOOT. It is an interactive website that turns students' devices (smartphones, laptops, tablets) into a student response system. Questions and answer choices are displayed from your projector, and students are able to respond to the questions by using by tapping or clicking on one of the answers displayed on their device [26]. Figure 2 below provides a picture of this interactive game [27].

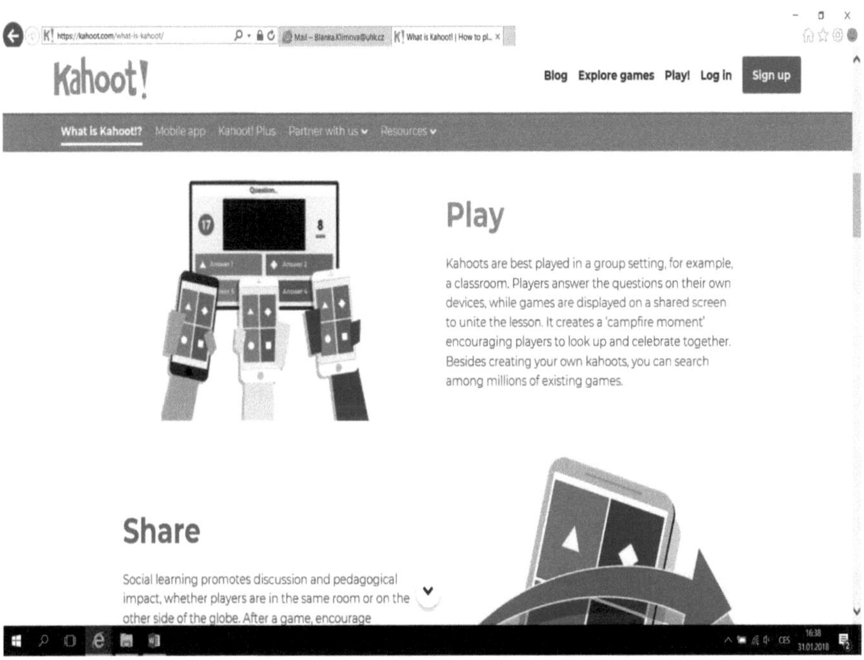


**Fig. 2.** A picture of KAHOOT platform

Figure 3 below summarizes the key advantages and disadvantages of the computer games for foreign language learning.

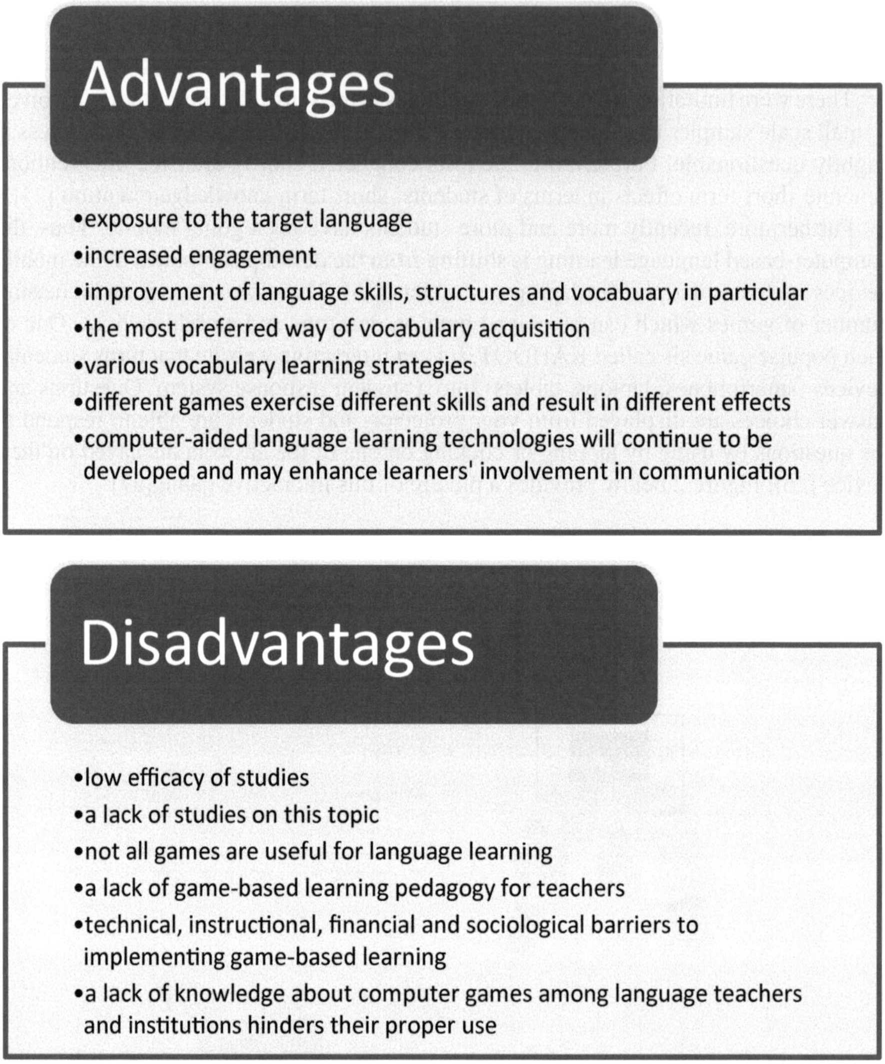


**Fig. 3.** Key advantages and disadvantages of the computer games for foreign language learning (authors' own processing)

Further research in the area of the use of computer game-based foreign language learning should focus on the other aspects (e.g., the development of productive language skills such as speaking and writing, as well as pedagogical methods and techniques) than just the vocabulary acquisition in foreign language learning. In addition, this research should include longitudinal randomized controlled studies.

Of course, there are certain limitations of this article such as a relatively small number found on the research topic. In addition, the studies use different methodological approaches to the solved issue, which may consequently cause the overestimated impact of the results and thus it may have a negative effect on the validity of the selected research studies [28].

## 4 Conclusion

The findings indicate that computer game-based foreign language learning appears to be especially effective in the vocabulary acquisition. They obviously generate a lot of advantages, for example, contact with foreign language environment, higher motivation for foreign language learning, or increased engagement in foreign language communication. On the other hand, there are also certain disadvantages of using technological devices in students' learning, for instance, a lack of students' concentration on the vocabulary acquisition and learning, inappropriate choice of the games which are not relevant for foreign language learning, unfamiliarity of computer games among teachers, or their unwillingness and anxiety to use them. Thus, in order to prove the effective-ness of the exploitation of computer games in foreign language learning, more research studies with larger subject samples should be conducted in this area.

**Acknowledgments.** This article is supported by SPEV project 2018, run at the Faculty of Informatics and Management, University of Hradec Kralove, Czech Republic. The authors especially thank Josef Toman for his help with data processing.

## References

1. Prensky, M.: The emerging online life of the digital native: what they do differently because of technology and how they do it (2004). http://www.bu.edu/ssw/files/pdf/Prensky-The_Emerging_Online_Life_of_the_Digital_Native-033.pdf
2. Letchumanan, K., Bee Hoon, T.: Using computer games to improve secondary school students' vocabulary acquisition in English. Soc. Sci. Humanit. **20**(4), 1005–1018 (2012)
3. Higgings, S., Xiao, Z.M., Katsipataki, M.: The impact of digital technology on learning: a summary for the education endowment foundation. Full report, UK, Durham University (2012)
4. Uzun, L.: An evaluative checklist for computer games used for foreign language vocabulary learning and practice: vocaword sample. Novitas-ROYAL **3**(1), 45–59 (2009)
5. Klimova, B.: Games in the teaching of English. Procedia – Soc. Behav. Sci. **191**, 1157–1160 (2015)
6. Findley, J.: Game-based learning vs. gamification: do you know the difference? (2016). http://www.trainingindustry.com/learning-technologies/articles/game-based-learning-vs-gamification-do-you-know-the-difference.aspx
7. Vasileiadou, I., Makrina, Z.: Using online computer games in the ELT classroom: a case study. Engl. Lang. Teach. **10**(12), 134–150 (2017)
8. Ashraf, H., Motlagh, F.G., Salami, M.: The impact of online games on learning English vocabulary by Iranian (low-intermediate) EFL learners. Procedia – Soc. Behav. Sci. **98**, 286–291 (2014)
9. Calvo-Ferrer, J.R.: Educational games as stand-alone learning tools and their motivational effect on L2 vocabulary acquisition and perceived learning gains. Br. J. Edu. Technol. **48**(2), 264–278 (2015)

10. Yudintseva, A.: Game-enhanced second language vocabulary acquisition strategies: a systematic review. Open J. Soc. Sci. **3**, 101–109 (2015)
11. Caro, K., Mendinueta, N.R.: Lexis, lexical competence and lexical knowledge: a review. J. Lang. Teach. Res. **8**(2), 205–213 (2017)
12. Franciosi, S.J.: The effect of computer game-based learning on FL vocabulary transferability. Educ. Technol. Soc. **20**(1), 123–133 (2017)
13. Alyaz, Y., Genc, Z.S.: Digital game-based language learning in foreign language teacher education. Turk. Online J. Distance Educ. **17**(4), 130–146 (2016)
14. Aghlahara, L., Tamjid, N.H.: The effect of digital games on Iranian children's vocabulary retention in foreign language acquisition. Procedia Soc. Behav. Sci. **29**, 552–560 (2011)
15. Peterson, M.: Computerized games and simulations in computer-assisted language learning: a meta-analysis of research. Simul. Gaming **41**, 72 (2010)
16. Turgut, Y., Irgin, P.: Young learners' language learning via computer games. Procedia Soc. Behav. Sci. **1**, 760–764 (2009)
17. Smith, G.G., Li, M., Drobisz, J., Park, H.R., Kim, D., Smith, S.D.: Play games or study? Computer games in ebooks to learn English vocabulary. Comput. Educ. **69**, 274–286 (2013)
18. Bado, N., Franklin, T.: Cooperative game-based learning in the English as a foreign language classroom. Issues Trends Educ. Technol. **2**(2), 1–17 (2014)
19. deHaan, J., Reed, W.M., Kuwada, K.: The effect of interactivity with a music video game on second language vocabulary recall. Lang. Learn. Technol. **14**(2), 74–94 (2010)
20. deHaan, J.: Teaching and learning English through digital game projects. Digit. Cult. Educ. **3**(1), 46–55 (2011)
21. Khaksari, Z., Javanmard, M.: Computer games and psychological motivation in adolescents. Adv. Nat. Appl. Sci. **8**(10), 119–125 (2014)
22. Gee, J.P.: Are video games good for learning? Nordic J. Digit. Lit. **1**(3), 172–173 (2006)
23. Goethe Institut. Educational Games: Possibilities and Limitations (2017). https://www.goethe.de/en/spr/mag/20395586.html
24. Guerrero, H.A.G.: Using video game-based instruction in an EFL program. Understanding the power of video games in education. Colomb. Appl. Linguist. **13**(1), 54–70 (2011)
25. Klimova, B.: Mobile phones and/or smartphones and their apps for teaching English as a foreign language. Educ. Inf. Technol. (2017). https://doi.org/10.1007/s10639-017-9655-5
26. McKee, K.C.: The Vocab Games: Kahoot! (2014). http://kennycmckee.com/the-vocab-games-kahoot/
27. KAHOOT (2017). https://kahoot.com/what-is-kahoot/
28. Melby-Lervag, M., Hulme, C.: There is no convincing evidence that working memory training is effective: a reply to Au et al. (2014) and Karbach and Verhaeghen (2014). Psychon. Bull. Rev. **23**(1), 324–330 (2016)

# Preparing for Examination: An Extended Implementation of a Generator that Uses the Same Questions to Form Tests

Doru Anastasiu Popescu[1(✉)], Daniel Nijloveanu[2], and Nicolae Bold[1]

[1] Department of Mathematics and Computer Science, University of Pitești, Pitești, Romania
dopopan@yahoo.com, bold_nicolae@yahoo.com

[2] Faculty of Management, Economic Engineering in Agriculture and Rural Development, University of Agronomic Sciences and Veterinary Medicine Bucharest, Slatina Branch, Slatina, Romania
nijloveanu_daniel@yahoo.com

**Abstract.** The preparation for an examination has a multitude of perspectives. Assessment in learning can be made using various methods and techniques. One of the most widespread methods of assessing the progress of learners is the multiple-choice test. In this paper, we present a web implementation of a generator of tests which uses same questions that are stored in a certain form (generally referred as the database of questions), an extension of a previously-presented implementation of the same system. The main difference and the novelty brought to the system is that the questions have a larger number of choices than a standard number chosen by a user, from which will be randomly chosen a fixed number of choices, the correct one(s) being amongst the chosen ones. Also, in order to avoid situations of learning based on the choice letter (a, b, c etc.), the variants will be shuffled every time, their position being changed whether the question is generated once more. One of the characteristics that differentiates it from other test generators is the distinctive environment that was created for, the generator being built for the particular context of the learning used within the studied academic environment.

**Keywords:** Test · Random · Learning

## 1 Introduction

Assessment by multiple-choice tests has its advantages and disadvantages. Despite its seeming superficiality, the multiple-choice test is widely-used but not limited to the educational and academic learning environments for its quickness in implementation and easiness in checking correct answers. Multiple-choice tests are also easily implementable electronically, included in web applications or any type of software, being one of the most widespread types of electronic assessment. Nonetheless, the usage of these tests has several drawbacks, the main being the fact that a test of this kind does not show the whole knowledge and the skills that the learner possess. Based on these facts,


S. K. S. Cheung et al. (Eds.): ICTE 2018, CCIS 843, pp. 35–43, 2018.
https://doi.org/10.1007/978-981-13-0008-0_4

multiple-choice tests are a good alternative to other types of assessment when a short and quick examination is made.

This paper extends a theoretical proposition of a system [2] which generates tests with a fixed number of questions that have a chosen number of variants by randomly selecting questions from a database of questions (which may be a proper database, a text file etc., depending on the implementation language). These questions are accompanied in the database by a various number of choices which are chosen in the desired number and generated in a shuffled arrangement, in order for the correct choice(s) to be positioned distinctively at a different runtime.

The main distinctive features of the system are the particular learning style that was the source idea of the generator and the introduction of the multiple choices over the fixed number of showed choices within the assessment process.

## 2 Literature Work

Assessment in learning is a strongly-studied subject in the literature. Assessment is a particular subject in a variated domain of electronic-based learning [9], due to the sensitivity of the subject and the implications in various fields [1]. On-line assessment raises a series of issues related to learning efficiency [6] or defining learning strategies [3]. Various methods and structures were used for solving similar issues of generating test items, such as genetic algorithms such as in [10, 12] or using several restrictions such as the degree of difficulty as in [11].

Multiple-choice tests are widely-used within on-line assessment because their easy transpose to an informatics implementation. Due to this main advantage, various models of multiple-choice e-learning tests were created [2, 5].

The usage of on-line assessment and educational systems has as one of the effects the formation of a learning style based on different principles than the traditional paper-based learning systems [7, 8]. The assessment can be made regardless the spatial or temporal context and the chosen domain, either formal education or adult training [15], with the condition of the existence of a device, usually connected to Internet, and the answer check can be made instantaneously. The massive gather of more actors of learning within such a platform leads to the creation of open learning environments [4] with a physical layer in the form of e-learning platform [13], which can have benefices or can raise ethical issues [14] on the educational evolution of the involved parts.

## 3 Short Description and Implementation

A short statement of the issue presented in this paper is:

- Given a set of *nrq* questions $q_i$, i = 1,*nrq* each question with its *nrc* number of choices set $x_j$, j = 1, *nrc*, it is required a multiple-choice test formed of k questions, each question having c choices.

The issue can be easily modeled using number representation and arrangements. Starting from the idea that each question is labeled with a number from 1 to total number of questions from the database and each choice labeled with a number from 1 to total number of choices for a question, the problem is reduced to:

- generating $k$ distinct questions;
- for each generated question, the generation of $c$ distinct choices with the requirement of the presence of the correct choice(s) amongst the generated ones;
- the shuffle of the chosen choices at the previous step.

For each question, the form of the generated sequence is $q\ x_1\ x_2 \ldots x_c$, where q is the selected question and $x_i$ is the selected choice. Actually, the subsequence $x_1\ x_2 \ldots x_c$ is an arrangement of the choices set of the question $q$. The obtained sequence is then decodified by outputting the question statement and the textual choices.

In order to show the usefulness of the described system, we have implemented it in a form of a web application, for $c = 3$. This application was used for the training of the senior students for their final degree examination and is built using PHP for programming and MySQL for the database. Figure 1 presents the graphical user interface for a user, while Fig. 4 shows the structure of the tables within the database.

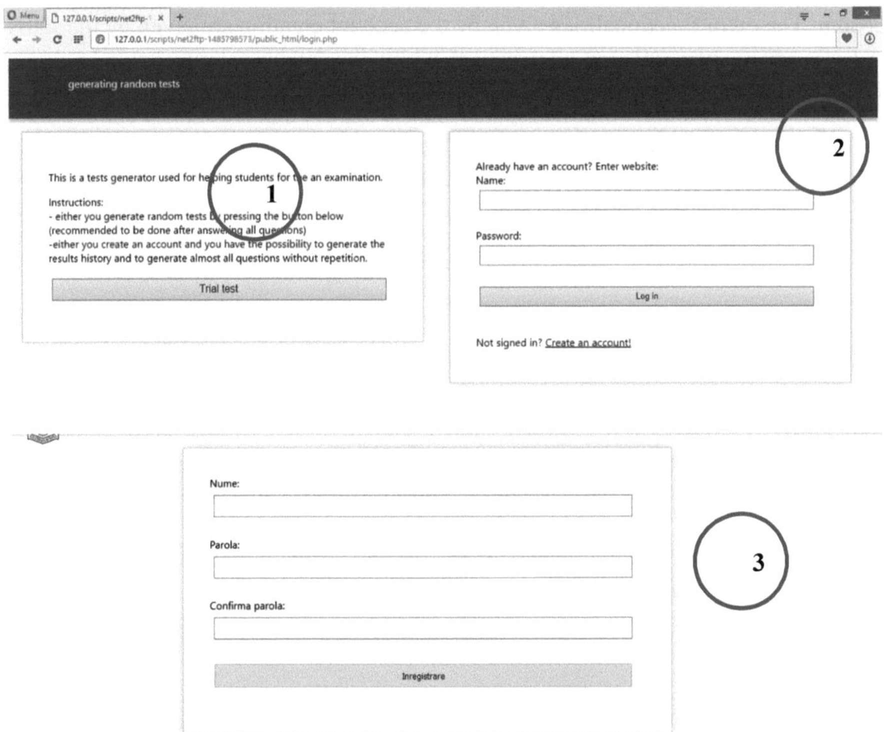


**Fig. 1.** Main panel of the GUI of the web implementation: (1) login-free trial test area; (2) members area (3) registration area

Within the application, the data structures that are used are the next:

- *nrq* is the number of question in the pool or database of questions;
- *q*[*nrq*] is the array of questions that stores all the questions within the database with their characteristics: index, statement, number of choices (*nrc*), correct answer;
- *k* is the size of the test, that is, the number of questions that must be chosen from all the *nrq* questions;
- *c* is the question size, that is, the number of choices that each question must have within the test; c must be larger than the minimum number of choices of all questions ($c \geq \min\{nrc\}$).
- *qs*[*k*] is the array that stores the questions that are selected for the current test;
- *vars*[*c*] is the array where the chosen choices for a certain question are stored;
- *viz*[*c*] is the array that stores whether the selected choice was chosen for output for a certain question; it can be 1 (if the choice was chosen at a given step) or 0 (otherwise).

In the pseudocode, the function rand(*a*,*b*) has the next meaning: it generates a random integer number in the interval comprised between a and b.

The user has basic functionalities, such as generating a trial test and creating an account. The extra functionalities given by the account creation are given by the statistical area and the generation of all questions within the database during a whole session of tests, which assures passing through all the questions (Fig. 2).

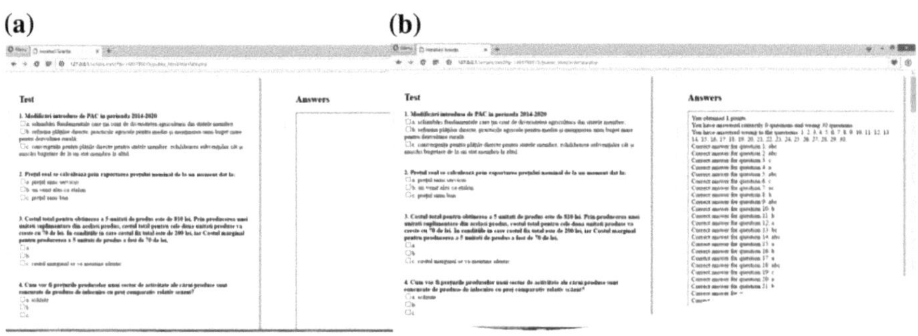


**Fig. 2.** Trial test window: (a) before solving; (b) after solving

A part of the function that generates the choices, namely that generates questions with a single correct choice is presented next (Fig. 3).

```
T ← rand (1,nrc)
ind_cor ← rand(1,c) //we choose next a position for the
correct choice `index` and we mark it as visited
vars[ind_cor] ← index
viz[index] ← true
fori = 1,c do
  ifi=  ind_cor then
    viz[ind_cor] ← true
  else
    whileviz[T] = true do
      T ← rand(1,nrc)
    vars[i] ← T
    viz[T] ← true
  endif
endfor
```

| | Log out |
|---|---|
| Number of completed tests | 5 |
| Number of correct answers | 0 / 150 ( 0.00% ) |
| Maximum number of correct answers to a test | 0 |
| Maximum points | 1.00 |
| Average number of points | 1.00 |
| Generated questions | |
| 4, 10, 24, 27, 33, 34, 38, 43, 46, 50, 52, 68, 84, 85, 91, 92, 100, 124, 144, 145, 146, 147, 179, 182, 189, 192, 193, 200, 203, 206, 236, 239, 244, 258, 265, 274, 276, 290, 291, 294, 298, 306, 309, 320, 322, 323, 326, 335, 345, 350, 351, 356, 367, 376, 383, 384, 387, 400, 401, 415, | |
| Number of generated questions from all the questions | 60 / 416 |

**Fig. 3.** Panel of the statistics of the user

The database stores the list of all questions and data related to the user. A structure of the database with its three tables is presented in Fig. 4.

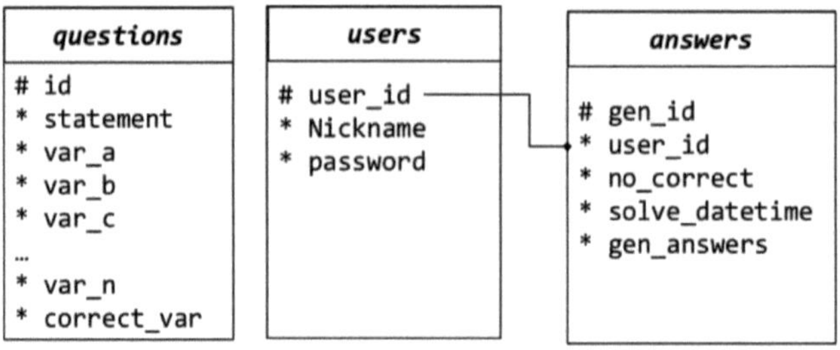


| ←T→ | nr | enunt | var_a | var_b | var_c | ras_cor2 | rasp_corect |
|---|---|---|---|---|---|---|---|
| Editare Copiază Șterge | 1 | 1. Pentru situatia agromarketingului, se pot face ... | a. aparitia unor efecte inflationiste, situatie ge... | b. neconcordanta intre productia de materie prima ... | c. productia industriala pentru unele mijloace de ... | abc | 1abc |
| Editare Copiază Șterge | 2 | 2. Care dintre etapele tranzitiei s-au manifestat ... | a. setea de reforma (reforma fondului funciar din ... | b. frica de reforma (1992-1996) | c. imperativul reformei (1997) | abc | 2abc |
| Editare Copiază Șterge | 3 | 3. Importanta cunoasterii accesului la o hrana san... | a. pe capacitatea de cumparare a consumatorilor ca... | b. pe capacitatea de productie a agricultorilor, c... | c. pe puterea de cumparare a natiunii care conditi... | abc | 3abc |
| Editare Copiază Șterge | 4 | 4. Care dintre nevoile de consum alimentar se mani... | a. nevoile fiziologice | b. nevoia de consideratie | c. nevoia de realizare | a | 4a |
| Editare Copiază Șterge | 5 | 5. In organizare studierii cererii de produse alim... | a. cercetarea continua a cererii | b. investigatiile de agromarketing vor urmari cons... | c. concluziile analizei cererii alimentare a popul... | abc | 5abc |
| Editare Copiază Șterge | 6 | 6. Comportamentul manifestat de consumator este co... | a. perceptia, informarea, atitudinea, motivatia, c... | b. perceptia, atitudinea, comportamentul, motivati... | c. comportamentul, perceptia, motivatia, atitudine... | a | 6a |
| Editare Copiază Șterge | 7 | 7. Care este elementul de care este atras, in prim... | a. calitate | b. aspect | c. perioada de returnare | b | 7b |
| Editare Copiază Șterge | 8 | 8. Cantitatile obtinute in cazul culturilor ecolog... | a. la fel ca la celelate culturi | b. mai mari | c. mai mici | c | 8c |

| ←T→ | cod_generare | cod_user | generate |
|---|---|---|---|
| Editare Copiază Șterge | 1 | 57 | 402,196,98,170,94,74,186,280,403,158,405,77,63,296... |
| Editare Copiază Șterge | 2 | 57 | 402,196,98,170,94,74,186,280,403,158,405,77,63,296... |
| Editare Copiază Șterge | 3 | 57 | 402,196,98,170,94,74,186,280,403,158,405,77,63,296... |
| Editare Copiază Șterge | 114 | 74 | 409,123,315,405,362,277,237,148,346,139,316,144,17... |
| Editare Copiază Șterge | 7 | 60 | 182,323,58,342,296,204,100,124,39,186,250,85,177,1... |
| Editare Copiază Șterge | 8 | 60 | 182,323,58,342,296,204,100,124,39,186,250,85,177,1... |
| Editare Copiază Șterge | 9 | 61 | 129,363,177,248,283,48,81,83,280,395,269,99,276,95... |
| Editare Copiază Șterge | 10 | 61 | 129,363,177,248,283,48,81,83,280,395,269,99,276,95... |
| Editare Copiază Șterge | 11 | 62 | 146,148,255,28,383,224,200,189,139,351,256,196,182... |
| Editare Copiază Șterge | 215 | 74 | 409,123,315,405,362,277,237,148,346,139,316,144,17... |

**Fig. 4.** Database tables structure

The relation between scripts is shown in Fig. 5.

The idea itself is quite simple, but the keys of the whole system are the introduction of false-leading choices and the permanent movement of the choices in order to avoid static learning of variants and to encourage logic thinking.

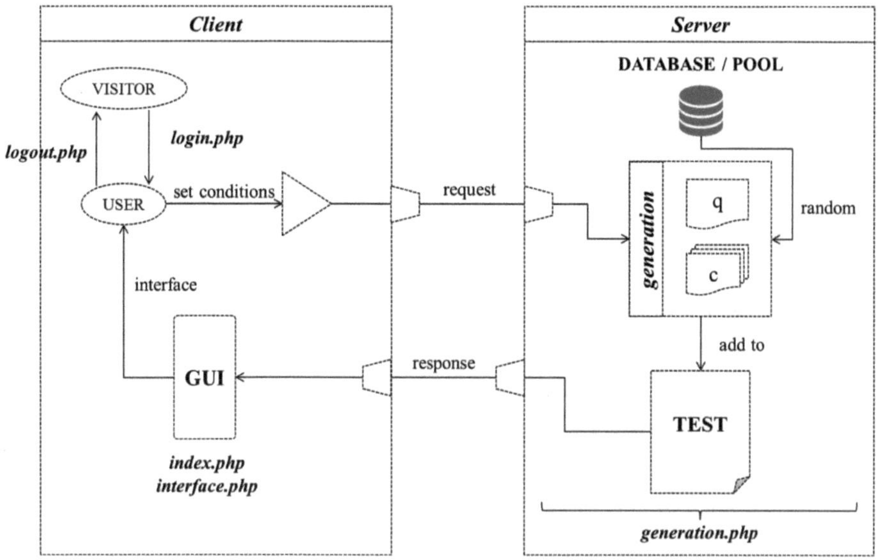


**Fig. 5.** Client-server-relation and scripts involved

# 4 Results

The overall idea of introducing electronic-based assessment brings an extra motivation for the student, for some basic psychological reasons. The e-based version is usable in any context for learning, being ready at any moment. This is why learning for an examination is enhanced by the easiness in usage and the development of wearables and portable devices (laptops, smartphones etc.).

The system was successfully introduced in the learning process for the final examination for the students in 4$^{th}$ year at the Faculty of Management, Economic Engineering in Agriculture and Rural Development at Slatina Branch. Unfortunately, a study could not be run in order to show the effects of the implementation over student learning enhancement, but students that ran tests on a daily basis had better results at the final exam than the average of all four years results. Some of the feedback of the students that used the system showed some of its advantages:

- quick learning of the theoretical aspects involved in learning
- avoids mechanical learning
- easiness and fastness in usage due to its electronic form
- adaptability to other contexts.

Figure 6 presents some data related to student trials before exam, taken from the solve log stored in the database.

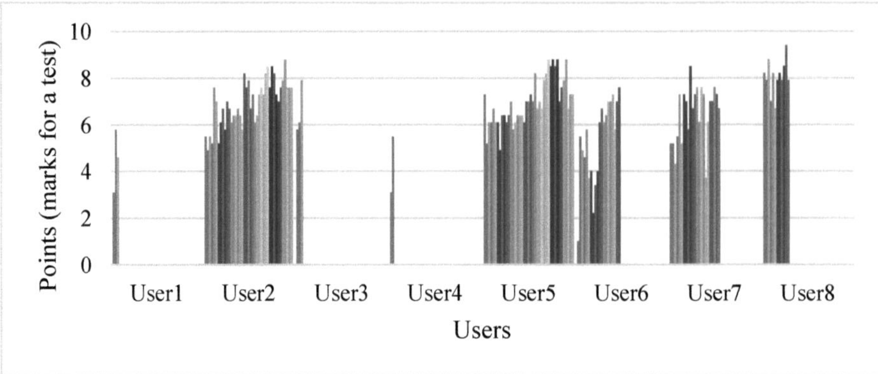


**Fig. 6.** Statistical data of trials for 8 users

We can observe that all the 8 users had a positive tendency regarding the chronological results. For a bigger number of taken tests, we can observe an emphasized positive tendency in raising the final mark, as seen in Fig. 7 for the User 5.

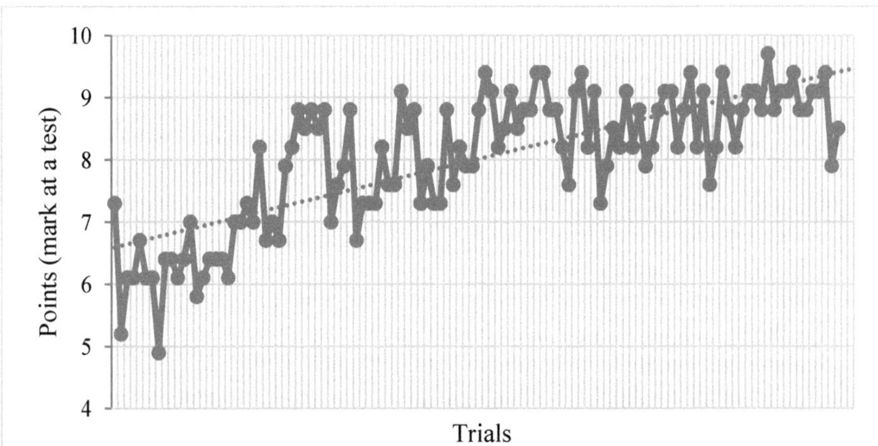


**Fig. 7.** Trials for user 5

## 5 Conclusions

A system of this type can have beneficial effects on the learning of the students involved. We recommend the usage of multiple-choice tests as a part of the preparation for an examination, due to its particular features in respect to learning. The system is fully updatable, many features can be added in order for the user to interact with other learners and to create a better understanding and integration within the assessment environment and, thus, to create a better experience for the user, because e-based learning is and will remain a debatable topic.

## References

1. Buchanan, T.: Online assessment: desirable or dangerous? Prof. Psychol.: Res. Practice **33**(2), 148–154 (2002)
2. Domşa, O., Bold, N.: Generator of variants of tests using the same questions. In: The 12th International Scientific Conference eLearning and Software for Education, Bucharest (2016)
3. Gaytan, J., McEwen, B.C.: Effective online instructional and assessment strategies. Am. J. Distance Educ. **21**(3), 117–132 (2007)
4. Holotescu, C.: A conceptual model for open learning environments. In: International Conference on Virtual Learning – ICVL (2015)
5. Mitkov, R., Ha, L.A.: Computer-aided generation of multiple-choice tests. In: Proceedings of the HLT-NAACL 2003 Workshop on Building Educational Applications Using Natural Language Processing, vol. 2, pp. 17–22 (2003)
6. Nicol, D.: E-assessment by design: using multiple-choice tests to good effect. J. Further High. Educ. **31**(1), 53–64 (2007). Changing perspectives on teaching
7. Popescu, E.: Adaptation provisioning with respect to learning styles in a web-based educational system: an experimental study. J. Comput. Assist. Learn. **26**(4), 243–257 (2010). Wiley
8. Roy, C., Wallace, P.: Paper–based versus computer–based assessment: key factors associated with the test mode effect. Br. J. Educ. Technol. **33**(5), 593–602 (2002)
9. Stodberg, U.: A research review of e-assessment. Assess. Eval. High. Educ. **37**(5), 591–604 (2012)
10. Popescu, D.A., Bold, N., Domsa, O.: Generating assessment tests with restrictions using genetic algorithms. In: 12th IEEE International Conference on Control and Automation, 1–3 June 2016, Kathmandu, Nepal, pp. 696–700 (2016)
11. Popescu, D.A., Bold, N.: Model of assessment using tests formed of questions with different theoretical and practical difficulty degrees based on a genetic algorithm. In: International Workshop on Social Computing in Digital Education (ITS 2016), Workshop Proceedings, pp. 39–43 (2016)
12. Popescu, D.A., Bold, N., Nijloveanu, D.: A method based on genetic algorithms for generating assessment tests used for learning. In: CICLING 2016, Konya, Turkey (2016)
13. Baron, C., Şerb, A., Iacob, N.M., Defta, C.L.: IT infrastructure model used for implementing an E-learning platform based on distributed databases. Qual.-Access Success J. **15**(140), 195–201 (2014)
14. Defta, C.L., Şerb, A., Iacob, N.M., Baron, C.: Threats analysis for E-learning platforms. **6**(1), 132–135 (2014)
15. Tiţa, V., Necula, R.: Trends in educational training for agriculture in olt county. Sci. Papers Ser. Manag. Econ. Eng. Agric. Rural Dev. **15**(4) (2015)

# Game-Based Vocabulary Learning in China and Hong Kong: Students' Evaluation of Different Word Learning APPs

Di Zou[1], Fu Lee Wang[2], Haoran Xie[1(✉)], and Lucas Kohnke[3]

[1] The Education University of Hong Kong, Hong Kong SAR, China
hxie@eduhk.hk
[2] Caritas Institute of Higher Education, Hong Kong SAR, China
[3] The Hong Kong Polytechnic University, Hong Kong SAR, China

**Abstract.** The present research firstly investigated how Chinese and Hong Kong students evaluated five commonly used word learning APPs. Data concerning their perceptions and experience of using these APPs were collected through interviews and questionnaire surveys. Questions concerning their expectations of effective word learning APPs were also asked. The collected data were coded and analyzed to identify common features or points mentioned by the students. The results showed that students highly value features like enabling users to choose specific target groups of words, having vivid visual aids, providing pronunciations, detailed and accurate definitions and examples, and allowing users to interact with other users. The second part of this research asked the students to compare a wording learning APP developed by The Hong Kong Polytechnic University to the APPs that they had used previously, evaluating the advantages and disadvantages of different word learning APPs. The results of the research are consistent with Zou's (2016, 2017) arguments that the availability of various aspects of word knowledge are conducive to effective word learning as it promotes greater degree of elaboration on the target vocabulary. Moreover, the results support Zou and Xie's (2018) argument that personalized learning is essential to learner engagement and learning effectiveness.

**Keywords:** Game-based vocabulary learning · Word learning APPs
Degree of elaboration · Personalized learning

## 1 Introduction

The effectiveness of computer assisted language learning (hereafter, CALL) has been widely investigated and acclaimed among language teachers, learners and researchers. Based on the large number of CALL practices and studies, game-based learning has become increasingly influential for language education, research on second language acquisition is also moving toward this direction (Chen et al. 2018). Being widely acknowledged as an essential part of second language acquisition, word learning has always been a very active area among linguistics and researchers (Zou 2012), and a wide range of studies have been conducted in the fields of game-based vocabulary learning


S. K. S. Cheung et al. (Eds.): ICTE 2018, CCIS 843, pp. 44–55, 2018.
https://doi.org/10.1007/978-981-13-0008-0_5

and vocabulary learning. With the popularity of mobile phones, the number of education APPs has been rapidly increased, and the number of students who use word learning APPs to facilitate their vocabulary learning has also been increasing. Playing an important role in assisting students in vocabulary acquisition, word learning APPs have drawn much attention from educators and researchers.

In this research, we developed a word learning APP to facilitate students' vocabulary learning. The features of this APP are introduced in the method. We also investigated how Hong Kong students evaluated five commonly used word learning APPs and asked them to compare our APP with other common APPs. Moreover, the advantages and disadvantages of different word learning APPs are discussed and analyzed. Additionally, a list of essential features for effective word learning APPs is suggested.

## 2 Literature Review

In the literature, there is a consensus that game-based learning applications are effective tools for ESL learners to acquire new vocabulary (Calvo-Ferrer 2015; Chen and Chung 2008; Rankin et al. 2006; Uzun et al. 2013). Most of the studies focused on vocabulary adopted a comparative methodology involving an experimental group and a control group and compared their performances in the pre- and post- vocabulary test. The experimental group was asked to play the game for a period of time in the classroom settings or in their own time whereas the control group learnt vocabulary with a paper-based drill-and-practice method. These studies have shown that the experimental group either significantly or substantively outperformed the control group in the post-test, suggesting that the educational games are more useful than the traditional method in helping students to learn and remember new vocabulary. For example, Rankin et al. (2006) investigated the benefits of a massive multiplayer online role-playing game as a pedagogical learning tool for intermediate and advanced ESL learners and revealed that the vocabulary of the students who played the game increased by 40%.

There might be a variety of reasons for these improvements:

First, games could provide considerable and enriched sources for ESL vocabulary learning. The multimodal representation of words in games provides learners with a visual context for understanding words and associating them with existing knowledge (Abrams and Walsh 2014). In addition, understanding the instruction of the game offers players extended opportunities to learn words that are not in their course.

Second, students' satisfaction and motivation are enhanced by the opportunity to learn while playing games. According to Pensky (2004), digital games can engage students because of its profound tempting form in design to include specific elements such as a storyline, goals, interaction, outcome and immediate feedback. The incentives such as rewards, points and top score lead boards provide intense motivation to players unmatched by non-game activities and environments (Kapp 2012). When students themselves own strong motivation to learn, the gaming system could offer satisfied learning mechanism for them (Chen and Chung 2008). For those who lack intrinsic motivation, their interaction with the game characters could increase their interest and motivation in the game, and in turn, help them to learn and remember English words more efficiently (Abu Bakar and Nosratired 2013; Bekleyen and Yilmaz 2011). As pointed out by Calvo-Ferrer (2015), compared with intrinsic motivation, extrinsic motivation and students' perceived learning gains has a great influence on students L2 vocabulary acquisition. Through games the conventional rote learning is shifted to a meaningful and enjoyable experience.

Third, students' interaction and collaboration are stimulated and promoted while playing the game together with peers. They are forced to interact with the game and other players by using appropriate vocabulary and language. Psychologically, the interaction induced from the game is facilitative to players' germane cognitive load and significantly increases vocabulary recall (Huang and Lin 2014). Interpersonally, students help each other to complete the game and learn new words from each other, consequently, their interpersonal relationship, self-confidence, will for collaboration and group work are improved (Uzon et al. 2013). As suggested by Sylven and Sundqvist (2012), intra-communication between the players and inter-communication between the game and the players can facilitate the input-output transfer process and make comprehension easier so that vocabulary of the game can be acquired incidentally and naturally.

Fourth, digital-based game learning is conducive to problem-solving and self-directed learning. Prior research has suggested that game-based learning has an important role in increasing the level of learning and can promote imagination in learners. The concrete challenges are normally tailored to a player's skill level. The increased difficulty can force the players to adopt new strategies to solve the problems and the immediate feedback can urge them to think critically (Abrams and Walsh 2014). In addition, gaming creates an environment where the learners learn without the interference of the teacher, affording them more time to train and practice at a self-paced speed. More importantly, it creates anxiety-free conditions as they are left on their own and not judged (Uzun et al. 2013).

## 3 Alphabet vs. Aliens

Mobile devises can provide educational opportunities for students to improve on course content/outcomes (in this case their lexical range and sentence structure), as well as interact with teachers and other colleagues wherever they are located (Cavus and Ibrahim 2008, 2009; Nihalani and Mayrath 2010). These interactions using mobile devices are even more accessible by the inclusion of social media for communication and enhance learning (Rodriguez 2011). Game-based language learning is conducive to English vocabulary development as it enhances learner motivation, interaction, and autonomy through the extended ubiquitous learning opportunities. A tailor-made game application for vocabulary learning is therefore in need for students to enlarge their vocabulary for academic studies in university.

In response to this call, we developed an APP named Alphabet vs. Aliens at The Hong Kong Polytechnic University (hereafter, PolyU), aiming to assist students to enhance their interest, sustain motivation and foster participation in independent language learning. This app was extensively used in the Excel@English Scheme (EES) which provided supplementary English language enhancement support for students who entered PolyU with a relatively low level of English Proficiency (DSE3, or equivalent). According to The Hong Kong Examinations and Assessment Authority, such scores are roughly equivalent to an IELTS score of 5.5. Moreover, the mobile app was promoted to Senior Year Admitted students (SYA) who were exempted from university English courses provided by the English language centre so that they can have the opportunity to improve and enhance their language abilities through independent learning.

Alphabet vs. Aliens@PolyU is innovative in the sense that it has the following features and educational benefits with learning content that suit the language levels and interests of PolyU students (see Table 1).

**Table 1.** Features and educational benefits of Alphabet vs. Aliens

| Features | Educational benefits |
|---|---|
| Available on both iOS and Android platforms | Students can expand the breadth and depth of vocabulary range |
| Moving level path | Receive extended opportunities to pursue autonomous learning within a supportive context |
| Multiplayer mode | Interact with other PolyU learners on the proposed game-mediated app while engaging in language learning |
| Block features (letters) | Stimulate collaboration while using and playing the games with peers |
| Social media connection/scoreboard | Increase imagination level of learning while playing the app |
| Comprehensive word list | Encourage students towards self-directed and independent learning |
| Engaging story line | |

The activities on the app are designed to be adapted-release (e.g. hint and clues) and responsiveness (e.g. immediate feedback) in order to cater to different level of learner characteristics and level of competence. Animation, multi-media, and scoring features will also feature in the app.

## 4 Five Common Word Learning APPs

In this research, we selected the following five commonly used word learning APPs (see Table 2). We asked ten students to explore these five APPs and interviewed them one months later to examine their experience of word learning with the APPs. Based on the previous literature and our investigation among students in China and Hong Kong, we summarized the following key features of these APPs.

**Table 2.** Word learning APPs and their key features

| APPs | Features | |
|---|---|---|
| ShanBay | 1. | Including a variety of target groups of words |
| | 2. | Providing personalized learning experience |
| | 3. | Demonstrating detailed and accurate definitions and examples |
| | 4. | Having sharing functions |
| | 5. | Recording learning progresses |
| Baicizhan | 1. | Using images to help learners better understand word meanings and establish links between words and the real world |
| | 2. | Enabling users to add friends, share leaning progresses, and have competitions |
| | 3. | Including a variety of target groups of words |
| | 4. | Enabling Android users to set word cards as lock screens |
| | 5. | Providing personalized learning experience |
| | 6. | Recording learning progresses |
| SuperMemo | 1. | Applying spaced repetition |
| | 2. | Having a database of questions and answers co-built by users |
| | 3. | Providing personalized learning experience |
| Youdao | 1. | Providing free and instant full text translations |
| | 2. | Integrating Collins Cobuild Advanced English-Chinese dictionary and authentic resources |
| | 3. | Providing very rich information, including definitions, bilingual examples and encyclopedic knowledge |
| | 4. | Offering audio pronunciations of words and example sentences by native speakers |
| Dictionary | 1. | Integrating several well-known dictionaries |
| | 2. | Offering translations from English to several languages |

## 4.1 Shanbay

As one of the most popular APPs among students, Shanbay has several important features that are facilitative to word learning. Firstly, it enables users to select different target groups of words based on their needs. These target groups are also consistent with almost all common stages of word learning for Chinese students, i.e., primary English, secondary English, College English Test 4 & 6, Test for English majors 4 & 8, Kaoyan, Test of English for International Communication, Test of English as a Foreign Language, International English Language Testing System, Graduate Management Admission Test, etc. There are also some target groups of words for specific purposes, for example, for public speech and business.

Secondly, Shanbay allows users to make their personalized daily learning plan, for example, to learn 20 new words and review 20 words that were learned previously. Based on the learners' personalized plan, Shanbay can automatically generate a certain number of target words for the learners to do self-assessment or quizzes. The self-assessment mode asks users to evaluate and rate their familiarity with a given word. If a user indicates that he or she is very familiar with the word, this word will not appear again; and if the user selects the option not so familiar, the learner will encounter the word again and again until he or she feels that the word has been well learned (Chen 2016). The testing mode of Shanbay does not provide users with multiple choices to facilitate their recalling of the meaning of a target word. This forces learners to remember the meanings of words, not the answers to the questions.

Thirdly, the definitions of words provided by Shanbay are adopted from the Collins Advanced Learner Dictionary. They are accurate and easy to understand. Some example sentences are also provided to better facilitate users' comprehension.

Lastly, Shanbay is easy to use. Learners can also form groups to learn collaboratively. Various ways for English learning are provided, and users can share their learning progresses with friends. To better motivate learners, Shanbay also awards users with medals. Online discussion forum is also provided to encourage communication among users of the APP.

### 4.2 Baicizhan

The most prominent feature of Baicizhan is that it uses images to help learners better understand word meanings and establish links between words and the real world. In addition to images, Baicizhan also provides TV and radio to engage users and assist their learning. Specifically, vocabulary TV of different topics is offered for fun; vocabulary radios which include pronunciations and explanations of words with examples, reading books, and listening practices are offered; articles are also available for users to read; and when users tap a word, its translation immediately comes out.

Another advantage of Baicizhan is that it enables users to add friends and share their leaning progresses with each other. Friends can also have word learning competitions, which is very engaging.

Like Shanbay, Baicizhan also enables users to select target groups of words based on their needs, and different groups of words correspond to different vocabulary sizes. Moreover, it can record users' learning progresses.

Fourthly, Android users can set word cards of Baicizhan as lock screens of their smart phones. This helps users make full use of their trivial time every day.

However, many users reported a shortcoming of Baicizhan. It is sometimes difficult to figure out what image matches the given word as meanings of some words are quite abstract and people may have different understandings of the same word (Huang and Reddy 2015). There are also words with multiple meanings and it is impossible to present all meanings in one image. Additionally, some images are unhelpful for word learning.

### 4.3 SuperMemo

SuperMemo applies spaced repetition to suggest necessary review of a word just before it is likely to be forgotten. The system works in this way: it firstly asks a user to scale from 0 to 5 to indicate how well or poorly the word is recalled; based on this score and the scores of the user's previous viewings, the system then makes a schedule for the review of the word.

The SuperMemo also has a database of questions and answers co-built by users. When reviewing information saved in the database, the program uses the SuperMemo algorithm to decide what questions to show the user. The user then answers the question and rates the recall. Through this way, personalized learning experience is provided. Furthermore, SuperMemo is not only a word learning app but also a program for the learning of mathematical formula, programming, poetry, history, etc.

Because of its scientific design, SuperMemo is effective in promoting word learning in the long-term. However, its user interface is not very user-friendly, and it is very difficult to customize (Godwin-Jones 2010; Schimanke et al. 2014).

### 4.4 Youdao

Youdao dictionary is a multilingual dictionary APP, providing free and instant full text translations for Chinese, English, Japanese, Korean, Spanish, Russian and French. It covers the world's largest Chinese encyclopedia and Wikipedia and is the first online dictionary which integrates the camera word searching function.

Collins Cobuild Advanced English-Chinese dictionary and authentic resources are built into the APP. Users of Youdao can expand their knowledge on words, phrases, idioms, buzzwords, synonyms, bilingual examples and trending stories. The large numbers of example phrases and sentences of target words, bilingual examples and encyclopedic knowledge for the words from Wikipedia can effectively help students thoroughly understand the meanings of the word (Min and Ping 2016).

Audio pronunciations of words and example sentences by native speakers are also available in Youdao. Users can also choose their tones and styles in the settings based on their preferences.

However, this APP do not provide interactive activities or monitoring mechanisms. Users can not share their learning progresses either.

### 4.5 Dictionary

Dictionary.com integrates several well-known dictionaries, including Collins English Dictionary, The Free Online Dictionary of Computing, The American Heritage New Dictionary of Cultural Literacy, The American Heritage Science Dictionary, etc. It also offers translations from English to a range of languages, for example, Arabic, Chinese, French, German, and Italian (Gao 2013).

It is one of the most commonly and frequently used APP among students in China and Hong Kong.

## 5 Evaluation of the Alphabet vs. Aliens

### 5.1 Users of Alphabet vs. Aliens@PolyU

Approximately one hundred students from PolyU used the Alphabet vs. Aliens@PolyU. These students aged between sixteen and eighteen. Thirty-two of them (twenty-one male and eleven female) participated in the focus group interviews and questionnaire surveys, which investigated their expectations and experiences of what is considered helpful and useful features of an application game for learning English. The interview results were coded and analysed to identify common features or points mentioned by the students concerning their perceptions, attitudes and expectations of an effective vocabulary learning APP.

## 5.2 Questions

The participants were asked to indicate to what extent they agreed with the following statements on a five-point Likert scale (strongly agree, agree, neutral, disagree, strongly disagree).

(1) Alphabet vs. Aliens @PolyU is fun to play.
(2) Alphabet vs. Aliens @PolyU is a stress-free way to learn English.
(3) Alphabet vs. Aliens @PolyU help me to become more confident in my learning.
(4) Alphabet vs. Aliens @PolyU allows me to improve on my English on my own time.
(5) Alphabet vs. Aliens @PolyU is more practical than using a vocabulary book.
(6) Alphabet vs. Aliens @PolyU help me to remember English vocabulary better.
(7) Alphabet vs. Aliens @PolyU give me confidence knowing I have an English language resource at hand at any time.
(8) Alphabet vs. Aliens @PolyU will help me to succeed at University.
(9) I will recommend Alphabet vs. Aliens @PolyU to others.

They were also asked to answer two open-ended questions.

(1) What aspects of English vocabulary do you think you have improved by using Alphabet vs. Aliens @PolyU.
(2) Please list three things you like and three things you dislike with Alphabet vs. Aliens@PolyU.

## 5.3 Evaluation of Alphabet vs. Aliens

The participants' evaluation of the nine statements as presented above is demonstrated in Table 3. It can be seen that very positive feedback has been received.

**Table 3.** The participants' evaluation of the nine statements

| Statement | The number of participants who | | | | |
|---|---|---|---|---|---|
| | Strongly agree | Agree | Neutral | Disagree | Strongly disagree |
| 1 | 18 | 12 | 0 | 2 | 0 |
| 2 | 21 | 11 | 0 | 0 | 0 |
| 3 | 15 | 7 | 5 | 5 | 0 |
| 4 | 20 | 11 | 0 | 1 | 0 |
| 5 | 9 | 16 | 3 | 4 | 0 |
| 6 | 11 | 12 | 2 | 6 | 1 |
| 7 | 20 | 12 | 0 | 0 | 0 |
| 8 | 15 | 10 | 4 | 2 | 1 |
| 9 | 20 | 10 | 2 | 0 | 0 |

The participants' answers to the two open-ended questions are: (1) their knowledge of the definitions, parts of speech, and spellings of vocabulary have been improved; (2) the like such features as many missions, hints, explanations, dictionary, and colors of the app.

This first round of interview results also showed that students highly value features like the story plot, graphic, vocabulary list and types of definitions for the design of vocabulary learning APPs, because they believed that rich information and contexts were conducive to word learning.

Based on these findings, the APP was further improved by adding synonyms, sentence contexts and extended definitions of the words. Our followed-up interviews indicated that students rated the improved version of the APP higher than the preliminary one. Such findings are consistent with Zou's (2016, 2017) arguments that the availability of various aspects of word knowledge are conducive to effective word learning as it promotes greater degree of elaboration on the target vocabulary. These findings also shed lights on the development of word learning APPs and may integrate with personalized vocabulary learning systems (Zou et al. 2016; Zou et al. 2017; Xie et al. 2016) in the future development.

## 5.4 Comparing Alphabet vs. Aliens to Other APPs

The second round of interview focused on the comparisons between the Alphabet vs. Aliens and other word learning APPs that the students had used in the past. The ten participants were asked to indicate what the advantages and disadvantages of the Alphabet vs. Aliens are. The results are demonstrated in the following Table 4. Six students stated that the Alphabet vs. Aliens was helpful for their learning of disciplinary words; ten noted that the APP provided long and clear definitions; six mentioned that Alphabet vs. Aliens was suitable for university studies; seven love the hints provided; six like the colorful interface; and eight commented on the good examples of words provided by Alphabet vs. Aliens.

**Table 4.** Advantages and disadvantages of Alphabet vs. Aliens

| Advantages | Disadvantages |
|---|---|
| Helpful with disciplinary words (6 students) | Cannot download the words (3 students) |
| Long and clear definitions (10 students) | No pronunciations (8 students) |
| Suitable for university studies (6 students) | Insufficient animations or visual aids (6 students) |
| Good hints (7 students) | No game-like features (5 students) |
| Colorful interface (6 students) | No flashcards (2 students) |
| Good examples of words (8 students) | No specific lists for academic words (5 students) |

Compared to other APPs, learners felt that Alphabet vs. Aliens did not have features like enabling users to download the words (3 students), providing pronunciations (8 students) and animations or other visual aids (6 students), including game-like features (5 students), flashcards (2 students), or specific lists for academic words (5 students).

When the students were asked to report their learning experience, three mentioned that Alphabet vs. Aliens was fun to play; six felt it helpful but challenging to find the right words; ten reported that Alphabet vs. Aliens helped them think of new words; seven were surprised about their spelling performance; three students felt that Alphabet vs. Aliens was not easy to use and if it is easier, they could learn better; four students stated that the hints were helpful when they were stuck; and seven said they would play Alphabet vs. Aliens more often as they know more about this APP now (Table 5).

**Table 5.** Learning experience

| |
|---|
| Enjoyed playing it as it was fun (3 mentioned it was fun) |
| Helpful but very challenging to find the right words (6 mentioned challenging) |
| Made me think of new words (10 mentioned new words) |
| I thought I was better at spelling (7 were surprised about their spelling) |
| Not easy to use; too complicated design (3 students) |
| It was good I could use hint when I was stuck (4 mentioned hints specifically) |
| I will play this app more often now that I know about it (7 students) |

All ten participants had very positive attitudes towards Alphabet vs. Aliens and confirmed that they would recommend Alphabet vs. Aliens to their friends. Five students explained that this was because Alphabet vs. Aliens helped them learn more vocabulary, three felt that Alphabet vs. Aliens was good for their studies, and one mentioned that Alphabet vs. Aliens helped him with IELTS exam (Table 6).

**Table 6.** Attitudes towards Alphabet vs. Aliens

| | | |
|---|---|---|
| Would you recommend Alphabet vs. Aliens? Why? | Yes. 10 students | Helps us learn more vocabulary (5 students) |
| | | Good for our studies (3 students) |
| | | Help me with IELTS exam (1 student) |

# 6 Conclusion

This research investigates several word learning APPs and compares them with our own APP, Alphabet vs. Aliens. Similarities of popular word learning APPs include enabling users to choose specific target groups of words, having vivid visual aids, providing pronunciations, detailed and accurate definitions and examples, and allowing users to interact with other users. Ours interview results also showed that students highly valued such features. These results support Zou and Xie's (2018) argument that personalized learning is essential to learner engagement and learning effectiveness.

Limitations of this research includes the small number of participants and word learning APPs investigated. Future studies are suggested to examine a wider range of APPs and recruit more participants. How word learning APPs provide personalized learning experience is also a topic of interest.

**Acknowledgement.** This study was fully supported by the Start-Up Research Grant (RG 54/2017-2018R) of the Education University of Hong Kong and a grant from Research Grants Council of Hong Kong Special Administrative Region, China (UGC/FDS11/E03/16).

## References

Abrams, S.S., Walsh, S.: Gamified vocabulary: online resources and enriched language learning. J. Adolesc. Adult Literacy **9**(1), 49–58 (2014)

Abu Bakar, N., Nosratirad, E.: Sustaining vocabulary acquisition through computer game: a case study. Asian Soc. Sci. **9**(5), 1911–2017 (2013)

Bekleyen, N., Yilmaz, A.: The impact of computer-assisted language learning on vocabulary teaching. In: Seventh International Computer & Instructional Technologies Symposium. Firat University, Elazig-Turkey (2011)

Calvo-Ferrer, J.R.: Educational games as stand-alone learning tools and their motivational effect on L2 vocabulary acquisition and perceived learning gains. Br. J. Educ. Technol. **48**(2), 264–278 (2017)

Cavus, N., Ibrahim, D.: A mobile tool for learning English words. In: Paper Presented at the 5th International Conference on Electrical and Computer Systems, Lefke, Cyprus (2008)

Cavus, N., Ibrahim, D.: M-learning: an experiment using SMS to support learning new English language words. Br. J. Educ. Technol. **40**(1), 78–91 (2009)

Chen, C.M., Chung, C.J.: Personalized mobile English vocabulary learning system based on item response theory and learning memory cycle. Comput. Educ. **5**(2), 624–645 (2008)

Chen, M.H., Tseng, W.T., Hsiao, T.Y.: The effectiveness of digital game-based vocabulary learning: a framework-based view of meta-analysis. Br. J. Educ. Technol. **49**(1), 69–77 (2018)

Chen, X.: Evaluating language-learning mobile apps for second-language learners. J. Educ. Technol. Dev. Exchange **9**(2), 39–51 (2016)

Gao, Y.: On the appification of dictionaries: from a Chinese perspective. In: Proceedings of the eLex 2013 Conference, Tallinn, Estonia, pp. 213–224 (2013)

Godwin-Jones, R.: Emerging technologies from memory palaces to spacing algorithms: approaches to second language vocabulary learning. Lang. Learn. Technol. **14**(2), 4–11 (2010)

Huang, L.L., Lin, C.C.: Three approaches to glossing and their effects on vocabulary learning. System **44**, 127–136 (2014)

Huang, X., Reddy, S.C.: NEWordS: a news search engine for English vocabulary learning. Int. J. Sci. Technol. Res. **4**(8), 271–273 (2015)

Kapp, K.: The Gamification of Learning and Instruction: Game-Based Methods and Strategies for Training and Education. Wiley, Hoboken (2012)

Min, H., Ping, Y.: The research on the application of mobile learning into college English teaching. Int. J. Liberal Arts Soc. Sci. **4**(5), 110–114 (2016)

Nihalani, P., Mayrath, M.: Statistics I: findings from using an iPhone app in a higher education course (2010). https://s2.slidedocument.org/uploads/DPDSO2017/09/15/soNjIXmQJR/d8346c34663b203d08bf4f49a2f3960f.pdf. Accessed 1 Feb 2017

Pensky, M.: Digital Game-Based Learning. McGraw Hill, New York (2004)

Rankin, Y., Gold, R., Gooch, B.: 3D role-playing games as language learning tools. In: Gröller, E., Szirmay-Kalos, L. (eds.) Proceedings of EuroGraphics 2006, vol. 25, no. 3. ACM, New York (2006)

Rodriquez, J.E.: Social media use in higher education: key areas to consider for educators. J. Online Learn. Teach. **7**(4), 539–550 (2011)

Schimanke, F., Mertens, R., Vornberger, O.: Spaced repetition learning games on mobile devices: foundations and perspectives. Interact. Technol. Smart Educ. **11**(3), 201–222 (2014)

Sylven, L.K., Sundqist, P.: Gaming as extramural English L2 learning and L2 proficiency among young learners. ReCALL **24**(3), 302–321 (2012)
Uzun, L., Cetinavci, U.R., Korkmaz, S., Salihoglu, U.: Developing and applying foreign language vocabulary learning and practicing game: the effect of vocaword. Digit. Culture Educ. **5**(1), 50–70 (2013)
Xie, H., Zou, D., Lau, R.Y., Wang, F.L., Wong, T.L.: Generating incidental word-learning tasks via topic-based and load-based profiles. IEEE Multimedia **23**(1), 60–70 (2016)
Zou, D.: A study of the components of the involvement load hypothesis: how involvement load should be allocated to "Search" and "Evaluation". Unpublished Ph.D. dissertation, City University of Hong Kong, Hong Kong (2012)
Zou, D.: Comparing dictionary-induced vocabulary learning and inferencing in the context of reading. Lexikos **26**, 372–390 (2016)
Zou, D.: Vocabulary acquisition through cloze exercises, sentence-writing and composition-writing: extending the evaluation component of the involvement load hypothesis. Lang. Teach. Res. **21**(1), 54–75 (2017)
Zou, D., Xie, H.R.: Personalized word-learning based on technique feature analysis and learning analytics. J. Educ. Technol. Soc. (2018)
Zou, D., Xie, H., Rao, Y., Wong, T.L., Wang, F.L., Wu, Q.: A comparative study on various vocabulary knowledge scales for predicting vocabulary pre-knowledge. Int. J. Distance Educ. Technol. **15**(1), 69–81 (2017)
Zou, D., Xie, H., Wong, T.L., Wang, F.L., Wu, Q.: The augmented hybrid graph framework for multi-level e-learning applications. In: Cheung, S., Kwok, L., Shang, J., Wang, A., Kwan, R. (eds.) ICBL 2016. LNCS, vol. 9757, pp. 360–370. Springer, Cham (2016). https://doi.org/10.1007/978-3-319-41165-1_32

# Perceived Online Learning Environment and Students' Learning Performance in Higher Education: Mediating Role of Student Engagement

Zhang Tao[1], Bin Zhang[2], and Ivan Ka Wai Lai[3](✉)

[1] Guangxi Teachers Education University, Nanning 530001, China
t173538073@126.com
[2] Zhuhai College, Jilin University, Zhuhai 519000, China
zhangbin1218@sina.com
[3] City University of Macau, Macau, China
ivanlai@cityu.mo

**Abstract.** Colleges and universities have focused on increasing the number of online courses and programs offered to remove the obstacles in terms of time and space. Partial Least Squares Structural Equation Modeling (SEM) is used to explore the relationships among the parameters. The results of this study indicate a positive relationship between perceived online learning environment and university students' learning performance mediated by students' engagement. Therefore, educators should develop online student engagement strategies in order to increase online student engagement. Furthermore, for improving online students' learning performance, educators should invest their resources to develop a good online learning environment.

**Keywords:** Online learning environment · Learning performance · Engagement Online courses

## 1 Introduction

Recently, through the ease and comfort of computers and other internet devices, colleges and universities have focused on increasing the number of online courses and programs offered (Meyer 2012; Chauhan 2014) to remove the obstacles in terms of time and space (Marino et al. 2008; Stahl et al. 2006). However, at the meantime, the student drop-out rate of online learning is very high (Park and Choi 2009; Shea and Bidjerano 2014). The aim of this study is to test the relationship between perceived online learning environment (OLE) and university students' learning performance mediated by students' engagement. Partial Least Squares Structural Equation Modeling (PLS-SEM) is used to explore the relationships among the parameters.

This article is organized as follows. As a theoretical base of the study, the OLE is firstly described and the learning performance is then outlined. Then, the research model is constructed and hypotheses regarding the effects of perceived designed-related, system-related, content-related, and contact-related OLE on students' LP under the


S. K. S. Cheung et al. (Eds.): ICTE 2018, CCIS 843, pp. 56–64, 2018.
https://doi.org/10.1007/978-981-13-0008-0_6

mediating of student's engagement are developed. The empirical results of PLS-SEM analysis are presented. Finally, findings, conclusion, limitations, and future research directions are discussed.

# 2 Theoretical Background and Hypothesis Development

## 2.1 Perceived Online Learning Environment (OLE) and Learning Performance (LP)

Online learning is defined as access to learning experiences via the use of some web-based technological tools (Reeves et al. 2002; Carliner and Shank 2016). OLE is referring to that learning is occurring in a specific web-based area (Asunka 2008; Barnard-Brak et al. 2010; Zhang and Kenny 2010 and Moore and Kearsley 2011). Students' perceptions of their learning environment influence the quality of performance they achieve (Suksudaj et al. 2015). OLE also emphasizes that students are more advantageous compared with students in conventional classroom environments (Busato et al. 1998; Stein et al. 2005), which make it possible for students and teachers to share knowledge and ideas without having to be at the same place at the same time. Interaction technologies in online learning, like Electronic Classroom Response System (ECRS) and Information Communication Technology (ICT) Facility (Gan and Balakrishnan 2017), can enhance the academic performance of students (Reinecke 2017; Nouh 2016). On the other hand, some empirical studies indicated that students' academic performance does not vary based on the learning environment (Brock et al. 2008), some other studies have demonstrated that students' interest generated by multimedia can negatively affect learning (Bartsch and Cobern 2003; Mayer et al. 2001). Therefore, the following hypothesis is proposed:

H1: Perceived online learning environment is positively related to students' learning performance.

## 2.2 Perceived Online Learning Environment and Student Engagement

Student engagement has been defined as "the extent of students' involvement and active participation in learning activities" (Yang 2011), "the effort, both in time and energy, students commit to educationally purposeful activities" (Greene et al. 2008), or "student psychological investment in learning in terms of motivational interpretations and goals as described in achievement goal theory" (Järvelä et al. 2008). The theoretical models of the student engagement consist of behavioral engagement, psychological engagement and cognitive engagement (Peng 2016). One of the critical features of student engagement is described as "the institution deploys its resources and organizes the curriculum and other learning opportunities to get students to participate in activities" (national survey of student engagement, NSSE), the online learning environment is one kind of resources institution managed. So there is a correlation between OLE and students' engagement.

H2: Perceived online learning environment is positively related to students' engagement.

### 2.3 Student Engagement and Learning Performance

Student engagement is widely recognized as an important influence on learning achievement (Kahu 2013), and has been cited as having an overall positive correlation with academic achievement (Fredricks et al. 2004). In fact, "engagement in educationally purposeful activities" was listed as one of eight measures of student success (Kuh 2001). In light of the above discussion, student engagement should be associated with learning performance. The online learning mostly occurs depending on the engagement of the learners (Delen et al. 2014), the engagement is affected by OLE, so learning engagement may mediate the relationship between OLE and learning performance. According to the proposed hypotheses, the research model is showed in Fig. 1.

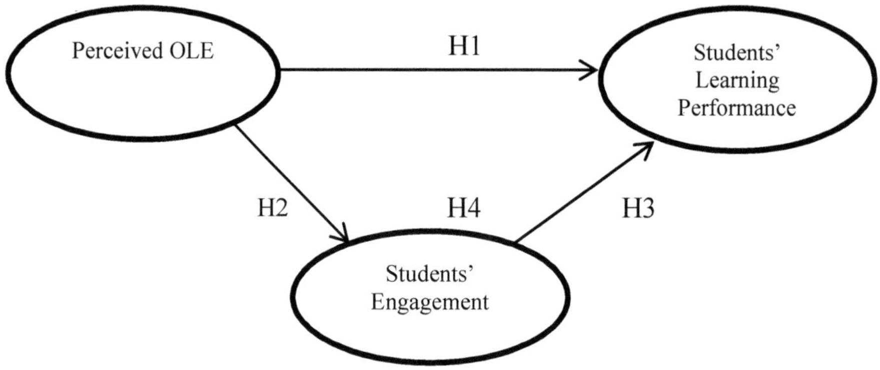


**Fig. 1.** The research model

H3: Students' engagement is positively related to students' learning performance.

H4: Students' engagement mediates the relationship between perceived online learning environment and students' learning performance.

## 3 Research Methodology

### 3.1 Instrument Development

For the survey instrument, existing measures in related literature were identified which had been repeatedly tested and where strong content validity was exhibited. These measures were then adapted to this research. The process of pretesting was launched in an institution with a sample size of 50 college students. Then, the instrument was refined based on the pretest results and suggestions from interviewees. To make sure the participants understanding the survey instrument, some explanations of the constructs will be provided. The instrument and reference sources are shown in Table 1.

**Table 1.** Construct, items and reference research

| Construct | Items | Reference research | Question |
|---|---|---|---|
| Perceived OLE | Content | Cheong (2005) | I think that the information I got is valuable from last online course |
| | System | | I think that my last online course provided very reliable service |
| | Image (interface) | Volery and Lord (2000) | I think the webpage of last online course is friendly |
| | Ease of use | Davis (1989) | I would find it easy to get the system to do what I want it to do |
| Student engagement | Accomplishment | Boekarts et al. (2000) | I finished my last online course fully |
| | Learning joyfully | Skinner et al. (2008) | I enjoy learning new things in last online course |
| | Level of effort | | I worked as hard as I can in last online course |
| Learning performance | Achievement | Xu et al. (2010) | I got a very well academic score in last online course |
| | Satisfaction | Lin (2012) | I feel satisfaction on last online course |
| | Willing to re-use | Cheong (2005) | I intend to use online course as much as possible |

## 3.2 Data Collection

The study was conducted using an internet-based survey. The participation in the survey was voluntary. Participants could withdraw from the survey at any time. After collecting the data, data were coded and analyzed using mixed methods.

A total of 229 participants, who were students in a bachelor-level or above, has been invited to complete the survey. 55 responses were dropped due to incomplete responses or have no experience about online learning. The total number of valid responses was 174 which included 4.0% freshmen, 21.3% sophomores, 25.3% juniors, 37.9% seniors, and 11.5% graduated students. Among the 174 respondents, 19.5% were males and 80.5% were females.

### 3.3 Measurement Mode

Data analysis was performed using PLS-SEM. It is because PLS-SEM has greater power for small sample sizes than covariance-based method. It also does not have a strict demand of normal distribution assumption on sample data. In this study, SmartPLS version 3.2.7 was used (Hair Jr., et al. 2016). Follow the recommendation from Hair et al. (2012) PLS bootstrap resampling procedure with an iteration of 5,000 sub-samples replacement from the initial sample 174 was performed. All the p-values are 0.000, so the model is stable.

## 4 Data Analysis

### 4.1 Reliability and Validity

Measurement reliability was assessed using internal consistency scores, calculated by the Cronbach's Alpha value. Internal consistencies of all variables are considered acceptable since all $\alpha \geq 0.70$, signifying acceptable reliability. As can be seen in Table 2, the composite reliability for all constructs exceeds 0.7. Thus, all constructs in the model exhibit good internal consistency. Discriminant validity was assessed based on the squared correlations between variables and the square root of each construct's average variance extracted (AVE), when the AVE is greater than squared correlations, the discriminant validity is approved. The results show in Table 2 is suggesting discriminant validity is satisfied.

**Table 2.** Reliability and discriminant validity

| | Discriminant validity | | | | | |
|---|---|---|---|---|---|---|
| | Cronbach's alpha | Composite reliability | AVE | Learning performance | Perceived OLE | Student engagement |
| Learning performance | 0.731 | 0.881 | 0.787 | 0.887 | | |
| Perceived OLE | 0.712 | 0.838 | 0.634 | 0.627 | 0.796 | |
| Student engagement | 0.776 | 0.871 | 0.692 | 0.692 | 0.387 | 0.832 |

The $\chi^2$/degree of freedom ratio is 2.763, smaller than the value of 3 which is recommended by Schermelleh-Engel et al. (2003), and the Standardized Root Mean Square Residual (SRMR) Index = 0.091, is smaller than 0.1 which recommended by Kline et al. (2011) and Hu and Bentler (1999). The two indices are above the acceptable fit of the structural model (Cangur and Ercan 2015).

### 4.2 Structural Model for Hypotheses Testing

The hypotheses proposed above were tested collectively using PLS-SEM. The values of R-square represent the amount of variance explained by the independent variables.

The estimates of the path coefficients indicate the strengths of the relationships between the dependent and independent variables. Together, the values of R-square and the path coefficients indicate how well the data support the hypothesized model.

Figure 2 illustrates the value of R-square and the path coefficients of the proposed research model. Learning performance is found to be significantly determined by the two exogenous variables perceived OLE and student engagement. The value of R-square is 0.631 which means that the above mentioned variables explain 63.1% of variance in the learning performance. Likewise, student engagement is found to be slightly determined by perceived online learning environment with an R-square of 0.150. Thus, the perceived online learning environment explains 15.0% of variance in the student engagement.

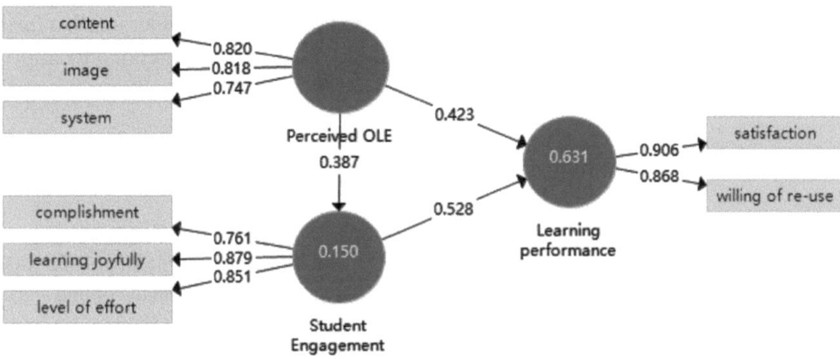


**Fig. 2.** Path analysis.

Hypotheses 1 explore the relationship between perceived OLE and students' performance, which posited that perceived OLE should influence the student performance positively, this hypotheses is supported ($\beta = 0.423$, $p \leq 0.01$).

PLS results provide support for H2, which asserts that online learning environment has an obvious positively impact on student engagement ($\beta = 0.387$, $p \leq 0.01$).

Students' engagement was positively associated with learning performance ($\beta = .528$, $p \leq 0.01$).

Online learning environment had a significantly positive influence on learning performance mediated by student engagement.

Thus, all the 4 hypotheses are supported by the PLS results.

## 5 Discussions and Conclusion

Although a number of studies have examined the relationship between learning environment and students' learning performance in traditional education, a fewer literature revealed the relationship between OLE and students' learning performance with the mediating effect of students' engagement. In the terms of theory building, this study shows the importance of students' engagement in the online education. For the online education, it does not like traditional education where students must attend the class and teachers can force students' participation, it is hard to control students' participation in the online environment. Therefore, educators should develop online student engagement strategies in order to increase online student engagement. Gamification is the one that can keep online students engaged. Students like to play games and get rewards when they complete the exercises after learning a course.

The results of the study indicate that for having a good student learning performance, a good OLE is very important. The educators should invest their resources to develop attractive contents, establish good online learning platforms and internet infrastructure, and build a good online education image.

In this study, the value of R-square of students' engagement is small. This implies that students' engagement would be influenced by other factors. Therefore, further research is expected to find out the factors for enhancing the online student engagement.

This study was conducted in Guangxi, China and the sample size was small, a further study with larger sample size in more provinces of China is recommended to improve the data representativeness.

## References

Asunka, S.: Online learning in higher education in Sub-Saharan Africa: Ghanaian university students' experiences and perceptions. Int. Rev. Res. Open Distrib. Learn. **9**(3), 1–23 (2008)

Barnard-Brak, L., Paton, V.O., Lan, W.Y.: Profiles in self-regulated learning in the online learning environment. Int. Rev. Res. Open Distrib. Learn. **11**(1), 61–80 (2010)

Bartsch, R.A., Cobern, K.M.: Effectiveness of PowerPoint presentations in lectures. Comput. Educ. **41**(1), 77–86 (2003)

Boekarts, M., Pintrich, P.R., Zeidner, M. (eds.): Handbook of Self-Regulation: Theory, Research and Applications. Academic, San Diego (2000)

Brock, L.L., Nishida, T.K., Chiong, C., Grimm, K.J., Rimm-Kaufman, S.E.: Children's perceptions of the classroom environment and social and academic performance: a longitudinal analysis of the contribution of the Responsive Classroom approach. J. Sch. Psychol. **46**(2), 129–149 (2008)

Busato, V.V., Prins, F.J., Elshout, J.J., Hamaker, C.: Learning styles: a cross-sectional and longitudinal study in higher education. Br. J. Educ. Psychol. **68**(3), 427–441 (1998)

Cangur, S., Ercan, I.: Comparison of model fit indices used in structural equation modeling under multivariate normality. J. Modern Appl. Stat. Methods **14**(1), 14 (2015)

Carliner, S., Shank, P. (eds.): The E-Learning Handbook: Past Promises, Present Challenges. Wiley, Hoboken (2016)

Chauhan, A.: Massive open online courses (MOOCS): emerging trends in assessment and accreditation. Digit. Educ. Rev. **25**, 7–17 (2014)

Cheong, I.A.: Educating pre-service teachers for a sustainable environment. Asia-Pacific J. Teach. Educ. **33**(1), 97–110 (2005)

Davis, F.D.: Perceived usefulness, perceived ease of use, and user acceptance of information technology. MIS Q. **13**(3), 319–340 (1989)

Delen, E., Liew, J., Willson, V.: Effects of interactivity and instructional scaffolding on learning: self-regulation in online video-based environments. Comput. Educ. **78**, 312–320 (2014)

Frederick, H.R.L.K.S.: Cracking the paradox of Chinese learners: looking into the mathematics classrooms in Hong Kong and Shanghai. How Chin. Learn Math.: Perspect. Insiders **1**, 348 (2004)

Gan, C.L., Balakrishnan, V.: Enhancing classroom interaction via IMMAP–an interactive mobile messaging app. Telematics Inform. **34**(1), 230–243 (2017)

Greene, T.G., Marti, C.N., McClenney, K.: The effort—outcome gap: differences for African American and hispanic community college students in student engagement and academic achievement. J. High. Educ. **79**(5), 513–539 (2008)

Hair Jr., J.F., Hult, G.T.M., Ringle, C., Sarstedt, M.: A Primer on Partial Least Squares Structural Equation Modeling (PLS-SEM). Sage Publications, Thousand Oaks (2016)

Hair, J.F., Sarstedt, M., Ringle, C.M., Mena, J.A.: An assessment of the use of partial least squares structural equation modeling in marketing research. J. Acad. Market. Sci. **40**(3), 414–433 (2012)

Hu, L.T., Bentler, P.M.: Cutoff criteria for fit indexes in covariance structure analysis: conventional criteria versus new alternatives. Struct. Equ. Model.: Multidisciplinary J. **6**(1), 1–55 (1999)

Järvelä, S., Veermans, M., Leinonen, P.: Investigating student engagement in computer-supported inquiry: a process-oriented analysis. Soc. Psychol. Educ. **11**(3), 299–322 (2008)

Kahu, E.R.: Framing student engagement in higher education. Stud. High. Educ. **38**(5), 758–773 (2013)

Klein, K.J., Knight, A.P., Ziegert, J.C., Lim, B.C., Saltz, J.L.: When team members' values differ: the moderating role of team leadership. Organ. Behav. Hum. Decis. Process. **114**(1), 25–36 (2011)

Kuh, G.D.: Assessing what really matters to student learning inside the national survey of student engagement. Change: Mag. High. Learn. **33**(3), 10–17 (2001)

Lin, W.S.: Perceived fit and satisfaction on web learning performance: IS continuance intention and task-technology fit perspectives. Int. J. Hum.-Comput. Stud. **70**(7), 498–507 (2012)

Marino, S., Hogue, I.B., Ray, C.J., Kirschner, D.E.: A methodology for performing global uncertainty and sensitivity analysis in systems biology. J. Theoret. Biol. **254**(1), 178–196 (2008)

Mayer, R.E., Heiser, J., Lonn, S.: Cognitive constraints on multimedia learning: when presenting more material results in less understanding. J. Educ. Psychol. **93**(1), 187 (2001)

Meyer, K.A.: The influence of online teaching on faculty productivity. Innovat. High. Educ. **37**(1), 37–52 (2012)

Moore, M.G., Kearsley, G.: Distance Education: A Systems View of Online Learning. Cengage Learning, Boston (2011)

Nouh, T., Anil, S., Alanazi, A., Al-Shehri, W., Alfaisal, N., Alfaris, B., Alamer, E.: Assessing correlation between students' perception of the learning environment and their academic performance. JPMA **66**(12), 1616–1620 (2016)

Park, J.H., Choi, H.J.: Factors influencing adult learners' decision to drop out or persist in online learning. J. Educ. Technol. Soc. **12**(4), 207–217 (2009)

Peng, W.: Research on model of student engagement in online learning. EURASIA J. Math. Sci. Tech. Educ. **13**(7), 2869–2882 (2017)

Reeves, T.C., Benson, L., Elliott, D., Grant, M., Holschuh, D., Kim, B., Kim, H., Lauber, E., Loh, S.: Usability and Instructional Design Heuristics for E-Learning Evaluation (2002)

Reinecke, L., Eden, A.: Media use and well-being (2017)

Schermelleh-Engel, K., Moosbrugger, H., Müller, H.: Evaluating the fit of structural equation models: tests of significance and descriptive goodness-of-fit measures. Methods Psychol. Res. Online **8**(2), 23–74 (2003)

Shea, P., Bidjerano, T.: Does online learning impede degree completion? A national study of community college students. Comput. Educ. **75**, 103–111 (2014). https://doi.org/10.1016/j.compedu.2014.02.009

Skinner, E., Furrer, C., Marchand, G., Kindermann, T.: Engagement and disaffection in the classroom: part of a larger motivational dynamic? J. Educ. Psychol. **100**(4), 765 (2008)
Stahl, G.: Group Cognition: Computer Support for Building Collaborative Knowledge, pp. 451–473. MIT Press, Cambridge, MA (2006)
Stein, D.S., Wanstreet, C.E., Calvin, J., Overtoom, C., Wheaton, J.E.: Bridging the transactional distance gap in online learning environments. Am. J. Distance Educ. **19**(2), 105–118 (2005)
Suksudaj, N., Lekkas, D., Kaidonis, J., Townsend, G.C., Winning, T.A.: Features of an effective operative dentistry learning environment: students' perceptions and relationship with performance. Eur. J. Dental Educ. **19**(1), 53–62 (2015)
Volery, T., Lord, D.: Critical success factors in online education. Int. J. Educ. Manag. **14**(5), 216–223 (2000)
Xu, M., Benson, S.N.K., Mudrey-Camino, R., Steiner, R.P.: The relationship between parental involvement, self-regulated learning, and reading achievement of fifth graders: a path analysis using the ECLS-K database. Soc. Psychol. Educ. **13**(2), 237–269 (2010)
Yang, Y.F.: Engaging students in an online situated language learning environment. Comput. Assist. Lang. Learn. **24**(2), 181–198 (2011)
Zhang, Z., Kenny, R.: Learning in an online distance education course: experiences of three international students. Int. Rev. Res. Open Distrib. Learn. **11**(1), 17–36 (2010)

# In-game Card as Educational Reward (ICER) Moodle Plug-in: A Pilot Study

Rita Kuo[1(✉)], Maiga Chang[2], and Cheng-Li Chen[2]

[1] Department of Computer Science and Engineering, New Mexico Institute of Mining and Technology, Socorro, USA
rita.mcsl@gmail.com

[2] School of Computing and Information System, Athabasca University, Athabasca, Canada
maiga.chang@gmail.com, eric.chenglichen@gmail.com

**Abstract.** Reward plays an important role for engaging students in learning in traditional classroom. The research team has designed a Trading Card Game and uses the cards in the game as educational rewards to make the rewards more attractive to students. To ease and reduce teachers' workload in awarding students, the research team designs the In-game Card as Education Reward (ICER) plug-in for Moodle. Teachers are able and only need to pre-define the award criteria based on student performance in Moodle. Moreover, the research team has conducted a pilot to understand the acceptance that teachers have toward the use of the Moodle plug-in in a hands-on workshop jointly held in an advanced learning technology conference. The pilot result shows that most of the teachers believe that rewards can get students motivated in doing learning activities. In addition, teachers who have used Moodle before believe that students can easily learn how to use the plug-in.

**Keywords:** Motivation · Learning management system · Trading card game Educational game

## 1 Introduction

Rewards can positively affect students' learning performance (Winefield et al. 1984). Researchers have proved that giving rewards when students having good performance in the learning activities does improve their persistence of achieving the goals (Woolley and Fishbach 2016). However, if the reward is unattractive to students, it cannot help in terms of getting them engaged in learning (Marinak 2007). On the other hand, web-based learning application and research have grown rapidly (Cook et al. 2010). Web-based distance learning environment allows people access course content online from everywhere at any time. However, the use of rewards in the web-based distance learning situation becomes another issue; for instance, how to deliver the reward to the student if he or she lives on another side of earth and who is going to cover the postage for the delivery?

This research aims to design a reward management and delivery plug-in which adopt in-game (virtual) items as rewards for the web-based learning environment. With the plug-in's help, teachers can give rewards to students based on their learning activity


S. K. S. Cheung et al. (Eds.): ICTE 2018, CCIS 843, pp. 65–76, 2018.
https://doi.org/10.1007/978-981-13-0008-0_7

performances in the learning environment as what they do in the traditional classroom. Students can also easily get the rewards through the plug-in and understand their performance for each learning activity. To get a better reward, students will need to work harder in the upcoming learning activities.

The next section introduces how game-based learning can adopt educational reward mechanism. The proposed reward Moodle plug-in is illustrated in Sect. 3. Section 4 describes the pilot designed for assessing teachers' perceptions toward the rewards and the plug-in. The data analysis results from the pilot are discussed in Sect. 5. Section 6 summarizes this research and talks the possible future works.

## 2 Related Works

Game-Based Learning has become a popular research topic because researchers believe that playing not only can hold students' attention and make students learn concepts and knowledge at same time (Virvou et al. 2005; Boyle 1997). For example, Shakshouka Restaurant helps students understand financial concepts and develop math skills (Barzilai and Blau 2014). Researchers also use Age of Empires II: The Age of Kings to teach history in the social study class (Maguth et al. 2015). Moreover, Weatherlings Teaches students weather and climate by defeating their opponents through the prediction of weather based on the historical climate data (Klopfer et al. 2012; Sheldon et al. 2010).

Chen and colleagues have developed a discipline independent Trading Card Game (TCG) as educational reward system (Chen et al. 2009, 2017). Figure 1 shows the motivation enhancement cycle of using the TCG as educational reward system.

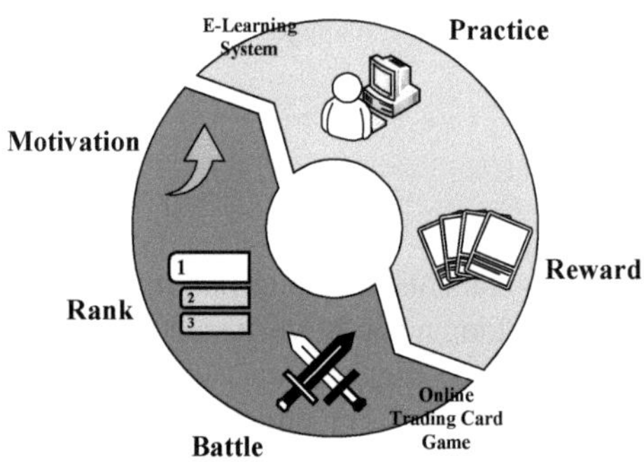


**Fig. 1.** Motivation enhancement cycle

Students get cards of the TCG after they complete the requirements in the learning activities (i.e., learning within an English vocabulary web-based learning system). Students can always play the game with their friends at any time they want. With rarer and higher level cards, students might win a match easier. They may, therefore, would like to collect more rarer and higher level cards from doing learning activities harder and actively.

Teachers can setup different criteria of awarding the cards for students. If students have a better performance in the learning activities, teachers can give them a higher level or rarer card which can help students have higher chance to defeat their opponents in a match when they play the game. For students who do not prefer to compete with others, they could collect the cards just as collecting coins and stamps; they might want to get all of the cards in their collection books.

## 3 In-game Card as Education Reward (ICER) Moodle Plug-in

The research team has design the In-game Card as Education Reward (ICER) Moodle Plug-in for delivering the cards in the TCG (Chen et al. 2017). Teachers can set up the criteria of giving rewards (i.e., cards in the TCG) according to students' performance through the plug-in. The plug-in will also need students' permission in sending reward request to the TCG. With the help of the built-in Educational Resource Information Communication (ERIC) API, students' privacy data in a course, such as student ID and marks, remain unknown to the TCG and its players (Chen et al. 2016). Figure 2 shows an example of how to use the ICER plug-in.

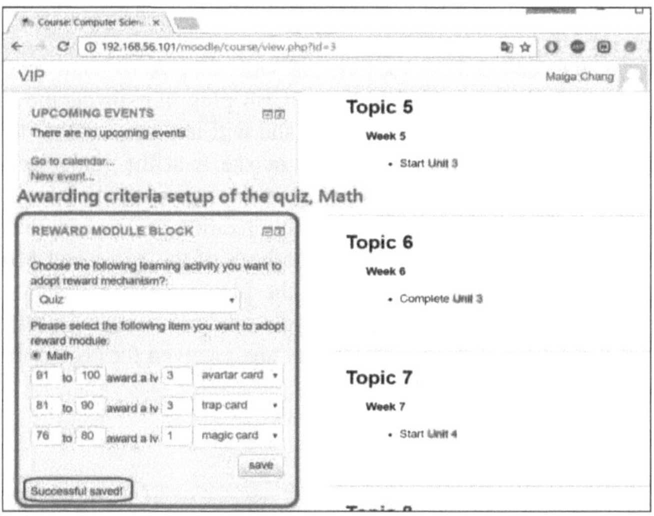


**Fig. 2.** Reward Module block for teachers to setup awarding criteria for the "Math" quiz

When a teacher signs in Moodle, he or she can see the Reward Module block as Fig. 2 shows. The teacher can decide which learning activity he or she would like to have the reward mechanism applied. After the teacher selects a learning activity, such as Quiz in Fig. 2, he or she can determine the criteria of giving cards. In this example, the teacher decides to give a level 3 avatar card to the students who receive marks between 91 to 100, a level 3 trap card to those who get marks between 81 to 90, and a level 1 magic card to the ones who obtain marks between 76 to 80. Students who get marks lower than 75 will not receive any reward according to this setting.

On the other hand, students should be able to receive the rewards after they finish the learning activity. Although Moodle will be aware of what rewards should be given to students, it still needs to have permission granted from the students to really send request of giving cards to the game server; in the meanwhile, student's identity in both Moodle and the game server should remain anonymous for each other. Therefore, when a student signs in Moodle, he or she can only see that his or her performance for the Math quiz has earned him or her a reward based on the award criteria predefined by the teacher as Fig. 3 (a) shows. He or she needs to authorize Moodle to further deliver the reward to the game.

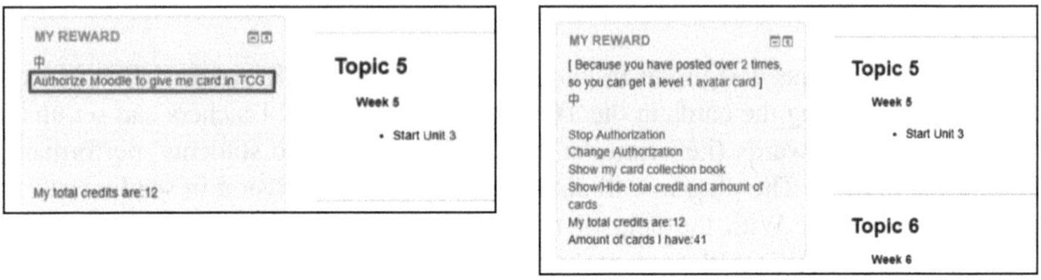


(a) (b)

**Fig. 3.** My Reward block in Moodle: (a) before authorizing Moodle to deliver cards to the game; (b) after the authorization.

After the student clicked the "Authorize Moodle to give me card in TCG" link in the My Reward block shown in Fig. 3(a), the ICER plug-in redirects the student to the Permission Granting page of the TCG. He or she will feel comfortable to enter his or her credential since he or she is aware of he or she is at the game server side. The student also needs to decide which permission he or she would like Moodle to have as Fig. 4(a) shows. Figure 4(b) shows that the authorization process requires the student to enter the authorization code into Moodle so both of the game and Moodle can be convinced that the authorization is made by the player and the student. As soon as Moodle is granted the permission of delivering cards to the game for the student, the student can see the details of the card that he or she received for his or her efforts for a particular learning activity as Fig. 3(b) shows.

(a) (b)

**Fig. 4.** Granting Moodle the permission for accessing the student's information in the game: (a) granting particular permission for Moodle; (b) entering authorization code generated by the game on Moodle.

## 4 Research Design

To understand how teachers perceive the educational reward and the use of ICER plug-in, the research team has several hypotheses illustrated in Fig. 5.

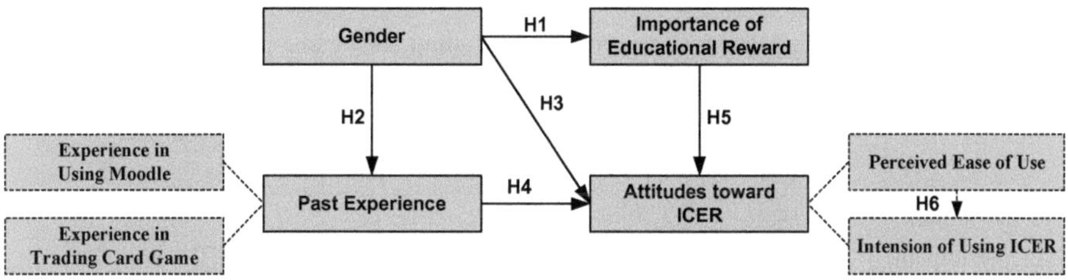


**Fig. 5.** Relations among factors in the hypotheses

- H1: Teachers' gender may affect their perceived importance of educational rewards.
- H2: Teacher's gender may affect their past experience in using Moodle and any trading card games.
- H3: Teacher's gender may affect their attitudes toward the ICER plug-in.
- H4: Teachers' past experience of using Moodle and any trading card games may affect their attitudes toward the ICER plug-in.
- H5: Teachers' perceived the importance of educational reward may affect their attitudes toward the ICER plug-in.
- H6: Teachers' perceived ease of use toward the ICER plug-in may affect their intention of using it.

To understand the acceptance that teachers, the research team collected their perceptions toward rewards and the plug-in with questionnaire in a hands-on workshop jointly held in an advanced learning technology conference in June 2017 in Beijing. Nineteen participants (7 males and 12 females) participated in the workshop and were seen and taught the ICER plug-in. In the end of the workshop, the participants were asked to fill out a questionnaire which asks for their perceived importance of educational rewards, ease of use toward the ICER plug-in, and intention of using the plug-in in the future.

After collected the data, the research team found out that eleven participants (57.9%) have heard Moodle before, but only five participants (26%) had experience of using Moodle (see Table 1).

**Table 1.** Descriptive statistics of participants' Moodle usage experience.

| | Have heard Moodle | | Have used Moodle | |
|---|---|---|---|---|
| | Yes | No | Yes | No |
| # of participant | 11 | 8 | 5 | 14 |
| % of participant | 57.9 | 42.1 | 26.3 | 73.7 |

On the other hand, fourteen participants (73.7%) had heard what trading card games are, and there are also fourteen participants had seen other people playing trading card games before. Only seven participants (36%) had played trading card games in the past (Table 2).

**Table 2.** Descriptive statistics of participants' trading card game playing experience.

| | Have heard | | Have played | | Have seen people play | |
|---|---|---|---|---|---|---|
| | Yes | No | Yes | No | Yes | No |
| # of participant | 14 | 5 | 7 | 12 | 14 | 5 |
| % of participant | 73.7 | 26.3 | 36.8 | 63.2 | 73.7 | 26.3 |

In the next step, the research team used SPSS 17.0 to verify the validity and reliability for the Importance of Education Reward, Perceived Ease of Use, and Intention of Using ICER factors in the questionnaire. The Cronbach's Alpha value is 0.769, which sits on "acceptable" range and shows the questionnaire is reliable (George and Mallery 2010). The principle component analysis was also used to test the validity of the questionnaire and the result is valid as Table 3 shows.

**Table 3.** Validity analysis result for the questionnaire.

| Item | | Factor | | |
|---|---|---|---|---|
| | | 1 | 2 | 3 |
| *Factor 1: importance of educational reward* | | | | |
| I8 | I believe students will work harder in the learning activities (e.g., doing homework, participating in discussion) if they can get rewards through working on them | .963 | | |
| I9 | I believe students prefer they can get rewards from all learning activities | .844 | | |
| I5 | It is workable to set up the reward mechanism toward a specific learning activity | .754 | | |
| *Factor 2: intention of using ICER* | | | | |
| I7 | I would like to use ICER Moodle Plug-in in my course | | .915 | |
| I6 | Once the student achieves the criteria of the getting rewards in the learning activity, he/she can get the cards from Trading Card Game as the reward | | .747 | |
| I2 | The process of how students authenticate Moodle dispatching cards in the Trading Card Game as reward is straightforward | | .746 | |

(*continued*)

**Table 3.** (*continued*)

| Item | | Factor | | |
|---|---|---|---|---|
| | | 1 | 2 | 3 |
| *Factor 3: perceived of ease of use* | | | | |
| I3 | The ways of getting cards in Trading Card Game through different learning activities are similar | | | .951 |
| I1 | Using ICER Moodle plug-in in Moodle is ease to use | | | .739 |
| I4 | I believe students can easily learn how to authenticate Moodle dispatching cards in the Trading Card Game as reward | | | .728 |
| Eigenvalue | | 3.359 | 2.180 | 1.558 |
| % of variance | | 37.318 | 24.223 | 17.314 |
| Overall $\alpha = 0.775$, total variance explained is 78.855% | | | | |

# 5 Evaluation and Discussion

## 5.1 Findings

The research team used t-test to verify hypothesis H1 to understand whether or not teachers' gender will affect their perceived importance of educational rewards. The results listed in Table 4 show that there is no significant difference between male and female teachers' believe in terms of the importance of the educational rewards; both groups agreed students will perform better in the learning activities with proper educational rewards.

**Table 4.** Independent t-test result for teachers' perceived importance of educational reward in gender.

| | Descriptive statistics | | | *t*-test | | |
|---|---|---|---|---|---|---|
| | N | Mean | SD | *t* | *df* | *p* |
| Male | 7 | 4.46 | 0.393 | 1.083 | 17 | 0.294 |
| Female | 12 | 4.18 | 0.619 | | | |

Regarding whether or not teachers' gender will affect their past experience in using Moodle and any trading card games (hypothesis H2), the research team used Chi-square test to examine the data. The results showed that there is no significant difference between male and female teachers' past experience of using both technologies. Tables 5 and 6 list the analysis results of the Chi-square tests.

The research team also wanted to know whether teachers' gender will affect their attitudes toward the ICER plug-in (i.e., hypothesis H3). The t-test analysis is applied and the results are shown in Table 7. Although the results show that there is no significant between male and female teachers in their attitudes toward the ICER plug-in, male teachers are slightly more positive in terms of Perceived Ease of Use factor, but, on the contrary, female teachers are more positive on the intention of using the ICER plug-in in the future.

**Table 5.** Chi-square test result for teachers' past Moodle usage experience in gender.

| | | Count | | | $\chi^2$ test | | |
|---|---|---|---|---|---|---|---|
| | | Yes | No | Total | $\chi^2$ | *df* | *p* |
| Have heard Moodle | Male | 4 | 3 | 7 | 0.003 | 1 | 0.663 |
| | Female | 7 | 5 | 12 | | | |
| Have used Moodle | Male | 2 | 5 | 7 | 0.029 | 1 | 0.634 |
| | Female | 3 | 9 | 12 | | | |

**Table 6.** Chi-square test result for teachers' past trading card game usage experience in gender.

| | | Count | | | $\chi^2$ test | | |
|---|---|---|---|---|---|---|---|
| | | Yes | No | Total | $\chi^2$ | *df* | *p* |
| Have heard TCG | Male | 5 | 2 | 7 | 0.029 | 1 | 0.634 |
| | Female | 9 | 3 | 12 | | | |
| Have played TCG | Male | 3 | 4 | 7 | 0.172 | 1 | 0.526 |
| | Female | 4 | 8 | 12 | | | |
| Have seen others playing TCG | Male | 5 | 2 | 7 | 0.029 | 1 | 0.634 |
| | Female | 9 | 3 | 12 | | | |

**Table 7.** t-test result for teachers' attitudes toward the ICER plug-in in gender.

| | | Descriptive statistics | | | *t*-test | | |
|---|---|---|---|---|---|---|---|
| | | N | Mean | SD | *t* | *df* | *p* |
| Perceived ease of use | Male | 7 | 3.810 | 0.537 | 0.992 | 17 | 0.335 |
| | Female | 12 | 3.528 | 0.626 | | | |
| Intention of using ICER | Male | 7 | 3.810 | 0.573 | −1.303 | 17 | 0.210 |
| | Female | 12 | 4.086 | 0.351 | | | |

Teachers' past experience in using Moodle and any trading card games might affect their attitudes toward the ICER plug-in (i.e., hypothesis H4). The research team used t-test to verify the hypothesis. The results in Table 8 showed that there is no significant difference in teachers' past experience of using Moodle toward their attitudes of using the ICER plug-in. However, when the research team applied t-test in each item, the results showed that teachers who have (M = 4.00, SD = 0.00) and have not (M = 3.71, SD = 0.756) used Moodle before have significant difference in their thought for "I2. The process of how students authenticate Moodle dispatching cards in the Trading Card Game as reward is straightforward" ($t(13) = 2.280$, $p = 0.040$).

The results listed in Table 9 indicate teachers' past experience in using trading card game has no significant difference in their attitudes toward the ICER plug-in. The research team also applies t-test to each of the items, and the results show that teachers who have (M = 3.71, SD = 0.469) and have not (M = 4.00 SD = 0.000) heard trading card games have significant difference for their thought on I2 ($t(13) = -2.280$, $p = 0.040$). There is also a significant difference ($t(13) = -2.280$, $p = 0.040$) between

**Table 8.** t-test result for teachers' attitudes toward the ICER plug-in in past experience in using Moodle.

| | | | Descriptive statistics | | | *t*-test | | |
|---|---|---|---|---|---|---|---|---|
| | | | N | Mean | SD | *t* | *df* | *p* |
| Have heard Moodle | EoU | Yes | 11 | 3.546 | 0.670 | −0.725 | 17 | 0.478 |
| | | No | 8 | 3.750 | 0.495 | | | |
| | Intention | Yes | 11 | 4.000 | 0.494 | 0.196 | 17 | 0.847 |
| | | No | 8 | 3.959 | 0.416 | | | |
| Have used Moodle | EoU | Yes | 5 | 3.934 | 0.276 | 1.348 | 17 | 0.195 |
| | | No | 14 | 3.524 | 0.649 | | | |
| | Intention | Yes | 5 | 4.134 | 0.380 | 0.865 | 17 | 0.399 |
| | | No | 14 | 3.929 | 0.475 | | | |

EoU: perceived ease of use; Intention: intention of using ICER

**Table 9.** t-test result for teachers' attitudes toward the ICER plug-in in past experience in using any trading card games.

| | | | Descriptive statistics | | | *t*-test | | |
|---|---|---|---|---|---|---|---|---|
| | | | N | Mean | SD | *t* | *df* | *p* |
| Have heard TCG | EoU | Yes | 14 | 3.572 | 0.659 | −0.723 | 17 | 0.479 |
| | | No | 5 | 3.800 | 0.379 | | | |
| | Intention | Yes | 14 | 3.976 | 0.480 | −0.106 | 17 | 0.917 |
| | | No | 5 | 4.002 | 0.408 | | | |
| Have played TCG | EoU | Yes | 7 | 3.716 | 0.487 | 0.456 | 17 | 0.654 |
| | | No | 12 | 3.583 | 0.668 | | | |
| | Intention | Yes | 7 | 3.904 | 0.600 | −0.571 | 17 | 0.575 |
| | | No | 12 | 4.029 | 0.361 | | | |
| Have seen others playing TCG | EoU | Yes | 14 | 3.691 | 0.479 | 0.715 | 17 | 0.484 |
| | | No | 5 | 3.466 | 0.900 | | | |
| | Intention | Yes | 14 | 3.976 | 0.480 | −0.106 | 17 | 0.917 |
| | | No | 5 | 4.002 | 0.408 | | | |

EoU: perceived ease of use; Intention: intention of using ICER

teachers who have (M = 3.71, SD = 0.469) and have not (M = 4.00 SD = 0.000) seen other people playing trading card games to the same question.

To evaluate the hypothesis H5, the research team uses Pearson correlation to find out the linear dependence between teachers' perceived the importance of educational reward and their attitudes toward ICER. Two sub-factors are examined in the attitudes toward ICER, which are Perceived Ease of Use and Intension of Using ICER plug-in. The results (see Table 10) show that there is no significant relation between teachers' perceived the importance of educational reward and the perceived ease of use of ICER plug-in; the relation between teachers' perceived the importance of education reward and the intention of using ICER plug-in in the future is also not significant.

**Table 10.** Correlation analysis between teachers' perceived the importance of educational rewards and two sub-factors of their attitudes toward the ICER plug-in.

| | Perceived ease of use | Intention of using ICER |
|---|---|---|
| Pearson correlation | 0.117 | 0.381 |
| Sig. | 0.634 | 0.108 |
| N | 19 | 19 |

Pearson correlation is also applied to validate the hypothesis H6 and the result show that there is no relation between teachers' perceived ease of use toward the ICER plug-in and their intention of using it in the future, $r = 0.294$, n = 19, $p = 0.222$.

## 5.2 Discussion

Based on the data analysis results, we have the following findings:

1. Most of the participants believe educational rewards are important.
   Teachers have given high score (M = 4.29, SD = 0.55) for the Importance of Educational Reward factor. The result shows that most of the teachers believe educational rewards can enhance students' performance in learning activities. However, participants have less intention of using the ICER Plug-in (M = 3.98, SD = 0.45) in their classes.
   One of the possible reason is only five of the participants (26.3%) have used Moodle before; teachers who are not using Moodle will have less intention of using the ICER plug-in as Table 8 shows. Another possible reason is that teachers believe the process of integrating the ICER plug-in could be more straightforward (Ease of Use factor: M = 3.63, SD: 0.60). If we can simply the process of integrating ICER plug-in into Moodle or making the plug-in available directly in Moodle, teachers might have more intention of using it in the future.
2. Teachers who have used Moodle before believe students can easily learn how to use ICER plug-in in Moodle to get cards for their efforts done in learning activities.
   Although the analysis results show that there is no significant difference for hypothesis H5, teachers who have used Moodle before (M = 3.93, SD = 0.28) are more positive in average than those who have not (M = 3.52, SD = 0.65) in terms of how ease students can learn to authorize Moodle to giving themselves in-game cards as rewards. The result shows that if teachers or students have used Moodle before, they can learn how to use ICER plug-in in Moodle easily.
3. Teachers' past experience in any trading card games will not affect their attitudes toward ICER plug-in.
   Based on the results listed in Table 9, teachers' past experience in any trading card game will not affect the two sub-factors of their attitudes toward ICER plug-in. They rate positively for both Ease of Use (M = 3.63, SD = 0.59) and Intention of Using the Plug-in (M = 3.98, SD = 0.45). The results show that whether or not the teachers have heard or used any trading card games before, they believe the plug-in is easy to use and have intention of using this plug-in in their course.

4. Teachers' past experience in any trading card games will affect them believing in how easy students can learn the process of authorizing Moodle to give cards in the game as reward.
   The analysis results show that teachers who have not heard about trading card games or have not seen other people playing such games believe the process of students authorizing Moodle to give cards in the game as rewards is straightforward comparing to those who have heard trading card games or have seen other people playing trading card games; however, there is no difference between teachers who have and have not played the games before. The result show that whether the teacher have played any trading card game before or not, they still rate positively toward how easy when students learning the process of authorizing Moodle to give them cards as reward.
5. Teachers' perceived ease of use in ICER plug-in will not affect their intention of using ICER plug-in in the future.
   As the hypothesis H6 is rejected, there is no significant linear relation between teachers' perceived ease of use in ICER plug-in and their intension of using the plug-in in the future. The result show that even few of the participants believe the workflow of using ICER plug-in can be improved (two participants rated lower than Neutral in average for the Ease of Use sub-factor, they still give positive responses toward the Intention of Using the plug-in.
6. Teachers has positive attitudes toward the ICER plug-in in both genders.
   Because there is no significant difference between male and female teachers in their past experience of using Moodle and trading card games as Tables 5 and 6 show, the result indicates that even teachers who don't have experience of using the two techniques male teachers are still believe the plug-in is easy to use and female teachers still have high intention of using the plug-in in their classes (see Table 7).

# 6 Conclusion

The research team has developed an In-game Card as Educational Reward (ICER) Moodle Plug-in to connect Moodle with an existing trading card game, TCG. Teachers can use the plug-in to define the criteria of how students get rewards when they do learning activities in Moodle; students can also be aware of when and why a reward they receive for a particular learning activity. The plug-in also keeps students' private data like student ID and marks in Moodle remaining unknown from the game.

The research team has conducted a pilot to understand teachers' perceptions toward the educational rewards and the use of the plug-in. The pilot is done in a hands-on workshop jointly held in an advanced learning technology conference in June 2017 in Beijing with nineteen teachers. The analysis results of the collected data show that most of the teachers believe educational rewards are important. Although the perceived ease of use towards the plug-in is in moderate score, teachers who have experience of using Moodle believe that the use of the plug-in in Moodle is easy to learn for students.

The next step of the research is to understand students' perceptions toward the plug-in. Moreover, the research team would like to know whether or not students believe the adoption of the plug-in in Moodle can help them do better and harder in different online learning activities. We would like to know if students' learning motivation can be improved when the plug-in is used in a course.

**Acknowledgement.** The authors want to thank Mitacs Globalink Research Award for supporting graduate student doing the relevant research abroad.

## References

Barzilai, S., Blau, I.: Scaffolding game-based learning: impact on learning achievements, perceived learning, and game experiences. Comput. Educ. **70**(2014), 65–79 (2014)

Boyle, T.: Design for Multimedia Learning. Prentice Hall, London (1997)

Chen, C.-L., Chang, M., Chang, H.-Y.: Educational Resource Information Communication API (ERIC API): the case of Moodle and online tests system integration. In: Proceedings of 3rd International Conference on Smart Learning Environments (ICSLE 2016), pp. 225–229 (2016)

Chen, C.-L., Zhao, Y., Luo, A., Chang, M., Qian, D., Kuo, R., Chang, H.-Y.: Educational reward Moodle plug-in. In: Proceeding of 21st Global Chinese Conference on Computers in Education (GCCCE 2017), pp. 211–218 (2017)

Chen, P., Kuo, R., Chang, M., Heh, J.-S.: Designing a trading card game as educational reward system to improve students' learning motivations. In: Pan, Z., Cheok, A.D., Müller, W., Chang, M. (eds.) Transactions on Edutainment III. LNCS, vol. 5940, pp. 116–128. Springer, Heidelberg (2009). https://doi.org/10.1007/978-3-642-11245-4_11

Chen, P., Kuo, R., Chang, M., Heh, J.-H.: The effectiveness of using in-game cards as reward. Res. Pract. Technol. Enhanced Learn. **12**, 15 (2017)

Cook, D.A., Garside, S., Levinson, A.J., Dupras, D.M., Montori, V.M.: What do we mean by web-based learning? A systematic review of the variability of the interventions. Med. Educ. **44**(8), 765–774 (2010)

George, D., Mallery, P.: SPSS for Windows Step by Step: A Simple Guide and Reference 18.0 Update, 11th edn. Allyn & Bacon, Boston (2010)

Klopfer, E., Sheldon, J., Perry, J., Chen, V.H.: Ubiquitous games for learning (UbiqGames): weatherlings, a worked example. J. Comput. Assist. Learn. **28**(5), 465–476 (2012)

Maguth, B.M., List, J.S., Wunderle, M.: Teaching social studies with video games. Soc. Stud. **106**(1), 32–36 (2015)

Marinak, B.A.: Insights about third-grade children's motivation to read. Coll. Read. Assoc. Yearb. **28**, 54–65 (2007)

Sheldon, J., Perry, J., Klopfer, E., Ong, J., Chen, V.H.H., Tzuo, P.W., Rosenheck, L.: Weatherlings: a new approach to student learning using web-based mobile games. In: Proceedings of 5th International Conference on the Foundations of Digital Games, pp. 203–208. ACM (2010)

Virvou, M., Katsionis, G., Manos, K.: Combining software games with education: evaluation of its educational effectiveness. Educ. Technol. Soc. **8**(2), 54–65 (2005)

Winefield, A.H., Barnett, J.A., Tiggemann, M.: Learned helplessness and IQ differences. Pers. Individ. Differ. **5**(5), 493–500 (1984)

Woolley, K., Fishbach, A.: For the fun of it: harnessing immediate rewards to increase persistence in long-term goals. J. Consum. Res. **42**(6), 952–966 (2016)

# Automatic Correction of Definite Article Redundancy Error in the English Compositions of College Students

Lei Wang[1(✉)] and Ting Wang[2]

[1] School of Foreign Languages, Peking University, Beijing 100871, China
wangleics@pku.edu.cn

[2] No. 1 Senior High School of Liaoyang, Liaoyang 111000, Liaoning Province, China
cherrywangting@126.com

**Abstract.** Scholars have conducted research on the errors made by language learners in writing both theoretically and practically, and they have made considerable breakthroughs in Second Language Acquisition (SLA) with respect of writing. The learners' use of articles in English writing displays a certain pattern with factors such as influence from a learner's mother language, personal idiosyncracy or common misunderstanding. Thus it is feasible to judge whether an article is used correctly in a certain context on a rule basis. This paper adopts a rule-based method, which lets the computer learn how to use articles from empirical sources and automatic correct the Definite Article Redundancy Errors (DAREs) committed by students in their English compositions. With the help of both grammatical and contextual information, the rules in our system are deduced from authentic examples and possess authority and accuracy. The system also allows teachers to add or alter these rules flexibly by either examining the actual cases or updating their professional knowledge as they wish. By doing this, we hope the quality and efficiency of marking compositions in Chinese colleges will be improved.

**Keywords:** Automatic correction · Definite Article Redundancy Error
College English writing

## 1 Introduction

As one of the two ways of expression, writing reflects one's cognitive, thinking and logical abilities and plays a central role in learning another language. However, in spite of the considerable effort and investment in the English education of various levels around China, both parents and students have seen neither fruitful outcome nor optimistic prospect. Compared with the other three abilities, i.e. listening, speaking and reading of English learners, writing presents the poorest performance among students in various academic requirements, whilst the very ability is in high demand in most of examinations or tests for both academic and professional purposes.

Second language learners display various types of errors in their compositions and the misuse of articles is among those typical ones committed by Chinese students under


S. K. S. Cheung et al. (Eds.): ICTE 2018, CCIS 843, pp. 77–85, 2018.
https://doi.org/10.1007/978-981-13-0008-0_8

a unified education system. This can be attributed to the lack of this particular word class in Chinese language and most often students are at a loss when using English articles.

Researchers both home and abroad have conducted research on the mechanism of committing errors when using certain words. Among them the theory of Error Analysis (EA) has made significant progress in Second Language Acquisition (SLA) and shifted linguistic study of language learning and teaching from external environment to the observation and investigation of learners themselves [1]. For second language learners who attempt to learn and use English articles, EA can still serve as a powerful instrument of guidance. In the secondary education of China, teachers spare no efforts in letting students know well about how to use English articles correctly and testing students' command of articles has always been a focus. For instance, questions about article usage appear often in the test papers of National Matriculation English Test (NMET).

*Example 1*

She is ____ newcomer to ____ chemistry but she has already made some important discoveries. (NMET 1994)

A. the; the B. the; / C. a; / D. a; the

*Example 2*

The cakes are delicious. He'd like to have ____ third one because ____ second one is rather too small. (NMET Shanghai 2002)

A. a; a B. the; the C. a; the D. the; a

As the English instructors for both high school and Chinese college students, the authors spend much time on marking students' compositions in work and finds the article errors in students' writing make up a large proportion of the total errors. In the 150 compositions of over 27,000 words collected for this study, the article errors account for around 60% and the redundancy the definite article "the" in front of nouns or noun phrases is a typical error.

Therefore, it is necessary to analyze and summarize the redundancy errors in article usage committed by Chinese college students. If the automatic recognition of article redundancy in English writing of college students can be realized, the quality and efficiency of composition marking by teachers can be greatly improved.

## 2 Literature Review

Plenty of research has been done on the use of the English definite article "the". Pica [2] seriously questioned the "orthodox" instruction on the use of articles in the textbooks in America and attempted to arouse public awareness of the problems that had emerged in the US grammar education. Master [3] laid a special emphasis on raising teachers' consciousness in teaching articles in students' writing. Lee et al. [4] studied the acquisition of the definite article "the" of three Chinese children and obtained different findings compared with the former study results about foreigners' learning English. Robertson [5] specifically investigated the variability in the use of the English article system by Chinese learners of English.

With the development of education in China, research on article usage of Chinese students begins to flourish. Wang [6] made an attempt to put the definite article in the discourse/text perspective and investigated the cohesion and coherence of the definite article in the linguistic, situational and cultural context. Li and Cai [7] specially studied the article errors in college students' writing. Wang [8] studied the use of the definite article in the sub-corpus St2, St4 and St6 from the Chinese Learners' English Corpus (CLEC) and revealed that the non-generic use of the definite article "the" present different levels of difficulty for Chinese learners and thus they are not acquired at the same time in the process of acquisition. With the improvement of students' English level, the number of missed obligatory use and unnecessary use reduces obviously. However, most of these research has laid an emphasis on the function or grammatical attributes of articles from a descriptive approach but not from a quantitative one.

As for study on the automatic processing of English articles, Knight et al. [9] proposed a method based on decision tree in selecting articles for nouns, while Chang [10] did the same job by applying a method of transformation-based error-driven learning mechanism. Experiments showed that they can both improve the accuracy of selecting articles for machine translation systems. Ning [11] treated articles as tags and described the problem as a task of sequence tagging, which is one of the strategies of machine learning. The work adopted attributes such as word, POS and MI information of before-and-after words. The experiment showed that $F$-value reaches 80% with a corpus of patent extracts which includes 91,106 articles.

## 3 The Characteristics of College English Writing and Rules of Using Definite Article

In China, College English is a credit course and the Ministry of Education stipulated general guidelines and curriculum for it, which is included in its *College English Curriculum Requirements* [12]. In terms of writing, it requires:

> For writing, a student should propose his/her opinion on general topics and is able to write English abstracts for academic papers; can write short academic papers with depiction of various charts and tables; can write a composition of no fewer than 160 words with content, opinion, logic and fluency.[1]

Therefore, we can see that college English writing is restricted in terms of both content and structure and it is plausible to deduce the correct usage of articles based on a complete set of rules. Figure 1 is the writing part of College English Test Band 4 (CET 4), which is a popular English test taken by many Chinese students.

[1] In fact, there are three levels of requirements in *College English Curriculum Requirements*, which are "basic", "relatively high" and "high". We only give "relatively high" here as an example.

**2013年12月全国大学英语四级考试试卷**

**Part Ⅰ Writing (30 minutes)**

**Directions:** For this part, you are allowed 30 minutes to write a short essay entitled What Electives to Choose. You should write at least 120 words but no more than 180 words following the outline given below in Chinese:

1. 各大学开设了各种各样的选修课；
2. 学生因为各种原因选择了不同的选修课；
3. 以你自己为例……

**What Electives to Choose**

Student's response ____________________

**Fig. 1.** The writing part for College English Test Band 4

Many college students expect to continue their study abroad, especially those countries with good universities such as the US or the UK. To do that they have to take English tests such as TOEFL organized by Educational Testing Service (ETS) or IELTS organized by the British Council. Both tests include a writing part. Let's take TOEFL for example. Its writing part[2] requires (See Fig. 2):

**SAMPLE TEST**

Read the question below. In a real test, you will have 30 minutes to plan, write, and revise your essay. Candidates with disabilities may request a time extension. Typically, an effective response will contain a minimum of 300 words.

Question: Do you agree or disagree with the following statement?

A teacher's ability to relate well with students is more important than excellent knowledge of the subject being taught. Use specific reasons and examples to support your answer.

**REQUIREMENT**

For the second task, you will demonstrate your ability to write an essay in response to a question that asks you to express and support your opinion about a topic or issue. Your essay will be scored on the quality of your writing. This includes the development of your ideas, the organization of your essay, and the quality and accuracy of the language you use to express your ideas.

**Fig. 2.** Requirement of the wring part of TOEFL

In the two sample responses given by ETS official website, they contain 447 words and 329 words respectively.

[2] http://www.baidu.com/link?url=lOr8wvpkgvsUAr0dFcM7nvJfW9z7hyOkS2OaUdcSkGg-foPqUKBd3F3S1nW4vx6SHWMmc2ABN0g7ALv7J8NWIYq.

In the English education of Chinese universities, teachers often assign writing tasks to students who select English courses of various levels. Let's take Level 3 of College English Course in Peking University for example. Teachers will assign writing tasks at the beginning of each semester along with clear requirements and ask students to submit their work to a certain website by a certain deadline. The following is the writing requirement of Level 3 (Fig. 3):

> *Students are able to take notes, answer questions and writing abstracts in English; can write a short essay of 150–180 words within half an hour about certain topics and summaries with coherent content and correct grammar.*

**WRITING INSTRUCTION**

Write a composition based on the following topic with no less than 150 words and no more than 200 words. (Please mark your total words at the end and submit your work to our website.)

TOPIC: How can student-teacher relationship be improved in college?

**One student's response:**

As education developing quickly, there is a rising problem on student-teacher relationship.

Some students have words with their teachers during the (UDA) class or even worse. They talk less and hardly greet in the school. If the exacerbation of the relationship continues, the(UDA) education will not even exist. It should be taken seriously.

In my opinion, three reasons lead to this phenomenon. First, the typical one-way education model. It makes students receivers rather than participants. Second, less communication. There is widespread apathy among the(UDA) students. And finally, the reduction of mutual trust between teachers and students. Teachers and students merely dream about the resurgence but they never put it into practice.

To solve this problem, communication must be established. Only when they talk to each other, can they trust each other. They need to know what exact role they play. Friendship appears. Then the(UDA) indifference will no longer be there. Once they become friends, teaching will be more effective and enjoying.

**Fig. 3.** The writing requirement of Level 3 and one sample response (There are other errors in this student's composition that are erased from the sample for its irrelevance to our research. "UDA" is the tag used for "Unnecessary Definite Article", i.e. DARE, by the author in marking students' compositions.)

From the above we can see that the compositions required for college students have a maximum of 200 words and in practice students only use limited vocabulary.

The curricula of college English education require students to pass CET 4 and will not compel students to learn English beyond its requirements. But if a student passes band 4 and wants to take band 6, he or she is free to further learn English and teachers are exempted from the responsibility to instruct him or her. The *College English Curriculum Requirements* [12] also provide suggested vocabulary for both teaching and learning and the following Fig. 4 lists parts of the vocabularies for both CET 4 and CET 6[3]:

| Band 4 vocabulary | | Band 6 vocabulary | |
|---|---|---|---|
| abandon | vt. 放弃 | abbreviation | n.节略，缩写，缩短 |
| ability | n.能力；能耐，本领 | abide | vt.遵守 vt.忍受 |
| able | a.有能力的；出色的 | abolish | vt.废除，取消 |
| abnormal | a.不正常的；变态的 | absent | a.不在意的 |
| aboard | ad.在船(车)上；上船 | absorption | n.吸收；专注 |
| about | prep.关于；在...周围 | abstract | a.理论上的 n.抽象 |
| above | prep.在...上面；高于 | absurd | a.不合理的，荒唐的 |
| abroad | ad.(在)国外；到处 | abundance | n.丰富，充裕 |
| absence | n.不在场；缺乏 | accessory | n.同谋 a.附属的... |
| absent | a.不在场的；缺乏的... | academic | a. 学术的 |

**Fig. 4.** Suggested vocabulary of CET 4 and CET 6 (part)

From the above vocabulary lists we can see that students generally apply a limited vocabulary when writing compositions in the above-mentioned writing tests. The words used by students in our compositions that exceed the CET 4 vocabulary range are merely 64 and the CET 6 are 37[4].

More importantly, the prompts in these tests are often related to students' life as is shown is Table 1, which further restricts students' register in writing from the pragmatic perspective.

**Table 1.** The statistics of composition corpus[a]

| No. | Nouns or verbs | Counts |
|---|---|---|
| 1 | people | 840 |
| 2 | know | 684 |
| 3 | life | 654 |
| 4 | world | 564 |
| 5 | China | 501 |
| … | … | … |

[a]Here the composition corpus refers to the compositions in Table 3 in Sect. 4.

Therefore, we adopt a rule-based method and take both pragmatic and semantic factors into account in order to make accurate judgment about the redundancy of definite

[3] http://wenku.baidu.com/view/ae44f24d33687e21af45a910.html.

[4] Only nouns and verbs are counted.

article "the" in students' compositions. The set of rules is generalized from several authoritative grammar books together with experience from teachers of secondary and higher education. Meanwhile, we allow teachers to add or alter the rules flexibly according their actual teaching practice based on their professional knowledge. Table 2 provides some examples of the set of rules.

**Table 2.** The set of rules for identifying DAREs

| ID | Rule | Formal description | Example |
|---|---|---|---|
| 1 | Noun or NP followed by "of"[a] | If noun or NP + "of", then "the" + noun or NP | We must deal with the problem of inflation |
| 2 | Noun or NP followed by "that" | If noun or NP + "that", then "the" + noun or NP | I agree with the view that music is important |
| 3 | Most of + the + Noun or NP | If "most of" + noun or NP, then "the" + noun or NP | Most of the problems are solved |
| 4 | No "the" before abstract noun | If abstract noun, then NOT "the" + abstract noun | history, music, love, freedom, power |
| 5 | "the" before special noun or NP | If special noun or NP, "the" + special noun or NP | the United States, the poor, the whole country |
| … | … | … | … |

[a]To make it convenient to formalize, the DAREs are identified actually by the principle of violating the rules in the table.

## 4 System, Experiment and Discussion

Our system was developed in collaboration with the Institute of Computational Linguistics at Peking University. Even though it is still in progress, we manage to input the compositions by college students during the fall semester of 2013–14 at Peking University. These compositions were written by students studying an English course to fulfill their credit requirement as one of the semester assignments. On average, each composition has around 200 words and the errors committed by students in these compositions were marked by their instructor who is specialized in English language teaching, and in particular, the DARE errors in them were marked with the tag "UDA". The statistics of the marked compositions is shown in the following Table 3.

**Table 3.** Information of students' compositions

| | |
|---|---|
| No. of compositions | 152 |
| Total no. of words (tokens) | 27,360 |
| Frequencies of words (types) | 2,357 |
| No. of article errors | 183 |
| No. of DAREs | 112 |

Figure 5 provides a flowchart that shows how a student's composition is processed and the DAREs will be detected and corrected automatically. We hope that with this system teachers' workload of marking students' writing can be alleviated.

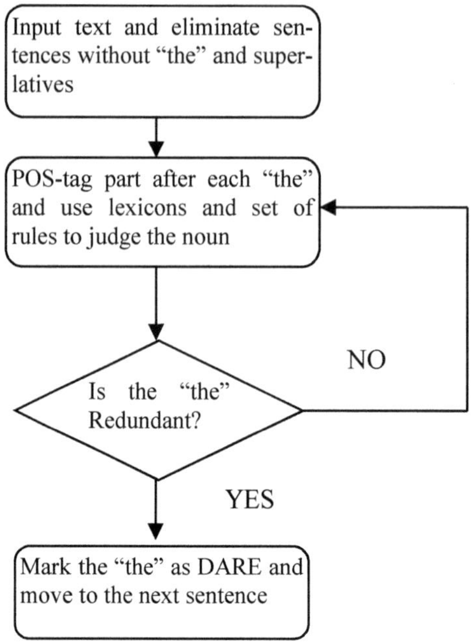


**Fig. 5.** The flowchart showing how a student's composition is processed

After the compositions were input into our system, the following result was obtained as is shown in Table 4.

**Table 4.** Experiment result

| Precision | Recall | $F$-value ($F = 1$) |
|---|---|---|
| 74.2% | 89.1% | 80.8% |

The advantage of rule-based systems is their accuracy. Therefore, the definite articles that should appear in front of some noun phrases were identified fairly accurately, such as "the China" (which is wrong) and "the United States" (which is correct). Most of the misjudgments happened to those abstract nouns that is hard to determine the presence of a proceeding definite article, such as "the education", "the concept". What made it even more difficult was the co-reference, i.e. to decide whether the second mention of the same noun would need the "the". Sometimes when the rules were applied, the "seesaw" phenomenon also occurred; thus our rules need further modifications in order to facilitate the decision process and correctly eliminate the redundant definite articles.

## 5 Conclusion and Future Work

Articles are one of the word classes that second language learners encounter at the very early phase of learning. Thanks to Corder [13] who believed the errors committed by L2 learners be summarized and analyzed so that their common characteristics can be identified and treated from a positive perspective. We now also think in learning or using a foreign language, errors shall be regarded as the mark of learners' L2 progress. By doing this work, we hope to standardize a pattern on the basis of which both educators and researchers are able to adjust their pedagogical approaches or research methods.

So far we have been working on a solution for auto-correcting the article redundancy error in students' writing. Nevertheless, this is only the first step forward because the use of articles is very complicated and involves complex grammatical, semantic and pragmatic knowledge. And even the word class itself include definite articles and indefinite articles. In the short run, we plan to work on the missing of definite articles in students' writing, while in the long run we will deal with an overall solution of article errors in students' compositions at both high school and college level.

**Acknowledgment.** This work is supported by the grant "Research on Teaching College English Writing and Modern Educational Technology (2013)" from Beijing College English Research Association.

## References

1. Ellis, R.: Understanding Second Language Acquisition. Oxford University Press, Oxford (1985)
2. Pica, T.: The article in American English: what the textbooks don't tell us? In: Wolfson, N., Judd, E. (eds.) Sociolinguistics and Language Acquisition, pp. 222–233. Newbury House, Rowley (1983)
3. Master, P.: Consciousness raising and article pedagogy. In: Belcher, D., Braine, G. (eds.) Academic Writing in Second Language Essays on Research and Pedagogy, pp. 183–204. Ablex, Norwood (1995)
4. Lee, K., et al.: Referential place-holding in Chinese children's acquisition of English articles. Appl. Psycholinguist. **15**, 29–43 (1994)
5. Robertson, D.: Variability in the use of the English article system by Chinese learners of English. Second Lang. Res. **16**, 135–172 (2000)
6. Wang, J.: Cohesion and coherence of the definite article at level discourse/text. J. Sichuan Int. Stud. Univ. **17**(6), 68–71 (2001)
7. Li, J., Cai, J.: The article errors in Chinese students' writing based on corpus. J. PLA Foreign Lang. Coll. **6**, 8–62 (2001)
8. Wang, J.: The acquisition of non-generic use of definite articles of Chinese learners. J. Foreign Lang. Educ. **26**(3), 22–26 (2005)
9. Knight, K., et al.: Automated postediting of documents. In: Proceedings of AAAI 1994 (1994)
10. Chang, B., Liu, Y., Liu, Q.: Research on article selection in Chinese-English machine translation. J. Chin. Inf. Process. **12**(2), 8–14 (1998)
11. Ning, W., Cai, D., Zhang, G., Ji, D., Miao, X.: Research on article choice based on conditional random fields. J. Chin. Inf. Process. **22**(6), 20 (2008)
12. Department of Higher Education, Ministry of Education of China: College English Curriculum Requirements. Shanghai Foreign Language Education Press (2007)
13. Corder, S.P.: Error Analysis and Interlanguage. Oxford University Press, Oxford (1976)

# Mobile Learning and Flipped Classrooms

# A Study on the Pattern and Trend of Students' Typical Usage of Mobile Devices in Learning Activities

Simon K. S. Cheung(✉)

The Open University of Hong Kong, Good Shepherd Street, Homantin, Kowloon, Hong Kong
kscheung@ouhk.edu.hk

**Abstract.** This paper investigates the pattern and trend of university students' typical usage of mobile devices for learning purposes. Based on the surveys conducted to the full-time students at the Open University of Hong Kong in the past 5 years, it is revealed that the majority of students usually use mobile phones for communication using social media whilst less than half usually use mobile phones in reading e-books and doing assignments. Tablet computers are usually used for connecting to learning portals and reading e-books. Notebook computers are still used for conventional usage, such as doing assignment. It is also revealed that the use of tablet computers for doing assignment becomes popular because of the availability of cloud-based storage. The use of mobile phones for connecting to learning portals becomes popular since many mobile apps for learning portals are available. As compared to mobile phones, tablet computers and notebook computers become less popular for communication using social media. The results affirm that the pattern and trend of typical usage depends on not only the nature of the learning activities but also the functional features, limitations and technological development of mobile devices.

**Keywords:** Mobile learning · Mobile devices · Learning activities
Mobile device usage

## 1 Introduction

In the past decade, mobile devices have been widely used by university students for learning purposes. They generally include mobile phones, tablet computers and notebook computers, which are portable or handheld computers with an operating system, network and communication utilities for internet access, e-mail, social media, software applications, and data storage.

In Hong Kong, both the internet penetration and mobile device penetration used to stay at very high percentages. As reported in a recent census's thematic household survey, in Hong Kong, the Internet penetration rate for the age group between 15 and 24 is 99.8%, and 99.3% of the same age group possess a mobile phone with internet access [1, 2]. Among many other regions and countries in Asia, Hong Kong has the almost the highest internet penetration rate and mobile device penetration rate, as reported by the World Bank [3].


S. K. S. Cheung et al. (Eds.): ICTE 2018, CCIS 843, pp. 89–100, 2018.
https://doi.org/10.1007/978-981-13-0008-0_9

Given the over 99% internet penetration rate and mobile device penetration rate for the age group between 15 and 24 in Hong Kong, it can be inferred that almost every full-time university student possesses at least a mobile device with internet access. This enables mobile or ubiquitous learning, which emphasizes learning anywhere and anytime [4–6]. The successful adoption of mobile learning indeed depends on not only the technological feasibility of mobile learning but also the students' needs of flexible learning [7–10]. With the advent of the latest mobile technology and the growing needs of flexible and mobile learning, the popularity of using mobile devices for learning purposes has become obvious.

The Pearson Student Mobile Device Survey is a comprehensive survey conducted in 2011 to 2015 with an aim to better understand how students use mobile phones, tablet computers, notebook computers and other mobile devices for learning purposes [11]. The targets are college students in the United States. According to the survey, in 2015, 85% of students owned a mobile phone and 89% of students owned a notebook computer while 52% of students owned a tablet computer. The percentages had been steadily increased from 2011, especially on the ownership of tablet computers. It is also reported that, for learning purposes, notebook computers were still the most often used mobile devices, and that more students often use mobile phones than tablet computers. In figures, 87%, 64% and 40% of students often use notebook computers, mobile phones and tablet computers, respectively.

The author conducted similar surveys on the students' usage of mobile devices at the Open University of Hong Kong for several years. Dated back to 2011/12, in terms of the ownership of mobile devices, 83% of distance-learning students and 92% of full-time students owned a mobile phone while 63% of distance-learning students and 59% of full-time students owned a notebook computer [12, 13]. Also, only 34% of distance-learning students and 16% of full-time students owned a tablet computer. Until 2014/15, the figures had not varied a lot, except that the percentage of full-time students owning a tablet computer had been increased by more than double [14]. It is reported that, over the academic years from 2012/3 to 2014/15, the typical usage of mobile phones, tablet computers and notebook computers had been stabilized. Mobile phones were often used for e-mail, social media and internet browsing, but not often used for reading e-books and doing assignments. Tablet computers were often used for connecting to learning portals and reading e-books but not for doing assignments. Notebook computers are often used in all learning activities [12–14].

This paper investigates the university students' usage of mobile devices, based on the annual surveys conducted to the full-time undergraduate students at the Open University of Hong Kong. It aims to identify the student's typical usage of mobile phone, tablet computers and notebook computers in different learning activities, such as connecting to learning portals, accessing e-books, communication using e-mail and social media, doing assignments, and browsing the internet for other online resources, as well as to observe the trend and changes in the usage over the past several years. The rest of this paper is structured as follows. Section 2 is an overview of mobile devices, which are generally characterized by their technical features and limitations. Section 3 reports the results of the surveys in the past 5 academic years. Section 4 discusses the pattern and trend of the typical usage, based on the survey results. Section 5 briefly concludes this paper.

## 2 Overview of Mobile Devices

Mobile devices generally refer to hand-held or portable electronic computing devices with the processing capability comparable to a personal computer. These mobile devices are characterized by a number of features, including a flat screen display, a touch-pad or touch-screen interface, a virtual or physical keyboard, a weight of less than 2 kg, and the provision of network interfaces to access the internet through Wi-Fi network, and 3G or 4G cell network. Similar to other computing devices, mobile devices have an operating system and data storage, on which software applications can be installed and operated. Typical bundled software applications include e-mail, social media, online communication tools, calendar, internet browser, e-book reader, multimedia player, note taking utilities, etc.

Mobile devices are generally classified into 3 categories, namely, mobile phones, tablet computers and notebook computers. In this paper, the students' usage of each of these 3 categories of mobile devices for learning are investigated. For the purpose of this study, the following definitions are used for mobile phones, tablet computers and notebook computers.

***Mobile Phones.*** Mobile phones broadly refer to smart phones which provide not only the telephony functions but also internet access and computing functionality. Mobile phones are characterized by a flat screen with a touch-screen interface and a virtual keyboard. Typical operating systems for mobile phones are Android and iOS. A typical mobile phone has a flat screen display of less than 6-inch width, supporting touch-screen navigation. Owing to the small screen size which is not conducive for reading e-books, many mobile phones do not provide e-book reader. The weight is less than 1 kg. Almost all mobile phones have the built-in camera and multimedia player. A mobile phone can be continuously used for several hours to half a day if its battery is fully charged. Network accesses are supported, including Wi-Fi network, 3G or 4G cell network. Representative examples are the Apple iPhone [15], Samsung Galaxy Note [16] and Sony Xperia [17].

***Tablet Computers.*** Tablet computers broadly refer to both tablet computers and slate computers, but not netbook computers which come with a fixed (and non-detachable) physical keyboard. Like mobile phones, tablet computers are characterized by a flat screen with a touch-screen interface and a virtual keyboard. Some tablet computers provide a detachable physical keyboard. However, tablet computers do not provide the conventional telephony functions. Typical operating systems for tablet computers are Android, iOS and Windows. A typical tablet computer has a flat screen display of 7 to 12-inch width, supporting touch-screen navigation. The weight is around 1 kg. A tablet computer can be continuously used for several hours to half a day if its battery is fully charged. For network interface, tablet computers are usually equipped with Wi-Fi network interface. It is not common for tablet computers to provide 3G or 4G cell network support. Representative examples are the Apple i-Pad [18], Samsung Galaxy Tab [19] and Microsoft Surface [20].

***Notebook Computers.*** Notebook computers broadly refer to notebook computers, netbook computers and laptop computers which are functionally identical to desktop personal computers. They have a fixed (and non-detachable) physical keyboard, with a touch-pad or track stick as the pointing device for navigation. A typical notebook computer has a screen display of 10 to 17-inch width. The weight ranges from 1 to 2 kg, depending on the screen size. Many conventional notebook computers resemble the desktop computers, operating on Windows or Mac OS and the traditional desktop software applications. Some notebook or netbook computers operate on Android or iOS. In recent years, notebook computers tend to use solid state memory which consume lesser power than the traditional hard disk drives. A typical notebook computer with solid state memory can be continuously used for 4 to 8 h. Almost all notebook computers provide both wired and wireless network interface, but not supporting 3G or 4G cell network. Representative examples are the Lenovo ThinkPad [21], Apple MacBook [22] and Sony VAIO [23].

Table 1 summarizes the characteristics and technical features of mobile phones, tablet computers and notebook computers.

**Table 1.** Summary of the characteristics technical features of mobile devices

| Features | Mobile phones | Tablet computers | Notebook computers |
|---|---|---|---|
| Screen size | Less than 6 inch | 7 to 12 inch | 10 to 17 inch |
| Disk storage | Solid state memory | Solid state memory | Solid state memory, or hard disk drives |
| Input device | Virtual keyboard | Virtual keyboard, or detachable keyboard | Physical and fixed (non-detachable) keyboard |
| Pointing device | Touch screen | Touch screen, or touch-pad of a detachable keyboard | Touch screen, touch-pad or track-stick of a non-detachable keyboard |
| Weight | Less than 1 kg | Around 1 kg | 1 to 2 kg |
| Battery life | 8 to 12 h | 8 to 12 h | 4 to 8 h |
| Network adaptor | Wi-Fi network, and 3G or 4G cell network | Wi-Fi network; seldom 3G or 4G cell network | Wi-Fi network, and wired network |
| Operating system | Mobile OS, such as Android and iOS | Mobile OS, such as Android and iOS | Conventional PC OS, or mobile OS |
| Application software | Mobile applications on Android and iOS | Mobile applications on Android and iOS | Typical PC applications, or mobile applications |

In recent years, there are some new mobile phones with a larger screen size, say 6 or 7 inch, called phablets [24]. On the other hand, notebook computers become more portable with longer battery life, after the adoption of solid-state memory instead of hard disk drives for reducing the weight and minimizing the consumption of power. Some notebook computers also support a detachable physical keyboard, and can be used perfectly as tablet computers without the physical keyboard as they support touch-screen with a virtual keyboard. Unquestionably, the boundary between mobile phones and tablet computers as well as the boundary between tablet computers and notebook computers become blurred.

For our study, phablets, which have telephony functions, are regarded as mobile phones. Notebook computers refer to those with a physical fixed (and non-detachable) keyboards that cannot be used as a tablet computer.

## 3 Survey on the Use of Mobile Devices for Learning Purposes

This section reports the survey on the students' typical usage of mobile devices for learning purposes, conducted at the Open University of Hong Kong over the past 5 academic years.

The Open University of Hong Kong is a public university in Hong Kong offering both undergraduate and postgraduate programmes in full-time face-to-face mode or part-time distance-learning mode [25]. The university has been using a full-fledged online learning environment for 20 years, where students had used to retrieve course materials and learning resources, perform quizzes and tests, submit assignments and communicate with the instructors and peer classmates. For several years, an annual survey has been conducted to the undergraduate students at the Open University of Hong Kong on their typical usage of mobile devices in different learning activities, usually at the beginning of an academic year.

In this paper, the focus is placed on the full-time undergraduate students, using the surveys over the past 5 academic years, i.e. 2012/13, 2013/14, 2014/15, 2015/16 and 2016/17. For each year, a set of randomly selected students were invited to participate an online survey in the form of multiple-choice questionnaires. The survey has two parts. In the first part, students were asked on their possession of mobile devices, and their daily usage in terms of hours per day. In the second part, there are three sets of identical questions, asking if mobile devices are usually used in the following learning activities. One set of questions is for mobile phones, and the other two are for tablet computers and notebook computers.

- accessing e-mails related to study;
- connecting to the learning portal for retrieving learning materials, enquiring learning-related information, submitting assignments, etc.;
- reading e-books or learning resources in e-format;
- communicating with other through social media or online chat;
- doing assignments or other learning tasks;
- browsing the internet for online learning materials.

The first part of the survey results are summarized in Tables 2 and 3, which report the possession of mobile devices and the daily usage, respectively.

The second part of the survey results are summarized in Tables 4, 5 and 6. They show the percentages of students who usually use mobile phones, tablet computers and notebook computers in different learning activities.

**Table 2.** Possession of mobile devices.

| Mobile devices | % of students possessing the devices for learning purposes | | | | |
|---|---|---|---|---|---|
| | 2012/13 (n = 385) | 2013/14 (n = 368) | 2014/15 (n = 359) | 2015/16 (n = 279) | 2016/17 (n = 370) |
| Mobile phones | 95% (367) | 93% (342) | 94% (337) | 98% (274) | 97% (360) |
| Tablet computers | 29% (111) | 37% (137) | 43% (153) | 43% (121) | 42% (154) |
| Notebook computers | 53% (204) | 53% (194) | 64% (228) | 65% (181) | 65% (239) |
| Nil | 0% (0) | 1% (2) | 0% (0) | 0% (0) | 1% (3) |

**Table 3.** Daily usage of mobile devices.

| Daily usage in hours per day | % of students using mobile devices for learning purposes | | | | |
|---|---|---|---|---|---|
| | 2012/13 (n = 385) | 2013/14 (n = 368) | 2014/15 (n = 359) | 2015/16 (n = 279) | 2016/17 (n = 370) |
| More than 3 h | 69% (265) | 72% (265) | 69% (247) | 73% (204) | 78% (288) |
| 2 to 3 h | 13% (51) | 14% (50) | 17% (62) | 14% (38) | 14% (51) |
| 1 to 2 h | 12% (48) | 10% (37) | 11% (38) | 11% (30) | 6% (23) |
| Less than 1 h | 5% (21) | 4% (16) | 3% (12) | 3% (7) | 2% (8) |

**Table 4.** Usage of mobile phones in different learning activities.

| Learning activities | % of students usually use mobile phones in the learning activities | | | | |
|---|---|---|---|---|---|
| | 2012/13 (n = 367) | 2013/14 (n = 342) | 2014/15 (n = 337) | 2015/16 (n = 274) | 2016/17 (n = 360) |
| Accessing e-mails | 76% (279) | 75% (257) | 75% (252) | 80% (218) | 80% (288) |
| Learning portal | 74% (271) | 77% (265) | 79% (267) | 89% (238) | 90% (324) |
| Reading e-books | 44% (163) | 44% (150) | 47% (157) | 50% (136) | 51% (182) |
| Social network | 93% (342) | 94% (323) | 94% (316) | 94% (258) | 98% (351) |
| Doing assignments | 29% (106) | 30% (101) | 23% (78) | 33% (91) | 29% (106) |
| Browsing internet | 73% (268) | 76% (261) | 74% (251) | 75% (206) | 79% (284) |

**Table 5.** Usage of tablet computers in different learning activities.

| Learning activities | % of students usually use tablet computers in the learning activities | | | | |
|---|---|---|---|---|---|
| | 2012/13 (n = 111) | 2013/14 (n = 137) | 2014/15 (n = 153) | 2015/16 (n = 121) | 2016/17 (n = 144) |
| Accessing e-mails | 66% (73) | 64% (88) | 61% (94) | 69% (83) | 66% (95) |
| Learning portal | 74% (82) | 73% (100) | 75% (115) | 79% (95) | 77% (111) |
| Reading e-books | 64% (71) | 68% (93) | 67% (102) | 70% (85) | 63% (91) |
| Social network | 71% (79) | 63% (86) | 65% (99) | 60% (72) | 60% (86) |
| Doing assignments | 50% (56) | 39% (53) | 48% (73) | 57% (69) | 60% (87) |
| Browsing internet | 73% (81) | 69% (94) | 71% (109) | 71% (86) | 72% (103) |

**Table 6.** Usage of notebook computers in different learning activities.

| Learning activities | % of students usually use notebook computers in the learning activities | | | | |
|---|---|---|---|---|---|
| | 2012/13 (n = 204) | 2013/14 (n = 194) | 2014/15 (n = 228) | 2015/16 (n = 181) | 2016/17 (n = 239) |
| Accessing e-mails | 64% (130) | 62% (120) | 68% (155) | 66% (119) | 74% (177) |
| Learning portal | 79% (161) | 74% (143) | 77% (176) | 78% (142) | 80% (193) |
| Reading e-books | 70% (142) | 67% (130) | 70% (160) | 69% (125) | 71% (169) |
| Social network | 67% (136) | 54% (105) | 59% (135) | 59% (107) | 59% (140) |
| Doing assignments | 99% (201) | 93% (181) | 98% (224) | 98% (177) | 98% (235) |
| Browsing internet | 70% (142) | 65% (127) | 72% (164) | 67% (121) | 67% (160) |

## 4 Pattern and Trend of Typical Usage

This section discusses the pattern and trend of university students' typical usage of mobile devices, based on the survey results.

It is shown in Table 2 that the percentage of students possessing mobile phones for learning purposes has been consistently high (over 90%), and even reached 97% or 98% recently. The percentage of students possessing tablet computers and notebook computers for learning purposes have become stabilized at around 40% and 65% respectively. For the daily usage of mobile devices for learning purposes, as shown in Table 3, there is an increasing trend over the past 5 academic years. The majority of students (near 80%) used to use mobile devices for more than 3 h per day in different learning activities.

In Table 4, the students' typical usage of mobile phones are communication using e-mail and social media, and connecting to learning portal and browsing the internet. The usage on online communication has been consistently high (over 75% and over 90% on e-mail and social media, respectively) over the past 5 years. This is because the handheld mobile phones are portable and can access the network anytime and anywhere, through Wi-Fi network, 3G or 4G cell network interfaces. It is also shown that students do not usually use mobile phones for reading e-books and doing assignments. This aligns to the physical limitations of mobile phones, such as small screen size and no full-size physical keyboard. Besides, as many mobile apps for learning portals are available, more and more students usually use mobile phones for connecting to the learning portals.

It is shown in Table 5 that around 60% of students usually use tablet computers in all the learning activities, except doing assignments. There are however no particular learning activities that tablet computers were usually used by a large percentage (over 80%) of students. For reading e-books, it is clear that more students usually use tablet computers than mobile phones. Besides having a larger flat screen comparable to the size of printed books, tablet computers generally provide an e-book reader with some enhanced features, such as online dictionary and pronunciation, which are advantages over the traditional books. Among other learning activities, the least percentage of students usually use tablet computers for doing assignments. One reason is the lack of a physical keyboard. Another reason is the lack of memory storage. However, some new models of tablet computers offer detachable physical keyboards. Cloud-based storage is now provided for mobile users. Perhaps for these reasons, the percentage rose from around 50% to 60% last year.

Notebook computers are usually used by students as shown in Table 6. Over 70% of students usually use notebook computer in all learning activities, except for social networking (less than 60% of students usually use notebook computers for social networking). As most of the notebook computers do not connect to 3G or 4G cell networks, it not convenient for social networking, where instant communication is preferred. This is also why only around 70% of students usually notebook computers for e-mail communication and internet browsing. Except on the portability and cell network connection, notebook computers offer many advantages over mobile phones and tablet computers, such as the provision of a physical keyboard, more memory storage, and more capacity of operating the conventional software applications. These advantages are especially useful for doing assignments, as reflected in Table 6 that a very large percentage (98% or 99%) of students usually use notebook computers for doing assignments.

Based on the above observations, the pattern of students' typical usage of mobile devices can be derived. Table 7 summarizes the percentage of students usually using mobile phones, tablet computers and notebook computers in different learning activities. A higher percentage of students usually using a particular type of mobile devices for a particular learning activity implies that the type of mobile devices is frequently used for the learning activity. In contrast, a lower percentage implies that the type of mobile is not frequently used for the learning activity. In numerical terms, over 80% is generally regarded as very frequent, 60% to 80% as frequent, 40% to 60% as less frequent, and less than 40% as not frequent.

**Table 7.** Pattern of students' usage of mobile devices in different learning activities.

| Learning activities | % of students usually using mobile devices in learning activities (in 5 years) | | |
|---|---|---|---|
| | Mobile phones | Tablet computers | Notebook computers |
| Accessing e-mails | Frequent (75% to 80%) | Frequent (61% to 66%) | Frequent (62% to 74%) |
| Learning portal | Frequent (74% to 90%) | Frequent (73% to 79%) | Frequent (74% to 80%) |
| Reading e-books | Less frequent (44% to 51%) | Frequent (63% to 70%) | Frequent (67% to 71%) |
| Social network | Very frequent (93% to 98%) | Frequent (63% to 71%) | Less frequent (54% to 67%) |
| Doing assignments | Not frequent (23% to 33%) | Less frequent (39% to 60%) | Very frequent (93% to 99%) |
| Browsing internet | Frequent (73% to 79%) | Frequent (69% to 73%) | Frequent (65% to 72%) |

Following the notion, as shown in Table 7, mobile phones are very frequently used for social networking, less frequently used for reading e-books, and not frequently used for doing assignments. Tablet computers are less frequently used for doing assignment. Notebook computers are very frequently used for doing assignment, and less frequently used for social networking. This pattern of usage is similar to the one derived by the author in [14].

Although the pattern of typical usage of mobile devices is quite stabilized, there are changes which mimic salient trend of typical usage of mobile devices over the past 5 years. Whilst these changes are mostly insignificant, some become more frequently used (upward trend), and some become less frequently used (downward trend) in particular learning activities, as shown in Table 8.

**Table 8.** Trend of students' usage of mobile devices in different learning activities.

| Learning activities | Trend of usage of mobile devices in learning activities in terms of frequency | | |
|---|---|---|---|
| | Mobile phones | Tablet computers | Notebook computers |
| Accessing e-mails | Insignificant | Insignificant | Insignificant |
| Learning portal | Upward trend | Insignificant | Insignificant |
| Reading e-books | Insignificant | Insignificant | Insignificant |
| Social network | Insignificant | Insignificant | Insignificant |
| Doing assignments | Insignificant | Upward trend | Insignificant |
| Browsing internet | Insignificant | Insignificant | Insignificant |

Regarding the changes in the pattern of students' usage of mobile devices for learning purposes in the past 5 years, one significant trend is that more and more students usually use mobile phones for connecting to the learning portals. An underlying reason is that, in recent years, many learning management system developers have provided mobile apps for the learning portals. These mobile apps provide functionality on learning management, such as class calendar and examination calendar, timetables and announcements are more convenient for students to access through mobile phones anywhere and anytime.

Another significant trend is that more and more students usually use tablet computers for doing assignments. In recent years, cloud-based storage has become popular for users to store some working files on cloud when using mobile devices. Besides, detachable physical keyboards have become popular accessories for tablet computers. These keyboards are small, portable, and can be even foldable. With the provision of detachable keyboards and cloud-based storage, tablet computers can be used as good as notebook computers, and this explains the increasing trend of using tablet computers in doing assignments.

## 5 Conclusion

Todays, mobile devices have been widely used. Almost every student owns at least a mobile device for learning purposes. In this paper, we investigate the pattern and trend of students' typical usage of mobile devices for learning purposes. Following a brief review of mobile devices which include mobile phones, tablet computers and notebook computers, this paper reports the surveys on the usage of mobile devices conducted to the full-time undergraduate students in the Open University of Hong Kong in the past 5 academic years. Based on the survey results, the pattern and trend of usage are derived and reported.

In summary, the majority of students usually use mobile phones for communication using e-mail and social media, whilst less than half usually use mobile phones in reading e-books and doing assignment. In contrast, mobile tablets are not as popular as mobile phones for communication using e-mail and social media. They are usually used for connecting to learning portals and reading e-books. Notebook computers are still used for conventional usage, such as doing assignments, reading e-books, and browsing the internet for learning resources. These observations on the pattern of students' usage of mobile devices indeed align with the observations obtained in an earlier study by the author [14].

Over the past 5 academic years, it is observed that more and more students usually use mobile phones for connecting to learning portals, and use tablet computers for doing assignments. This is because the availability of many mobile apps of learning portals or learning management systems, and the availability of some cloud-based storage and the provision of detachable keyboards for some tablet computers. On the other hand, there are no significant changes on the pattern of usages of notebook computers in different learning activities.

The findings reflect that the pattern of how mobile phones, tablet computers and notebook computers are used for learning purposes have become stabilized, and the usages depend on the nature of the learning activities and the technical features as well as limitations of the mobile devices. The findings also reflect that the trend of usages depend on the latest technological development of the mobile devices. It is hoped that the findings can provide some insights on the students' typical usage of mobile devices for learning purposes in Hong Kong.

## References

1. Census and Statistics: Information Technology Usage and Penetration, Thematic Household Survey Report No. 62, Census and Statistics Department, Hong Kong Special Administrative Region (2017)
2. Census and Statistics: Hong Kong Monthly Digest of Statistics, November 2017 Issue, Census and Statistics Department, Hong Kong Special Administrative Region (2017)
3. World Bank: Report on Internet Penetration, Data Bank, World Bank (2017). databank.worldbank.org
4. Ellis, K.: Moving into m-learning. Train. J. **40**(10), 56 (2003)
5. Crompton, H.: A historical overview of mobile learning: toward learner-centered education. In: Berge, Z.L., Muilenburg, L.Y. (eds.) Handbook of Mobile Learning, pp. 3–14. Routledge, Abingdon (2013)
6. Winters, N.: What is mobile learning? In: Sharples, M. (ed.) Big Issues in Mobile Learning, Workshop Report, Kaleidoscope Network of Excellence Mobile Learning Initiative, pp. 7–11. University of Nottingham, Nottingham (2007)
7. Cheung, S.K.S.: A case study on the students' attitude and acceptance of mobile learning. In: Li, K.C., Wong, T.L., Cheung, S.K.S., Lam, J., Ng, K.K. (eds.) ICTE 2014. CCIS, vol. 494, pp. 45–54. Springer, Heidelberg (2014). https://doi.org/10.1007/978-3-662-46158-7_5
8. Cheung, S.K.S., Yuen, K.S., Tsang, E.: A study on the readiness of mobile learning in open education. In: Proceedings of IEEE International Symposium on IT in Medicine and Education, pp. 133–136. IEEE Press (2011)
9. Lam, J., Yau, J., Cheung, S.K.S.: A review of mobile learning in the mobile age. In: Tsang, P., Cheung, S.K.S., Lee, V.S.K., Huang, R. (eds.) ICHL 2010. LNCS, vol. 6248, pp. 306–315. Springer, Heidelberg (2010). https://doi.org/10.1007/978-3-642-14657-2_28
10. Lam, J., You, J., Cheung, S.K.S.: A review of the use of mobile learning in education. In: Proceedings of International Conference on ICT in Teaching and Learning, pp. 271–276. SIM University (2010)
11. Poll, H.: Pearson student mobile device survey: college students. Pearson Higher Education, June 2015
12. Cheung, S.K.S.: A survey on the use of mobile devices for learning purposes. Int. J. Innov. Learn. **16**(2), 192–202 (2014)
13. Cheung, S.K.S.: A study on the use of mobile devices for distance learning. In: Cheung, S.K.S., Fong, J., Kwok, L.-F., Li, K.C., Kwan, R. (eds.) ICHL 2012. LNCS, vol. 7411, pp. 89–98. Springer, Heidelberg (2012). https://doi.org/10.1007/978-3-642-32018-7_9
14. Cheung, S.K.S.: Students' typical usage of mobile devices in learning activities. In: Lam, J., Ng, K.K., Cheung, S.K.S., Wong, T.L., Li, K.C., Wang, F. (eds.) ICTE 2015. CCIS, vol. 559, pp. 63–72. Springer, Heidelberg (2015). https://doi.org/10.1007/978-3-662-48978-9_6
15. iPhone: Website of iPhone, Apple (2017). https://www.apple.com/iphone
16. Galaxy: Website of Galaxy Note (2017). https://www.samsung.com/us/mobile/phones
17. Xperia: Website of Xperia, Sony (2017). https://www.sonymobile.com/global-en/xperia
18. iPad: Website of iPad, Apple (2017). https://www.apple.com/ipad
19. Galaxy: Website of Galaxy Tab (2017). https://www.samsung.com/us/mobile/tablets
20. Surface: Website of Surface, Microsoft (2017). https://www.microsoft.com/surface
21. ThinkPad: Website of ThinkPad Series, Lenovo (2017). https://www.lenovo.com/hk/en?menu-id=ThinkPad_Laptops

22. MacBook: Website of MacBook, Apple (2017). https://www.apple.com/macbook
23. VAIO: Website of Sony VAIO, Sony (2017). http://www.sony.com.hk/en/electronics/computers/ vaio-laptops
24. Wikipedia: Definition of Phablet, Wikipedia (2017). https://en.wikipedia.org/wiki/Phablet
25. OUHK: Website of the Open University of Hong Kong, the Open University of Hong Kong (2017). http://www.ouhk.ed.hk

# The Acceptance of "Flash Class" – Mobile Mini-lessons Through WeChat

Ting Yang[1], Hao Zhong[1], Qingmin Mok[1], Ivan Ka-Wai Lai[2(✉)], and Kwan-Keung Ng[3]

[1] School of Business, Macau University of Science and Technology, Taipa, Macau
ytt163@126.com, benchunggz@foxmail.com, kirodemon@163.com
[2] Faculty of International Tourism and Management, City University of Macau, Taipa, Macau
ivanlai@cityu.mo
[3] University of Sunderland, Hong Kong, China
steven.ng@sunderland.edu.hk

**Abstract.** The aim of this study is to identify the factors that influence the acceptance of "Flash Class" - mobile mini-lessons through WeChat. The empirical results were obtained in a sample of 187 university students in China. The results of PLS analysis indicate that performance expectancy, effort expectancy, social influence, hedonic motivation, and habit directly affect the acceptance of using "Flash Class" through WeChat for students learning English. The results of multi-group analysis also indicate that gender moderates the effect of effort expectancy on user behavioural intention. This study makes several suggestions to the "Flash Class" developers for improving their designs according to the listed factors in order to satisfy the learners' needs.

**Keywords:** Mobile mini-lesson · Mobile instant message
Mobile learning platform · UTAUT2

## 1 Introduction

In China, a mobile instant messaging and social network app such as WeChat is not only used as an instant communication application, but also extended to a mobile learning platform for students. Nowadays, 'Flash Class' is a new innovative service in WeChat, which allows teachers to quickly make mobile mini-lessons and share them with students. There is an increasing number of students who are using it to learn and share English knowledge directly through WeChat because this way of mobile learning is more convenient, faster, and relatively stress-free for students to learn English. In order to recruit more students to participate this app, the purpose of this study is to examine the factors that can significantly explain the acceptance of "Flash Class" based on the Unified Theory of Acceptance and Use of Technology 2 (UTAUT2) model. This study will examine the impacts of the factors of UTAUT2 including Performance Expectancy (PE), Effort Expectancy (EE), Social Influence (SI), Facilitating Conditions (FC), Hedonic Motivation (HM), Price Value (PV), and Habit (HB) on the behavioural


S. K. S. Cheung et al. (Eds.): ICTE 2018, CCIS 843, pp. 101–108, 2018.
https://doi.org/10.1007/978-981-13-0008-0_10

intention (BI) toward using "Flash Class" through WeChat for students learning English. Furthermore, it also examines the differences in students' gender as a moderator factor that influences the effects of PE, EE, SI, FC, HM, PV, and HB on BI.

# 2 Literature Review

## 2.1 The Unified Theory of Acceptance and Use of Technology 2 (UTAUT2)

An essential factor which determines the success or failure of a new technology is the acceptance of users. Hence, it is crucial for the "Flash Class" developers to know users' needs and the acceptance level of users. There are various researches aimed at the factors which predicted user acceptance of a technology such as Technology Acceptance Model (TAM) (Davis 1989), Diffusion of Innovation (Rogers 1995), The Unified Theory of Acceptance and Use of Technology (UTAUT) (Venkatesh et al. 2003). The UTAUT was developed by unifying eight different theories including the Theory of Reasoned Action (TRA) (Ajzen and Fishbein 1980), TAM, the Motivational Model (MM) (Davis et al. 2006), the Theory of Planned Behaviour (TPB) (Ajzen 1985), a combined theory of Planned Behaviour/Technology Acceptance Model (C-TPB-TAM), the Model of PC Utilization (MPCU) (Thompson et al. 1991), Innovation Diffusion Theory (IDT) (Moore and Benbasat 1996), and Social Cognitive Theory (SCT) (Compeau et al. 1999). The UTAUT model has four core determinants of usage and intentions, including PE, EE, SI, and FC. It also includes four moderators of key relationships: gender, age, experience, and voluntariness of use. The UTAUT has been used to describe technology acceptance in the organizational context. Recently, Venkatesh et al. (2012) extended UTAUT to UTAUT2 which was focused on individual perspectives in technology adoptions. Hence, the UTAUT2 has been adopted for exploring self-technology service, smart mobile device adoption, and learning management software acceptance (Raman and Don 2013). Since the purpose of this research is to explore the possible factors influencing individual users' adoptions, so the UTAUT2 model will be adopted to explore the factors that can significantly explain the acceptance of "Flash Class" through WeChat for students.

# 3 Research Hypothesis

As discussed above, PE, EE, SI, FC, HM, PV, and HB may have positive effects on BI toward using "Flash Class" through WeChat for students learning English; and students' gender may as a moderator that influences the effects of PE, EE, SI, FC, HM, PV, and HB on BI. The following hypotheses were developed. Figure 1 shows the research model.

H1: Performance expectancy (PE) has a direct effect on user behavioural intention toward using "Flash Class" through WeChat for students learning English.
H2: Effort Expectancy (EE) has a direct effect on user behavioural intention toward using "Flash Class" through WeChat for students learning English.

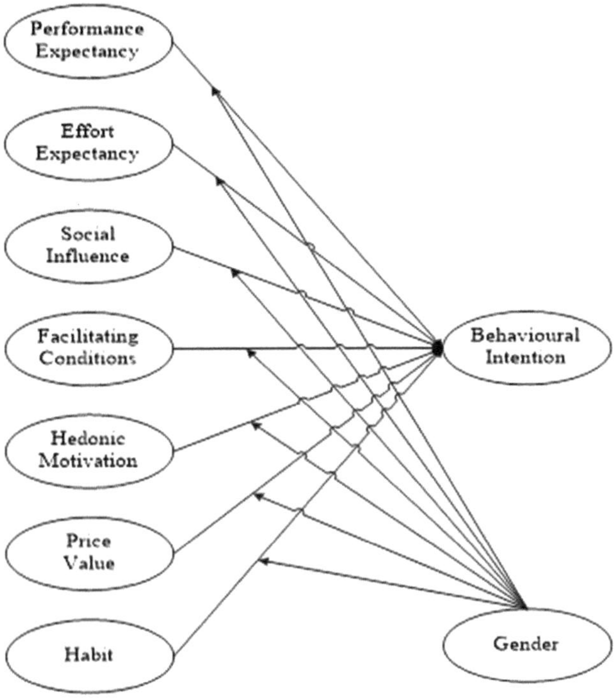


**Fig. 1.** Research model

H3: Social Influence (SI) has a direct effect on user behavioural intention toward using "Flash Class" through WeChat for students learning English.
H4: Facilitating Conditions (FC) have a direct effect on user behavioural intention toward using "Flash Class" through WeChat for students learning English.
H5: Hedonic Motivation (HM) has a direct effect on user behavioural intention toward using "Flash Class" through WeChat for students learning English.
H6: Price Value (PV) has a direct effect on user behavioural intention toward using "Flash Class" through WeChat for students learning English.
H7: Habit (HB) has a direct effect on user behavioural intention toward using "Flash Class" through WeChat for students learning English.
H8: Students' gender moderates the effects of PE, EE, SI, FC, HM, PV, and HB on user behavioural intention toward using "Flash Class" through WeChat for students learning English.

## 4 Findings

Through the online surveys in September 2017, totally 187 valid data were collected from university students. The measurable items for PE, EE, SI, FC, HM, PV, HB and BI were adopted from Venkatesh et al. (2012). Table 1 shows the sample characteristics.

**Table 1.** Demographic information (n = 187)

| | | Frequency | % | | | Frequency | % |
|---|---|---|---|---|---|---|---|
| Gen | Male | 54 | 28.9 | Age | 18 | 17 | 9.1 |
| | Female | 133 | 71.1 | | 19 | 53 | 28.3 |
| Edu | Year-1 | 5 | 2.7 | | 20 | 43 | 23 |
| | Year-2 | 88 | 47.1 | | 21 | 29 | 15.5 |
| | Year-3 | 40 | 21.4 | | 22 | 27 | 14.4 |
| | Year-4 | 37 | 19.8 | | 23 | 2 | 1.1 |
| | PG year-1 | 5 | 2.7 | | 24 | 6 | 3.2 |
| | PG year-2 | 12 | 6.4 | | 25 | 3 | 1.6 |
| | | | | | Over 25 | 7 | 3.7 |

54 respondents (28.9%) were males, 133 respondents (71.1%) were females. Most of the respondents were aged between 19 (28.3%) and 20 (23.0%).

Table 2 presents the means, standard deviations, and Partial Least Square (PLS) loadings of each measurement item. All factor loadings of each construct exceed 0.7, which reached the recommended level. Table 3 shows the values of Cronbach's alpha, average variance extracted (AVE), construct reliability (CR), and correlation analysis of eight constructs. The AVE and CR values of all constructs exceed 0.6 and 0.8, respectively. And all values of correlation are less than 0.85, so eight constructs are relatively independent of one another. These results confirm the data reliability and validity of the discriminants.

Figure 2 shows the results of PLS analysis. The value of $R^2$ of the research model is 0.749 that can be described as 'substantial' (Hair and Sarstedt 2011). In summary, PE,

**Table 2.** Mean, standard deviation, and PLS loading (5-point Likert scale)

| | Mean | Std. dev. | Factor loading | | Mean | Std. dev. | Factor loading |
|---|---|---|---|---|---|---|---|
| BI1 | 3.18 | 0.883 | 0.869 | HT1 | 2.85 | 0.994 | 0.910 |
| BI2 | 3.14 | 0.929 | 0.889 | HT2 | 2.81 | 1.008 | 0.882 |
| BI3 | 3.24 | 0.886 | 0.914 | HT3 | 2.78 | 0.939 | 0.908 |
| BI4 | 3.26 | 0.893 | 0.845 | HT4 | 2.96 | 0.952 | 0.888 |
| EE1 | 3.45 | 0.856 | 0.877 | PE1 | 3.29 | 0.813 | 0.888 |
| EE2 | 3.4 | 0.813 | 0.843 | PE2 | 3.41 | 0.859 | 0.877 |
| EE3 | 3.42 | 0.841 | 0.835 | PE3 | 3.21 | 0.878 | 0.903 |
| EE4 | 3.59 | 0.878 | 0.744 | PV1 | 3.04 | 0.812 | 0.875 |
| FC1 | 3.79 | 0.993 | 0.801 | PV2 | 3.09 | 0.853 | 0.896 |
| FC2 | 3.78 | 0.844 | 0.829 | PV3 | 3.08 | 0.854 | 0.891 |
| FC3 | 3.71 | 0.923 | 0.790 | SI1 | 2.9 | 0.959 | 0.832 |
| FC4 | 3.27 | 0.865 | 0.750 | SI2 | 2.98 | 0.989 | 0.910 |
| HM1 | 3.24 | 0.815 | 0.891 | SI3 | 3.15 | 0.933 | 0.883 |
| HM2 | 3.15 | 0.809 | 0.912 | | | | |
| HM3 | 3.21 | 0.799 | 0.905 | | | | |

**Table 3.** Reliability, validity, correlations and square roots of AVEs

| | Cronbach's Alpha | AVE | CR | BI | EE | FC | HM | HT | PE | PV | SI |
|---|---|---|---|---|---|---|---|---|---|---|---|
| BI | 0.902 | 0.774 | 0.932 | *0.880* | | | | | | | |
| EE | 0.844 | 0.683 | 0.896 | 0.610 | *0.826* | | | | | | |
| FC | 0.817 | 0.629 | 0.871 | 0.399 | 0.592 | *0.793* | | | | | |
| HM | 0.887 | 0.815 | 0.930 | 0.738 | 0.664 | 0.542 | *0.903* | | | | |
| HT | 0.919 | 0.805 | 0.943 | 0.768 | 0.444 | 0.296 | 0.693 | *0.897* | | | |
| PE | 0.868 | 0.791 | 0.919 | 0.692 | 0.636 | 0.404 | 0.662 | 0.615 | *0.889* | | |
| PV | 0.865 | 0.787 | 0.917 | 0.614 | 0.503 | 0.443 | 0.680 | 0.673 | 0.476 | *0.887* | |
| SI | 0.847 | 0.767 | 0.908 | 0.668 | 0.481 | 0.357 | 0.622 | 0.631 | 0.553 | 0.540 | *0.876* |

EE, SI, HM, and HT are all significantly related to BI, indicating that H1, H2, H3, H5, and H7 are supported, but H4 and H6 are unsupported, H8 is partially accepted where gender moderates the effect of EE on BI toward using "Flash Class" through WeChat for students learning English.

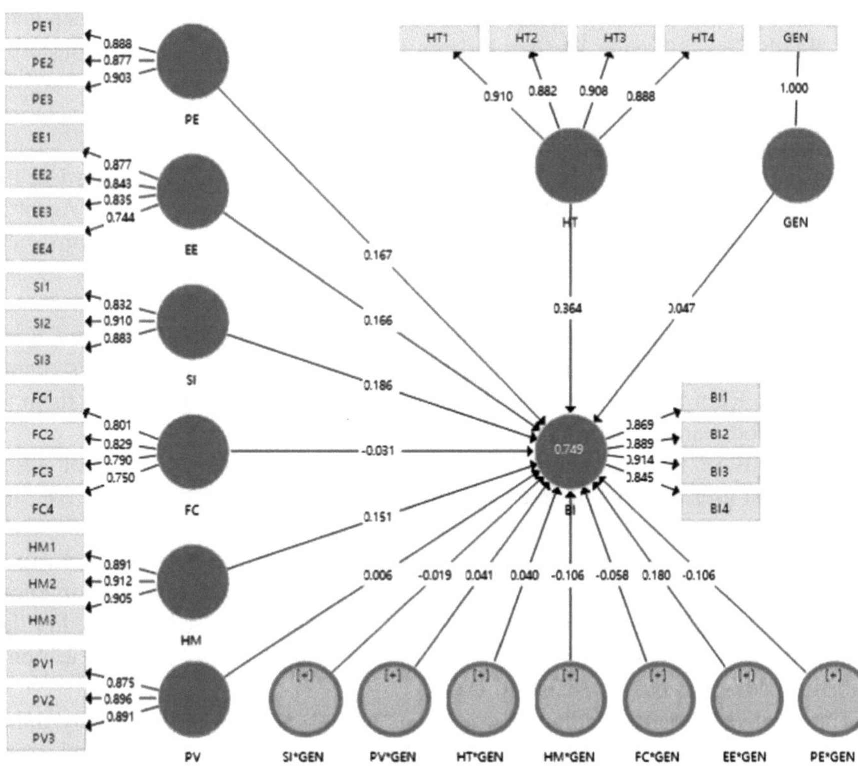


**Fig. 2.** Results of PLS analysis

## 5 Discussion and Conclusion

Habit is the strongest predictor of user behavioural intention toward using "Flash Class" through WeChat for students learning English ($\beta = 0.364$, t-statistics = 5.219). Performance expectancy, effort expectancy, social influence, and hedonic motivation are also the determinants of user behavioural intention toward using "Flash Class" through WeChat for students learning English ($\beta = 0.167$, t-statistics = 2.654; $\beta = 0.166$, t-statistics = 2.553; $\beta = 0.186$, t-statistics = 2.679; $\beta = 0.151$, t-statistics = 2.052 respectively). The results also indicate that gender is a moderator which influences the effect of effort expectancy on user behavioural intention toward using "Flash Class" through WeChat for students learning English ($\beta = 0.180$, t-statistics = 2.473).

Performance expectancy shows a significant effect on user behavioural intention toward using "Flash Class" through WeChat for students learning English. This indicates that students as the potential users have realized the benefits they can get from using "Flash Class" through WeChat for learning English. The mobile mini-lessons can be used to supplement the textbooks for students to learn English.

The influence of effort expectancy on user behavioural intention toward using "Flash Class" through WeChat for students learning English is significant. It shows that students would like to use "Flash Class" because they believe that it is easy and convenient for them to use "Flash Class" through WeChat for learning English.

Social influence has a significant effect on user behavioural intention for students using "Flash Class" through WeChat to learn English. Students will be influenced by their friends, classmates, and teachers who used the "Flash Class" for learning English and were satisfied with its learning effect. Students would accept their acquaintances' suggestions to use "Flash Class" to learn English.

The influence of hedonic motivation on user behavioural intention toward using "Flash Class" through WeChat for students learning English is significant. Accordingly, students believe that they can better learn English in more interesting forms such as audio, picture, text, and multiple-choice exercises, thus, they would like to use "Flash Class".

The effect of habit on user behavioural intention toward using "Flash Class" through WeChat for students to learn English is significant. This explains that students would like to learn English anytime, anywhere through WeChat, which helps them to develop a good learning habit of English.

The results of this research explore that gender moderates the effect of effort expectancy on user behavioural intention toward using "Flash Class" through WeChat for students learning English. In order to further explain the differences between males and females, the multi-group analysis (MGA) was used to analyse the samples. Table 4 shows the results of MGA of gender groups. There is a significant difference in effort expectancy (coef. Diff = −0373, p-value = 0.982) between males and females. For the female group, they will incline to use "Flash Class" through WeChat for learning English because it is easy for them to use.

The results show that facilitating conditions and price value insignificantly influence on user behavioural intention. At the present stage, students have a good experience in using WeChat, so they don't think they will have any problem in using "Flash

**Table 4.** Males vs females

| | Males (n = 54) | | Females (n = 133) | | MGA | P-value |
|---|---|---|---|---|---|---|
| | Coefficients | t-statistics | Coefficients | t-statistics | | |
| EE → BI | −0.088 | 0.617 | 0.285 | 3.952 | −0.373 | 0.982 |
| FC → BI | 0.053 | 0.557 | −0.066 | 0.977 | 0.119 | 0.149 |
| HM → BI | 0.326 | 2.110 | 0.077 | 0.925 | 0.249 | 0.069 |
| HT → BI | 0.307 | 1.933 | 0.400 | 5.116 | −0.093 | 0.705 |
| PE → BI | 0.297 | 2.337 | 0.103 | 1.433 | 0.195 | 0.091 |
| PV → BI | −0.069 | 0.436 | 0.035 | 0.488 | −0.104 | 0.730 |
| SI → BI | 0.185 | 1.101 | 0.192 | 3.058 | −0.007 | 0.474 |

Class" through WeChat platform to learn English. Moreover, since most of the "Flash Class" English courses through WeChat are free of charge, therefore, there is no significant impact on price value factor.

In conclusion, the results of PLS analysis indicate that PE, EE, SI, HM, and HT have direct effects on user behavioural intention toward using "Flash Class" through WeChat for students learning English and gender moderates the effect of effort expectancy on user behavioural intention. This study also gives several suggestions to the "Flash Class" developers for improving their designs according to the above factors in order to satisfy the learners' needs.

## References


Ajzen, I.: From intentions to actions: a theory of planned behaviour. In: Kuhl, J., Beckman, J. (eds.) Action-Control: FROM Cognition to Behaviour. SSSP Springer Series in Social Psychology, pp. 11–39. Springer, Heidelberg (1985). https://doi.org/10.1007/978-3-642-69746-3_2

Ajzen, I., Fishbein, M.: Understanding Attitudes and Predicting Social Behaviour. Prentice-Hall, Englewood Cliffs (1980)

Compeau, D., Higgins, C.A., Huff, S.: Social cognitive theory and individual reactions to computing technology: a longitudinal study. MIS Q. **23**(2), 145–158 (1999)

Davis, F.D., Bagozzi, R.P., Warshaw, P.R.: Extrinsic and intrinsic motivation to use computers in the workplace. J. Appl. Soc. Psychol. **22**(14), 1111–1132 (2006)

Davis, F.D.: Perceived usefulness, perceived ease of use, and user acceptance of information technology. MIS Q. **13**(3), 319–340 (1989)

Hair, J.F., Sarstedt, M.: PLS-SEM: indeed a silver bullet. J. Mark. Theory Pract. **19**(2), 139–152 (2011)

Moore, G.C., Benbasat, I.: Integrating diffusion of innovations and theory of reasoned action models to predict utilization of information technology by end-users. In: Kautz, K., Pries-Heje, J. (eds.) Diffusion and Adoption of Information Technology, pp. 132–146. Chapman and Hall, London (1996)

Raman, A., Don, Y.: Preservice teachers' acceptance of learning management software: an application of the UTAUT2 model. Int. Educ. Stud. **6**(7), 157–164 (2013)

Rogers, E.M.: Diffusion of Innovations, 4th edn. Free Press, New York (1995)

Thompson, R.L., Higgins, C.A., Howell, J.M.: Personal computing: toward a conceptual model of utilization. MIS Q. **15**(1), 124–143 (1991)

Venkatesh, V., Morris, M.G., Davis, G.B., Davis, F.D.: User acceptance of information technology: toward a unified view. MIS Q. **27**(3), 425–478 (2003)

Venkatesh, V., Thong, J.Y.L., Xu, X.: Consumer acceptance and use of information technology: extending the unified theory of acceptance and use of technology. MIS Q. **36**(1), 157–178 (2012)

# Designing and Evaluating Postgraduate Courses Based on a 5E-Flipped Classroom Model: A Two-Case Mixed-Method Study

Khe Foon Hew(✉), Yanzhen Zhu, and Chung Kwan Lo

Division of Information and Technology Studies, Faculty of Education, The University of Hong Kong, Pok Fu Lam, Hong Kong SAR, China
kfhew@hku.hk

**Abstract.** In recent years, the flipped classroom approach has attracted much attention from educators around the world. However, we still understand little about how we can structure the pre-class, and in-class activities in a coherent way that could engage students. The purpose of this study is to examine the use of the 5-E instructional model in order to foster students' active learning in a flipped learning environment. A two-case mixed-method study was conducted, involving the teachers and students from two different postgraduate courses *Engaging Adult Learners*, and *E-Learning Strategies*. Both the quantitative and qualitative data collection methods such as student survey and interviews were conducted. The results suggested that 92% of participant strongly agreed or agreed that flipped classroom is more engaging than traditional classroom instruction, and 81% reported that the flipped classroom approach gave them more time to discuss issues or solve problems. Interview data suggested three main reasons for the overall positive student perception of flipped classroom's impact on their learning.

**Keywords:** Flipped classroom · Inverted classroom · 5E instructional model Postgraduate education

## 1 Introduction

Flipped classroom has become increasingly popular in recent years. In a flipped classroom, in-class teacher led instruction is replaced with individual homework or group activities (Pierce and Fox 2012), and learning content was introduced prior to class. More and more studies have been conducted to investigate the practices of flipped classroom. In fact, the number of published papers has been significantly increasing after 2012 (Giannakos et al. 2014).

Scholars, for example have implemented and examined the use of flipped classrooms in mathematics (Young 2015), economics (Vazquez and Chiang 2015), nursing (Simpson and Richards 2015), pharmacy (Pierce and Fox 2012), biochemistry (Ojennus 2016), engineering (Hotle and Garrow 2016), and computer science (Mok 2014).

Yet despite the increasing number of empirical studies that examined the use of flipped classroom, several research gaps still exist. First, a majority of studies have


S. K. S. Cheung et al. (Eds.): ICTE 2018, CCIS 843, pp. 109–120, 2018.
https://doi.org/10.1007/978-981-13-0008-0_11

hitherto focused on undergraduate students in the Western world such as the USA (Bishop and Verleger 2013). Relatively few studies have been conducted on postgraduate learners in an Asian country. Second, there is still no adequate conceptual-based framework to guide the overall design and implementation of flipped classroom in actual practice (Abeysekera and Dawson 2015; Karabulut-Ilgu et al. 2017; Song et al. 2017). Song et al. (2017), for example, lamented that a large number of studies failed to present theoretical or conceptual underpinnings for their pedagogical designs of flipped classroom.

This study aims to overcome the aforementioned research gaps. Specifically, we report the use of the 5-E instructional model to foster students' active learning in two flipped courses. But before presenting the two flipped classes, we first provide an overview of the 5-E instructional model.

## 2 Conceptual Framework: 5E Instructional Model

The 5-E instructional model (Table 1) is originally proposed in science education (see Bybee et al. 2006 for a review). Prior research (e.g., Balci et al. 2006; Bilgin et al. 2013) shows that the 5-E model can lead to a positive effect on students' science achievement. Currently, the 5-E instructional model is widely used in various subject areas. In her undergraduate research methods course, Mullins (2017) used this model to structure the learning activities. Each activity was inquiry-based and a series of questions was designed following the five phases. For example, guiding questions were set to facilitate students' exploration of the provided information such as charts and narrative materials. Mullins (2017) compared this 5-E supported instructional approach to traditional teaching. In the course exam, she found that students in the 5-E supported learning environment outperformed those in a traditional lecture setting.

**Table 1.** Phases of the 5-E instructional model

| Phase | Remark |
|---|---|
| Engage | Serves to interest the students in the material and engage them in the process of learning; it usually took the form of simply introducing students to a real-world scenario, phenomenon, or problem |
| Explore | Allows the students to explore the content and construct their own understanding before introducing any terminology |
| Explain | The instructor introduces terminology to facilitate concept building |
| Elaborate | Requires the students to apply their new conceptual understanding to problem situations in order to broaden the domain and strengthen the framework of these concepts |
| Evaluate | Can be both formative (e.g., online quiz) and/or summative assessments (e.g., unit exam) that test students' understanding of the concepts they have just learned |

### 2.1 Using 5E in Previous Flipped Classroom Studies

However, in the contexts of flipped learning, very few published studies grounded their flipped classroom design in some established frameworks of instructional design (Abeysekera and Dawson 2015; Karabulut-Ilgu et al. 2017; O'Flaherty and Phillips 2015). Lo (2017) thus proposes using 5-E instructional model to design flipped History courses. He first argues that the engagement and evaluation phases should be delivered both outside and inside the classroom. In other words, teachers should recall prerequisite knowledge for video lectures and in-class learning activities as well as assess students' out-of-class learning and in-class learning outcomes. He further suggests providing online resources for students' exploration and explaining the materials through instructional videos before class meetings. The in-class time can thus focus on the elaboration phase in which students can apply their knowledge to problem-solving. However, Lo (2017) acknowledges the need of conducting empirical research which examines the efficacy and challenges of using 5-E instructional model in flipped learning.

In fact, only a scarcity of studies used the 5-E instructional model to inform their flipped classroom design. In their master-level engineering course, Svensson and Adawi (2015) used pre-class videos to implement the engagement and exploration phases whereas the in-class time was dedicated to the explanation, elaboration, and evaluation phases. For example, their students were required to explain what they had explored during class preparation and the teacher clarified their misconceptions (Svensson and Adawi 2015). At the end of their course, 23 out of 35 students responded to their course survey. Most of the respondents (91.3%) agreed that the flipped lessons could improve their learning and lead to a better understanding of concepts. However, without a control group (e.g., a non-flipped class), it is questionable to conclude that such positive result is due to the proposed course design.

In Jensen et al. (2015) study of undergraduate biology education, both their flipped class and non-flipped class were designed using the 5-E instructional model. They first defined two components of their course: (1) The content attainment part which covered the engagement, exploration, and explanation phases; and (2) the concept application part which focused on the elaboration and evaluation phases. In their non-flipped class, students' content attainment was completed inside the classroom and the concept application part was handled after class. In the flipped class, students' content attainment was facilitated before class through video lectures and the concept application was done inside the classroom. As a result, Jensen et al. (2015) found that there were no significant differences between these two classes in terms of learning gains and student satisfaction. Although they argue that flipped learning offers no additional benefits over a 5-E supported non-flipped approach, they recommend further research to confirm their findings.

## 3 Method

The present study aims to extend our collective understanding of flipped learning in two ways. First, we extended our study to a Hong Kong university context; more specifically to two different postgraduate courses: (a) *Engaging Adult Learners*, and (b) *E-Learning*

*Strategies*. Second, we investigated the use of the 5-E instructional model in order to foster students' active learning. The following three questions guided the present study:

(a) What are the students' attitude toward flipped classroom? Attitudes, or people's overall evaluations of an entity are important to study because they have predictable and very powerful effects on behavior (Greenwald 1989).
(b) What are students' opinions about the impact of the flipped classroom on their learning?
(c) What suggestions for improvement do students have for flipped classroom?

A multiple case study approach was employed in this study. Yin (2013) maintains that the case study approach is most appropriate when it investigates a contemporary phenomenon within its real-life context. The phenomenon under investigation is the implementation of 5-E supported flipped classrooms in two postgraduate courses. The phenomenon will be studied in real-life contexts.

### 3.1 Course 1: E-Learning Strategies

Participants in this course were 21 graduate students between ages 22 and 28. This course explored issues relevant to the design and management of e-learning in educational contexts encompassing five specific types of learning outcomes. It investigated the various instructional strategies that could promote the mastery of each aforementioned types of learning. The course was based on 8 sessions of 3 h duration each. Lessons in the first 5 sessions were flipped and the last three sessions were for student in-class class presentations.

Figure 1 shows an example of how the 5-E instructional model was utilized in the *E-Learning Strategies* course. For example, in Topic 3: Attitude learning, we posted a video that contrasted good attitude and negative attitude as a pre-class activity. This video served as a trigger to **engage** students. Students then **explored** and **explained** the topic of attitude by reflecting on their own experiences by answering three questions before class: (a) have you ever ever have a negative attitude? (b) What's the situation? (c) How did you change the negative attitude?

During the in-class session, the instructor facilitated discussions on questions, such as "what is attitude and how can we change it", and "how do we write good lesson objectives, including attitude learning" The instructor also facilitated discussions on the strategies that good instructors use to teach attitude learning. These questions, scenarios, and discussions served as trigger points to **elaborate** on good instructional design practices. To **evaluate** the students' understanding of the contents, they were asked to work in groups of fours to create their own actual lesson on Moodle.

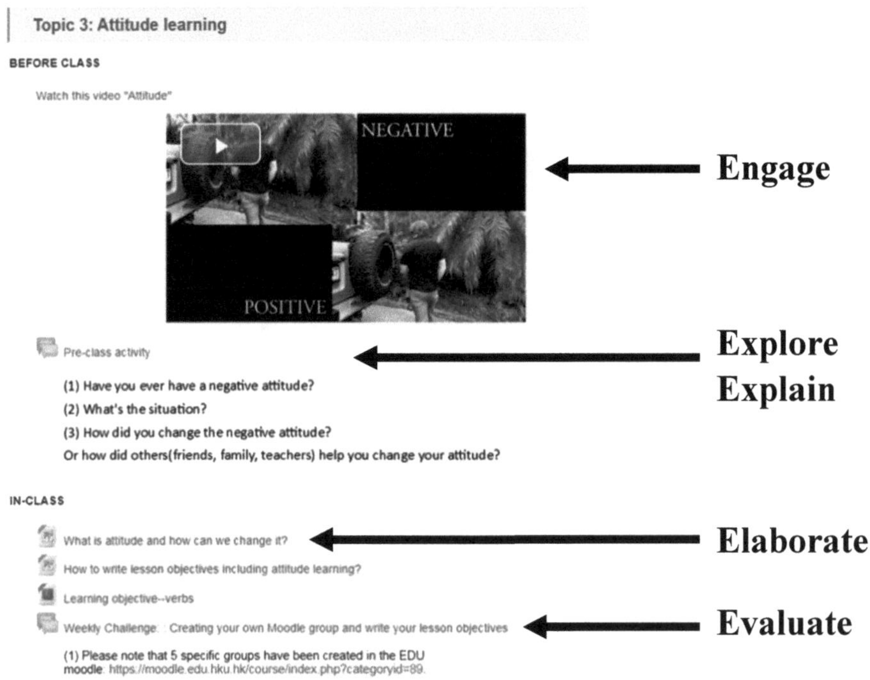


**Fig. 1.** An example of how the 5E model was used in the *E-Learning Strategies* course

### 3.2 Course 2: Engaging Adult Learners

Participants in this course were 26 graduate students between ages 22 and 40. This course introduced participants to the key characteristics of adult learners. It also discussed the applications of various strategies that are particularly pertinent to adult education such as self-directed learning, workplace learning, and transformational learning theory. Participants were required to design a course based on one of these strategies. The course was based on 8 sessions of 3 h duration each. Lessons in the first 4 sessions were flipped, while the last four sessions were used for individual consultations with the instructors, as well as for student in-class class presentations.

Figure 2 shows an example of how the 5-E instructional model was utilized in the *Engaging Adult Learners* course. For example, in Topic 4: How do we engage adults in online learning environments, we posted a video that described the increasing demand for e-learning, and posted the following question as a pre-class activity: "Imagine you are applying for a position as an adult educator in a large organization. In the interview, you are asked to voice 3 important questions that we should consider if we wish to design an e-learning course for adult learners. What would you say?" The video and question served as a trigger to **engage** students before class. Students **explored** the question by reflecting on their own experiences, and/or searching for relevant literature. Students then **explained** their viewpoints by posting them on the class WeChat.

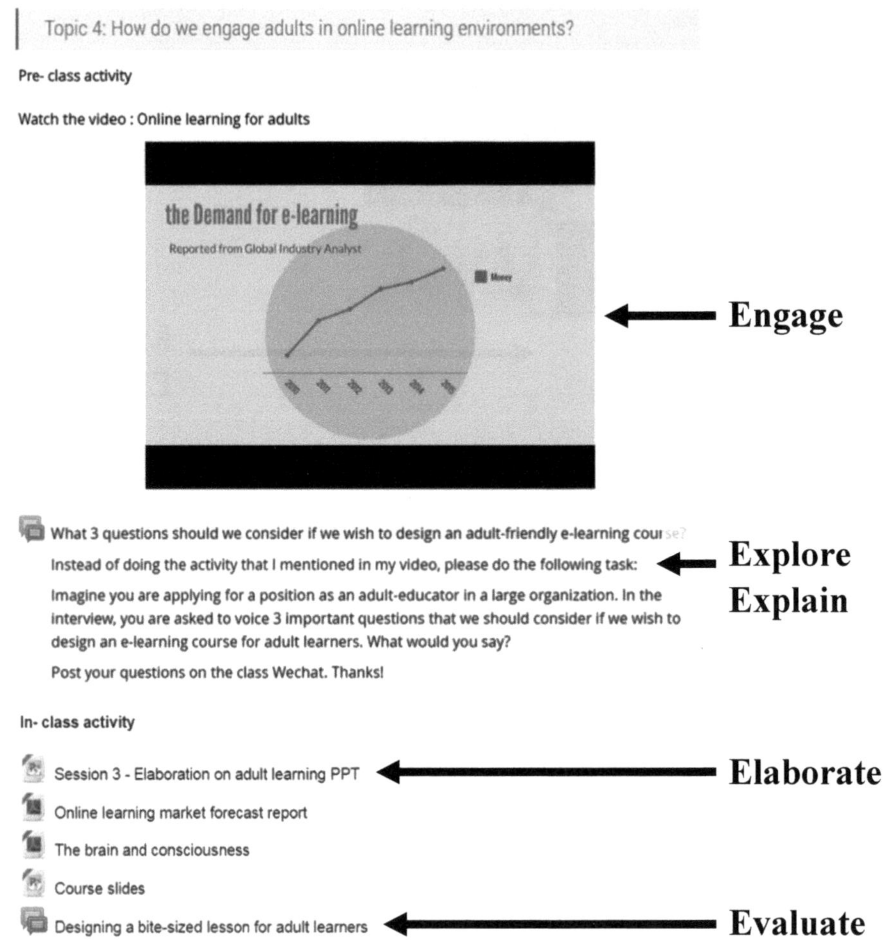


**Fig. 2.** An example of how the 5E model was used in the *Engaging Adult Learners* course

During the in-class session, the instructor facilitated in-depth discussions on issues including the six main factors that engage adult learners in an online course, key reasons why adults drop out of online course, and the implications of human brain for online learning. These issues served as trigger points to **elaborate** on strategies to engage adult learners. To **evaluate** the students' understanding of the contents, they were asked to design a bite-sized lesson for adult learners. Requirements for the lesson included: having only one learning objective, learning time between 5-10 min, making the lesson relevant to adults, using problem-centered and active learning strategies, and using at least one attention-grabbing strategy.

### 3.3 Data Collection and Analysis

Data were collected from two sources: a questionnaire and semi-structured interviews. The questionnaire consisted of 12 Likert-scale questions; and was administered at the end of the two courses. The questions made comparisons between the flipped classroom and the traditional classroom and focused on students' learning experience in the flipped course delivery. Descriptive statistical analyses were conducted on the survey data in order to determine the students' perception of flipped classroom.

Interviews were also used because the participants' perceptions and opinions of the flipped classroom approach could not be observed, but had to be explained by the participants themselves. In this study, we used the semi-structured interview format, where the interviews were focused and guided by interview questions such as how has the flipped classroom approach impacted your learning, how do you prepare for this class differently than other non-flipped classes, what did you find most helpful to your learning during the in-class time, what did you find least helpful to your learning during the in-class time, how has the flipped classroom approach differed from other classes as to how you interact with your classmates, how has the flipped classroom approach differed from other classes as to how you interact with your instructor, and what is your overall perceptions toward flipped learning?

## 4 Results and Discussion

Overall, the results indicate that graduate students' perception of flipped classroom tends to be positive and graduate students were actually more engaged in this innovative classroom. Answers to the research questions are discussed respectively in this section.

### 4.1 What Are the Students' Attitude Toward Flipped Classroom?

Table 2 summarizes the results of the questionnaire. The results indicate that 92% of participant strongly agreed or agreed that flipped classroom is more engaging than traditional classroom instruction, and 95% reported that they would recommend the flipped classroom approach to their friends. Eighty-six percent of participants indicated that flipped classroom gives me greater opportunities to communicate with other students, while 83% agreed or strongly agreed that they liked watching the lessons on video. Ninety-three percent of participants reported that they liked doing the online activities at their own pace, and 81% reported that the flipped classroom approach gave them more time to discuss issues or solve problems. Close to 80% of participants perceived that the flipped classroom approach improved their learning significant. Although 83% of participants reported that they liked to watch lessons on videos, only 64% said that they preferred a video-recording of the lesson to a traditional teacher-led lesson.

**Table 2.** Results of the questionnaire survey (n = 42 participants)

| Item | SD | D | N | A | SA |
|---|---|---|---|---|---|
| The Flipped Classroom is more engaging than traditional classroom instruction | 2% | 2% | 2% | 52% | 40% |
| I will recommend Flipped Class to my friends | 2% | 0% | 2% | 52% | 43% |
| The Flipped Classroom gives me greater opportunities to communicate with other students | 0% | 7% | 7% | 50% | 36% |
| I like watching the lessons on video | 0% | 2% | 14% | 29% | 55% |
| I like doing the online activities at my own pace | 0% | 5% | 3% | 38% | 55% |
| I prefer a video-recording of the lesson to a traditional teacher-led lesson | 0% | 5% | 31% | 36% | 29% |
| I like to self-pace myself through the course | 0% | 5% | 12% | 38% | 45% |
| I am more motivated to learn in the Flipped Classroom | 0% | 5% | 21% | 33% | 40% |
| The Flipped Classroom gives me more time to discuss issues or solve problems | 2% | 2% | 14% | 33% | 48% |
| The Flipped Classroom has improved my learning significantly | 2% | 2% | 17% | 40% | 38% |

## 4.2 What Are Students' Opinions About the Impact of the Flipped Classroom on Their Learning?

Twenty-four participants consented to be interviewed. Qualitative analysis of the student interview data suggested three main reasons for the overall positive student perception of flipped classroom's impact on their learning. These reasons include: promoting more in-depth learning, cultivating self-directed learning, and improving peer communication and collaboration.

*Promoting More In-depth Learning.* In a flipped course, students are required to learn some course materials before class meetings by reading, or watching instructional videos. More in-class time can thus be spent on active learning activities such as group discussion and problem-solving activities. Completing pre-class activities helps prepare students for the class activities (Madden and Martinez 2015). Students also had time to review the videos at their own pace (Ojennus 2016). Students with limited understanding of the materials could revisit the videos many times (Mok 2014). In addition, there are greater opportunities for students to apply knowledge in solving problems in flipped classes (Madden and Martinez 2015). Students overall reported that a flipped classroom can promote more in-depth learning than a traditional classroom:

> "I can master the basic knowledge before the class, so during the in-class time, there is no time wasting on surface learning. I can learn the knowledge and skills deeply through in-class discussion." (Participant #4)

> "The pre-class activities help me better understand the topic in class so I can better engage in it during in-class sessions." (Participant #1)
> "The flipped classroom approach gives the instructor more time collecting students' feedback based on their answers or sharing so the instructor could adjust the teaching approach and find where they should emphasis during the class time." (Participant #15)

*Cultivating Self-directed Learning.* Self-directed learning is "a process in which the individual takes the initiative, with or without the help of others, in diagnosing their learning needs, formulating learning goals, identifying human and material resources for learning, choosing and implementing appropriate learning strategies, and evaluating learning outcomes" (Knowles 1975, p. 18). The use of pre-class activities in a flipped classroom implementation can help cultivate students' self-directed learning as suggested by the following comments:

> "I would watch the videos that professor provides. After watching the videos, if I can't fully understand the points, I would like to search on the internet and read other articles and videos about it." (Participant #5)
> "It ability as we need to watch videos to learn new concepts before class." (Participant #11)

*Improving Peer Communication and Collaboration.* Flipped classroom also helps increase interactions with the instructor and classmates during in-class sessions (Ojennus 2016). Many of the in-class activities such as group improved my self-learning discussion promoted students' interactions with their peers:

> "Non-flipped classes require students to learn basic knowledge in class, so professors spend more time on giving lectures, and less time is distributed on group discussion. I think flipped classroom provides more opportunities for us to communicate and collaborate with classmates, which is beneficial for our deep learning." (Participant #5)
> "There are not only opportunities for discussing and collaborate with students in the same group but also we can interact with all classmates. The use of social media messaging WeChat in this course is totally a new and engaging way." (Participant #4)
> "A lot more interaction, cooperation and collaboration with classmates than non-flipped classes. Since everyone comes to class with good preparation, people are confident to share their own ideas in class." (Participant #12)

### 4.3 What Suggestions for Improvement Do Students Have for Flipped Classroom?

Notwithstanding the overall positive participant satisfaction, there are several suggestions for improvement concerning the use of flipped classroom in practice. First, some students were burdened by the apparent increase in workload because they were asked to complete the pre-class activities. Several previous studies reported that some students were unhappy being asked to do work before class that was traditionally done in a face-to-face class format (Simpson and Richards 2015). These students consider the out-of-class activities as burdensome in terms of time (Young 2015). Therefore, one participant in the current study proposed that:

> "The pre-class tasks should not be very hard. The time that is required to complete it shouldn't be too long." (Participant #3)

Hence, we recommend that instructors consider covering the more basic and introductory materials through instructional videos as a pre-class task, while the more difficult content being handled inside the classroom (Anderson and Brennan 2015). Furthermore, we recommend instructors carefully consider the total time required to complete all the pre-class tasks. Although it may be difficult to predict the optimum workload for out-of-class activities, a majority of students tend to spend about 20 min on these tasks (McGivney-Burelle and Xue 2013; Vazquez and Chiang 2015).

The second suggestion for improvement is to consolidate the main points after each in-class sessions:

> "My suggestion is adding a consolidation part in class. That is, before dismissing class, instructor or students themselves could summarize what have been learnt today. Otherwise, sometimes we get distracted by discussion and collaboration." (Participant #11)

In the present study, the instructor mainly focused on facilitating in-depth discussions on important issues, or providing students the opportunities to work together on group activities during the in-class sessions. Consolidation of the main or important points raised in the discussions and group activities was, unfortunately, left out in many of the sessions. We therefore recommend that instructors leave some time for the students to reflect individually at the end of every in-class session, and provide a closure of the session by highlighting the main takeaways.

The third suggestion for improvement is to provide opportunity for students to ask the instructor questions during the pre-class sessions:

> "After watching the video, maybe classmates are confused about some concepts. If we can make full use of the online discussion forum to post questions there, it will help us learn more." (Participant #5)

The lack of opportunity to ask questions and get immediate feedback may hinder understanding of the video material at the time the material is presented (Hotle and Garrow 2016). Although students may ask questions later during in-class sessions, they may have forgotten what they wish to ask because most students did not take notes while watching the videos (Hotle and Garrow 2016). Lo et al. (2017) therefore suggested that instructors provide support through online discussion boards or other social networking sites such as Twitter in their flipped courses. Using these technologies would allow instructors and peers to provide timely feedback outside the classroom.

## 5 Conclusion

In the past several years, we have witnessed an unprecedented growth in the use of flipped classrooms. Yet, despite having various studies of flipped classroom, we still understand little about how we can structure the pre-class and in-class activities in a coherent way that could engage students. In the present study, we examine the use of the 5-E instructional model in two different postgraduate courses *Engaging Adult Learners*, and *E-Learning Strategies*.

A total of 42 students completed the questionnaire survey. Overall, our findings suggested that most students preferred the flipped learning approach, and reported that flipped learning is more engaging than the traditional classroom instruction. Analysis of 24 student interview data suggested three main reasons for the overall positive student perception of flipped classroom's impact on their learning: promoting more in-depth learning, cultivating self-directed learning, and improving peer communication and collaboration. Despite the overall positive perceptions, students highlighted three main suggestions for improvement: designing the pre-class activities so that they would not be too difficult for students to manage in terms of content complexity and time duration, consolidating the main points after each in-class sessions, and providing opportunities for students to get immediate feedback from instructors during the pre-class sessions.

The findings of this study should, however, be viewed with some caution due to the relatively small participant sample size. Future research examining a larger sample size of postgraduate students would be useful to help us generalize the results. Although it is useful to understand students' perception and preference of using flipped classroom, it is also important to examine using experiments whether the postgraduate students can acquire and use the knowledge comparable to traditional classroom setting. We also plan to examine how the use of different video formats may affect postgraduate student learning in flipped classrooms. Commonly used video formats include PowerPoint slide presentation with voice-over, video screencast of the instructor writing code in a text-editor, video of instructor drawing freehand on a digital tablet video captured from a live classroom lecture, instructor recorded in a studio with no audience, and close-up shots of instructor's head filmed at an office desk (Guo et al. 2014). Investigating the various video formats is important because it can help us utilize the right format to develop video lectures that can engage students.

## References

Abeysekera, L., Dawson, P.: Motivation and cognitive load in the flipped classroom: definition, rationale and a call for research. High. Educ. Res. Dev. **34**(1), 1–14 (2015)

Anderson, L., Brennan, J.P.: An experiment in "flipped" teaching in freshman calculus. PRIMUS **25**(9–10), 861–875 (2015)

Balci, S., Cakiroglu, J., Tekkaya, C.: Engagement, exploration, explanation, extension, and evaluation (5E) learning cycle and conceptual change text as learning tools. Biochem. Mol. Biol. Educ. **34**(3), 199–203 (2006)

Bilgin, I., Coşkun, H., Aktaş, I.: The effect of 5E learning cycle on mental ability of elementary students. J. Baltic Sci. Educ. **12**(5), 592–607 (2013)

Bishop, J.L., Verleger, M.A.: The flipped classroom: a survey of the research. In: 120th ASEE National Conference and Exposition, Atlanta, GA (Paper ID 6219). American Society for Engineering Education, Washington, DC (2013)

Bybee, R.W., Taylor, J.A., Gardner, A., Van Scotter, P., Powell, J.C., Westbrook, A., Landes, N.: The BSCS 5E Instructional Model: Origins and Effectiveness. BSCS, Colorado Springs (2006)

Giannakos, M.N., Krogstie, J., Chrisochoides, N.: Reviewing the flipped classroom research: reflections for computer science education. In: Proceedings of the Computer Science Education Research Conference, pp. 23–29. ACM (2014)

Greenwald, A.G.: Why are attitudes important? In: Pratkanis, A.R., Breckler, S.J., Greenwald, A.G. (eds.) Attitude Structure and Function, pp. 1–10. Lawrence Erlbaum Associates, Inc., Hillsdale (1989)

Guo, P.J., Kim, J., Rubin, R.: How video production affects student engagement: an empirical study of MOOC videos. In: Proceedings of the First ACM Conference on Learning @ Scale Conference, pp. 41–50 (2014)
Hotle, S.L., Garrow, L.A.: Effects of the traditional and flipped classrooms on undergraduate student opinions and success. J. Prof. Issues Eng. Educ. Pract. **142**(1) (2016). Article no. 05015005
Jensen, J.L., Kummer, T.A., Godoy, P.D.D.M.: Improvements from a flipped classroom may simply be the fruits of active learning. CBE-Life Sci. Educ. **14**(1) (2015). Article no. 5
Karabulut-Ilgu, A., Jaramillo Cherrez, N., Jahren, C.T.: A systematic review of research on the flipped learning method in engineering education. Br. J. Educ. Technol., 1–14 (2017). http://onlinelibrary.wiley.com/doi/10.1111/bjet.12548/full
Knowles, M.S.: Self-Directed Learning: A Guide for Learners and Teachers. Follet, Chicago (1975)
Lo, C.K.: Toward a flipped classroom instructional model for history education: a call for research. Int. J. Culture Hist. **3**(1), 36–43 (2017)
Lo, C.K., Hew, K.F., Chen, G.: Toward a set of design principles for mathematics flipped classrooms: a synthesis of research in mathematics education. Educ. Res. Rev. **22**, 50–73 (2017)
Madden, M.L., Martinez, I.T.: The flipped library classroom at Georgia State University: a case study. Georgia Libr. Q. **52**(1), 13–20 (2015)
McGivney-Burelle, J., Xue, F.: Flipping calculus. PRIMUS **23**(5), 477–486 (2013)
Mok, H.N.: Teaching tip: the flipped classroom. J. Inf. Syst. Educ. **25**(1), 7–11 (2014)
Mullins, M.H.: Actively teaching research methods with a process oriented guided inquiry learning approach. J. Teach. Soc. Work **37**(4), 309–321 (2017)
O'Flaherty, J., Phillips, C.: The use of flipped classrooms in higher education: a scoping review. Internet High. Educ. **25**, 85–95 (2015)
Ojennus, D.D.: Assessment of learning gains in a flipped biochemistry classroom. Biochem. Mol. Biol. Educ. **44**(1), 20–27 (2016)
Pierce, R., Fox, J.: Vodcasts and active-learning exercises in a "flipped classroom" model of a renal pharmacotherapy module. Am. J. Pharm. Educ. **76**(10) (2012). Article no. 196
Simpson, V., Richards, E.: Flipping the classroom to teach population health: increasing the relevance. Nurse Educ. Pract. **15**(3), 162–167 (2015)
Song, Y., Jong, M.S.Y., Chang, M., Chen, W.: Guest editorial: "HOW" to design, implement and evaluate the flipped classroom? A synthesis. Educ. Technol. Soc. **20**(1), 180–183 (2017)
Svensson, L., Adawi, T.: Designing and evaluating a flipped signals and systems course. In: Proceedings of the 14th European Conference on e-Learning, Hatfield, UK, pp. 584–591 (2015)
Vazquez, J.J., Chiang, E.P.: Flipping out! A case study on how to flip the principles of economics classroom. Int. Adv. Econ. Res. **21**, 379–390 (2015)
Yin, R.K.: Case Study Research: Design and Methods, 5th edn. SAGE, Los Angles (2013)
Young, A.: Flipping the calculus classroom: a cost-effective approach. PRIMUS **25**(8), 713–723 (2015)

# Wine Appreciation Apps: Tools for Mobile Learning and Ubiquitous Learning

Kenneth Shiu-Pong Ng[1(✉)], Ivan Ka-Wai Lai[1,2], and Kwan-Keung Ng[3]

[1] Faculty of International Tourism and Management, City University of Macau, Taipa, Macau
kennethng@cityu.edu.mo, ivanlai@cityu.mo

[2] School of Business and Hospitality Management, Caritas Institute of Higher Education, Tseung Kwan O, New Territories, Hong Kong

[3] University of Sunderland, Hong Kong, China
steven.ng@sunderland.edu.hk

**Abstract.** Although Wine Appreciation Apps (WAA) are aimed for wine enthusiasts to understand how to appreciate and enjoy wines, these apps are very useful for university students, who are studying wine courses, to obtain wine knowledge. However, these apps are not popular as supplementary tools for students to study wines. Therefore, this research aims to identify the factors that influence students' behavioral intention toward using WAA for supplementing their learning in wine courses. The research is based on UTAUT model. According to the conditions of WAA, a new variable 'flexibility' is added. In the previous research, system flexibility has been used for web-based training research on the intention of users, defined as to use the web-based systems anytime and anywhere. 200 valid data were collected by questionnaire survey. Data analysis was performed by using PLS. The results of the study indicate that Performance Expectancy, Effort Expectancy, Social Influence, Facilitating Conditions, and Flexibility are the factors that influence learners' behavioral intention toward using WAA. This research has verified the applicability of UTAUT on studying the mobile learning and ubiquitous learning. This study also provides some recommendations for WAA developers to enhance the design of WAA. It provides a new model for studying the mobile learning and ubiquitous learning.

**Keywords:** UTAUT · Flexibility · Mobile learning · Wine appreciation

## 1 Introduction

Food and beverage management is one of the popular divisions in the hospitality and tourism education. Many famous institutions are providing short-term training courses and long-term degree programs. For instance, Le Cordon Bleu provides a wide range of Culinary Arts courses from fine-dining to pastry in many locations (Le Cordon Bleu Programs 2017). And The Hong Kong Polytechnic University designs a 1.5 year Master of Science program in International Wine Management (HKPolyU 2017). Many of these traditional courses and programs, no matter short-term or long-term, are face-to-face courses. However, owing to the development of mobile technology, people learn from


S. K. S. Cheung et al. (Eds.): ICTE 2018, CCIS 843, pp. 121–129, 2018.
https://doi.org/10.1007/978-981-13-0008-0_12

mobile apps become more and more prevalent. Mobile apps can be used for education in various aspects; one successful area is language learning, according to Chinnery's (2006) survey, the language learning mobile apps can be used for vocabulary practice, quiz delivery, online tutoring, video playback, file sharing and so on. And also, when people are using mobile apps to learn, the course contents can be personalized, as the apps can automatically sync the user's learning status, and allow the lessons to be adjusted based on user's performance. Furthermore, when the mobile apps provide options for multi-languages, students can choose their native language to study and it is not easy to be achieved in the face-to-face classrooms (Godwin-Jones 2011).

As of March 2017, there are over 2.8 million apps in Google Play and 2.2 million apps in Apple App Store (Statista 2017), and some of the categories are popular such as games, business, education, book and so on. Given that the gaining attention and popularity in mobile technologies increases in the education sectors, many studies are suggested and educators are encouraged to involve in designing the educational mobile apps (Hsu et al. 2012). In the hospitality industry, although there are some apps being designed to learn restaurant management or hotel management, they are not popular enough as supplementary tools for students to study; especially apps are limited in the study of wine. Therefore, based on the Unified Theory of Acceptance and Use of Technology (UTAUT) model, this study attempts to examine the factors influencing students' behavioral intention (BI) toward using wine appreciation apps (WAA) as supplementary tools for studying via Partial Least Squares (PLS) software.

## 2 Literature Review

### 2.1 The Unified Theory of Acceptance and Use of Technology

Venkatesh et al. (2003) proposed the UTAUT model that aims to explain user behavioral intentions to use new technology and subsequent usage behavior. According to this theory, four critical constructs are direct determinants of user behavioural intention. These four constructs are: Performance Expectancy (PE), Effort Expectancy (EE), Social Influence (SI), and Facilitating Conditions (FC). PE is defined the degree to which a person believes that using a particular system would enhance his or her job performance; EE is defined as the degree to which a person believes that using a particular system would be free of effort; SI is defined as the degree to which an individual perceives that important others believe he or she should use the new system; and FC are defined as the degree to which an individual believes that an organizational and technical infrastructure exists to support use of the system (Venkatesh et al. 2003). In the previous research, system flexibility has been used for web-based training research on the intention of users (Alrawashdeh and Al-Mahadeen 2014). Flexibility of e-learning system was defined as the degree to which an individual believes that he/she can access the system from anywhere at any time (Hsia and Tseng 2008). Thus, this research includes Flexibility (FL) into the UTAUT to survey if it also has a significant impact on the BI.

## 2.2 Apps Using in Learning in Hospitality Industry

Given the rapid development of smartphone technology, smartphones and apps are widely used in many areas of learning. For instance, Dickinson et al. (2014) suggested that the app primary functions in tourism industry can be information, two-way sharing, context awareness, internet of things, and tagging. And it enhances the temporal alignment among people, and provides tourists more information, knowledge and awareness before travel, during travel and post travel. One of the reasons why App using becomes more and more prevalent in recent years as it is regarded as a seamless learning, a learning style that the learners can learn in various kinds of environment, and they can switch the way of learning from on to another easily, without limitation of time and space (Wong 2012). With the technology of mobility, learning apps allow learners to facilitate learning activities out of the classroom and connect and communicate with other peers through the apps. Furthermore, the added equipment on mobiles such as internet connection, embedded camera, GPS receiver and RFID, can also assist on student's learning (Jeng et al. 2010). However, mobile apps are limited by the small screen size, WI-FI environment, battery capacity, computational power and so on (Chen et al. 2008). Therefore, it is crucial to examine how to adapt the knowledge in one area for delivering students in order to achieve the learning outcomes. In the hospitality industry, mobile learning shows many advantages. Firstly, when scheduling training is a big challenge in hospitality industry due to the job nature, the mobile training can be arranged 24 h, 7 days and it reduces face-to-face scheduling and coordination. Secondly, employees from different departments with different learning styles can learn from the same mobile app. Third, the update policies or standards can be spread to all of the students quickly after something important changed. Even though there are apparent advantages in mobile learning in hospitality industry, it is still in the process of developing, especially there is no specific research studying the mobile learning in the hospitality industry (Fig. 1).

**Fig. 1.** WAA example 1 (tomsguide.com 2017)

Thus, this research was conducted on one specific mobile application, the Wine appreciation app for mobile learning, where students can use this app to search for information, communicate with peers, and learn some courses. Based on the UTAUT model, this study examines the student's behavioral intention to use this new technology in learning wine knowledge, in order to testify the factors that influence student's acceptance and use of the mobile learning technology in the hospitality industry (Fig. 2).

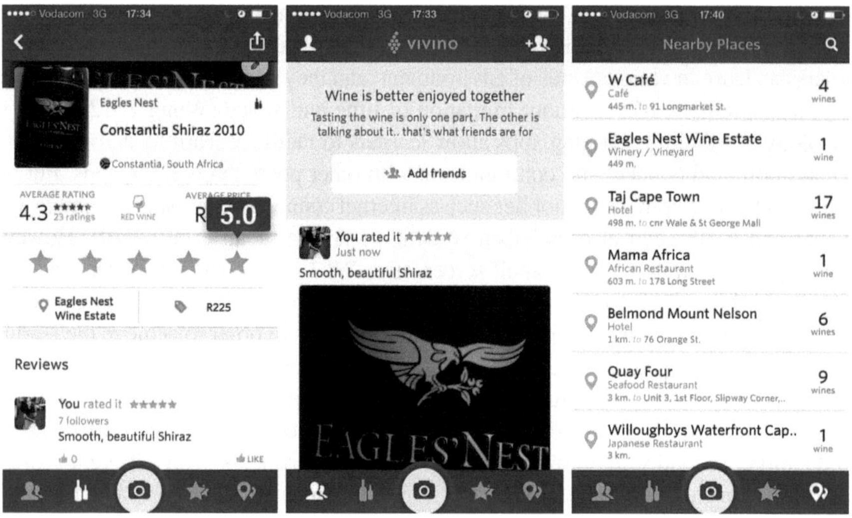


**Fig. 2.** WAA example 2 (Capetownmylove.com 2014)

## 3 Research Hypothesis

As aforementioned, UTAUT model that aims to explain user behavioral intentions to use new technology and subsequent usage behavior; FL is proposed to be the fifth key construct that would contribute any significant impact as similar as the other four constructs (PE, EE, SI, and FC) on university students' BI (BI) for using WAA for mobile learning. Flexibility refers to the ability to react to a wide range of possible environments with few penalties in terms of time, effort, cost or performance (Sethi and Sethi 1990; Upton1995). In this study, FL is defined as the degree to which a university student believes that he/she can access the WAA from anywhere at any time for mobile learning. Figure 3 shows the research model. There are FIVE research hypotheses which are listed as follows:

H1: PE has a significant influence on university students' BI for using WAA as supplementary tools for studying a Wine course.
H2: EE has a significant influence on university students' BI for using WAA as supplementary tools for studying a Wine course.
H3: SI has a significant influence on university students' BI for using WAA as supplementary tools for studying a Wine course.

H4: FC has a significant influence on university students' BI for using WAA as supplementary tools for studying a Wine course.
H5: FL has a significant influence on university students' BI for using WAA as supplementary tools for studying a Wine course.

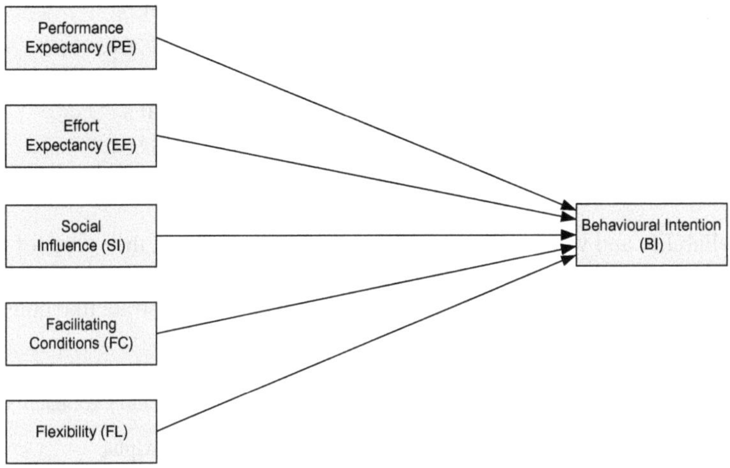


**Fig. 3.** Research model

Twenty questionnaires have been sent out to qualified respondents for a pilot test; after collecting the respondents' comments, the questionnaire has been further revised for official research. Total 200 sets of questionnaires have been collected from university students in Macau in September 2017. Total 183 valid data were analyzed via PLS software because 17 questionnaires were removed due to invalid responses and/or uncompleted responses.

## 4 Findings

Referring to the analysis of descriptive information of these 183 responses, 66% of respondents are female students and 72% respondents are Year 4 students; 36% of respondents are at the age of 21, 21% of respondents are at the age of 18. Questionnaires used a 7-point Likert-type scale. The mean scores of PE, EE, FC, and FL are ranged from 5.40 to 5.70; however, SI has received the lowest scores among these six constructs; specially on SI-2 "Classmates think that I should use WAA to supplementing classroom learning in a Wine course" and SI-3 "People around me think that I should use WAA to supplementing classroom learning in a Wine course", the mean scores of these questions are 4.99 and 5.03 respectively. The mean and standard deviation scores of these six constructs are shown in Table 1.

**Table 1.** Mean and standard deviation of measurable items

| | PE 1 | PE 2 | PE 3 | FC 1 | FC 2 | FC 3 |
|---|---|---|---|---|---|---|
| Mean | 5.396 | 5.456 | 5.374 | 5.231 | 5.297 | 5.582 |
| S.D. | 1.057 | 1.019 | 1.096 | 1.201 | 1.124 | 1.210 |
| | EE 1 | EE 2 | EE 3 | FL 1 | FL 2 | FL 3 |
| Mean | 5.445 | 5.495 | 5.577 | 5.538 | 5.555 | 5.764 |
| S.D. | 1.092 | 1.138 | 1.096 | 1.030 | 1.107 | 1.002 |
| | SI 1 | SI 2 | SI 3 | BI 1 | BI 2 | BI 3 |
| Mean | 5.396 | 5.033 | 4.995 | 5.577 | 5.621 | 5.604 |
| S.D. | 1.133 | 1.181 | 1.193 | 1.070 | 1.061 | 1.133 |

The reliability and validity test results are reported in Table 2, the values of Average Variance Extracted (AVE) and Cronbach's Alpha are more than 0.5 and 0.7 respectively in both BI, EE, FC, FL, PE, and SI; therefore, the results demonstrate that construction of the questionnaires and responsès are reliable and acceptable.

**Table 2.** Average Variance Extracted (AVE), composite reliability, and Cronbach's Alpha

| | AVE | Composite reliability | Cronbach's Alpha |
|---|---|---|---|
| BI | 0.853 | 0.945 | 0.914 |
| EE | 0.769 | 0.909 | 0.85 |
| FC | 0.814 | 0.929 | 0.886 |
| FL | 0.791 | 0.919 | 0.868 |
| PE | 0.786 | 0.917 | 0.864 |
| SI | 0.75 | 0.9 | 0.833 |

In addition, regarding the correlation analysis, please refer to the latent variable correlations table in Table 3; the correlation values among these six constructs are all lower than 0.85 which reflect the correlations among these six constructs are reasonable and acceptable.

**Table 3.** Latent variable correlations analysis

| | BI | EE | FC | FL | PE | SI |
|---|---|---|---|---|---|---|
| BI | *0.923* | | | | | |
| EE | 0.517 | *0.877* | | | | |
| FC | 0.607 | 0.491 | *0.902* | | | |
| FL | 0.688 | 0.747 | 0.553 | *0.889* | | |
| PE | 0.703 | 0.589 | 0.62 | 0.682 | *0.887* | |
| SI | 0.638 | 0.696 | 0.616 | 0.569 | 0.704 | *0.866* |

The bootstrapping analysis in SmartPLS programme with 183 responses to 5000 samples was performed to assess the significance of the path coefficients among these five constructs. According to the PLS-SEM results, the p-values of PE, SI, FC, and FL are less than 0.05. Therefore, H1, H3, H4, and H5 are supported However H2 has been neglected as its p-value is over 0.05. Table 4 and Fig. 4 show the results of the Partial Least Squares Structural Equation Modeling (PLS-SEM).

**Table 4.** Results of PLS-SEM analysis

| FACTOR → BI (Behavioural Intention) | Beta value | p-value | |
|---|---|---|---|
| H1: Performance Expectancy → BI | 0.266 | 0.000 | Accept |
| H2: Effort Expectancy → BI | −0.023 | 0.739 | Reject |
| H3: Facilitating Conditions → BI | 0.161 | 0.012 | Accept |
| H4: Social Influence → BI | 0.176 | 0.004 | Accept |
| H5: Flexibility → BI | 0.333 | 0.000 | Accept |

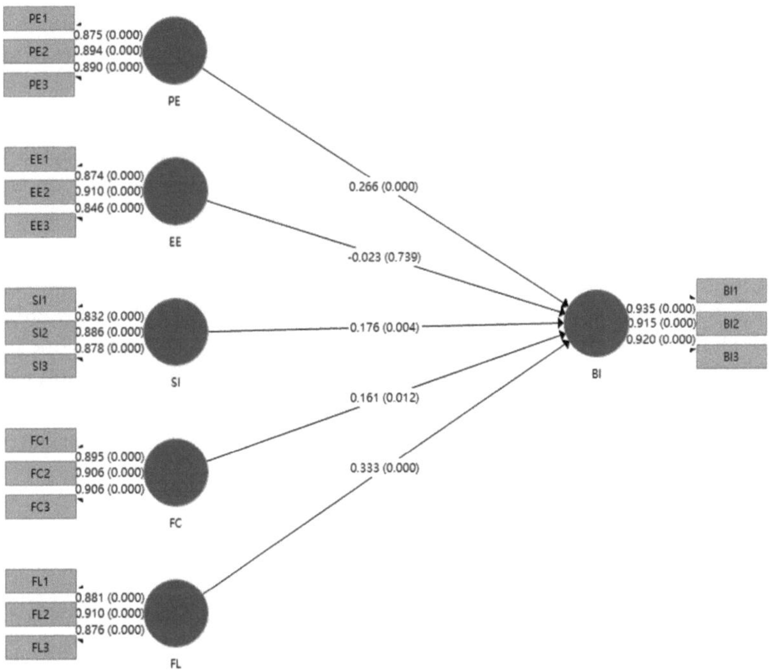


**Fig. 4.** Results of PLS-SEM analysis

Overall speaking, according to the above reports, Flexibility (FL) has demonstrated as one of the significant influences on university students' BI toward using WAA in addition to PE, FC, and SI in UTAUT.

## 5 Discussion and Conclusion

Technology is coming to become a major tool in education nowadays especially in higher education and vocational training that needs not only basic theories in the text-book. Practical knowledge like demonstration of serving food and wine and for many areas, for example, hospitality service training, property management and also kinds of industry related to service can be a more efficient way for people to learn in all ages and nationality as visual reflection is always a common language in the world; thus, by adopting mobile apps which becoming most popular way in daily life usage of communication will also become a major trend for people more willing and easy to learn knowledge and skills.

This research aims to use the UTAUT model via PLS software to analyze university students' BI for using WAA. The research results generate a body of knowledge on identifying those salient factors which influence the BI of university students toward using WAA; especially in the research it reflects that as mobile phone apps have been introduced for more many years and results shows that EE is not a very important issue when people decided to use apps like WAA. The research results may also facilitate the service industry to identify important factors for attracting more organization to use the mobile apps for improving the flexibility, efficiency and also service quality of staffs in their work.

This research aims to analyze the BI for using the WAA among university students by adopting the UTAUT model. Even though the five research hypotheses are all supported by the research results above, researchers would recommend conducting a broader research to other customer segments, such as hotel restaurant staff, wine lovers, white-collar workers, professions, and elderly groups as these groups are increasing their interest on wines for different reasons. In addition to the university students' group. Researchers recommend conducting further research to identify factors for motivating the BI of all these customers groups toward using WAA so as to assist the wine industry to promote their wine products by increasing the wine knowledge of potential customers and also the flexibility of purchase. Last but not least researchers would recommend a boarder research on other Apps except in Wine learning and it will contribute in the areas of Apps design for Apps developers.

## References


Alrawashdeh, T.A., Al-Mahadeen, V.M.: Extended UTAUT to examine the acceptance of web based training systems by public sector employees. Int. J. Interact. Mob. Technol. **7**(1), 4–9 (2014)

Capetownmylove.com: Wine appreciation made easy with Vivino, 08 May 2014. http://www.capetownmylove.com/2014/05/08/wine-appreciation-made-easy-with-vivino/

Chen, G.D., Chang, C.K., Wang, C.Y.: Ubiquitous learning website: scaffold learners by mobile devices with information-aware techniques. Comput. Educ. **50**(1), 77–90 (2008)

Chinnery, G.M.: Going to the MALL: mobile assisted language learning. Lang. Learn. Technol. **10**(1), 9–16 (2006)

Dickinson, J.E., Ghali, K., Cherrett, T., Speed, C., Davies, N., Norgate, S.: Tourism and the smartphone app: capabilities, emerging practice and scope in the travel domain. Curr. Issues Tour. **17**(1), 84–101 (2014)

Godwin-Jones, R.: Emerging technology: mobile apps for language learning. Lang. Learn. Technol. **15**(2), 2–11 (2011)

HKPolyU: The Hong Kong Polytechnic University Academic Programs (2017). http://hotelschool.shtm.polyu.edu.hk/eng/academic/programs_overview.jsp?ID=41&Tag=1&Program=pgd&SubProg=msc&SA=posthk
Hsia, J.W., Tseng, A.H.: An enhanced technology acceptance model for e-learning systems in high-tech companies in Taiwan: analyzed by structural equation modeling. In: The Proceeding of the International Conference on Cyberworlds, pp. 39–44, 6–8 October 2014, Santander, Cantabria, Spain (2008)
Hsu, Y.C., Rice, K., Dawley, L.: Empowering educators with Google's Android App Inventor: an online workshop in mobile app design. Br. J. Edu. Technol. **43**(1), 1–5 (2012)
Jeng, Y.L., Wu, T.T., Huang, Y.M., Tan, Q., Yang, S.J.: The add-on impact of mobile applications in learning strategies: a review study. Educ. Technol. Soc. **13**(3), 3–11 (2010)
Le Cordon Bleu Programs: Le Cordon Bleu Programs (2017). https://www.cordonbleu.edu/programmes/en
Sethi, A., Sethi, S.: Flexibility in manufacturing: a survey. Int. J. Flex. Manuf. Syst. **2**(4), 289–328 (1990)
Statista: Number of apps available in leading app stores as of March 2017 (2017). https://www.statista.com/statistics/276623/number-of-apps-available-in-leading-app-stores/
Tomsguide.com: Tom's Guide: Best Apps for wine lovers, 30 June 2017. https://www.tomsguide.com/us/pictures-story/915-best-apps-for-wine-lovers.html
Upton, D.: What really makes factories flexible? Harv. Bus. Rev. **73**(4), 74–84 (1995)
Venkatesh, V., Morris, M.G., Davis, G.B., Davis, F.D.: User acceptance of information technology: toward a unified view. MIS Q. **27**(3), 425–478 (2003)
Wong, L.H.: A learner-centric view of mobile seamless learning. Br. J. Edu. Technol. **43**(1), E19–E23 (2012)

# Engaging Learners in a Flipped Information Science Course with Gamification: A Quasi-experimental Study

Biyun Huang(✉), Khe Foon Hew, and Peter Warning

Faculty of Education, The University of Hong Kong, Pok Fu Lam Road, Hong Kong
lucy99@connect.hku.hk, {kfhew,pwarning}@hku.hk

**Abstract.** In educational context, gamification is increasingly used as a pedagogical tool to increase learner engagement and motivation. However, there is still a lack of evidence about the long-term benefits of using gamified interventions in flipped classroom. This study examined the effects of a gamified intervention on student engagement in a 10-week flipped information science course. Prior to the intervention, the authors systematically reviewed the motivation theories that are relevant to game psychology, and proposed a goal-access-feedback-competition-collaboration (GAFCC) design model to scaffold the invention design. Both quantitative and qualitative data were collected and analyzed to evaluate the impact of gamification. Results showed that the gamified group completed more out-of-class discussion activities than the control group within the expected time. Self-report data (i.e. survey data) indicated that more than half of the respondents in the gamified group expressed that gamification added fun to this course, and encouraged them to reflect on their learning strategies. This study provided evidence that gamification strategies guided by the GAFCC model can enhance students' behavior engagement and motivation in the flipped activities. The implications and limitations of this study, and future trends are discussed as well.

**Keywords:** Gamification · Flipped classroom · Information science education Student engagement

## 1 Introduction

Gamification is gaining increasingly more attention as a pedagogical tool to increase learner engagement and motivation in K12 to higher education settings. Findings and reports indicated that gamified interventions have the potential to stimulate learners to participate more course activities (e.g. Huang and Hew 2015), attempt more difficulty tasks (e.g. Hew et al. 2016), and enhance student engagement in an ICT course (e.g. Çakıroğlu et al. 2017). Can gamification be a possible solution for engaging students in flipped classrooms?

Several literature review studies reported (e.g. Betihavas et al. 2016; Lo et al. 2017) that student disengagement is one of the major challenges of flipped classroom. O'Flaherty and Philips (2015) pointed out that in flipped classrooms students were less


S. K. S. Cheung et al. (Eds.): ICTE 2018, CCIS 843, pp. 130–141, 2018.
https://doi.org/10.1007/978-981-13-0008-0_13

likely to engage in out-of-class activities, which were deficient in interactivity and formative feedback mechanism. They further warned that the disengagement in out-of-class activities could lead to student unpreparedness, and result in increased student diversity in face-to-face learning session. That is, the students who are prepared in the out-of-class activities may be even stronger, and the less prepared students may feel much harder to keep up with other learners in flipped courses. He et al. (2016) reported that students had bipolar perception on the value of flipped learning activities, some students favored flipped instruction and some students were quite critical of the flipped instruction. To ease the problem of student disengagement (i.e. behavioral engagement and emotional engagement), this study explores whether gamification could be a possible approach for encouraging student participation with the flipped activities, as well as adding fun to the learning process.

## 2 Relevant Studies

### 2.1 Gamification and Game Design Elements

Gamification was initially defined as the "use of game design elements in non-game context" to "design a gameful experience" (Deterding et al. 2011). This definition helped distinguish gamification from full-fledged games by stressing the characteristics of using "elements" in non-game context. The benefits of integrating game design elements with learning context was that it can potentially enhance engagement and promote learning, and it could be cost-effective comparing to developing a full-fledged game.

In gamification design, game design elements are the building blocks of games, and play an important role in designing a gameful experience (Deterding et al. 2011). However, there yet has reached a standardized definition of game design elements (Dicheva et al. 2015). Bunchball (2010) classified game elements into two levels, namely "game mechanics" and "game dynamics". They refer "game mechanics" to the mechanisms for designing a gamified activity, such as points, badges, and leaderboards, and refer "game dynamics" to the motivations or desires enabled by gamification, such as self-expression, and altruism. Werbach and Hunter (2012) categorized game elements into three layers, dynamics (i.e. the big picture of a gamified system, such as emotions, constraints), mechanics (i.e. the processes that players engaged in), and components (i.e. the most concrete level of gameful design, such as badges, points).

Despite the differences in classifying the design elements, it seems commonly agreed that the most concrete level of game design elements are elements like badges, points, leaderboards, etc. In this study, we define game elements as the basic and concrete elements in gameful experience design, which could be directly visualized (Sailer et al. 2017). The examples of game elements include, points, badges, leaderboards, performance graphs, level, unlocking content, storyline, avatar, and quests (individual, or group quests) (Antin and Churchill, 2011; Sailer et al. 2017; Werbach and Hunter 2012). The game elements entail various motivational functions, and when appropriately implemented with the context, it could meet certain human needs and promote expected behavior (Bunchball 2010; Antin and Churchill 2011; Sailer et al. 2017).

## 2.2 Flipped Learning with Gamification

Flipped classroom is defined as an instructional approach where students read new materials or watch instructional videos outside of class, free up in-class time for explanation, discussion or problem solving activities, and finish some additional practices (if any) after class (Bergmann and Sams 2009; Nederveld and Berge 2015). See Fig. 1. for the flipped classroom model. In flipped classroom, students can learn at their own pace and have the autonomy in deciding when to access the learning materials (O' Flaherty and Philips 2015), and it can reduce the course difficulty by exposing learners to self-directed learning materials before class (He et al. 2016). As a large chunk of learning where traditionally happens in class under instructors' supervision has now inverted into students' self-directed learning, the engagement in the out-of-class session becomes a key premise for guaranteeing the success of flipped learning (Dicheva and Dichev 2016).

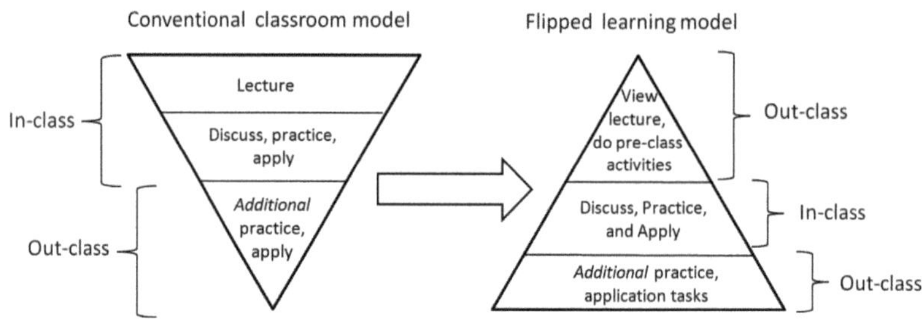


**Fig. 1.** Flipped classroom model (adapted from Nederveld & Berge, 2015, p. 165).

With the purpose of engaging learners in participating flipped activities, researchers suggested that instructors give marks to learners' self-check quizzes (e.g., Tune et al. 2013) or their submitted questions (e.g., Albert and Beatty 2014). While marks may enhance students' participation in a way, students may feel pressure or anxiety in completing those flipped learning activities. Can gamification be used as a pedagogical tool to encourage active participation in the out-of-class activities without introducing much pressure? Only a handful of studies pioneered in integrating gamification with the in-class learning session in flipped classrooms, and there is a scarcity of empirical studies exploring the impacts of utilizing gamification for the out-of-class flipped learning activities.

Mortensen and Nicholson (2015), to the best of our knowledge, is the first study that empirically applied gamification in a flipped introductory equine science course. In their study, they used gamification to encourage learners to participate in-class knowledge reinforcement activities, and reported that learners in the flipped course scored higher than the traditional group (i.e. non-flipped group) in academic and critical thinking tests. Their study demonstrated that gamification could be applied to the in-class learning session so as to enhance students' in-class learning experience. However, they did not use gamification for the out-of-class learning activities. The effect of using gamification for scaffolding out-of-class learning is not yet known.

Dicheva and Dichev (2016) recommended using a gamified mentored active learning model to facilitate the interplay between extrinsic incentives and the intrinsic motives of learners, with the ultimate goal of engaging learners in actively participating the pre- & post- class activities. The theoretical base of this model is self-determination theory and flow theory. Nevertheless, no empirical data was reported based on this model.

Yildirm (2017) integrated gamification strategies into an undergraduate level blended pre-service teacher education course. The study reported that in the gamified group students achieved better academic achievements and had better attitudes than the non-gamified group. In this design, gamification was used for both in-class activities and out-of-class activities. Still, the effect of gamification on students' out-of-class learning activities was not yet explored.

Different from previous empirical studies, our study focuses on exploring effective ways of using gamification to scaffold out-of-class learning activities in flipped classrooms. The research questions are:

1. What is the effect of gamification on students' behavior engagement in out-of-class discussion activities in flipped classrooms?
2. What are the students' perceptions toward the use of gamification in a flipped classroom?

## 2.3 Underpinning Theories of Gamification Design

Gamification design is the process of using game-design and game psychology in non-game contexts to engage users and motive target behaviors (Ng 2014). The most widely quoted psychological theory in gamification studies is self-determination theory (Nacke and Deterding 2017). Meanwhile, goal-setting theory (e.g. Landers et al. 2017) and flow theory (e.g. Han 2015) are also gaining more attention in recent years. In addition to the aforementioned theories, we included social comparison theory (Festinger 1954) and behavior reinforcement theory (Skinner 1953) for review. The intention was to gain an overall picture of how the individual motivation mechanism functions from both individual's layer and social layer.

Goal setting theory (Locke and Latham 2002), flow theory (Csikszentmihalyi 1978), and behavior reinforcement theory (Skinner 1953) explained the elements for constructing a motivating experience from the individual's layer. According to Locke and Latham (2002), goal influences people's motivation and task performance. Long-term and short-term goals, feedback to one's performance, and assistance in evaluating one' performance are measures for building up a motivating environment. It seems that there are some overlapping parts in flow theory and goal setting theory. Flow theory (Csikszentmihalyi 1978) posits that clear goals, immediate feedback, suitable level of challenges, and perceived usefulness of challenges are important elements in building up full involvement and intrinsic enjoyment. Behavior reinforcement theory (Skinner 1953) introduced how incentives could be used to motivate individuals and reinforce positive behavior.

Self-determination theory (Deci and Ryan 2010) and social comparison theory (Festinger 1954) explains the establishment of a motivating experience from both the individuals' perspective and social perspective. Self-determination theory (SDT) posits that autonomy, competence, and relatedness are three important psychological needs of people. Therefore, a sense of choice, and the psychological freedom in participating activities; feeling effective in building up competence when engaging with the context; and the perception of security, belongingness to a community helps in developing higher level motivation and engagement (Deci and Ryan 2010). Social comparison theory elaborated individuals' need for self-evaluation and individuals would compare their opinions with others. In a social context, an individual might even make efforts to achieve uniformity in actions or opinions within the group or community (Feinstger 1954).

Based on the synthesis of the five psychological theories, we proposed a goal-access-feedback-challenge-collaboration (GAFCC) gamification design framework. It emphasizes that (1) clear and achievable goals, (2) access for building up competence, (3) immediate feedback, (4) suitable level of challenges, and (5) chances for collaboration and interaction are essential elements for designing a motivating experience. Game elements, such as badges, points, progress bar, individual or team challenges could be the enabler of these five motivating elements. The relationship among game elements, motivating elements, and motivational needs is illustrated in Fig. 2. In the following part, we will introduce our research context, research methods and the gamified invention design based on the GAFCC design framework.

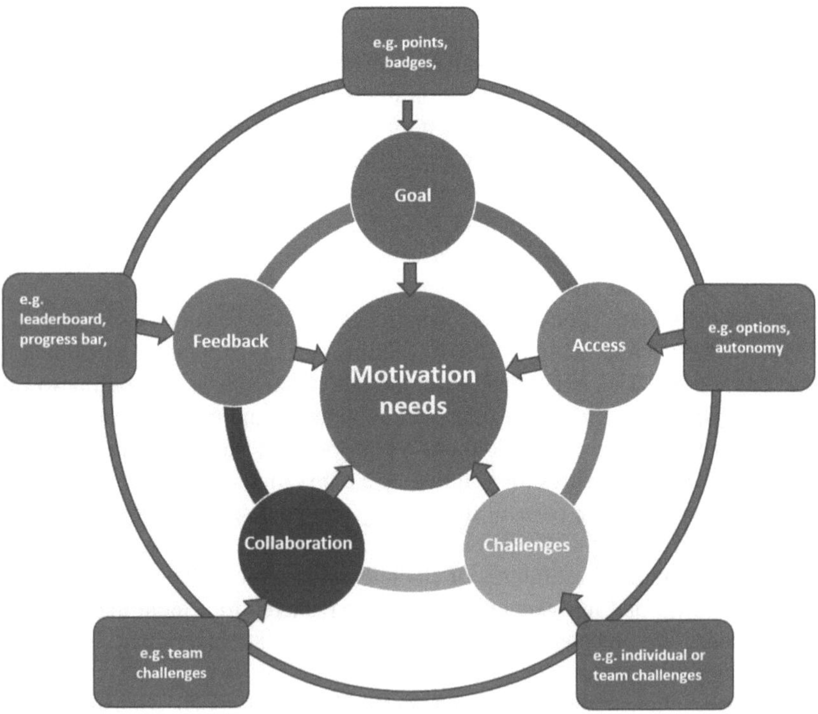


**Fig. 2.** Goal-access-feedback-challenge-collaboration gamification design framework

# 3 Methods

## 3.1 Research Context

Information science course is a fundamental course devoted to effective communication of knowledge and information management through scientific inquiry and professional practice. In this course, students need to achieve such targets as distinguishing information properties, applying information management models to create and transfer information. It is a course that addresses both theory and practice. In order to provide more active learning opportunities for students, the course instructor designed flipped learning activities (e.g. pre-class activity, pre-class reading materials, and post-class forum activity), and hosted on Moodle system. Nevertheless, simply providing students with the materials online without any incentives did not attract many students to complete the post-class activities on time, and students did not seem to engage in the post-class discussions. To invite more participation to the flipped activities and bring fun to the class, we integrated gamification as a pedagogical tool to this course.

**Fig. 3.** Motivating elements and selected game elements

The gamified intervention design followed the goal-access-feedback-challenge-collaboration (GAFCC) design framework. To indicate the short-term goals of each lesson, early bird badges were used to encourage learners to participate the pre-class individual activities, super-efficient badges and communicator badges were used to stimulate learners to participate the post-class forum discussion activities and interact with peers. To challenge learners, level up badges were used to encourage learners to persist in completing all the target activities. To address feedback, leaderboards were used to provide feedback to learner status and enable self-evaluation and competition. See Fig. 3. for the motivating elements and the selected game elements for this course.

### 3.2 Data Collection and Instruments

A quasi-experiment was administrated to test the effectiveness of this gamified intervention. This study involved two classes of first year undergraduates, one class as control group (flipped classroom, n = 48), and one class as treatment group (flipped classroom with gamified intervention, n = 48). In order to answer the research question "what is the effect of gamification on students' behaviour engagement in out-of-class group discussion activities in flipped classrooms", students' participation data on discussion forum were collected. Descriptive data analysis and Chi-square test were conducted to compare the number of postings, and the percentage of students that commented or replied to the postings on the discussion forums. To answer the research question "what are the students' perceptions toward the use of gamification in a flipped classroom", a learner perception on gamification strategies survey questionnaire was conducted in the treatment group (i.e. flipped classroom with gamified intervention). This survey questionnaire is a 5-point Likert-scale, and invites participants to choose from "strongly agree" to "strongly disagree" to indicate their motivation in this learning setting. The sample questions include "I think gamification added fun to this course", "I made more efforts on learning in a gamified setting than a non-gamified setting". Open ended questions were also used to collect students' feedback.

## 4 Results

### 4.1 Participation in Out-of-Class Discussion Activities

Student participation data on post-class group activities were collected and analyzed. In total, this course included 9 weekly post-class forum activities. In the gamified group, students were informed that commenting on each other's postings for more than 3 times would win a weekly communicator badge. In the control group, students were encouraged to make comments to others' postings, but participating or not participating the activities would not receive any badges.

Number of postings. Descriptive data showed that the gamified group submitted more postings within an expected time (i.e. submit at the end of each week) than the control group in all the examined weeks. For example, at the end of the third week, gamified group submitted 61 comments, whereas the control group submitted only 17 comments. See Fig. 4.

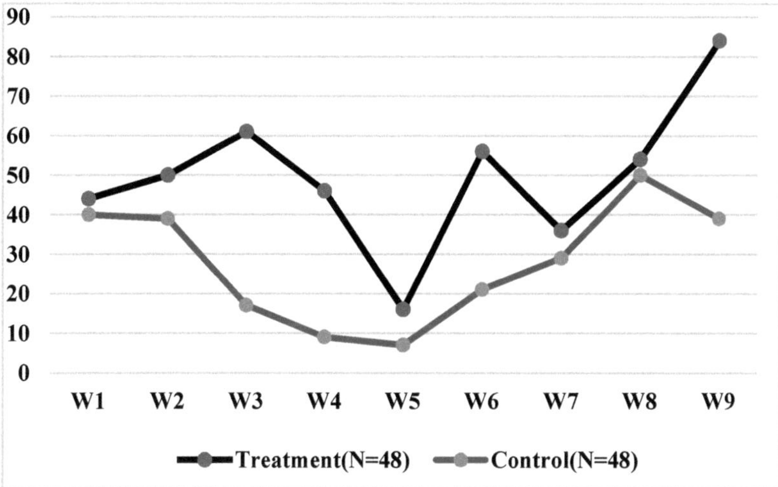


**Fig. 4.** Postings submitted by the end of each week (i.e. within an expected time)

**Table 1.** Chi-square test results for weekly forum activity participation

| | N | Participation | Chi-square | p-value |
|---|---|---|---|---|
| Week1 | Treatment (N = 48) | 65% | $X^2(1) = 1.08$ | p = 0.30 |
| | Control (N = 48) | 54% | | |
| Week2 | Treatment (N = 48) | 50% | $X^2(1) = 0.04$ | p = 0.84 |
| | Control (N = 48) | 48% | | |
| Week3 | Treatment (N = 48) | 58% | $X^2(1) = 14.11$ | p = 0.00 |
| | Control (N = 48) | 21% | | |
| Week4 | Treatment (N = 48) | 67% | $X^2(1) = 37.82$ | p = 0.00 |
| | Control (N = 48) | 6% | | |
| Week5 | Treatment (N = 48) | 10% | $X^2(1) = 1.39$ | p = 0.24 |
| | Control (N = 48) | 4% | | |
| Week6 | Treatment (N = 48) | 67% | $X^2(1) = 16.78$ | p = 0.00 |
| | Control (N = 48) | 25% | | |
| Week7 | Treatment (N = 48) | 31% | $X^2(1) = 0.05$ | p = 0.83 |
| | Control (N = 48) | 33% | | |
| Week8 | Treatment (N = 48) | 65% | $X^2(1) = 1.08$ | p = 0.30 |
| | Control (N = 48) | 54% | | |
| Week9 | Treatment (N = 48) | 90% | $X^2(1) = 26.23$ | p = 0.00 |
| | Control (N = 48) | 40% | | |

Percentage of students participated in out-of-class discussion activities. Descriptive data showed that more percentage of students in the gamified group participated in weekly forum discussion than the control group, except for week 7. See Table 1 for the proportion of students who participated in the forum discussions within an expected time (i.e. by the end of each week). Chi-square tests were conducted to analyze the difference of forum discussion participation. Chis-square test results indicated that there were statistically significant differences in students' participation between the two groups in week 3, 4, 6, 9. For example, in tutorial 3, a significant interaction was found ($x^2(1) = 14.11$, $p = 0.00$) between the two groups. This indicated that more students in the gamified group participated in the commenting activity than the non-gamified group in the third week. For another example, in tutorial 9, significant differences were found between the gamified group and the non-gamified group ($x^2(1) = 26.23$, $p = 0.00$). See Table 1 for details. Results showed that utilizing gamification strategies in flipped classroom was effective in promoting students' participation in forum discussion activities before the deadline elapsed.

### 4.2 Student Perception Toward Gamification

In this study, we used an 8-item learner perception on gamification survey to examine learners' engagement with the flipped classroom. It examined students' perception on gamification from such categories, perceived impact on interest, perceived impact on behavior engagement, perceived impact on cognitive engagement. The reliability test indicated that the standard Cronbach's Alpha was 0.94 (n = 39, 8 items), and the internal consistency for the examined items was 0.94. This showed that the internal validity of this survey questionnaire was high.

The survey questionnaire results showed that 61% (n = 24) of the participants agree or strongly agree that they were stimulated to reflect on their learning strategies, and 59% (n = 23) of the participants either agree or strongly agree that gamification added fun to this course. In this gamified setting, 51% (n = 20) of the participants felt that they were clearer about their learning goals than in a non-gamified setting. Among the surveyed participants, 54% (n = 21) expressed that they were clearer about their learning progress, and 51% (n = 20) stated that they made more efforts in the gamified setting than a non-gamified setting. See Fig. 5. for details. Overall, the survey questionnaire results indicated that more than a half of the students had positive perception on the gamification design.

Students' responses to the open-ended question "overall, do you think it is necessary to add in gamification strategies into courses? why" were collected and analyzed. There were 31 out of 39 survey participants who responded to this question. Result showed that 26 out of 31 respondents (84%) expressed positive attitude in adding gamification strategies. Among them, 71% (n = 22) participants gave an absolute "Yes", and 13% (n = 4) participants said "maybe", "kind of". The main reasons provided by the participants were gamification was "fun" and "interesting", and it provided "a good way to track progress". The other reasons were that gamification "can encourage active participation of students" and "provided a platform to discuss". In gamified settings, students would be gain "tiny little achievements" along the learning process, and they "would be more willing to learn". However, 16% (n = 5) participants were against the idea of integrating gamification into class. For example, one student stated that he or she could think of the benefits of adding gamification. Some survey respondents provided suggestions on improving the gamification design. One participant suggested that instructors could introduce the gamification design at the beginning of the course, and explicitly write the game rules into the course outline. Because this would enable students to remember the rules easily throughout the whole semester. Another respondent recommended that instructors could add some "real awards" to reward students.

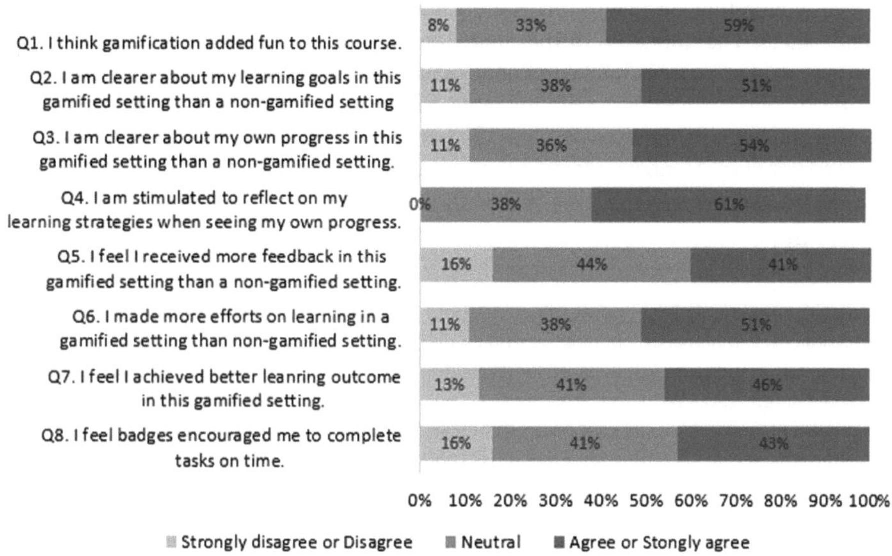


**Fig. 5.** Motivation with gamification in the flipped classroom

## 5 Discussion and Conclusion

Students' participation data showed that more students in the gamified group completed the post-class forum discussion activities than the control group. It is evident that the gamified group submitted more postings than control group. The data showed that gamification was effective in encouraging students early or on time participation in flipped classroom. It could be used for enhancing students' preparedness and timely participation for each lesson. Survey questionnaire data revealed that more than half of the students were motivated by the gamification design, and were encouraged to reflect on their learning strategies. Though a number of students hold a neutral view on the impact of gamification on their learning, the findings suggest that adding gamification to flipped classroom did not generate much negative impact. It was mostly positive or neutral. As long as half of the participants were positively influenced by the game elements, we believe it is worthwhile for an instructor to keep exploring possible appropriate ways to optimize engagement with gamification. The future research question could be how to motivate an even larger number of students to participate in the flipped activities (e.g. post-class forum activities).

Students' responses to the open ended questions showed that a large number of the participants could see the benefits of adding gamification to flipped classroom. But a small number of students could not feel the significance of adding gamification to their course. In order to motivate more active participation in future courses, the instructor or instructional designer could consider introducing the purpose for integrating game elements at the beginning of courses, and see whether this effort would help more students see the value of having gamification in courses.

The exploration on integrating gamification with flipped classroom is still at its infancy stage. The limitation of this study was that the experiment was carried out in only one course. To investigate and understand more about the effects of gamification in flipped courses, there is a need for more empirical studies guided by psychological theories and learning theories. We look forward to more studies that try different gamification strategies to enhance learning in flipped classroom settings.

## References


Albert, M., Beatty, B.J.: Flipping the classroom applications to curriculum redesign for an introduction to management course: impact on grades. J. Educ. Bus. **89**(8), 419–424 (2014)

Antin, J., Churchill, E.F.: Badges in social media: a social psychological perspective. In: CHI 2011 Gamification Workshop Proceedings, pp. 1–4. ACM, New York (2011)

Bergmann, J., Sams, A.: Remixing chemistry class: two Colorado teachers make vodcasts of their lectures to free up class time for hands-on activities. Learn. Lead. Technol. **36**(4), 22–27 (2009)

Betihavas, V., Bridgman, H., Kornhaber, R., Cross, M.: The evidence for 'flipping out': a systematic review of the flipped classroom in nursing education. Nurse Educ. Today **38**, 15–21 (2016)

Bunchball, I.: Gamification 101: an introduction to the use of game dynamics to influence behavior. White paper, 9 (2010)

Çakıroğlu, Ü., Başıbüyük, B., Güler, M., Atabay, M., Memiş, B.Y.: Gamifying an ICT course: influences on engagement and academic performance. Comput. Hum. Behav. **69**, 98–107 (2017)

Csikszentmihalyi, M.: Intrinsic rewards and emergent motivation. In: The Hidden Costs of Reward: New Perspectives on the Psychology of Human Motivation, pp. 205–216 (1978)

Deci, E.L., Ryan, R.M.: Self-Determination. Wiley, Hoboken (2010)

Deterding, S., Dixon, D., Khaled, R., Nacke, L.: From game design elements to gamefulness: defining gamification. In: Proceedings of the 15th International Academic MindTrek Conference: Envisioning Future Media Environments, pp. 9–15. ACM, September 2011

Dicheva, D., Dichev, C.: An active learning model employing flipped learning and gamification strategies. In: Proceedings of First International Workshop on Intelligent Mentoring Systems, pp. 1–6 (2016)

Dicheva, D., Dichev, C., Agre, G., Angelova, G.: Gamification in education: a systematic mapping study. J. Educ. Technol. Soc. **18**(3), 75 (2015)

Festinger, L.: A theory of social comparison processes. Hum. Relat. **7**(2), 117–140 (1954)

Han, H.C.: Gamified pedagogy: from gaming theory to creating a self-motivated learning environment in studio art. Stud. Art Educ. **56**(3), 257–267 (2015)

He, W., Holton, A., Farkas, G., Warschauer, M.: The effects of flipped instruction on out-of-class study time, exam performance, and student perceptions. Learn. Instr. **45**, 61–71 (2016)

Hew, K.F., Huang, B., Chu, K.W.S., Chiu, D.K.: Engaging Asian students through game mechanics: findings from two experiment studies. Comput. Educ. **92**, 221–236 (2016)

Huang, B., Hew, K.F.: Do points, badges and leaderboard increase learning and activity: a quasi-experiment on the effects of gamification. In: Proceedings of the 23rd International Conference on Computers in Education, pp. 275–280, November 2015

Landers, R.N., Bauer, K.N., Callan, R.C.: Gamification of task performance with leaderboards: a goal setting experiment. Comput. Hum. Behav. **71**, 508–515 (2017)

Lo, C.K., Hew, K.F., Chen, G.: Toward a set of design principles for mathematics flipped classrooms: a synthesis of research in mathematics education. Educ. Res. Rev. **22**, 50–73 (2017)

Locke, E.A., Latham, G.P.: Building a practically useful theory of goal setting and task motivation. Am. Psychol. **57**(9), 705–717 (2002)

Mortensen, C.J., Nicholson, A.M.: The flipped classroom stimulates greater learning and is a modern 21st century approach to teaching today's undergraduates. J. Anim. Sci. **93**(7), 3722–3731 (2015)

Nacke, L.E., Deterding, S.: The maturing of gamification research. Comput. Hum. Behav. **71**, 450–454 (2017)

Nederveld, A., Berge, Z.L.: Flipped learning in the workplace. J. Workplace Learn. **27**(2), 162–172 (2015)

Ng, K.: Bio (2014). https://keizng.wordpress.com/

O'Flaherty, J., Phillips, C.: The use of flipped classrooms in higher education: a scoping review. Internet High. Educ. **25**, 85–95 (2015)

Sailer, M., Hense, J.U., Mayr, S.K., Mandl, H.: How gamification motivates: an experimental study of the effects of specific game design elements on psychological need satisfaction. Comput. Hum. Behav. **69**, 371–380 (2017)

Skinner, B.F.: Science and Human Behavior. Simon and Schuster, New York (1953)

Tune, J.D., Sturek, M., Basile, D.P.: Flipped classroom model improves graduate student performance in cardiovascular, respiratory, and renal physiology. Adv. Physiol. Educ. **37**(4), 316–320 (2013)

Werbach, K., Hunter, D.: For the Win: How Game Thinking Can Revolutionize Your Business. Wharton Digital Press, Philadelphia (2012)

Yildirim, I.: The effects of gamification-based teaching practices on student achievement and students' attitudes toward lessons. Internet High. Educ. **33**, 86–92 (2017)

# Instructional Design of Multimedia Courseware Design and Production Based on Flipped Classroom in Universities - Take the Trigger as an Example

Dong Qian(✉)

Graduate School of Education, Peking University, Beijing, China
st16625m@gse.pku.edu.cn

**Abstract.** Under the flipped classroom teaching mode, students watch micro video resources to learn autonomously before class, cooperate with each other by sharing doubts and exchanging ideas for better understanding of knowledge, and share learning achievements after class. "Multimedia courseware design and production" course is practical and widely used as a professional course for students majoring in educational technology in universities. In this paper, we take the use of PPT in the trigger as an example, based on the flipped classroom teaching mode. We hope to enhance the students' autonomous learning ability, and cultivate their cooperative spirit of inquiry.

**Keywords:** Flipped classroom · Multimedia courseware design and production Instructional design · Trigger

## 1 Concepts of Flipped Classroom

### 1.1 Concept of Flipped Classroom

Flipped classroom is also called reversal class and upside down the classroom, which was first proposed in 2000 and developed initially in 2011. For the concept of flipped classroom, some scholars focus on the application of information technology and learning resources. They consider flipped classroom as a new teaching model in the information technology environment, where teachers provide educational videos as a main form of learning resources. Students finish watching and learning educational videos and other learning resources before class. Teachers and students interact with each other about questions of homework and complete the inquiry activities [1]. Some scholars emphasize the flipping of teaching progress. They summarize the concept that flipped classroom is a new teaching model, where students watch videos to exchange teachers' instruction in the classroom, and put more effort on finishing exercise and interact with each other. It flips the teaching in class while students do homework after class [2]. Some scholars believe that flipped classroom is also called reversal class that changes the roles of teachers and students in traditional teaching, and re-plans time schedule in class [3]. Still, some scholars think flipped classroom as a kind of means


S. K. S. Cheung et al. (Eds.): ICTE 2018, CCIS 843, pp. 142–153, 2018.
https://doi.org/10.1007/978-981-13-0008-0_14

that teachers use technical resources to create teaching content, and students learn under the guidance before class. Teachers and students discuss with each other to solve problems. Teachers are no longer just a knowledge senders and students are not just passive knowledge receivers [4].

### 1.2 Features of Flipped Classroom

As a new type of teaching mode, compared with traditional teaching mode, there are three features of flipped classroom:

First of all, in flipped classroom teaching model, teachers transform from classroom manager in traditional classroom into instructors and facilitators of students' study. Students change from passive receivers of knowledge in traditional classroom into active investigators.

Secondly, the traditional teaching environment is changed. In traditional class, students are not the subject of the classroom and active learners. Students do not have enough time to carry out inquiry activities limited by the instructional design of teachers and passive participation of students and classroom time is relatively tight [5]. Flipped classroom flips the position of teach and learn, namely, from "teaching before learning" to "learning before teaching", which makes students enter the classroom with problems. It may help facilitate communication between teachers and students and cultivate ability of independent thinking and collaboration among students.

Thirdly, flipped classroom can help realize an individual learning method and student-centered teaching way. It transforms the traditional teaching idea from "teacher-centered" teaching method to "student-centered". It transforms the traditional resources from textbook, blackboard-writing to rich resources, such as knowledge map, micro lesson video and so on. In learning style, flipped classroom breaks the learning style from tradition individual way to group learning, that is, it encourages students to set up groups and collaborate with each other and do inquiry activities in depth. The evaluation method is no longer a traditional way to test by paper examination only. Students can independently choose their evaluation way.

## 2 Instructional Design of Flipped Classroom in University Curriculum

### 2.1 Limitations of Traditional Classroom Instructional Design

The general process of traditional classroom instructional design is that teachers carry out pre-class preparation, and then determine the instructional objectives, combined with teaching content, instructional objectives, learner characteristics. They choose appropriate teaching environment and methods and design teaching activities. The teachers teach while students listen to teachers in class. The students complete their homework, and teachers finish teaching evaluation and reflection after class. From the above general process, we can see that there are some limitations in traditional classroom instructional design.

First, in traditional classroom, more attention is paid on teaching nor learning. The instructional design is all around "how teachers teach", ignoring "how students learn".

Secondly, traditional way of teaching emphasizes on passive learning, which is not benefit for students' independent thinking. One of the mistakes of traditional education model is to emphasize passive learning rather than encouraging students to participate actively in learning. Another mistake is that standardized education does not fully develop the ability of associate learning as much as possible [6]. In traditional classroom instructional design, most teachers deliver knowledge and different students passively accept knowledge according to the unified teaching rhythm of teachers. In addition, the students' active participation in the teaching activities are less, which makes it difficult to mobilize the initiative and enthusiasm of students.

Thirdly, teachers cannot be aware of the students' studies in time, and students' problem can't be solved timely. On one hand, in traditional classroom instructional design, teachers teach in class for most of the time, which make it not easy to detect students' learning gap, and cannot detect the course schedule constraints timely. Students in the learning process of questions cannot be solved in time with the course teaching content forward. The students' lack of understanding of the previous learning content affects the learning of the content behind. On the other hand, some students are afraid or unwilling to ask teachers questions or communicate with them so teachers cannot know if the students understand what they have taught. Some students try to solve problems independently. But they are faced with the difficulties of spending more time and energy finding past textbooks, learning material lost and other difficulties, which affect students' learning progress.

Fourth, it cannot satisfy the needs of students' individualized learning. The instructional design in traditional classroom of course schedule is unified, teachers impart knowledge according to the predetermined instructional design. Students learn in accordance with the unified pace, which causes some students have mastered the learning content, however, some students cannot keep up with teachers. In addition, students are unable to decide where to learn, what time to learn, what to learn, how long it is.

## 2.2 An Analysis of Feasibility of Introducing Flipped Classroom into University Curriculum

**School Level**

Colleges and universities can introduce and apply flipped classroom teaching model under the strong support of environment and resources. It is of practical significance to introduce the instructional design of college curriculum based on flipped classroom model.

**Teacher Level**

College teachers have higher educational level and knowledge level. They have stronger learning ability and can be easier to accept new ideas and try new things, which makes it easier to apply flipped classroom model into practice. Secondly, college and university teachers mostly use multimedia teaching equipment to prepare lessons and they can skillfully use modern teaching media and have strong information literacy, which provides great possibility to introduce the instructional design of college curriculum based on flipped classroom model. Finally, with the help of flipped classroom teaching model, students preview before class, participate activities in class and review after class. It is possible to enrich more interaction between teachers and students, such as discussions and inquiry activities which can be conductive to improve class listening, enhance communication.

**Student Level**

College students have accumulated a certain degree of knowledge. To some extent, they have a strong self-learning ability and information literacy. In other words, compared with students those before university, college students are more likely to adapt to flipped classroom teaching model. Next, college students have different backgrounds that there are certain differences in learning, such as learning content, learning content and so on. Flipped classroom can better meet the learning characteristics of college students. Finally, college curriculum arrangement is flexible, the free time of college students' is different. Flipped classroom can meet students' individual needs and arrange their learning independently.

It is necessary and feasible to do instructional design based on flipped classroom of the college curriculum through the narration of three aspects of the above schools, teachers and students.

## 2.3 Flipped Classroom Instructional Design

Flipped classroom instructional design model is in accordance with teaching steps: before class, in class and after class. Each step is divided into teacher activities and student activities.

**Pre-class Instructional Design**

*Teacher activities*

Teachers need to write documents that will be used in students' autonomous learning stage, such as learning manual, knowledge map, guiding case, video lectures etc. and complete making multimedia teaching courseware and video recording. After this, teachers need to share all the teaching resources for students' learning.

The core idea of micro course is to promote students' individuality, autonomy and efficiency of learning [7]. In the process of making micro videos, teachers should pay attention to the segmentation of knowledge reasonably, such as the content of the speech need to be clear and easy to understand, the frame is full of change and with unflagging passion.

*Student activities*

Student activities before class are divided into three stages: autonomous learning, practical inquiry, summary and reflection. Students first acquire and save learning resources provided by teachers and they know learning method and steps through learning manual, and then they learn autonomously and carry on the practice inquiry under the guidance of knowledge map. In the process of practice inquiry, they find problems and try to solve them in many ways. At last, they review the learn contents, collect and record learning queries, submit learning portfolios and set a question and its corresponding answers that related to the curriculum content.

**Instructional Design in Class**

*Teacher activities*
Teacher first ask questions to students for discussion in class. During this period, teachers walk in the classroom and provide help for students, for example, conduct individual tutoring and answer questions to the group. Then teachers put forward the common problems encountered by students in this class and explain it to the whole. After this, teachers arrange a series of task and help students complete them. Next, teachers need to guide students to complete personal evaluation and group evaluation. It should be noted that teachers can't simply think that "question is communication" or "the more students discuss, the better the effect is", they need to pay close attention to the quality and depth of communication. [8].

*Student activities*
Students set up a learning group in class and discuss the questions. Each group discusses the question and takes a representative to make a statement. Furthermore, students need to complete the tasks. If there are any problem, they can ask their classmates for help or seek their teachers to individual tutor. After completing the task, students need to sum up what they have learned and finish evaluation of learning performance which contains self-group evaluation, inter group evaluation and teacher evaluation [9].

**After-class Instructional Design**

*Teacher activities*
Teachers need to sort out students' materials after class, such as learning queries, common problems, works etc. On the basis of this, they should finish self-evaluation, reflect on the shortcomings in the teaching process and optimize teaching constantly.

*Student activities*
After class, students need to summarize what they have learned in class and write their learning experiences of the part that they are interested in.

## 3 Instructional Design of Multimedia Courseware Design and Production Based on Flipped Classroom in Universities

In this paper, we take undergraduates of Lanzhou University whose major are educational technology as objects. We carry out the instructional design based on flipped classroom in the course of multimedia courseware design and manufacture as an example, take the use of trigger in PPT for example.

### 3.1 Teaching Analysis

**Teaching Content Analysis**

The course of multimedia courseware design and manufacture is a professional development course, which devotes to improve the multimedia practical operation ability of students majored in educational technology [10]. This course is of strong practice, and the operation steps are coherent. Besides, it is easy to learn, but difficult to go deep. Various commands need to cooperate with each other, which requires students to practice more. As a function in PPT, trigger is a way to control animation execution in the "custom animation" choice to realize functions of man-machine interface. It is often used in the production of interactive multimedia courseware, which helps expand the slide capacity, control the process, and increase the interest of the slide.

**Teaching objectives analysis**

*Knowledge and skill objective*

1. understand the concept, mark, principle and function of trigger.
2. speak the concept and function of trigger in their own language.
3. master the steps of making triggers in PPT.
4. induce problems that should be paid attention to in the process of making triggers.
5. complete the trigger cases in PPT independently.

*Process and method objective*

1. make a thorough inquiry of triggers themselves.
2. participate in group discussions actively and communicate with others.

*Emotion, attitude and value objective*

1. stimulate students' interest in the course of learning.
2. build confidence in the design and manufacture of multimedia courseware.
3. cultivate imagination and creativity.
4. enjoy sharing their works, appreciate the works of others, and enhance the spirit of cooperation and inquiry.
5. enhance ability of self-learning and practical operation.

**Analysis of Learner Characteristics**

The learners of this course are second-year students majored in educational technology in Lanzhou University. They are 21–23 years old. At this age, students enter concrete operational stage of Piaget's theory, who are with strong understanding, independent thinking, comprehensive analysis, self-learning. Besides, they have their own learning methods. According to the teaching plan of educational technology, sophomores have already learned the leading course the University of the information technology infrastructure in the first year, which has certain theoretical basis and practical experience for learning PPT software. In other words, at this time, students have already had some professional basic theoretical knowledge. What's more, compared with most of the other major students, they have more access to software operations which means they have less technical barriers during the process of their study.

### Teaching Environment Analysis

*Network environment*

Lanzhou University campus network construction began in 1996. After many years of improvement and development, Lanzhou University campus network has been built in a large scale and covered five school zones, such as the main campus, medical campus, Yuzhong campus etc. At present, the number of full network access computers has reached nearly 30000 units (including more than 17000 in students' apartments, more than 9000 in staff offices, and more than 3000 in family district of teaching and administrative staff). Apart from this, the network has grown at an annual rate of 5% and now it has been built with full support for IPv4/IPv6. Based on access to CERNET and CNGI-CERNET2, it may realize IPv4/IPv6 universal access to campus network users and IPv4/IPv6 universal service of campus network information resources, which makes it a new teaching and research of information infrastructure in Lanzhou University [11]. Above all, the network of Lanzhou University provides strong support and service for teachers and students.

*Computer room*

There are forty computers for students and on computer for teachers. All of the computers are equipped with Windows XP operation system and Microsoft PowerPoint software. Besides, all of the computers can connect to the Internet, and more importantly, there is a temporary transfer in the computer room, which is convenient to share information, transfer files, and release tasks and submit homework for teachers and students. There are 10 computers in each longitudinal row in the computer room and the interval is about 1.1 m. So it is easy to carry out collaborative and group learning.

## 3.2 Teaching Activities Design

### Instructional design of teaching activities before class

*Teaching activities*

(a) Write documents

Teachers write learning manual, knowledge map, requirements of case manufacture, course questions and answers which builds scaffolding for students to learn and test learning performance. Also teachers provide students learning methods and frameworks, and guide students to learn the course of "use of trigger in PPT".

(b) Make courseware

Teachers make the courseware and write the corresponding notes to prepare for the video recording. Because the course of multimedia courseware design and manufacture is a practical course, when teachers are making courseware, they should pay attention to present more cases relatively, so that students can have a better understanding on it. At the same time, teachers need to collect the materials needed in the courseware for the students to apply in their own practice.

(c) Record videos

Teachers record a total of two videos of the content. The main content of the first lecture is the concept of trigger and the process of making a trigger. First, introduce the concept of trigger through asking "do you know what is trigger? which arouses students' thinking and then describe the concept by the combination of graphic and text. Combined with three cases of punishment game, audio switch controlling, video switch controlling, the concept of trigger is further explained. Next, take punishment game for example to demonstrate how to make triggers in PPT and summarize the whole process of it. Finally, a summary is made and bring questions to students to arouse their thinking further.

The second lecture is to explain the signs, principles and functions of trigger. It starts with looking back on the first lecture and then it shows what content they will learn in this part. Then the video demonstrate seven cases of how can triggers use in practical scenes, like literacy games, picture enlargement, guidance or tagging, linking questions, judgement questions, multiple choice questions and raising and dropping flag, which helps stimulate students' interest in learning through these cases. Finally, according to the cases, there is a summary of the mark, principle, function of trigger.

(d) Share resources

Teachers share documents, videos and other materials with the help of network and mobile equipment.

*Student activities*

(a) Obtain and save learning resources shared by teachers

Students obtain and save learning resources shared by teachers, such as learning manual, knowledge, micro lesson video, materials and so on.

(b) Learn and practice autonomously by resources provided

students read learning manuals first to know learning method and specific steps of this course. Under the guidance of knowledge, students learn with questions and practice autonomously by resources provided by teachers.

(c) Find problems in the process of practice and try to solve them

In the process of autonomous learning, students watch videos, surf the Internet, read books, communicate with students and try varieties of ways to solve problems. During this period, students sort out problems that they still can't be solved.

(d) Review and summarize

Students review what they have learnt, sum up the knowledge point, fill in the blanks in the knowledge, answer questions raised at the end of the video and check the answers.

(e) Submit learning outcomes and problems

To urge the students to learn before class and test learning effect, students need to submit their learning portfolios which at least include learning outcomes and problems these two parts. Learning outcomes include students' learning cases, other teaching materials collected and an original cased of PPT triggers. Learning problems include questions they have met in the process of learning and problems they can't solve.

In order to ensure that the students have watched the videos and brought questions into the classroom, each student needs to put forward at least one most valuable and meaningful topic that he personally believes is related to the course content. Making problem is a process of deepening understanding, and asking questions need to have a strong ability to use knowledge. On the one hand, it urges students to expand their study, improve their ability to use the curriculum, on the other hand, it encourages students to explore and think more. It is worth mentioning that a part of discussion topics of teacher's discussion in class come from this. It breaks through the traditional mode of students ask questions and teachers solve questions and it advocates students to answer questions about the solution, change from solve problems to raise issues and the develop the model of students' mutual teaching and mutual learning [12]. When the student's topic is chosen by teacher, the student's pride and confidence will be promoted. In addition, in the course of classroom discussion, listening to the ideas of other students and teachers will bring fresh new ways of thinking, which helps to deepen the understanding and improve the ability to use it.

**Instructional design of teaching activities in class**

(a) Provide topics for discussion, form a learning group

Teachers provide topics for discussion, part of which from teacher's personal experience, and the other comes from students' learning outcomes so as to increase their enthusiasm and self-confidence. We give the following topics for reference as follows: a. Where do you think the trigger can be used? Please give an example and draw a sketch map. b. What do you think should be paid attention to in the process of making triggers? c. What do you think of the role of PPT in college teaching?

(b) Solve problems and interact with each other

During the discussion, teachers observe the performance of students and help them solve problems. There are three ways for teachers to solve problems: the first is individual tutoring, teachers give one-on-one tutoring to problematic students, which increases the pertinence of problem solving and helps achieve individualized guidance. The second way is answer questions by group. Teachers participate in group discussion or observe the discussion of each group to know the common problems encountered by different groups. The third one is answering common questions in class. Teachers put forward and solve problems according to individual tutoring and group answer questions in class, prompting students what they have ignored, so that students can get new insights in problem solving. After the discussion, students actively speak as representatives and participate in the exchange of issues.

(c) Arrange tasks and practice themselves

Assignments can not only detect the students learning effect and push students to learn before class, but help students find problems in the process of complete the task. In the process of flipped classroom model instructional design, the assignment is to finish the case "picture magnifying effect". Students who finish first can help others, or under teachers' guidance, think how to improve cases of original trigger works submitted by individual.

(d) Show cases, exchange and evaluate outcomes

With the help of multimedia projection facilities, teachers show the original trigger works made before class to students, and encourage students to speak actively, to evaluate students' work, point out where is worth learning and what needs to be improved. On the basis of this, students put forward some opinions and suggestions, which make students learn from each other and to broaden their ideas. Finally, teachers systematically comb what they have learned and skills in class and lead students to evaluate their learning outcomes.

**Table 1.** The flipped classroom instructional design of the application of triggers

| | Teacher activities | | Student activities |
|---|---|---|---|
| Before class | Write documents | Write learning manual, knowledge map, lecture of micro lesson video, answers and questions etc | 1. Obtain and save learning resources shared by teachers<br>2. Learn and practice autonomously by resources provided<br>3. Find problems in the process of practice and try to solve them<br>4. Review and summarizes<br>5. Submit learning outcomes and problems |
| | Make courseware | Make courseware of the course | |
| | Record video | Record two videos | |
| | Resource sharing | Share documents, videos and other materials to students | |
| In class | Provide topics for discussion | One from teachers' personal experience, and one from students' learning outcomes | 1. Form a temporary study group<br>2. Discuss problems raised by teacher<br>3. Seek individual tutors in group or teachers<br>4. Complete the tasks arranged by teacher<br>5. Inductive knowledge point of fabrication skills and scenarios<br>6. Appreciate the case displayed by teacher<br>7. Evaluate the learning results |
| | Solve problems | Individual tutoring;<br>Answer questions by group;<br>Answer common questions | |
| | Assign tasks | See who do fast | |
| | Exchange works | Sum up skills;<br>Show works students do before class;<br>Evaluate and discuss about works of students | |
| After class | Collation | Collect students' works, learning problems, sort out materials | 1. Write learning experience<br>2. Optimize and upload personal works<br>3. Choose to answer the teacher's question<br>4. Expand learning by choosing what they are interested in |
| | Evaluation | Self-evaluation; student evaluation | |
| | Introspection | Reflect questions and improve them | |
| | Optimization | Sum up common problems, launch discussion, provide extended learning materials | |

**Instructional design of teaching activities after class**

*Teacher activities*

1. collation: collecting students' works, learning problems, sorting out materials as cases and materials afterwards.
2. evaluation: teachers evaluate the students' learning effect before class, discussion in class, completion of tasks and self-evaluation of individual teaching level.
3. introspection: teachers reflect on the deficiencies in the process of instructional design based on flipped classroom and write teaching reflection.
4. Optimization: teachers sum up the common problems of students, launch discussion of specific topics and make the best answer.

In addition, teachers provide extended learning materials for students, which make them choose the part that they are interest in to expand learning.

*Student activities*
At the end of the course, students sum up what they have learned and optimize their personal works and then hand it to teachers again. Except that, they can select the part that they are interested in to expand learning or answers questions provided by teachers.

## 4 Conclusion

In this case, we show the whole process of instructional design based on flipped classroom model, which can help teachers use flipped classroom into their own class to help their students learn more effectively. Besides, it's important to pay attention to the details in this model, such as appropriate learning manual to give let students know how to learn, submit problems before class to ensure the learning outcome before class. While in this case, we know that it is useful for courses with lots of steps in the design (Table 1).

## References

1. Zhong, X., Song, S., Jiao, L.: Research on instructional design based on the concept of flipped classroom in information environment. Open Educ. Res. (01), 58–64 (2013)
2. Yi, C., Zhao, C.: Research on instructional design and application based on flipped classroom model. Mod. Educ. Technol. (02), 49–54 (2014)
3. Jin Lei, Z., Ying, W., Baohui, Z.: Research on the model of flipped classroom. J. Distance Educ. **4**, 46–51 (2012)
4. Liu, Y., Nie, Y.: Research on the instructional design of flipped classroom. Mod. Educ. Technol. (02), 61–66 (2015)
5. Deng, X.: Research on the design and application strategy of the flipped classroom teaching model. East China Normal University (2015)
6. Khan, S.: The Flipped Classroom of Khan Academy. Zhejiang People's Publishing House, Zhejiang (2014). Liu Jing
7. Qiuhua, T.: Micro course and its development strategy. Curric. Teach. Mater. Method **5**, 30–34 (2009)

8. Yang, L.: Research on the design and practice of flipped classroom learning activities. Zhejiang Normal University (2014)
9. Guo, Y.: Study on the application of flipped classroom in higher educational. Hebei Normal University (2015)
10. Wenjuan, M.: The design of the special subject learning website of "multimedia courseware design and production" course. China Educ. Inf. **24**, 60–62 (2013)
11. Information Technology Services of Lanzhou University[EB/OL]. http://its.lzu.edu.cn/lzupage/2014/09/09/N20140909171054.html. Accessed 09 Sept 2014
12. Deng, X.: Research on the design and application strategy of the flipped classroom teaching model. East Normal University (2015)

# Instructional Design and Teaching Practices

# Can Entrustable Professional Activities Drive Learning: What We Can Learn from the Jesuits

Spencer H. L. Wan(✉)

School of Medicine, Western Sydney University, Penrith, Australia
honlamwan@gmail.com

**Abstract.** Entrustable Professional Activities (EPAs) has recently been the buzzword in medical education and in the realm of the healthcare professions. Medical professional bodies and medical educators worldwide envision the development of EPAs as a promising approach to overcome the difficulties in assessing their trainee's competencies in a work-integrated learning (WIL) clinical environment. Albeit numerous research has been done on how EPAs can be used as a stopwatch type of competencies assessment method helping to ensure medical trainees are judged to be the best based on well-tested as well as agreed-upon meaningful standards, the prime and essential question of how best EPAs could drive students' daily self-directed learning for their continuous professional development of expertise remains largely unanswered. Amid this leading-edge development in the competency-based medical education (CBME) along with the important role healthcare has to play in the 21st century's global society, there is an increasing need to understand current processes of change and the impact this will have on preparing medical professionals and on healthcare in the coming future. With this endeavour in mind, this paper provides an update on the progress of this gradually establishing approach to competency-based medical education, identifies the essence of this emerging novel workplace-based assessment method in relations to a review of the contemporary competency-based medical education, and finally explores how Jesuit's wisdom could be used in furthering EPAs' potential impact on attainment of medical education's mission.

**Keywords:** Entrustable professional activities (EPA) · Work-integrated learning (WIL) · Jesuit · Medical education · Competency-based assessment process · Clinical settings

## 1 Background

There is an interesting phenomenon in the contemporary medical education worldwide-the seemingly endless quest for the adoption of a competency-based medical education (CBME) as a better alternative to the traditional time-based education.

Over centuries, there have been numerous calls for reform in medical education and had stimulated countless project efforts at international, national and state levels, large and small, aiming to move forward medicine to a competency-focused model ever since


S. K. S. Cheung et al. (Eds.): ICTE 2018, CCIS 843, pp. 157–167, 2018.
https://doi.org/10.1007/978-981-13-0008-0_15

the release of the Abraham Flexner's legacy report (Flexner et al. 1910) on how future doctors should be prepared (Frank et al. 2010a, b; Hodges 2010; Cooke et al. 2009; Irby et al. 2010). Apparently, these past reforms were undertaken for good reasons, however, they had not attained educational excellence in the training and development of doctors as envisioned by Flexner (Hodges 2010). This is also evident in the ongoing researches and expanding literature around gaps in the competence of medical graduates and new residents and on preparedness and readiness of medical graduates for their actual practices in hospital and clinics (Chen et al. 2015a, b). And not until recently that, the development of Entrustable Professional Activities (EPAs) has been seen by many as a practical approach to the implementation of competency-based medical education.

## 2 Medicine as Professional Education

One way of understanding the rationales behind these changes and their revolution processes and the aftermaths is to first consider the nature of medicine as a professional education.

In much the same way of educating professionals in all other disciplines, medical education has a mission of both preparing and readying graduates for precise professional performance practices (in medicine/medical care) along with an indispensable social responsibility of in service of the public. Apart from proficiency of knowledge, ensuring students to have strong moral values and personal qualities of putting the patient's interest first, and responsible care of patients are central to medical education excellence. In other words, the education of medical professional is not solely about transmitting abundant scientific knowledge, but also imparting gradually both cognitive and procedural clinical skills for the care of the changing needs of patients. While broadening medical students' scientific knowledge can enable them to form solid clinical reasoning basis, providing them with the opportunity to practise clinical skills under the appropriate guidance of experienced doctors.

The seeds of in search of medical education excellence and medical education reform can be traced back to the time of William Halsted in 1890s. At that time, the prevailing medical training was fundamentally in the form of apprenticeship, and thereby the kind of training that a doctor encounters can be as diverse as the practices, locations and personalities of the doctors and surgeons offering the training. In an effort to standardise and turn medical training into a profession, Halsted stipulated a set of medical training requirements to include merit-based acceptance, fixed training duration, structured curriculum content and mandatory supervised practice toward the end of training (CanMed 2010).

Another wave of change was led by Flexner who had raised the North American medical education into a university level undergraduate medical programme with strong science grounding as well as a curriculum content that was amenable to a classroom testing methods for knowledge and an evaluation of performance of clinical skills (Hodges 2010). Since then, the medical education has been mostly based on a curriculum that is subject-centred and time-based with knowledge as main focus of summative evaluations and rigorous assessment. Despite there was an exponential expansion of a doctor's bodies of knowledge and skills for their medical practices as compared to Flexner's time, it has been difficult for medical schools to integrate the knowledge, skills and values necessary for their students' proficient practices into medical education programmes at either undergraduate (UME) or residency (PGME) levels. Importantly, there was growing concern that medical graduates may have acquired extraordinary knowledge, while the real final test of their level of authentic proficiency, however, will not be merely what they know but what they can actually perform at the workplace - in the context of real-life medical practice.

Just as the calls for reform in the past, competency-based medical education (CBME) was proposed as a renewed interest in tackling these concerns at a time when the environmental forces for changes were once again strongly felt. In 2010, the Carnegie Foundation for the Advancement of Teaching made another strong call-to-action aiming to standardise learning outcomes, individualise learning processes; develop of habits of inquiries and improvement; promote progressive formation of professional identities; and suggest multiple forms of integrations of knowledge, skills and values (Cooke et al. 2010). The call was so influential that some educators even regarded the contemporary competency-based medical education as an evolution from the outcomes movement in the 20th century and it has generated a shift in focus to accountability, curricular outcomes, and lessening the reliance on set courses and number of work hours in curricular design in the hope of reshaping medical education. Recently, competency-based model is perceived as one of the most appealing new medical education development and approach for meeting 21st century's major stakeholders' needs, improving efficiency and reducing costs to the healthcare and educational systems (Frank et al. 2010a, b, Takahashi et al. 2011).

A careful review of the literature uncovered that several determining factors may has been contributing to the momentum of the ongoing reforms and undermining the effectiveness and efficient attainment of the mission of medical education.

- Complexity of medical competence: lies at the heart of medicine as a professional practice are the complexity of competence required for the actual practice (i.e., with elements of work-integrated learning and workplace performance outcomes), the difficulties in determining and assessing whether those competencies have been adequately acquired and effectively applied (i.e., performed) by the learner in the reallife medical practice (i.e., whether the learner is truly competent), and their paramount impacts on the well-being of human life-ultimately, it's a life art and science. Frankly, this may be one of the reasons for the prevalence and dominance of the apprenticeship model with a time-based focus in the history of medical education;
- Distinctiveness of work-integrated learning, workplace curriculum and workplace performance: the learning of medicine demands for a well-designed contextual-based workplace curriculum and environment for the learning and the assessment of work-integrated learning (WIL), for which is a crucial element posing additional problems to the provision of adequate supervised medical practice.
- Medicine as a formal professional education is relatively young and is still on her way of in search of excellence in the teaching, learning and delivery of desirable impacts and outcomes;

- Apparently, the teaching, learning and assessment of medicine as a professional education has become increasingly complex as they were designated to fulfil the ever changing demands and needs of the society.

# 3 Entrustable Professional Activities and CBME

To understand what Entrustable Professional Activities are and where they fit, it is necessary to first analyse the competency-based system they belong to.

As Frank described the competency-based model as, *"…an approach to preparing physicians for practice that is fundamentally oriented to graduate outcome abilities and organised around competencies derived from an analysis of societal and patient needs. It de-emphasises time-based training and promises greater accountability, flexibility and learner-centeredness."* (Frank et al. 2010a, b: 636).

Competency is commonly defined as *"the ability to do something successfully and efficiently,"* (MedEdWorld Glossary) and competency-based medical education (CBME) was perceived by many as one of the most important development in the field for the past two decades since it was considered a big step forward helping to move away from using the hours worked to serve as a simple proxy that has been shown to result in incompetence of medical students and residents.

It is evident in the growing literature that CBME has been increasingly adopted by medical profession as a pragmatic approach to medical education. Basically, CBME is generally perceived as an outcome oriented model that can guide the educational process toward acquisition of the knowledge, skills, and attitudes required for effective professional practice in service of the public by focusing on both the processes and outcomes of medical education rather than the duration or the total time of a doctor's training. In this approach, it involves competency goals setting, curricular and experiences designed to help students attain the designated goals, integrating instruction in the full range of competencies throughout the educational milestones, guiding and evaluating student learning through formative assessment of competence, and revising standards and activities in light of student competence outcomes (CanMED).

# 4 Discussion

## 4.1 Assessing Competency and Challenges of Workplace Assessments

With recent emphases of patient-centred care and workplace-based assessment (WBA) in medicine, implementing effective methods of evaluating competency in clinical settings has become an integral part of the evaluation of students in contemporary competency-based medical education.

The challenge lies in the effective measurement of a student's actual performance in the workplace given limited direct observation in the real-world setting.

Although tools for direct observation of medical trainees performing clinical skills on patients in simulated settings such as OSCE and Mini-Clinical Evaluation Exercise (Mini-CEX) has been well-established with proven validity (Kogan et al.

2009), limitations such as time constraints in busy workplace environment (Day et al. 1990) still persist.

## 4.2 Understanding EPAs

Entrustable professional activity is a rapidly expanding method for assessing medical trainees. It is defined as 'tasks or responsibilities that faculty entrust to a trainee to execute, unsupervised, once he or she has obtained adequate competence' (Ten Cate and Billett 2014; El-Haddad 2016).

As it was suggested, EPA tasks aim to measure the general attributes of trainees performing day to day activities to establish competency rather than completing a checklist of hurdle requirements (Ten Cate et al. 2007).

In addition, EPAs are context or speciality specific as they should be articulated in terms of explicit, actual units of work and "job to be done" that are suitable for focused entrustment decisions (Ten Cate et al. 2007).

After EPAs are identified, they can be matched to a coordinated set of domains of competence in forming speciality specific assessment framework. Supervisors can then use the framework along with a pre-determined supervision scale for focused entrustment decisions.

Although EPAs do not aim to measure competencies directly, EPAs do provide a link between work outcomes (i.e. performance) and competencies (i.e. abilities) at work if they are carefully chosen and clearly defined in terms of representative components of professional work in the workplace and are coordinated in relation to the most relevant domains of competence (Ten Cate and Billett 2014; Ten Cate et al. 2015).

Specifically, instead of directly assessing each of the many separate and abstract competencies required to undertake a complex professional job, this approach takes supervisor's "entrustment" decision and the learner's performance in daily work activities into account as a surrogate measure of the learner's competence.

## 4.3 The Case for EPAs

Moving into the 21st century, the rise of competency-based medical education curricular has prompted a transformation in the realm of education at medical schools with heavy emphasis on performance outcomes, from individual practices to national standards, and from pre-clinical to clinical training and professional career pathways (Frank et al. 2010a, b).

Numerous research has been done on the concept of defining competence, competency-based medical education, competency-based assessment methods and tools, and competency and performance assessment in the workplace. While a wide range of competencies assessment methods, tools and approaches are proposed including 360-degree assessment, multi-source feedback (MSF), patient-input, workplace-based assessment, and Observed Structured Clinical Examinations (OSCEs) and Mini-Clinical Examinations (Mini-CEXs) etc., there's still a lack of consensus on how best to measure and assess trainees and students' competencies in a real-world setting (i.e. workplace) and in medical education with work-integrated learning in particular (Kwan et al. 2016).

For many medical schools, it was typical for their programmes to use a combination of discrete measurement methods and tests to assessing their trainees and students' competencies, and more than often their assessment results were problematics with obvious limitations on reliability and caused diverse levels of performance expectation for graduate's transition among medical education institutions (Govaerts et al. 2007; Govaerts et al. 2013).

Noting this inadequacy, medical educators, academic researchers and practitioners around the globe have been actively seeking alternative viable and practical competence assessment approaches, and most importantly exploring ways to reach agreeable standards in managing professional competence assessments at both local and national levels.

Of these massive and intensive efforts, EPAs have been singled out as one of novel, promising and practical approach toward effective competence assessments for work integrated learning (WIL) type of education, and especially medical education and professional training (Kwan et al. 2016; Chen et al. 2015a, b; Englander et al. 2016; El-Haddad 2016).

Since the direct measurement of competence is not the objective of EPA, but rather the measurement of trust based on general attributes of trainees performing day to day activities, EPA does not require the cumbersome process of defining each aspect of competence (Ten Cate et al. 2007).

Research to date has revealed that many leading medical schools, accreditation institutions and medical education community worldwide in the United States, Canada, Germany, Netherland have already incorporated their own institutional list of EPAs in both their undergraduate and postgraduate medical education curriculums, and ongoing pilot studies of its effective implementation in various disciplines/environments are also underway (Kwan et al. 2016; Chen et al. 2015a, b).

## 4.4 The Potentials of UME Level of EPAs

Medical professional bodies such as the Association of American Medical Colleges (AAMC) and the Canadian Medical Educational Directives for Specialists (CanMEDs) have published reports that a substantial progress has been achieved in evaluating, validating and expanding on this EPA framework approach.

For example, a list of 13 Core Entrustable Professional Activities (core EPAs) for Entering Residency framework was offered by the AAMC. A five-year-long pilot on this core EPAs framework has begun with ten medical schools across the United States for a better transition of undergraduate to graduate medical education (Englander et al. 2016).

As regards, the academic research community has called for follow-ups and longitudinal researches on its effective applications and implementations across various medical professional disciplines and along the physician professional training and development continuum and especially at undergraduate level (Chen et al. 2015a, b; El-Haddad 2016).

## 5 Entrustable Professional Activities and the Way Forward

The advent of entrustable professional activity (EPA) is already taking place in both North America and Europe, and the UK and Canada, but for the present moment, it is just an enhanced assessment tool that can help training programs implement a broader competency-based educational model (Takahashi et al. 2011). By incorporating EPAs, there seems to be an assumption that competency-based medical education will enable the medical field to guide the workplace's training and assessment of the medical students so that upon graduation they will demonstrate competence in the multiple domains of practice required to meet the needs of the 21st century global society, but this has yet to be proven. Let alone the fundamental problem is that what we come to think of as medical/professional competency and academic ability and medical/professional culture may vary over time depending on the desires of the stakeholders at the time (McGaghie et al. 1978). This may be one of the reasons why there have been centuries relentless callings for redefining medical competency and medical professionalism for better patient care.

Although the recent development of competency-based medical education (CBME) can be regarded as a huge step forward by moving from time-based to competence-based, from inputs focused to outputs focused, and from assuming to assessing, and when it is equipped with the promising development of EPAs, may relieve the difficulties in assessing trainee's competencies in a work-integrated learning (WIL) clinical environment and may stimulate their clinical learning, it is still a great challenge to tackle the clinical inertia culture (guidelines culture) - the source of difficulties in entrustment decision making while assuring those essential stimulations necessary for driving students' daily self-directed clinical learning for their continuous professional development (Takahashi et al. 2011; McGaghie et al. 1978; Ten Cate 2016).

Also, this may be the reason why it seems that it was so close yet so far from solving the problems and/or meeting the patients' needs almost every time when reform and change were sought.

## 6 EPAs and Mission of Medical Education: Where We Stand and What Else Needs to Be Done

It is clear from the above review of medical education reforms that previous reforms were largely aroused and taken in response to forces for change at the time. Dating back to the time of Flexner's report, medical leaders and medical educators have had initiated and pioneered numerous unprecedented changes to medical education in meeting those prevailing healthcare needs of the patients and the society at the time.

Entrustable professional activities (EPAs) and of more recently entrustment decision making in clinical training have reframed both the concept and the approach to the assessment of competence through an alignment of entrustment decisions with what clinical teachers and trainees actually do as part of their daily essential work tasks/activities-the heart of clinical assessment and training (i.e., clinical training and practice in reality). Put it simply, EPA seems to be a better received approach and a readily understood concept as it deals with one of the most important, practical and recurring questions that clinical teachers have about their trainees in the process of clinical training-to trust or not to trust them in on-the-spot safety patient care.

Perhaps the EPA approach has helped to identify the key concept to the assessment of clinical training in the workplace, but more importantly it has reminded us the indispensable role of clinical training in the entire professional medical education process. As recognised by Flexner, clinical training is an essential phase for a trainee's transformation, through thoughtful authentic patient encounters to attain deeper understanding of knowledge and know-how, they can apply and refine their skills, learn to determine their deliberate self-improvement needs and progression's direction. Thus, it's not just about assessment, supervision and entrustment decisions, the underlying benefits of the EPAs concept can be further derived when it is used to inspire dedicated ongoing actions of clinical teachers and trainees for their self-improvements, for refreshing their professional skills, and for fostering their pursues of excellence in their professional practice of medicine both in the course of clinical training and beyond, of which is the ultimate goal of all medical education.

It is well recognised that, the Jesuits subscribe to an unique Jesuit's philosophy of which has inspired their dedicated efforts towards their mission in education, and that has in fact ensured their lasting lead in education in diverse cultures and across different countries with a long standing tradition that has spanned over 450 years. As such, it is considered that the Jesuit's philosophy and its principles should be useful for inspiring, guiding and nurturing dedicated and responsible clinical teachers and students in their applications of EPAs for attaining meaningful clinical trainings and reaching excellence in their future professional practices while ensuring safe medical practices.

## 7 Jesuit's Medical Education, Jesuit's Heritage and EPAs

Ensuring quality educational outcomes is not a simple task, there is a huge difference in the development of medical professionals as compared to the development of professional skills and expertise. Clearly, the assessment of workplace performance and/or work-integrated learning require not solely well-developed standards (fixed targets), but also that certain extent of expert judgements, and the assessment of the learner's quality of performance requires information regarding the individual as a whole person than just discrete technical skills or functional aspect alone.

With respect to medical education, the Jesuits have a pretty distinguishing view and rich heritage of how to nurture commitment to health care's excellence from all involved (students, faculty, and all medical professionals). Generally, Jesuit medical education is largely based on the experience and heritage of the Jesuit Founder-Loyola. Since 1592, person-centered focus has been promoted as a hallmark of Jesuit education and that has led to several specific practical actions and later became their heritage and formed their unique Jesuit culture and character. As it is described by the Jesuits, its founder advocated the urgency to share what his followers and he received, and to use their learning and leadership, their life experience and values, and compassion in service to the people in need of these special qualities of life and hope. Thus, it is this culture that helped to form the mission of all Jesuit's medical schools and hold them accountable to their unwavering desire and relentless commitment to do better in all that they do in patient care.

And through this 'Magis Standard', that "calls them to be their very best by placing themselves at the service of four core values" namely respect, care, concern, and cooperation for better patient care ("Loyola Univ. Health Sys. - Mission & Ministry - Medical Education & Health Care in the Jesuit Tradition" 2008).

Essentially, the Jesuit's unique emphasis on thoughtful steward leadership, their interactive way of teaching and learning, and ongoing self-reflection on experience are the invisible drives behind their relentless improvement efforts in all they do as they strive for excellence in patient care beyond treating disease to the healing of the human spirit in the communities they serve.

It is envisaged that these Jesuit's culture and characteristics are essential to advancing the design of work-integrated learning, workplace-based clinical curriculum and thereby the formation of flexible and adaptable EPAs that can enable entrustable decision making, tackle clinical inertia culture, stimulate self-directed and cooperative learning, and avoid what Hodges amused as a modern 'i-Doc' model. Because this 'i-Doc' model is thought to be a new way to organise medical education but essentially modelling on an industrialism's mindset, with which medical schools still concentrate solely on one aspect of capabilities- functions (McGaghie et al. 2014; Takahashi et al. 2011) of various batches of end products, not of a human being (medical school graduate, resident or practising physician), to manufacture "highly desirable products adapted to user needs and desires" (Hodges 2010). Therefore, it is expected that Jesuit's wisdom could be better unveiled and used in furthering EPAs' potential impact on attainment of medical education's mission.

## References


Association of Faculties of Medicine of Canada: The future of medical education in Canada (FMEC): a collective vision for MD education. Association of Faculties of Medicine of Canada (AFMC) (2010)

Chen, C.A., Kotliar, D., Drolet, B.C.: Medical education in the United States: do residents feel prepared? Perspect. Med. Educ. **4**(4), 181–185 (2015a)

Chen, H.C., van den Broek, W.S., Ten Cate, O.: The case for use of entrustable professional activities in undergraduate medical education. Acad. Med. **90**(4), 431–436 (2015b)

Cooke, M., Irby, D.M., O'Brien, B.C.: Future Directions for Medical Education: Educating Physicians: Professional Formation and Insistence on Excellence. Jossey-Bass, San Francisco (2009)

Cooke, M., Irby, D.M., O'Brien, B.C.: Educating Physicians: A Call for Reform of Medical School and Residency, vol. 16. Wiley, Hoboken (2010)

Day, S.C., Grosso, L.J., Norcini, J.J., Blank, L.L., Swanson, D.B., Horne, M.H.: Residents' perception of evaluation procedures used by their training program. J. Gen. Intern. Med. **5**(5), 421–426 (1990)

El-Haddad, C., Damodaran, A., McNeil, H.P., Hu, W.: The ABCs of entrustable professional activities: an overview of 'entrustable professional activities' in medical education. Intern. Med. J. **46**(9), 1006–1010 (2016)
Englander, R., Flynn, T., Call, S., Carraccio, C., Cleary, L., Fulton, T.B., Minter, R.M.: Toward defining the foundation of the MD degree: core entrustable professional activities for entering residency. Acad. Med. **91**(10), 1352–1358 (2016)
Flexner, A., Pritchet, H., Henry, S.: Medical education in the United States and Canada bulletin number four (The Flexner Report). The Carnegie Foundation for the Advancement of Teaching, New York (1910)
Frank, J.R., Mungroo, R., Ahmad, Y., Wang, M., De Rossi, S., Horsley, T.: Toward a definition of competency-based education in medicine: a systematic review of published definitions. Med. Teach. **32**(8), 631–637 (2010a)
Frank, J.R., Snell, L.S., Cate, O.T., Holmboe, E.S., Carraccio, C., Swing, S.R., Harden, R.M.: Competency-based medical education: theory to practice. Med. Teach. **32**(8), 638–645 (2010b)
Govaerts, M.J.B., Van de Wiel, M.W., Schuwirth, L.W.T., Van der Vleuten, C.P.M., Muijtjens, A.M.M.: Workplace-based assessment: raters' performance theories and constructs. Adv. Health Sci. Educ. **18**(3), 375–396 (2013)
Govaerts, M.J., Van der Vleuten, C.P., Schuwirth, L.W., Muijtjens, A.M.: Broadening perspectives on clinical performance assessment: rethinking the nature of in-training assessment. Adv. Health Sci. Educ. **12**(2), 239–260 (2007)
Hodges, B.D.: A tea-steeping or i-Doc model for medical education? Acad. Med. **85**(9), S34–S44 (2010)
Irby, D.M., Cooke, M., O'brien, B.C.: Calls for reform of medical education by the carnegie foundation for the advancement of teaching: 1910 and 2010. Acad. Med. **85**(2), 220–227 (2010)
Kogan, J.R., Holmboe, E.S., Hauer, K.E.: Tools for direct observation and assessment of clinical skills of medical trainees: a systematic review. JAMA **302**(12), 1316–1326 (2009)
Kwan, J., Crampton, R., Mogensen, L.L., Weaver, R., van der Vleuten, C.P., Hu, W.C.: Bridging the gap: a five stage approach for developing specialty-specific entrustable professional activities. BMC Med. Educ. **16**(1), 117 (2016)
Loyola University Health System - Mission & Ministry - Medical Education & Health Care in the Jesuit Tradition. Lumc.edu (2008). http://www.lumc.edu/depts/ministry/education.htm. Accessed 6 Dec 2017
McGaghie, W.C., Miller, G.E., Sajid, A.W., Telder, T.V.: Competency-Based Medical Education: Origins and Prospects: An Introduction. World Health Organisation, Geneva (1978)
McGaghie, W.C., Issenberg, S.B., Barsuk, J.H., Wayne, D.B.: A critical review of simulation-based mastery learning with translational outcomes. Med. Educ. **48**(4), 375–385 (2014)
Royal College of Physicians and Surgeons of Canada: Competence by Design (CBD): moving towards competency-based medical education (2014). http://www.royalcollege.ca/portal/page/portal/rc/resources/cbme
Takahashi, S.G., Waddell, A., Kennedy, M., Hodges, B.: Innovations, integration and implementation issues in competency-based education in postgraduate medical education. Memb. FMEC PG Consort. **33**, 17–18 (2011)
Ten Cate, O., Scheele, F.: Competency-based postgraduate training: can we bridge the gap between theory and clinical practice? Acad. Med. **82**(6), 542–547 (2007)

Ten Cate, O., Billett, S.: Competency-based medical education: origins, perspectives and potentialities. Med. Educ. **48**(3), 325–332 (2014)

Ten Cate, O., Chen, H.C., Hoff, R.G., Peters, H., Bok, H., van der Schaaf, M.: Curriculum development for the workplace using entrustable professional activities (EPAs): AMEE guide no. 99. Med. Teach. **37**(11), 983–1002 (2015)

Ten Cate, O., Hart, D., Ankel, F., Busari, J., Englander, R., Glasgow, N., Touchie, C.: Entrustment decision making in clinical training. Acad. Med. **91**(2), 191–198 (2016)

The MedEdWorld Glossary. www.mededworld.org/Glossary.aspx

# The K-12 Learn-to-Code Movement is Leaving Current Graduates Behind: Status and a Case Study

Theodor Wyeld[1(✉)] and Minoru Nakayama[2]

[1] Flinders University, Adelaide, Australia
theodor.wyeld@flinders.edu.au
[2] Tokyo Institute of Technology, Tokyo, Japan

**Abstract.** There is a movement towards teaching children how to code. This is not a new idea. It has been promoted since the 1980s. It is only very recently, however, that the need to know how to code has become crucial. University-age students need to know how to code to achieve employment after graduation. Post-graduation jobs increasingly require some understanding of how programs work and are developed. Since the early 2000s there has been an increasing demand for graduating students with coding skills. They have attempted to meet this demand by teaching themselves some coding skills (such as for web apps). But, many report they struggle to get past the basics. The tool used in this study immersed students in code in a way that was both fun and leverage existing interests. An online 2D games editor was used for students to learn how to build an app for their mobile device. They interacted directly with the code base and created solutions to problems. Before and after questionnaires showed a shift in sentiment from a fear of coding to a better understanding of code.

**Keywords:** Learning to code · Learning to program · Code anxiety

## 1 Introduction

Coding is being promoted as a way to encourage children to think about computing as a creative outlet. It is beginning to be included in the K-12 curriculum in schools globally. Children's socialising on digital networks demands some fundamental understanding of the technology, how it works, and even how to produce for it. Their enthusiasm for creating digital media to share is only matched by the communities that support the activity. Children increasingly modify, create, design, illustrate, animate and tell stories using digital media. This is extended into programmable toys, robots and other devices (Kafai and Baurke 2016). But, this explosion in programming activity at an early age has found their older siblings – between 18 and 25 – playing catch-up. It is this later group that are now at university age and know that the sort of jobs available after graduation increasingly require some understanding of programming; either coding or project managing. Their anxiety about gaining the requisite skills is real, yet largely ignored in curricular outside the traditional university computer science courses (Brooks 1986, 1995). This paper discusses the


S. K. S. Cheung et al. (Eds.): ICTE 2018, CCIS 843, pp. 168–178, 2018.
https://doi.org/10.1007/978-981-13-0008-0_16

implications of this and, in brief, a project which attempted to address the deficit by introducing students to coding in a non-threatening albeit realistic development environment. It used a before and after questionnaire to capture any shift in sentiment towards learning to code over the term of the project. It found that, it is possible to relieve some of the anxiety experienced by exposing students to coding from IT and non-traditional IT backgrounds alike. While this reports on only one method of introducing students to coding, the need to provide for an authentic environment whereby students could hold an expectation of succeeding was paramount to its success.

## 1.1 The Need to Learn to Code

The idea that children should be learning how to code from an early age is not new. Since the time of accessible computing in the late 1970s and early 80s Papert (1980) was advocating its role in the curriculum. Papert (1980) saw computer systems as a new medium for learning. He saw it as a shift away from passive knowledge acquisition to actively promoting individual creativity. The computer provided a logical environment for exploring creativity at a new level. Papert's work with Piaget (see Ackermann 2001) exposed him to different ways of approaching how children learn. Papert (1980) felt a need to shift education from instruction to natural-inquiry; children should be free to construct their own knowledge. His Logo programming language was designed to compliment a child's egocentric position and movement by developing their nascent theories about geometry. He was not simply suggesting that children should learn coding as another language. Rather, he saw computer programming as a way to restructure maths and grammar such that it accommodates the child's natural tendencies to learn as a creative pursuit. Learning to code is in this sense not an end in itself but a means to explore the role of computing in modern society. He subscribed to the constructionist philosophy that computers are merely an epistemological tool to inspire and express creative ideas. He claimed, like Minsky (1988) proposed, the computer's ability to simulate reality, and processes outside of reality, mirrors human thought processes – it provides insights into our own ways of thinking and changes them in the process. Although many schools attempted to incorporate at least some of Papert's ideas in the 1980s, few persisted. It is only recently that there has been a renewed push for coding to be added to the curriculum in early education. However, there is also a burgeoning cohort of university-aged students who need to know how to code as a pre-condition of employment post-graduation.

## 1.2 The Rise of the Need to Code

The rise of high-tech innovation hubs in places like Silicon Valley, Bangalore, Shenzen (Startup Warehouse), Dublin (Silicon Docks), Tokyo, Taipei, and Seoul, led to a shortage of coders after the early 2000s. The growth in demand for coders was more than 30% between 2007 and 2012, and is predicted to grow at 22% between 2012–2022. Most recently, a group has formed called the 'learn to code' movement (see code.org; codeconquest; codecademy; meetup.com; codelikeagirl.org; Silicon Valley Coding School; Disrupting Engineering Education). They are pushing for coding to be taught in schools. They have support from a wide variety of high-profile advocates such as the mayor of NY, Michael Bloomberg, Microsoft founder Bill Gates, Facebook founder Mark Zuckerberg, and President Obama, pushing for legislation to include computer science in every public-school curriculum.

The rise in the perceived need to learn how to code is based on the success of entrepreneurs such as Elon Musk and Mark Zuckerberg. They are often cited as extraordinary success stories that others should try to emulate. But, some argue coding is not the new literacy – coding is simply the extension of existing skills in a new framework (Farag 2016). The framework is one usually reserved for those who work in it directly. But, increasingly, nearly everything we interact with has some code base. And, knowing how to code helps us understand how it works (see Petzold 2000). But, even if you don't need to know how a car works to drive it, it does help if you have any chance of understanding how to fix it when it breaks down. In this sense, knowing how code works also helps you know what questions to ask even if only to direct others to do the coding for you.

### 1.3 How Graduating Students are Teaching Themselves Code

Many contemporary graduates are coming to the realisation that in order to secure employment they need to know how to code (see Althoff 2017). Some learn bootstrap (a front end responsive framework for building websites – WordPress was built on it). CSS is another place they start learning how front-end code affects websites. Websites in general are a good place to start to learn coding as it is more about layout and structure than functionality *per se*. Other packages include: SQL, JavaScript, Ruby on Rails, HTML, Sass, Stylus, Meteor (a full stack JavaScript framework). For example, many of the blogs, news sites and eCommerce sites that the current graduates access are web applications. Content Management Systems (CMS) like Wordpress and Magento (which does eCommerce) make it easy to edit and build these sorts of web apps. However, the limits of a CMS are quickly reached. More advanced design or technical features require a more advanced understanding of the underlying code. JavaScript is a common method for adding the functionality.

### 1.4 Getting Past the Basics

The most common difficulty for beginners is getting past the basics. They may have learned some code but don't really know how to go about building their own programs from scratch. They might understand the theory but can't put it into code. They understand some core concepts but are not sure about where and when to use them. They don't know how to combine the various core concepts such as loops, arrays and variables. They feel lost after completing the basics. This can be caused by a number of factors. Often the learning environment is not the same as the actual developing environment. Hence, getting started in a real environment helps facilitate some self-guidance. The learning environment is often supported with lots of hints and technical advice. But, when it comes time to develop the code from scratch, none of that is there. Knowing the correct syntax does not guarantee they understand the underlying concepts. Too much help makes the programming look artificially easy. When students are left to do their own coding they may find they don't have a deep enough understanding of how to construct it.

Whether working from an IDE (Integrated Development Environment - compiler) or the command line, a real coding environment is more conducive to deep learning than simply writing pseudo code. It is actually from the active debugging and error fixing that learning begins (see Bonwell and Eison 1991; Prince 2004 on active learning). Copying and pasting other peoples' code is useful, but only if the learner understands what it does and how to fix it when it doesn't work.

### 1.5 What to Focus on

It is not enough to simply know how to code. Many students that have completed a course in coding do not feel they can actually write a program from scratch. They may understand these concepts and syntax but not how to put them together to solve a problem by building an actual program. Perhaps the learning environment had too much support. When this support is taken away, they feel lost. What matters is knowing what the problem is and how to implement a solution for it using code. The focus here should be on solving the problem rather than learning to code *per se* (Shermer 2005).

### 1.6 Coding Changes a Student's Way of Thinking

Coding should be fun. It should let students make things and build things. But it requires a lot of patience and hours of practice. Coding trains students to think in a certain way – but it is very narrow. Coding should not be seen as a goal in itself. It should instead be seen as a tool for solving problems (see comments by Peter Norvig, director of research at Google, norvig.com). Students are more likely to commit to learning to code if they have a problem they want to solve than learning to code for its own sake. But, while students can learn to code quickly, this doesn't make them a coder or engineer – it generally takes about 10 years to ever become expert in anything. However, even knowing the rudimentary basics of coding gives students a headstart in a world that relies on coding. In some ways, it's more important to know how coders think than actually being a coder.

### 1.7 Which Languages are in Greatest Demand?

The highest salaries paid to coders by language (usually linked to demand for knowledge of a particular language or shortage of those with that language) can be ranked as: 'Ruby on Rails', Python, C++, iOS, JavaScript, Java, C, PHP and SQL. But, one needs to be able to switch languages as the demand changes. And, one needs to know several languages. For example, even though Ruby and Python might appear to be the highest paying positions, most job ads list C, SQL and Java as also necessary. In fact, Ruby is not listed as often, meaning that, while Ruby may be highly paid, there are not many positions when compared to raw C. JavaScript and Python are often also listed (see Fig. 1). This is the case for established firms. For start-ups, the story is different (see Kelleher and Pausch 2005).

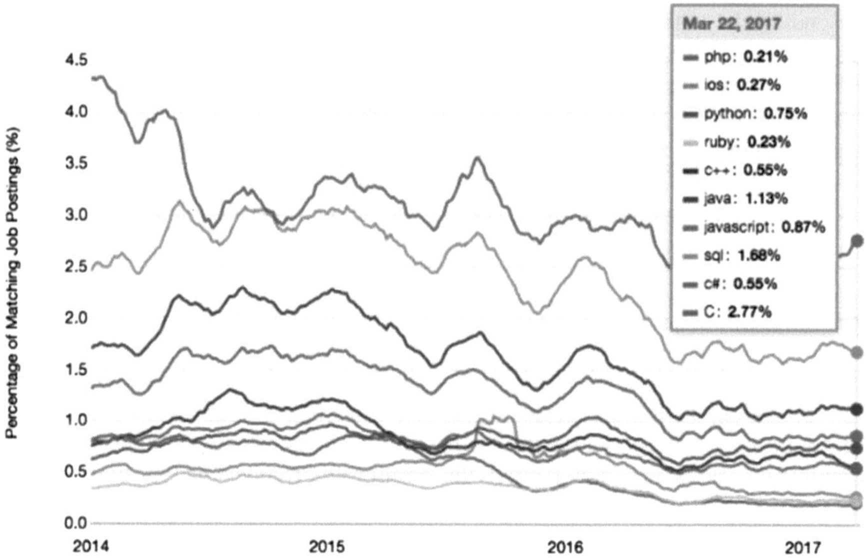


**Fig. 1.** Distribution of code languages as advertised between 2014 and 2017 (codementor.io, accessed 2017).

While 'Ruby on Rails' was the favoured language in 2015, in 2017 it tends to be JavaScript, Python and Java. These are easy to learn languages that can be used to produce prototypes quickly (see Fig. 2).

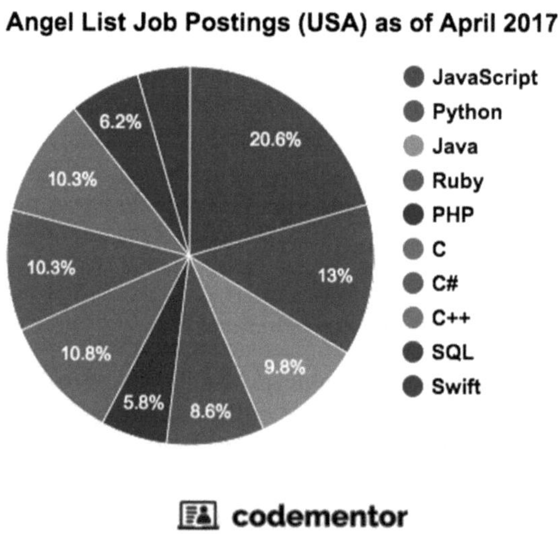


**Fig. 2.** Distribution of coder language preferences in startups for 2017 (codementor.io, accessed 2017).

In order to get ready for industry post-graduation, beginner learners need to know how to use repository or version control resources like GitHub. There they can post their projects and see what others are doing and share code. Employers often look at a potential employees history of programming activity. GitHub is one of the places they expect to find this history. Between StackOverflow and GitHub there are many resources for beginning learners.

## 1.8 The Future of Languages

The question of what language to learn now presents a dilemma. Languages fall into and out of favour depending on support and the sorts of apps needing to be developed. The shift from workstations in the 80s, to internet in the 90s, and mobile devices since the 2000s, has seen a lot of change in which languages are used. For example, now that JavaScript can be used for back-end development, and because it is relatively easy to learn, it is becoming increasingly popular. And, because some of the biggest sites were built in 'Ruby on Rails' (which is also easy to learn), they continue to need developers to maintain them (such as Airbnb, Twitch, Hulu and so on). However, Node.js is starting to take over from Rails, just as Rails took over from Python's Django, and so more growth in JavaScript is expected. By contrast, Python is the preferred language for educators and scientists. Hence, there will be continued growth in this language. It is an easy to learn and flexible language so it has wide appeal. As Android has captured such a large proportion of the mobile market, the demand for Java programmers has increased. Java is scalable, stable and has such an enormous collection of feature libraries that almost anything can be developed in it. It is also relatively easy to learn compared to C++. Therefore, Java will continue to grow over the years (see Krill 2014). On the other hand, where Objective-C was once the preferred developer environment for iOS, Swift has now largely taken over. Nonetheless, Objective-C and Swift are very similar, therefore, knowing how to code in both is an advantage. C is a low-level (machine code) language. As such, it is vital for programming at the operating system level. This is quite difficult to understand programming, conceptually and practically. Hence, there are few developers in this domain. But, it also means there are high-paid jobs to be had. However, demand can vary across the years, so it is important to be proficient in more than one language. An example of a language which fell out of favour only to come back is SQL. Other RDMS languages took over from SQL for a while on large database platforms, such as Hadoop, Spark and Cassandra. But, as the databases grew even larger, the non-SQL query languages used started to underperform. As such, SQL has made a come-back. Google's BigQuery now uses SQL. Spark also uses an SQL module for some of its products (ClustrixDB, DeepSQL, MemSQL, and VoltDB). SQL is important for managing and analysing big data. It is also an easy scripting language to learn. It is important to know how to leverage the access to big databases that SQL affords for front-end apps such as data-driven websites. Although C++ is much harder to learn than some of the high-level languages, its power and functionality make it a very important language in high demand. Along with C++, C# is another popular language. In particular, it is used in the gaming industry (Unity 3D). Once learned, it seems to generate its own following; that is, developers are loyal to developing everything they can in it. This means it is well supported by developer communities, but one has to be careful that they do not loose sight of the need to know other languages also.

## 2 The Case Study Project

From the literature on how best to facilitate learning to program, clearly it is important to set up an authentic developer environment with a 'real' project which both challenges students but also sets achievable goals. As such, our project was focused on supporting teams of students. They begin by accessing some preformed, working, code which they can customise to achieve their own goals. This gives them some autonomy to explore, create, edit, make mistakes and produce, all within a risk-free environment.

From the literature it seems text-based programs are a good place to start. But, they are often not very interesting. By introducing students to something familiar and fun they can push themselves and it holds their interest. Working with a GUI (Graphical User Interface – buttons, panels, sliders and so on) leverages the fact that many common programs implement GUIs (see Benyon et al. 2005; Preece et al. 2007). However, GUIs are not always implemented in the same ways. Some use object-oriented programming, others calls to the native graphics of the operating system. As JavaScript and HTML are often promoted as easy to learn languages in high demand in the industry it makes sense to develop in them.

Based on the apparent preference for learning JavaScript and HTML in a fun but realistic developer environment with teams, achievable goals, some autonomy, and an interface that employs graphics elements, we chose to use an online HTML games editor (see www.mogaed.com, use any 4 letters followed by any 4 numbers to login). The core of the project is for students to develop a 2D JavaScript game which launches in a browser, based on a working example which is evaluated by their class cohort.

The online games editor uses some standard buttons and graphic elements as buttons to demonstrate at least 2 different approaches to the same problem. By integrating HTML into the JavaScript this also showed how they can be integrated. JavaScript is used to generate HTML code. But, because JavaScript and HTML syntax is often similar, it is easy to get them confused – especially for where to put quotes as text wrappers etc. Hence, this project included both challenging elements and common solutions. Students started with some fully developed and functional code. Simply changing the variables and seeing what effect they had helped them understand how they function in the overall code.

### 2.1 Justification for Using a 2D Online Games Editor

From the literature we can identify some core competencies that the current cohort of students need and how to achieve them. The learning activity needs to be:

1. a fun activity;
2. an authentic experience – in a realistic developer environment;
3. able to help them overcome their anxiety about coding;
4. about working with pre-formed working code;
5. integrated with their existing everyday activities, such as game play;

6. about focusing on problem solving, not coding *per se*; and,
7. in a language that is in high demand yet easy to learn.

Structuring learning activities as enjoyable exercises leads to deeper learning outcomes (Bonwell and Eison 1991). By making the learning task enjoyable, students are more likely to engage and complete all the requirements (Prince 2004). Building a small 2D game on a mobile device is the sort of activity most students enjoy doing.

Working in teams (4–5 students per team, 4–5 teams per class), students can leverage each others' strengths whilst making up for deficits in knowledge. The diverse range of skills and backgrounds in a normally distributed student population fosters collaboration and sharing of skills and knowledge. This also parallels the sort of developer environments they are likely to encounter in the industry post-graduation.

Students express their anxiety about code by avoiding it. Presenting them with the raw code up front forces them to confront their fears. Often they simply haven't had the opportunity to engage in a coding exercise that isn't intimidating because they find the code largely incomprehensible and it is not clear how it works or what each part does. Starting with some pre-formed code that works straight up means they can experiment with some simple, clearly labeled, variables and see the effect immediately. This is intended to break down their barriers to learning to code.

The pre-formed code is in a rudimentary form that encourages exploration and experimentation. It is graphically primitive. The first task is to substitute the graphics elements with their own images. This allows them to personalise the game and take ownership of it.

Most students spend at least some of their day playing games on their mobile devices. It makes sense then that they should want to know how to build their own games. The simple editor used in this project lets them choose from a number of pre-formed games which they can customise and combine to create a version, or entirely different game, from.

Because the code is already pre-formed and the various variables and functions are clearly labelled, they can start to be creative immediately. In the creative pursuit of a personalised game, they need to think through what problems they need to overcome to achieve their goals. In this sense, they don't need to learn the code in detail – just enough to solve the problems they encounter.

The interface is fully functional and largely self-explanatory. They do not have to learn a new piece of software just to learn how to code. JavaScript and HTML were used. These are in high demand, encountered on a daily basis and easy to learn. The students do no need to complete the project knowing how to code, rather, they simply need to understand the role coding plays in problem solving. Along the way they pick up some coding knowledge.

The apps they develop are runnable on multiple platforms: PC, mobile device, tablet and so on. The development environment uses a PC with a mouse and keyboard, but the apps they develop can be run on touch control devices. The code is written in such a way as to accommodate the way different browsers treat code differently. As the variables are clearly labelled they can adjust them to see the effect immediately. The immediacy of the feedback promotes confidence in what they are doing. The editor includes error messaging. It shows the user what the problem is and where in the code it has arisen. This facilities easier problem solving at the code level. The interface is a simple, browser-based, text editor. As such, it avoids the added abstraction of the hidden functions in an IDE. It also means the environment variables, links, dependencies and so on do not need to be set up in advance. This removes much of the potential confusion around programming. The apps they develop include the core features of most graphics type applications – a GUI with buttons, graphics, changes and animation, substitution and methods or functions to activate elements such as moving enemies or scrolling player handlers. For a detailed overview of the online editor see: Wyeld and Barbuto (2014).

This project was first formed in 2009 using Flash. In 2014 it was recast as HTML4. Although HTML5 was available, at that time not all mobile devices implemented HTML5 fully. In 2018 it will shift to HTML5 and leverage the power of the 'canvas' function to open up other possibilities. This shift in codebase mirrors the developer world where languages are constantly evolving.

## 3 Discussion

From the results of the before and after questionnaires used in this case study we found a shift in sentiment from a fear of coding to a more relaxed approach to coding. However, for this group of students, they still reported being largely dependent on external help. This was expressed in their answers to the open-ended questions in the questionnaires about where to find help, the need for tutorials, and example code. But, this contradicts the abundance of these sorts of resources on the internet, such as Stackoverflow, Code.org, Code Mentor and so on. Hence, while it is possible to learn the basics of coding from these sources, having access to help, tutorials and example code appears to instead make them dependent on these resources rather than giving them the confidence to embark on their own coding projects unassisted. The project was designed to address this.

While the project provided a lot of learning scaffolding in the form of help, tutorials, and example code it also fostered inter-student interaction. In other words, it did not rely only on the resources available to the students to facilitate their code learning. Rather, it promoted active problem solving with the tools to implement solutions. It did this by forcing groups of students to work together towards a common goal and for other groups to peer-review their game productions as they were being developed. In this manner, they were focused on solving specific problems rather than learning code alone. In the process, they overcame some of their anxiety about working with code and how to implement changes, even though they may not have fully understood what the structure of the code was.

## 4 Conclusion

The after questionnaire was used to capture any shift in sentiment across this project. It required students to reflect on their experience in the project and comment on whether their attitudes to the same sorts of questions asked in the before questionnaire had changed. Students expressed a change in attitude to coding. They had changed their way of thinking about coding – from a mysterious, scary, magic 'code', to empowerment, and recognition that success is possible. Hopefully, some of the students will be inspired to practice more coding after this project.

From the before questionnaire we could see that many of the participants who took part in this project had used a game editor before. Yet, there was a clear shift in sentiment that indicated coding was less intimidating after completing the project. They felt more confident about coding and understanding what code does. However, they still demanded more in-code comments, coding examples, tutorials, and external help. This is symptomatic of the lack of confidence with the underlying principles of coding. For this group of students, their lack of fundamental skills prior to this project prevented them from taking charge of their own learning. They still felt reliant on external help after completing the project. This is despite a clear shift in sentiment in other ways. It remains to be seen whether their younger siblings, who are learning to code now, will feel the same in the next few decades. By learning the underlying principles of coding at an earlier age they should be less intimated by the complexities of coding later in their education. In the mean time, the current cohort of students needs to overcome their lack of confidence. This project went some way towards that goal. It provided a format whereby students could experiment with code in a non-threatening environment. However, clearly, their demand for more help is troubling. Hence, while this project alleviated some of this cohort's anxiety about coding, more investigation is warranted. Future projects may investigate whether text-based coding is the most useful format for learning to build apps. Other approaches might include node-based programming. Either way, clearly this is a pressing issue for which a solution is critical if this particular demographic is to achieve its goals of employment post graduation in a world that increasingly demands programming skills.

## References


Ackermann, E.: Piaget's constructivism, papert's constructionism: what's the difference? In: Proceedings Constructivism: Uses and Perspectives in Education, Cahier 8, pp. 85–94. Research Center in Education, Geneva (2001)

Althoff, C.: The Self-Taught Programmer: The Definitive Guide to Programming Professionally. Triangle Connection LLC, Mount Dora (2017)

Benyon, D., Turner, P., Turner, S.: Designing Interactive Systems: People, Activities, Contexts, Technologies. Pearson Education, London (2005)

Bonwell, C., Eison, J.: Active Learning: Creating Excitement in the Classroom, ASHE-ERIC Higher Education Report No. 1. George Washington University, School of Education and Human Development, Washington, D.C., USA (1991)

Brooks, F.P.: No silver bullet - essence and accidents of software engineering. In: Kugler, H.-J. (ed.) Proceedings of the IFIP Tenth World Computing Conference, pp. 1069–1076. Elsevier (1986)

Brooks, F.P.: The Mythical Man-Month: Essays on Software Engineering. Addison-Wesley, Boston (1995). First published 1975

Code Conquest - Free Coding Guide for Beginners. www.codeconquest.com. Accessed 22 Aug 2017

Code like a Girl - Providing girls with the tools, knowledge and support. https://codelikeagirl.org/. Accessed 22 Aug 2017

Codeacademy. www.codecademy.com/. Accessed 22 Aug 2017

Code.org: Leaders and trend-setters all agree on one thing. https://code.org/quotes. Accessed 22 Aug 2017

Code Mentor - What Programming Language Should a Beginner Learn in 2017? https://www.codementor.io/codementorteam/beginner-programming-language-job-salary-community -7s26wmbm6. Accessed 22 Aug 2017

Disrupting Engineering Education. www.42.us.org. Accessed 22 Aug 2017

Farag, B.: Please don't learn to code, TechCrunch (2016). https://techcrunch.com/2016/05/10/please-dont-learn-to-code/. Accessed 22 Aug 2013

Gamasutra - Better Games Through Usability Evaluation and Testing. http://www.gamasutra.com/view/feature/130745/better_games_through_usability_.php?print=1. Accessed 22 Aug 2017

Kafai, Y.B., Burke, Q.: Connected Code: Why Children Need to Learn Programming. The MIT Press, Cambridge (2016)

Kelleher, C., Pausch, R.: Lowering the barriers to programming: a taxonomy of programming environments and languages for novice programmers. ACM Comput. Surv. **37**(2), 83–137 (2005)

Krill, P.: Four reasons to stick with Java, and four reasons to dump it, Java World (2014). https://www.javaworld.com/article/2689406/java-platform/four-reasons-to-stick-with-java-and-four-reasons-to-dump-it.html. Accessed 22 Aug 2017

Learn, Share, Build - Stack Overflow. https://stackoverflow.com/. Accessed 22 Aug 2017

Meetup - Learn to Code - For Complete Beginners in Silicon Valley. www.meetup.com. Accessed 22 Aug 2017

Minsky, M.: The Society of Mind. Simon & Schuster, New York City (1988)

Papert, S.: Mindstorms: Children, Computers, and Powerful Ideas. Basic Books, Inc., New York (1980)

Norvig, P.: Director of research at Google. http://norvig.com

Petzold, C.: Code: The Hidden Language of Computer Hardware and Software. Microsoft Press, Redmond (2000)

Preece, J., Rogers, Y., Sharp, H.: Interaction Design: Beyond Human-Computer Interaction, 2nd edn. Wiley, Milton (2007)

Prince, M.: Does active learning work? A review of the research. J. Eng. Educ. **93**(3), 223–232 (2004)

Shermer, M.: The Feynman-Tufte Principle: a visual display of data should be simple enough to fit on the side of a van, in Scientific American (2005). https://www.scientificamerican.com/article/the-feynman-tufte-princip

Silicon Valley Coding School - Learn Coding. www.svcodingschool.com.au. Accessed 22 Aug 2017

Wyeld, T., Barbuto, Z.: Don't hide the code!: empowering novice and beginner programmers using a HTML game editor. In: Proceedings 18th International Conference on Information Visualisation (IV), Paris, France, July 2014, pp. 125–131 (2014)

# A Mind-Set Changing Project: Preparing Vocational and Professional Education and Training (VPET) Teachers with Technology Enhanced Learning (TEL) and E-pedagogies

Ricky Yuk-kwan Ng(✉) and Rechell Yee-shun Lam

Centre for Learning and Teaching, Vocational Training Council, 27 Wood Road, Wan Chai, Hong Kong SAR, China
{rickyng,rechelllam}@vtc.edu.hk

**Abstract.** Vocational and Professional Education and Training (VPET) emphasises in-class hands on practice and face-to-face theory delivery, e-learning and e-pedagogies are less common. The resistance normally rises from the argument of VPET's focuses on trade-specific hands on skills in authentic workplaces and the motto of 'practice makes perfect'. Nonetheless, with students' changing learning preferences and behaviours, the high accessibility of online and web-based information; VPET teachers are now confronting with challenges that trade-specific knowledge and demonstration of skills are widely available on internet and not solely transmitted by teachers. Furthermore, students' motivation and engagement in learning tasks are also issues that need to be addressed. In response, a mind-set changing teacher training project was introduced and this paper shares the empirical experience on nurturing VPET teachers' technology enhanced learning (TEL) and e-pedagogies competency so as to prepare them to cope with students' learning preferences and behaviours for teaching effectiveness. These series of training and engagement activities were carried out in four stages (1) Conceptualisation; (2) Familiarisation; (3) Acceptance and (4) Action. These training and activities enable teachers to adopt TEL and e-pedagogies in their daily teaching. Results of the project indicated that a well-planned scheme that aligned with the institution's strategy with gradual increment of intensity of e-elements infused in various training events allowed ease of acceptance and behavioural changes. Additionally, synergy from senior management, concurrent schemes, projects and awards to promote and encourage teachers to adopt TEL and e-pedagogies for innovative learning and teaching is also a critical factor in the teacher training scheme.

**Keywords:** Technology enhanced learning (TEL) · E-pedagogies
Vocational and Professional Education and Training (VPET) · Teacher training


S. K. S. Cheung et al. (Eds.): ICTE 2018, CCIS 843, pp. 179–187, 2018.
https://doi.org/10.1007/978-981-13-0008-0_17

## 1 Introduction

Teachers in Vocational and Professional Education and Training (VPET) stress in-class hands on practice and face-to-face theory delivery over the use of e-learning and e-pedagogies, although learning management platform (LMP) such as Moodle, Blackboard or other online tools were first introduced in the participating VPET institution of this study in the 1990s. It is not surprised to learn that most teachers' e-learning activities rest on uploading and downloading course materials on the LMP without touching on the fundamental concept of using online materials to supplement and complement learning back then. The resistance normally rises from the argument of VPET's focuses on trade-specific hands on skills in authentic workplaces and the motto of 'practice makes perfect'. VPET teachers also approached e-Learning with doubts. To them, it seemed not feasible to practice hands-on tasks online or on simulation systems and devices. In an earlier interview, Ng and Lam found that teachers questioned how students could practise a simple task like tightening and loosening nuts and bolts on a simulator. They asserted that "in real life, you need to use a certain degree of strength to tighten and loosen nuts and bolts but, with today's technology, you may not be able to achieve it unless you invest a fortune to develop the hardware and software. Another teacher said that people only live once – you will not hurt in simulated environments if you make mistakes but will surely be injured in real life" (Ng and Lam 2015, p. 6). Very often, mis-conception happened because e-Learning and technology enhanced learning aim not to replace face-to face contacts and hands-on practices, they rather facilitate understanding of procedures, skills and provide repeated access to venues that are normally prohibited because of safety or confidential purposes. Pedagogically, e-Learning and technology enhanced learning (TEL) when complimented with blended and flexible learning will generate effective teaching and better learning experience for students (Tsang et al. 2014; Ng et al. 2016, 2017). Nonetheless, with students' changing learning preferences and behaviours (they are enthusiasts in mobile devices, engaged in technologies and online activities for information retrieval 24 h a day), the advancement of online and web-based networking information communication technology technologies (ICT) and the easy accessibility of mobile devices such as smartphones and tablets that provide "just-in-time contemporary learning and can be accessed from any site" (Choy 2006, p. 2), VPET teachers are now confronting with challenges that trade-specific knowledge and demonstration of skills are widely available on internet. Students' motivation and engagement in learning tasks should also be looked into. In an earlier study, Ng and Lam (2015) found that the readiness of the teachers regarding TEL and e-pedagogies is a salient issue to be address. Furthermore, VPET stresses on mastery of hands-on skills but conversely, TEL and e-pedagogies emphasise self-paced online and virtual learning experiences; how would teachers be prepared to adopt the changes for teaching effectiveness? To further address the issue, a three-year mind-set changing project was introduced and this paper shares empirical experience on nurturing VPET teachers' TEL and e-pedagogies competency so as to prepare them to cope with students' learning preferences and behaviours for teaching effectiveness.

## 2 The Project

As teacher trainers in the Centre for Learning and Teaching (CLT) and responsible for teacher training and development in the participated VPET institution, the authors conducted environmental scan, analysed the institution, teachers and students' needs in order to advise the senior management team on the institution's e-learning strategy and direction. Allan and Seaman (2014) found that in United States, online learning growth significantly over the last decade and 66% of higher education institutions asserted that online education were their long-term strategy. Environmental scan found that e-Learning and TEL was adopted in Hong Kong's tertiary education institutions to facilitate learning. Although nearly 95% out of the 3,000 teachers in the participated institution in this study were using the LMP to supplement their teaching, the most frequent activities were uploading course information, notes and extended readings. It was noticed that only 10% of teachers further developed their own complimentary, extended and blended-learning activities such as online tutorials exercises, assessments, forums or video sources. Teachers always regarded TEL as extra workload because of the revision of existing teaching materials and the design of learning and teaching activities, without mentioning the technological know-how. A number of researchers agreed that the most common training needs of teachers rested on technology skills (Barczky et al. 2010; Arinto 2013; Lane 2013; Betts 2014). A survey on training needs was conducted by CLT with a number of 287 responses from teachers showed that more workshops on e-Learning/Information and Communications Technology (ICT) in education would equip teachers and instructing staff to adapt TEL in their daily teaching. Churchill (2017) also contended that how technologies will be used in daily teaching largely depends on teachers' understandings of the affordances and the possibilities of the technologies. On the other hand, students had different views on e-Learning. A study by the CLT in 2014 with 4,117 students studying in VPET indicated that all of them obtained information online via websites or social media. It was also found that more than 40% of them stayed online from 21 to 24 h every day. The average number of devices (phones, tablets, notebooks, computers) owned by each student is 1.82 (Centre for Learning and Teaching, Vocational Training Council, 2014). The results indicated the online learning preferences and learning habits of students and suggested to blend face-to-face teaching with e-Learning or TEL to further enhance student motivation and interaction. It echoed Cronje's point that "as students' knowledge of what technologies can enable, brings with it a need for flexibility. Students wants to be able to attend set lectures if they so wish, but they also want the ability to view (or-re-view) those lectures in the form of online videos or online audio podcasts" (Cronje 2016, p. 132). In addition to the data collected from teachers and students, the authors also reviewed the e-Learning, TEL and e-pedagogies training activities (seminars, programmes, workshops and sharing sessions) that were developed and offered by CLT over the last three years for an understanding of the teachers' participation and needs. In view of the percentage of acceptance and adaptation of e-Learning in daily teaching and with an aim to up-scale the usage of e-Learning as complimentary, extended or blended-learning activities, a project on implementation of E-Leaning and TEL was generated in 2014 and proposed to various committee for discussions. Under the proposal, an implementation plan adopting e-pedagogical approaches and TEL strategies would be rolled out to support the implementation of TEL. Members of various learning and teaching committees generally agreed to adopt E-learning and TEL to enhance effective learning and teaching, to enrich students' learning experiences and the institution's competiveness in the sector. It was also suggested using e-Learning and TEL to accommodate the demographic changes of pre-vocational to in-services learners to cope with the increasing life-long learning and continuous professional development needs. The 3-year Implementation of TEL Project from 2015 to 2018 which included a series of seminars and workshops and engagement activities was then endorsed. Accompanied with the training seminars and workshops were a number of activities including collaboration on development of learning and teaching aids using various kinds of technologies such as learning and teaching platform customisation, video broadcasting lectures, augmented and virtual reality (AR/VR) and wearable technology and mass open online course (MOOC). These series of training and engagement activities were considered as a mind-set changing project that was carried out in four stages (1) Conceptualisation, (2) Familiarisation, (3) Acceptance and (4) Action in order to enable teachers to adopt e-Learning and TEL and e-pedagogies in their daily teaching. To ensure participation, blessings from senior management of the institution were given to academic disciplines' leaders for smooth implementation of the project.

## 3 Implementation of the Project

A need analysis was conducted for an understanding of the teachers' engagement in e-Learning and TEL by first reviewing the training provided and teachers' participation. The year-round seminars and workshops offered by CLT were categorised into three different focuses namely (1) Developing as Professional, (2) IT Enhancement Programme and (3) Teaching, Learning and Assessment. Based on teachers' needs, the workshops numbers and titles varied over the years. A comparison of the number of headcount of the training workshops conducted in Academic Year (AY) 2014/15, AY2015/16 and AY2016/17 in the aforementioned categories is shown in the following table:

**Table 1.** Headcount of the training workshops in AY2014/15, AY2015/16 and AY2016/17

| Focuses | No. of headcount AY2014/15 | No. of headcount AY2015/16 | No. of headcount AY2016/17 |
|---|---|---|---|
| Developing as Professionals | 245 | 254 | 185 |
| IT Enhancement Programme | 574 | 1049 | 1098 |
| Teaching, Learning and Assessment | 3675 | 3250 | 3793 |

The results of AY2014/15 indicated that out of the three focuses, IT Enhancement Programme had the least participants (n = 574) when compared to the other two and that was resulted from the pre-conception of the needs and usefulness of e-Learning. Teachers' priorities were in Teaching, Learning and Assessment related training such as 'Classroom Management', 'Outcome-based Learning and Teaching', 'Planning for Active Classes', 'Design Multiple Choices Assessment' that enabled them to accommodate their urge needs in daily teaching practices. Short talked with teachers in training workshops showed that most teachers regarded e-Learning and TEL as extra workload and they would like to further modify their existing teaching materials if extra time (less teaching load), training and support were given. To address the above and as planned, the training and engagement activities in the project on implementation of E-Leaning and TEL (2015 to 2018) were to be carried out in four stages (1) Conceptualisation, (2) Familiarisation, (3) Acceptance and (4) Action, to gradually enable teachers to get to know e-pedagogies and adopt e-Learning and TEL and into their teaching practices.

### 3.1 'Conceptualisation' and 'Familiarisation'

In the 'Conceptualisation' and 'Familiarisation' stages in AY2015/16, training workshops on e-pedagogies and TEL were held regularly. To enhance participation and increase attraction, overseas and local guest speakers with expertise on e-Learning and TEL were invited to deliver seminars, workshops as well as sharing sessions to keep abreast participants' awareness and conceptualisation of the trend and usefulness of e-Learning and TEL. A range of seminars and workshops with topics on 'Harnessing Open and Flexible Resources (OER)', 'Mobile Design: Teaching Language and Literacy with Mobile Technologies', 'Situated Knowledge Building and Mobile Technologies in the third Space: Moving Beyond 21 Century Learning', 'e-Books Production for Teaching and Learning Packages', 'Design Video Resources to Facilitate Self-directed Learning in Flipped Classroom', 'AR/VR Technology for Education and Training' and 'Using MOOCs to Enhance Learning and Teaching' were organised with 612 headcounts. In addition to the above and with the aim to familiarise teaching staff with the LMP (Moodle), eleven workshops and three seminars ranged from 'Kickstart with Moodle', 'Gearing Up for Moodle', 'Use of VeriGuide for Assessment', 'Sharing Session on Moodle Customisation Project' and 'Moodle Information Session' were held with a number of 437 headcounts. Table 1 showed the total number of headcounts in the IT Enhancement Programme had recorded a significantly increase of 82.8% participation (n = 1049) in AY 2015/16 when compared to AY2014/15 (n = 574).

Using Kirkpatrick's (1994) four-level framework (Reactional, Learning, Behavioural and Results), the authors further evaluated the training activities' effectiveness and impacts on the teachers' readiness and acceptance to changes in their teaching practices. The model categorises the training outcomes to 'Reaction' focus on the trainees' satisfaction, 'Learning' on the acquisition of knowledge, skills, attitudes, 'Behaviour' addresses the improvement of behaviour on the job and 'Results' on trainees' achievement and productivity improvement. Feedback forms were used to collect instant reflections after each seminar and workshop in the first level (Reaction) and the second level (Learning) of analysis. In general, the overall rating on the structure, content relevancy, alignment to learning outcomes, facilitation and materials and resources provided in the seminars and workshop was 4.6 on a scale of 1 to 5 (1 = Strongly disagree, 5 = Strongly agree). Qualitative feedback such as ‘very practical and can be used during my class’, ‘the introduction app was very useful for teaching’, ‘Spark video is useful’ and ‘MOOC introduction is useful’ indicated the teachers were benefited in terms of conceptualisation, familiarisation and application of e-Learning and TEL. However, feedback such as ‘more different useful applications on ICT teaching can be introduced’, ‘the new tolls for teaching are quite good and should teach all teachers in order to facilitate the use of them’, ‘more practices are needed’, ‘more time for practicing the tools’ and ‘would like to have more consultation on applying AR/VR technology to enhance teaching’ revealed that teachers were eager to learn more in order to adopt the latest learning technologies in their teaching. Views on staff’s performance after the training were collected from senior staff of respective academic disciplines in various committees’ meetings for the third and fourth levels (Behaviour and Result) of analysis. Senior staff observed that there were increasing self-initiated e-learning projects by teaching staff, including customisation of the Moodle platform with online assessments and discussion forums to suit specific modules’ teaching needs, the embedded of videos as lecturing and instructional materials to enable flipped learning, the request for support and further consultation on developing TEL packages and resources. Most of the teachers realised and recognised the benefits of facilitating better learning and teaching experiences to both students and teachers. The above showed a promising behavioural change amongst teachers towards the adaptation of e-Learning and TEL.

### 3.2 ‘Acceptance’ and ‘Action’

With the results indicating general acceptance of using e-Learning and TEL from the training and feedback from meetings, the project had progressed into the ‘Acceptance’ and ‘Action’ stages in AY2016/17. Alongside with the on-going training seminars and workshops, sharing sessions of the self-initiated e-learning projects by teaching staff were organised to share experiences so as to consolidate the acceptance from a wider population of teachers. Making references to the successful projects, the sharing sessions also allowed teachers to reflect and plan for the applications of TEL in the coming ‘Action’ stage. As shown in Table 1, the training headcount on IT Enhancement Programme remained around 1098 with slight increment.

The authors once again evaluated the training activities’ effectiveness using Kirkpatrick’s (1994) four-level framework (Reactional, Learning, Behavioural and Results). The overall rating on the structure, content relevancy, alignment to learning outcomes, facilitation and materials and resources provided in the seminars and workshop was 4.5 on a scale of 1 to 5 (1 = Strongly disagree, 5 = Strongly agree). Qualitative feedback such as ‘the case studies enriched the seminar’, ‘new apps can be applied on helping us on teaching’, ‘the workshop can overcome how to use Mentimeter’, ‘would like to share with students off lecture’, ‘live demonstration and practice in computer lab could facilitate my learning’, ‘workshop clearly showed how to create online assignment’, and ‘all useful, very practical’ indicated teachers’ positive views on using TEL. Senior staff of respective academic disciplines also revealed that a number of their teaching staff were eager to apply what they have learnt to enrich their teaching contents and activities in various committees' meetings. The results indicated a gradually mind-set change and acceptance of the e-pedagogies and applications. In view of the above, it was considered the right time to progress the project into the 'Action' stage.

During the 'Action' stage, respective disciplines contributed subject contents while CLT provided instructional design and technological supports on production. A number of deliverables on the development of e-Learning and TEL resources that included customisation of Moodle platform, Mini-MOOCs, discipline-specific online learning resources, AR/VR applications, lecture capture system and wearable technologies (head-mounted devices and multi-function glasses such as HoloLens) were developed on a small piloting scale. These e-pedagogical approaches enable interaction and meaningful learning activities and tutorials that occur during the face-to-face time under teachers' guidance. Together with appropriate instructional design and technology as enabler, these approaches provide students with a large degree of learning autonomy and nurture students for a higher degree of self-directness, self-management, persistence and independency. During the implementation, the collaboration and support from different units was the key success factor. CLT provided advice on instructional design and production of innovative technologies, assist in the development of e-Resources for disciplines, deliver training workshops and seminars, and organise sharing sessions. The nominated teachers of nine disciplines provided the content of modules for the TEL development while the institution's information technology supporting division (ITSD) provided technical support and maintenance for those platforms and applications (Moodle, and Mini-MOOC). To ensure timely support, campuses' technical teams provided on-site technical and production services. The deliverable of the implementation of TEL in AY2017/18 is shown below:

1. A Task Force on Implementation of TEL was set up with CLT, ITSU, Disciplines nominated teachers and campuses' technical teams as Members to implement and report on the progress and effectiveness of application of TEL;
2. Production of one to two mini-MOOCs by each of the nine academic disciplines;
3. Nine sets of e-Resources for respective disciplines on selected modules;
4. Production of six AR exemplars and six wearable technology exemplars; and
5. Customised the Moodle platform to integrate the lecture capture system for one-stop access of all learning ad teaching resources and ease of management.

The above intended deliverables of the project were agreed between staff representatives of all levels and signified an institutional-wide mind-set and behavioural change. The project implied that an emerging concept change and paradigm shift in learning and teaching. It also addressed the increasing importance of e-pedagogies.

### 3.3 Lesson Learned

Results of the project indicated that a well-planned training scheme that aligned with the institution's strategy with gradual increment of intensity of e-elements infused in various training events and engagement activities allowed ease of acceptance and behavioural changes. As the project is still on-going and the above intended deliverables are in progress, the following salient points are yet to be further addressed. Firstly, a close communication for timely dissemination of up-to-date knowledge in technological advancement and experiences through sharing sessions, internal publications and various committees will ensure penetration to all levels of staff in the institution. Secondly, effective TEL lessons rest on the planning, instructional design and the appropriateness of the technology being used. The TPACK framework (Technologies, Pedagogies and Content Knowledge) (Herring et al. 2016) provided a promising guideline and method for content, instructional design and information technology experts for reference. Thirdly, technologies come and go, so does enthusiasm. Discrete consideration on the investment of resources on software, gadgets and facilities will minimise the risk of rapid outdating of technologies. To sustain motivation and engagement, it is suggested to launch concurrent schemes and awards to encourage and recognise teachers who adopt TEL and e-pedagogies for innovative learning and teaching. Lastly, the alignment of the e-Learning and TEL development to the institution's learning and teaching strategy as well as blessings from senior management are also one of the successful factors.

## 4 Conclusion

With an aim to promote e-Learning and TEL to teachers, this mind-set changing project demonstrated a good example for practice sharing. This paper started with the pressing needs of e-Learning and TEL in today's VPET and higher education institutions and argued the usefulness of TEL and e-pedagogies in VPET. A need analysis was conducted to diagnose teachers and students' learning and teaching preferences and habits followed by the proposal of the 3-year Implementation of TEL Project. The process, intended deliverables and progress were then described. Salient points were also mentioned in order to shed light for further development and research.

## References


Allen, I.E., Seaman, J.: Grade Change: Tracking Online Education in the United States. Babson Survey Research Group and Ouahog Research Group, Babson Park (2014)

Arinto, P.B.: A framework for developing competencies in open and distance learning. Int. Rev. Res. Open Distance Learn. **14**(1), 167–185 (2013)

Barczky, C., Buckenmeyer, J., Feldman, L.: Mentoring professors a model for developing online instructors and course in higher education. Int. J. E-Learn. **9**(1), 7–26 (2010)

Betts, K.: Factors influencing faculty participation and retention in online and blended education. Online J. Distance Learn. Adm. **17**(1), 1 (2014)

Choy, S.: Benefits of e-leaning benchmarks: Australian case studies. Technical report, Australian flexible learning framework, DEST (2006)

Churchill, D.: Digital Resources for Learning. STE. Springer, Singapore (2017). https://doi.org/10.1007/978-981-10-3776-4

Cronje, J.: Learning technology in higher education. In: Rushby, N., Surry, D.W. (eds.) The Wiley Handbook of Learning Technology. Wiley, UK (2016)

Herring, M., Koehler, M., Mishra, P.: Handbook of Technological Pedagogical Content Knowledge (TPACK) for Educators. Routledge, NY (2016)

Lane, L.M.: An open, online class to prepare faculty to teach online. J. Educ. Online **10**(1), 1–32 (2013)

Ng, R.Y.K., Lam, R.Y.S.: The possibilities of using mobile and flexible technologies to enhance workplace learning in vocational education and training (VET). In: The 2nd International Conference on Open and Flexible Education, the Open University of Hong Kong, Hong Kong, 16th to 17th July 2015, (2015)

Ng, R.Y.K., Lam, R.Y.S., Ng, K.K., Lai, I.K.W.: A cross-institutional study of vocational and professional education and training (VPET) students and teachers' needs of innovative pedagogical practices. In: 2016 International Symposium on Educational Technology (ISET 2016), Peking University, Beijing, China, 19th to 21st July 2016 (2016)

Ng, R.Y.K., Lam, R.Y.S., Ng, K.K., Lai, I.K.W.: Identifying the needs of flexible and technology enhanced learning in vocational and professional education and training's (VPET) workplaces. In: Ma, W., Chan, C.K., Tong, K., Fung, H., Fong, C. (eds.) New Ecology for Education — Communication X Learning, pp. 107–117. Springer, Singapore (2017). https://doi.org/10.1007/978-981-10-4346-8_9

Ng, R.Y.K., Lam, R.Y.S.: Using mobile and flexible technologies to enable, engage and enhance learning in vocational education and training (VET). In: IEEE International Conference on Teaching, Assessment, and Learning for Engineering (TALE 2015), United International College, Zhuhai, China, 10th to 12th December 2015, (2015)

Tsang, E., Yuen, K., Cheung, P.: Effective instructional design for mobile learning. In: Yuen, K.S., Li, K.C. (eds.) Emerging Modes and Approaches in Open and Flexible Education. Open University of Hong Kong Press, Hong Kong (2014)

# Teaching Effect of the Multi-mode Blended Learning Model from Students' Perceptions

Zexuan Chen[1,2(✉)]

[1] School of Foreign Studies, Southern Medical University, No. 1838, North of Guangzhou Avenue, Guangzhou, Guangdong Province, China
SerlinaChen@163.com

[2] School of Information Technology in Education, South China Normal University, No. 55, West of Zhongshan Avenue, Guangzhou, Guangdong Province, China

**Abstract.** Blended learning design face a number of key challenges, such as incorporating flexibility, stimulating interaction, facilitating students' learning processes, and fostering an affective learning climate. In this paper, a multi-mode blended learning model is developed, and the teaching effect is evaluated. It was conducted on the College English classes, which lasted for one semester. Reports from the students' self-assessment of their language proficiency levels indicate that the multi-mode blended learning approach brings the benefits of improved listening, speaking, reading, writing, and translating competence.

**Keywords:** Large classes · Multi-mode blended learning model College English · Language proficiency level

## 1 Introduction

The National Council of Teachers of English has been issuing position statements on smaller language class size to ensure better academic performance (NCTE 2014). However, as is noted Wang and Zhang (2011), the size of language class at any educational level of mainland China is increasing rapidly, due to the lack of quality teachers and educational resources. Chinese teachers at elementary or secondary schools have been confronting with the challenge of teaching a class with more than 50 students, whereas teachers at college level might even have a class with over 100 students (Wang and Zhang 2011). Large class seems to be one of the best policies to meet the challenge of increasing student-teacher ratio, however, it may in turn lead to compromised learning outcomes.

Technology-enhanced blended learning may become a pedagogical alternative, as it is featured with improved pedagogy, increased access/flexibility, increased cost effectiveness (Graham 2004), as well as the potential to increase students' learning outcomes (Dziuban et al. 2004), and improve the teaching of large groups (Marsh et al. 2003).

However, few researchers have been working on a holistic model which aims at tackling with the four key challenges faced with the design of blended learning (Boelens et al. 2017). Therefore, by taking into account the four challenges: incorporating flexibility, stimulating interaction, facilitating students' learning processes, and fostering an


S. K. S. Cheung et al. (Eds.): ICTE 2018, CCIS 843, pp. 188–199, 2018.
https://doi.org/10.1007/978-981-13-0008-0_18

affective learning climate (Boelens et al. 2017), the author of the present paper developed a multi-mode blended learning approach and conducted an empirical study to test out its teaching effect, in an attempt to work out a more productive blended learning model, and meanwhile find out a solution to alleviate the pressure caused by large classes.

## 2 Previous Blended Learning Models

Blended learning seems to be one of the potential solutions to improve the quality of instruction for large classes.

The term “Blended Learning” was originally used in the business world in connection with corporate training (Sharma and Barrett 2007), then was employed in higher education (MacDonald 2006) and lastly was applied in language teaching and learning (Whittaker 2013: 11). There is little consensus on the definition of blended learning (Smythe 2012) as scholars have different interpretations of the term itself.

Driscoll (2002) defines “Blended Learning” in four different concepts: (1) to combine or mix modes of Web-based technology to accomplish an educational goal; (2) to combine various pedagogical approaches to produce an optimal learning outcome with or without instructional technology; (3) to combine any form of instructional technology with face-to-face instructor-led training; (4) to mix or combine instructional technology with actual job tasks in order to create a harmonious effect of learning and working.

Most scholars echo the third definition and argue that: blended learning “combines online learning with face-to-face learning (Harriman 2004)”; “Blended Learning” is learning that “combine face-to-face instruction with computer mediated instruction” (Bonk and Graham 2006: 5), to name just a few.

Driscoll’s second and third definitions have pointed out the importance of pedagogy and instructors in the implementation of blended learning, which might guide instructors to focus on the pedagogical design and the rational combination of the online and face-to-face instructions.

Inspired by the literatures discussed above, the author would define the term “Blended Learning” as “a rational combination of online and face-to-face learning supported with instructional technology”.

According to Boelens et al. (2017), in many of the previous studies (Kerres and De Witt 2003; Olapiriyakul and Scherb 2006; Picciano 2009; Singh 2003; etc.), flexibility or learner control (of learning sequence) was limited to time- and place-independent activities; whereas the author of the present paper would like to propose more flexible switch between online and face-to-face learning, more flexible switch between in-class and out-of-class learning. Furthermore, learners reported that interaction during the blended learning process would lead to better learning outcomes (Joosten et al. 2014; Voegele 2014. etc.), however, only “slightly less than half” of the studies reviewed by Boelens et al. (2017) use instructional strategies to enhance interaction. In addition, Boelens et al. (2017) put forward four groups of instructional strategies to facilitate students’ learning processes, they are: orienting-planning, monitoring, adjusting, evaluating. Last but not least, they recommend five categories of instructional activities that develop an affective learning climate, they are: motivating, concentrating/exerting effort, attributing and judging oneself, appraising, dealing with emotions (Boelens et al. 2017).

However, it is a great pity that so far little studies have been focusing on designing a blended learning model in an attempt to optimize the whole learning environment. Furthermore, most previous studies seem to draw a clear boundary between face-to-face lecture and online learning or actually fail to explore the more sophisticated combination of online and face-to-face instruction (Köse 2010; Staker and Horn 2012). Last but not least, previous blended learning models seem to have little implications for managing large language classes.

## 3 The Multi-mode Blended Learning Model

As a matter of fact, the author of the present paper would like to argue that the multiple teaching and learning activities occur within a blended learning context could be complicated, all of the elements involved could be dynamically intertwined, and careful design of the blended learning model could probably lead to promising outcomes. Therefore, she designed a multi-mode blended learning model (see Fig. 1) to describe teaching procedures in the online and face-to-face learning sections, trying to meet the four challenges mentioned by Boelens et al. (2017), and put forward suggestions to more effective large class instructions as well.

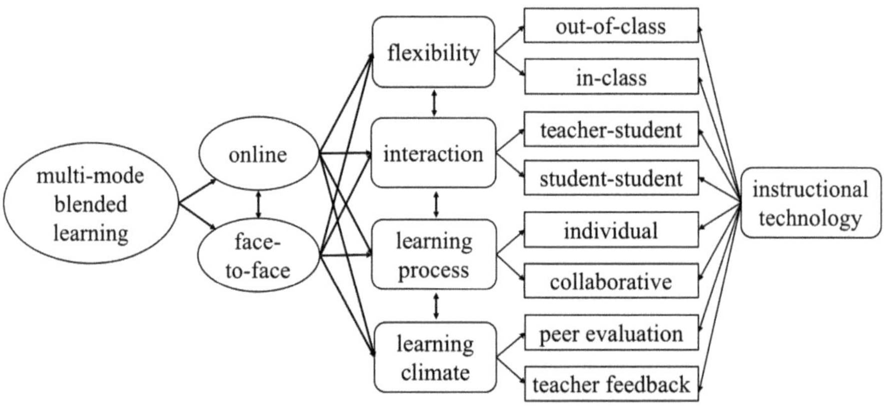


**Fig. 1.** The multi-mode blended learning model

Figure 1 shows the essential elements of the developed multi-mode blended learning model, which consists of two key components (online learning vs. face-to-face learning), four branches of blended learning design (flexibility, interaction, learning processes, learning climate), eight major elements (out-of-class learning vs. in-class learning, teacher-student interaction vs. student-student interaction, individual learning vs. collaborative learning, peer evaluation vs. teacher feedback) and a set of frequently-used instructional technologies.

As is indicated in Fig. 1, there are two sets of single-headed arrow (altogether eight arrows) pointing from the two key components to the four branches, indicating that both the online and face-to-face learning could be made good use of to deal with the four challenges categorized by Boelens et al. (2017). These eight single-headed arrows work together with four double-headed arrows to connect the two key components and the four branches within a closed loop, suggesting that the two components and the four branches are frequently interconnected and intertwined. Meanwhile, there are four sets of single-headed arrow pointing from the four branches to the eight major elements, and a set of single-headed arrows pointing from instructional technology to the eight elements, suggesting that the eight major elements could be freely combined to achieve different instructional objectives supported with web 2.0 instructional technology. Above all, this model aims at coping with the four blended learning design challenges and optimize the blended learning process for large language classes as well.

## 3.1 Incorporating Flexibility

This model encourages teachers to design and implement in-class and out-of-class blended learning activities flexibly.

Firstly, out-of-class activities could be mostly online learning activities conducted in Moodle—a learning management system (LMS). Students should be flexible in arranging suitable time (anytime), place (anywhere), pace (progressing at their own speed), and path (learning in their favorite order) to learn, to fulfill the online learning tasks.

Secondly, in-class activities could be a flexible combination of different elements in the model. For example, in order to enhance face-to-face communication skill and collaboration skill within the group in a face-to-face setting, the teacher might design a wiki-supported synchronous collaboration task or a pen and paper collaboration.

## 3.2 Facilitating Interaction

This model encourages both teacher-student and student-student interactions happening either out of/in class, online or in face-to-face settings.

Out-of-class teacher-student interaction occur mostly in Moodle, including teacher feedback on student works or individual questions, and teacher's participation on the forum discussion (posting a hashtag or following a hashtag), etc. Meanwhile, the teacher might invite the whole class to post to a forum in Moodle or on an online virtual "bulletin" board (e.g. Padlet), where teacher and students can interact synchronously online in a face-to-face setting.

Whereas out-of-class student-student interactions could be various, including face-to-face discussion, online discussion, or peer evaluation in Moodle, etc. Meanwhile, peer interactions in the class might take the form of online collaboration using Wiki technology (e.g. MindMeister, WhatsApp, Google Docs, etc.), as well as offline collaboration using paper and pen.

### 3.3 Facilitating Students' Learning Processes

As described in the developed multi-mode blended learning model, student learning activities include individual learning and collaborative learning.

Among which, individual learning is self-paced, personalized learning (text reading, audio listening, video watching, graph viewing, etc.). Students would be guided to complete individual learning tasks out of class, mostly in Moodle. While teacher would facilitate individual learning process by logging on Moodle regularly to check on their performance and learning progress, give different individuals prompt and personalized feedbacks or learning suggestions.

Collaborative learning could be fulfilled either online or in a face-to-face condition. Before/after class, groups might be assigned to explore on certain topics in a face-to-face setting or online, and complete a collaborative task (for example, create a video clip); whereas collaborative learning and student-student interaction in class might be achieved by having face-to-face brainstorming, discussion or online collaboration, etc. During which, teacher would walk around the classroom to provide every group with personal assistance and comments.

### 3.4 Fostering an Affective Learning Climate

Effective techniques can foster affective and safe learning climate while managing large class include offering clear guidance, prompt feedback, as well as encouraging peer learning.

Firstly, teacher-student interaction and prompt feedback are essential to the success of individual learning out of class, students would be guided to fulfill all the self-paced learning tasks and assignments in Moodle. Meanwhile, teacher would log on Moodle regularly to check on students' learning records and interact with students in Moodle forum, give comments to students' works, respond to students' personal messages or questions. All these efforts would play an important role in motivating and engaging students.

Secondly, peer evaluation in the form of either giving out a score or comment is beneficial for every participant. On the one hand, the experience of reviewing works submitted by peers is a great opportunity for students to communicate, to share, and ultimately, to learn from each other. On the other hand, peer evaluation work helps to enhance student-student bond, and consequently develop an affective learning climate within the blended learning context.

## 4 Teaching Large Classes with Multi-mode Blended Learning

During March–July, 2017, the author conducted an empirical study at one of the universities in Guangzhou, Guangdong Province of China to test out the teaching effect of the proposed model.

## 4.1 Research Question

By following the multi-mode blended learning model, the author taught college English to four large classes within a whole semester, in an attempt to answer the following research question: According to students' perceptions, is the model effective in improving their listening, speaking, reading, writing and translating skills?

## 4.2 Participants

Four classes of second year undergraduate students were randomly chosen to participate in the present study. They were all large classes with 80–100 students in each class (N = 360).

## 4.3 Research Instrument

The research instrument in the present study is a questionnaire, which was used as an instrument for both the pre-test and post-test surveys.

The questionnaire was developed in alignment with the Intermediate Requirement (second level of the requirements) for language skills put forward by the Higher Education Division of Ministry of Education (China) in the College English Curriculum Requirements (Higher Education Division of Ministry of Education, 2007: 38–40). It is composed of five parts (listening, speaking, reading, writing, and translating skills), with 3 items in every part, 15 items altogether.

The questionnaire in the pre-test and post-test surveys invited students to evaluate their own listening, speaking, reading, writing, and translating skills using 5-point Likert Scale (1 = very poor, 2 = poor, 3 = fair, 4 = good, 5 = excellent).

## 4.4 Experimental Procedure

The teaching experiment, lasted for one semester (16 weeks, 80 min every week), is based on a blended learning series course, consisting of one face-to-face course introduction at the very beginning of the semester, seven blended learning sections and one final exam at the end of the semester (see Table 1).

**Table 1.** Teaching schedule of the multi-mode blended learning of college English

| Week | CI | BL1 | | BL2 | | BL3 | | BL4 | | BL5 | | BL6 | | BL7 | | FE |
|---|---|---|---|---|---|---|---|---|---|---|---|---|---|---|---|---|
| | 1 | 2 | 3 | 4 | 5 | 6 | 7 | 8 | 9 | 10 | 11 | 12 | 13 | 14 | 15 | 16 |
| Online learning | | ✓ | | ✓ | | ✓ | | ✓ | | ✓ | | ✓ | | ✓ | | |
| F2F learning | | | ✓ | | ✓ | | ✓ | | ✓ | | ✓ | | ✓ | | ✓ | |

Note: "F2F" is short for "face-to-face", "CI" is short for "course introduction", "BL" is short for "blended learning", "FE" is short for "final exam".

Table 1 indicates that every two weeks makes a blended learning section, in which students would spend 80 min in the first week fulfilling the online learning tasks, and spend another 80 min in the following week to participate in face-to-face instruction.

As for assessment, the seven blended learning sections from Weeks 2–15 would keep record of students' performance (formative assessment), while the final exam serves as the summative assessment.

### 4.5 Data Collection and Analysis

Students were invited to fill out the pre-test survey questionnaire in Moodle at the very beginning of the semester, and answer the post-test survey questionnaire in Moodle at the end of the course. Students would choose from 1–5 (from "very poor" to "excellent") to describe their own situations.

According to Moodle record, 284 students out of the 360 participants (78.9%) filled out the questionnaire in the pre-test survey, and 173 students out of the 360 participants (48.1%) answered the questionnaire in the post-test survey (It is a pity that most of the students were busy preparing for the many final exams at the end of the semester and hence failed to fill out the questionnaire). In order to ensure consistency of the data, the author of the present paper excluded data from the participants that only answer the pre-test or the post-test survey questionnaire (Note that Moodle could automatically record the name and student ID of the questionnaire fillers). Finally, 145 pairs of pre-test and post-test questionnaires are ready for statistical analysis.

The data of the valid questionnaires were put into SPSS (23.0) for reliability analysis. Result indicated that the questionnaires enjoyed a relatively high reliability ($\alpha = 0.947$). After that, a paired samples T test was run to find out whether the students had benefited from the multi-mode blended learning model.

## 5 Teaching Effect

T test scores for the 15 items were collected (see Tables 2, 3, 4, 5 and 6), presenting both the average scores of pre-test and post-test questionnaires, and two-tailed P values.

### 5.1 Listening Skills

Table 2 presents the paired samples T test results of students' skills in understanding talks or lectures, radio or TV broadcasts, courses of specialty in English.

**Table 2.** Paired samples T test results of participants' listening skills

| Can understand English… | M (pre-test) | M (post-test) | P (two-tailed) |
|---|---|---|---|
| Talks or lectures | 3.3448 | 3.5724 | .002* |
| Radio or TV broadcasts | 2.4138 | 2.7034 | .007* |
| Courses of specialty | 2.1517 | 2.4276 | .017* |

Note: The mark "*" indicates significant difference.

Results from Table 2 suggest that participants have significant improvement in overall listening skills (P values are: 0.002 < 0.05, 0.007 < 0.05, 0.017 < 0.05, respectively). Therefore, the author of the present paper would argue that the teacher-student and student-student interaction in/out of class, especially the Moodle-based video watching activity before class (participants are allowed to replay the videos until they understand the teaching contents) is beneficial in improving students' listening skills. Actually, (Caruso et al. 2017) had similar findings and argued that online listening tasks were "a key element in the development of listening skills".

## 5.2 Speaking Skills

Table 3 presents the paired samples T test results of students' skills in speaking fluently in daily conversations, expressing complex emotions, opinions, and describing personal experiences in English.

**Table 3.** Paired samples T test results of participants' speaking skills

| Can... | M (pre-test) | M (post-test) | P (two-tailed) |
|---|---|---|---|
| Speak fluently in daily conversations | 2.6897 | 2.8828 | .081 |
| Express complex emotions, opinions | 2.4345 | 2.6966 | .025* |
| Describe personal experiences | 3.0690 | 3.2207 | .185 |

Note: The mark "*" indicates significant difference.

Results from Table 4 suggest that participants have made some but not significant progress in having daily conversations and describe personal experiences (P values are: 0.081 > 0.05, 0.185 > 0.5). This phenomenon might result from the teacher's failure to carry out related training. However, the paired samples T test suggests that participants have made significant progress in expressing complex emotions and opinions (P = 0.025 < 0.05). Therefore, the author of the present paper infers that the assignments and group collaboration that aim at developing higher-order thinking skills, fulfilled before and in the class, are helpful in improving students' communication skills and speaking skills.

## 5.3 Reading Skills

Table 4 presents the paired samples T test results of students' skills in reading English articles from popular newspaper, texts of intermediate level and summary of literature.

**Table 4.** Paired samples T test results of participants' reading skills

| Can read English... | M (pre-test) | M (post-test) | P (two-tailed) |
|---|---|---|---|
| Articles from popular newspapers | 2.7103 | 2.9931 | .013* |
| Texts of intermediate level | 2.6759 | 3.0345 | .003* |
| Summary of literature | 1.9448 | 2.3655 | .000** |

Note: The mark "*" indicates significant difference, while "**" indicates very significant difference.

As is noted in Table 4, participants have made significant improvement in the two subskills of reading articles from newspaper and texts with an intermediate level of difficulty (P values are: $0.013 < 0.05$, $0.003 < 0.05$, respectively). Meanwhile, participants reported great difficulty in understanding summary of literature in their areas of specialty, but have made very significant improvement ($P = 000 < 0.001$). Therefore, the author of the present paper infers that the videos on reading strategies provided in Moodle (participants are allowed to replay the videos until they master the strategies) are helpful for the students, and the reading tasks and assignments in Moodle provide students with opportunities to apply the strategies into practice, hence reinforce the reading skills. This finding supports previous study by Schechter et al. (2015) that blended learning approach is effective in enhancing reading skills.

## 5.4 Writing Skills

Table 5 presents the paired samples T test results of students' skills in writing practical texts on everyday topics, abstracts of thesis in specialty and well-structured short thesis in English.

**Table 5.** Paired samples T test results of participants' writing skills

| Can write English… | M (pre-test) | M (post-test) | P (two-tailed) |
|---|---|---|---|
| Practical texts on everyday topics | 3.0207 | 3.2897 | .023* |
| Abstracts of thesis in specialty | 2.0276 | 2.4138 | .000** |
| Well-structured short thesis | 2.3379 | 2.7586 | .000** |

Note: The mark "*" indicates significant difference, while "**" indicates very significant difference.

As is noted in Table 5, participants have made significant progress in writing practical texts on everyday topics ($P = 0.023 < 0.5$). At the same time, participants reported poor performance in writing English abstracts of thesis in their own specialties, and difficulty in writing well-structured short thesis in their own specialties. However, they have made very significant improvement ($P = 0.000 < 0.001$). This result echoes Milad's (2017) finding that blended learning could help students improve academic writing skills. In brief, the author of the present paper would argue that the videos on writing strategies provided in Moodle (participants are allowed to replay the videos until they succeed in developing the strategies), the asynchronous, synchronous forum/virtual "bulletin" board discussion, and online collaboration are beneficial for improving students' writing skills.

## 5.5 Translating Skills

Table 6 presents the paired samples T test results of students' skills in translating texts on general topics, literature in specialty and using proper translation techniques.

**Table 6.** Paired samples T test results of participants' translating skills

| Can … | M (pre-test) | M (post-test) | P (two-tailed) |
|---|---|---|---|
| Translate texts on general topics | 2.9241 | 3.1931 | .037* |
| Translate literature in specialty | 1.9310 | 2.3241 | .000** |
| Use proper translation techniques | 2.7655 | 3.0759 | .004* |

Note: The mark "*" indicates significant difference, while "**" indicates very significant difference.

As is noted in Table 6, participants have made significant progress in using appropriate translation techniques to translate texts on general topics (P values are: $0.037 < 0.05$; $0.004 < 0.05$). At the same time, participants reported poor performance in translating literature related to their own specialties. However, they have made very significant improvement in the subskill ($P = 0.000 < 0.001$).

Therefore, the author of the present paper infers that the videos on translating strategies provided in Moodle (participants are allowed to replay the videos until they master the strategies) are insightful for the students, and the translating tasks and assignments in Moodle provide students with opportunities to apply the strategies into practice, hence reinforce the translating skills.

### 5.6 Summary of the Section

According to the participants' reports, they are not so confident in their language proficiency so far, as average score of most items is lower than 3 or even lower than 2. However, they believe that they have made (very) significant improvement in terms of listening, speaking, reading, writing and translating skills. It is interesting to note that the participants believed that they have made significant (but not very significant) improvement in the fundamental subskills of listening, speaking, reading, writing and translating; however, they have made very significant progress in the ability to handle works related to their own specialties. Possible explanation for this phenomenon is that the teacher and students had given much weight to the skills of reading English literature, writing short thesis and translate literature in students' area of specialty.

## 6 Conclusion

The design of blended learning is confronted with four key challenges: incorporating flexibility, stimulating interaction, facilitating students' learning processes, and fostering an affective learning climate (Boelens et al. 2017). Meanwhile, large language class instruction in mainland China has posed great challenges to both teachers and students.

Therefore, the author of the present paper develops a multi-mode blended learning model to teach large classes. According to the proposed model, teachers could probably sub-divide a large class into groups and provide students with opportunities to carry out individual or collaborative learning out of/in class in either online or face-to-face condition supported with 2.0 technologies, and meanwhile offer students quick feedback and immediate help in either teacher-student interaction or student-student interaction and peer evaluation. Results of the empirical study, as is described in the present paper, prove that the developed multi-mode blended learning model is effective in improving college students' listening, speaking, reading, writing and translating skills in large class setting.

A tentative conclusion can be made that the multi-mode blended learning model could be applied to optimize the procedure of large class instructions and improve students' perceptions of their language proficiency as well. Further research would be done by the present author to gain hints on whether the developed model has succeeded in meeting the four key challenges summed up by Boelens et al. (2017).

## 7 Limitation

It's a little bit pity that the present study only collected 145 pairs of pre-test and post-test questionnaires out of the 284/360 participants that filled in pre-test questionnaires. In future's data collection, the researcher would try to collect data in a more effective way, for instance, by asking the students to fill in the questionnaire in the final face-to-face section.

**Acknowledgement.** My heartfelt thanks go to the four anonymous reviewers and Professor He Guangkeng and Professor Jiao Jianli from South China Normal University for their invaluable feedbacks on earlier versions of this paper.

## References

Boelens, R., Wever, B.D., Voet, M.: Four key challenges to the design of blended learning: a systematic literature review. Educ. Res. Rev. **22**, 1–18 (2017)

Bonk, C.J., Graham, C.R.: The Handbook of Blended Learning Environments: Global Perspectives, Local Designs. Jossey-Bass/Pfeiffer, San Francisco (2006)

Caruso, M., Colombi, A.G., Tebbit, S.: Teaching how to listen. blended for the development and assessment of listening skills in a second language. J. University Teach. Learn. Pract. **14**(1), 1–19 (2017)

Driscoll, M.: Blended Learning: Let's Get beyond the Hype (2002). http://www-07.ibm.com/services/pdf/blended_learning.pdf

Dziuban, C.D., Hartman, J.L., Moskal, P.D.: Blended Learning (2004). http://net.educause.edu /ir/library/pdf/erb0407.pdf

Graham, C.: Blended Learning Systems: Definition, Current Trends, and Future Directions (2004). www.publicationshare.com

Harriman, G.: What is Blended Learning (2004). http://www.grayharriman.com/blended_learning.htm

Higher Education Division of Ministry of Education: College English Curriculum Requirements. Foreign Language and Research Press, Beijing (2007)

Joosten, T.M., Barth, D., Harness, L., Weber, N.L.: The impact of instructional development and training for blended teaching on course effectiveness. In: Picciano, A.G., Dziuban, C.D., Graham, C.R. (eds.) Blended Learning: Research Perspectives, vol. 2, pp. 173–189. Routledge, New York (2014)

Kerres, M., De Witt, C.: A didactical framework for the design of blended learning arrangements. J. Educ. Media **28**, 101–113 (2003)

Köse, U.: A blended learning model supported with Web 2.0 technologies. Soc. Behav. Sci. **2**, 2794–2802 (2010)

MacDonald, J.: Blended Learning and Online Tutoring. Gower, Aldershot (2006)

Marsh, G.E., McFadden, A.C., Price, B.J.: Blended Instruction: Adapting Conventional Instruction for Large Classes (2003). http://www.westga.edu/~distance/ojdla/winter64/marsh64.htm

Milad, M.: Blended learning approach: integrating reading and writing research skills to improve academic writing. Arab J. Appl. Linguist. **3**(3), 23–55 (2017)

NCTE: Why Class Size Matters Today (2014). http://www.ncte.org/positions/statements/why-class-size-matters

Olapiriyakul, K., Scher, J.M.: A guide to establishing hybrid learning courses: employing information technology to create a new learning experience, and a case study. Internet High. Educ. **9**, 287–301 (2006)

Picciano, A.G.: Blending with purpose: the multimodal model. J. Asynchronous Learn. Netw. **13**(1), 7–18 (2009)

Schechter, R., Macaruso, P., Kazakoff, E.R., Brooke, E.: Exploration of a blended learning approach to reading instruction for low SES students in early elementary grades. Comput. Sch. **32**(3–4), 183–200 (2015)

Sharma, P., Barrett, B.: Blended Learning. Macmillan, Oxford (2007)

Singh, H.: Building effective blended learning programs. Educ. Technol. **43**, 51–54 (2003)

Smythe, M.: Toward a framework for evaluating blended learning. In: The 29th Annual ASCILITE Conference, Wellington, New Zealand, 25–28 November 2012

Staker, H., Horn, M.B.: Classifying K-12 blended learning (2012). http://www.innosightinstitute.org/innosight/wp-content/uploads/2012/05/Classifying-K-12-blended-learning.pdf

Voegele, J.D.: Student perspectives on blended learning through the lens of social, teaching, and cognitive presence. In: Picciano, A.G., Dziuban, C.D., Graham, C.R. (eds.) Blended Learning: Research Perspectives, vol. 2, p. 93e103. Routledge, New York (2014)

Wang, Q., Zhang, N.: Teaching Large Classes in China – English as a Foreign Language (2011). http://www.ntu.edu.vn/Portals/96/Phuong%20phap%20GD/Teaching%20large%20classes%20(7).pdf

Whittaker, C.: Introduction. In: Tomlinson, B., Whittaker, C. (eds.) Blended Learning in English Language Teaching: Course Design and Implementation. British Council, London (2013)

# Empirical Research on Co-construction of Core Teaching Practices

Jianglian Li(✉) and Xiaodong Xu

School of Information Technology in Education, South China Normal University, Zhongshan Avenue West, Tianhe District, Guangzhou, Guangdong, China
735247228@qq.com

**Abstract.** This paper identifies a collection of teaching knowledge and skills for effective teaching, called core practices. Firstly, the background, history and concept of core practices are introduced. Secondly, under an empirical research paradigm, we conduct three rounds of survey to identify the core teaching practices that are suitable for native teacher. These include finding and recording practices from front-line teachers, clustering and dividing practices by expert teachers, and identifying and defining practices by teacher educators. Finally, we conclude our study with examples, and discuss the future research direction.

**Keywords:** Teacher education · Co-construction · Core teaching practices

## 1 Core Teaching Practices and Context

As of now, it is generally believed that an effective teacher should possess knowledge, including subject knowledge, pedagogical knowledge, and TPACK (Technological Pedagogical and Content Knowledge). However, we found that teacher education is undergoing a major transformation—from specific and necessary teaching knowledge to teaching practices that needed specific knowledge and skills (Grossman et al. 2009a, b). Now more and more research on professional development of teachers focus on the "core" or "efficient" teaching practice approach (Forzani 2014). Teacher educators (Franke et al. 2006) consider that we need to rethink the content that pre-service teachers need to learn from the start by developing a set of high leverage practices for K-12 classroom (McDonald et al. 2013) so as to teach pre-service teachers and let them implement practices in class. Ball (2009) pointed out that high leverage practices which teachers can carry out in class through mastery and can bring great progress to students. High leverage practices are also known as core practices. At present, many researchers are trying to describe core teaching practices to provide an operable objective system for teacher education so that teachers can clearly identify specific contents they should require in teacher education and professional development. Native research suggests that teachers' knowledge is not only skill oriented, but more based on practice (Lu and Taisheng 2010). It is necessary for pre-service teachers to be trained in a systematic way of "learning to teach" (Xu et al. 2011). Based on the above development trend, this study is devoted to the exploration of the core teaching practices which are in line with native teacher culture and education policy.


S. K. S. Cheung et al. (Eds.): ICTE 2018, CCIS 843, pp. 200–210, 2018.
https://doi.org/10.1007/978-981-13-0008-0_19

"Core practice" was first mentioned by Franke et al. (2006) in the literature. Lampert (2001) present three kinds of practices including developing classroom culture, learning about student understanding and orchestrating classroom discussions that realize ambitious teaching in the monograph of "Teaching Problems and the Problem of Teaching". Later scholars believed that these practices which can be regarded as starting point of core practices research (Grossman 2009a, b). Developing classroom culture could be composed into a number of more discrete practices and instructional routines, including developing productive and professional relationships with students, helping students develop positive relationships with each other; managing transitions between activity structures, and creating classroom routines. Learning about student understanding might include strategies like eliciting student thinking during interactive teaching, anticipating student responses and eliciting further thinking. Orchestrating classroom discourse include asking questions or posing problems to begin a discussion, monitoring student participation during discussion, and responding to student ideas.

Core practices of this study refers to interacting production among teachers, students and teaching content in the classroom. At the same time, we believe that each core practice can be divided into more sub-practices, including skills, strategies and specific teacher knowledge, which belong to the knowledge but different from it. The former are the integration of specific knowledge, skills, specific teaching deeds that can bring great progress to the teachers by mastering them.

On the one hand, we hold that core practices, which exist in the way of practice representation, are applicable pedagogical knowledge. On the other hand, they are pathway of using subject knowledge and pedagogical knowledge and can promote the development of knowledge, skills and professional identity of teachers.

In recent years, researchers (Kloser 2014; Fogo, 2014; Troyan et al. 2013) have conducted the research on core practices. Researchers (TeachingWorks 2013a) of University of Michigan established 19 core practices can be used in different disciplines, grade and context; Kloser (2014) of University of Notre Dame described a set of core practices in science teaching. Fogo (2014) put forward 12 core practices in history teaching in the same way at the Stanford University. Researchers (Millican and Forrester 2017) of University of Texas and of University of Massachusetts System achieved a strong consensus on 3 core practices in music teaching. Canadian Researchers (Troyan et al. 2013) explored the application of core practices in foreign language teacher education.

Core practices are closely related to teaching and teacher culture, nevertheless overseas research results of core practices can't be applied to native teacher education. In order to help pre-service teachers adapt to their professional career as early as possible, we need to identify core practices that are suitable for our teacher culture and teaching situation. Based on the study of individualized and sustainable teacher professional development model, this study is intended to construct native core practices through investigation method.

## 2 Method

This study, which under the empirical research paradigm, refer the method of identifying core practices of University of Notre Dame and Stanford University—Delphi method. In order to increase the objectivity of investigation, we added a survey of finding core practices by front-line teachers in the first phase and use Delphi method in the other two phases. Finally we co-construct a set of core practices by three round of investigation.

### 2.1 Respondents

In the first phase of survey, 210 respondents are front-line teachers from nine subjects (covering Chinese, English, Politics, History, Geography, Math, physics, Chemistry and Biology), five schools (1 junior school, 2 senior schools and 2 elementary schools) and 3 cities in Guangdong Province.

In the second phase of survey, 10 respondents, which have rich subject teaching experience, are expert teachers who teach in different discipline. They participated many kinds of teacher training projects, such as "research helps teaching", "experts enter classroom" and "top teacher's workshop", in which they guide teachers as tutor to improve teaching performance according their theoretical knowledge and practical experience.

In the third phase of survey, 14 respondents are from different universities and research area in teacher education. They have long-term and close contact with the primary and secondary schools teachers. As theoretical mentor, they have ability of keen insight into actual teaching demand and deficiency and help teachers rethink teaching practices and turn experience into theory in order to make the teachers get ahead.

### 2.2 Procedures

The procedures are composed of the following three phases: front-line teachers discover and present teaching practices–verbalizing of practices; expert teachers cluster teaching practices– territorializing of practices; teacher educators define core practices – conceptualizing of practices. In the first phase of the survey, questionnaires were used to collect teaching practices that front-line teachers consider to be important and to describe them in the exact language. In the second phase of the survey, the Delphi method was adopted to collect the views of expert teachers on core practices. Based on the important teaching practices proposed by front-line teachers, the expert teachers further abstracted, selected and clustered core practices. In the third phase of investigation, the Delphi method was still adopted. Teacher educators further compared and analyzed core practices with the core practice standards, and made more scientific and accurate definition. Researchers construct the connotation and expression of core practices in the light of survey result.

# 3 Result and Analysis

## 3.1 Analysis of Phase I Survey Results

In the first phase, we encoded excerpts of front-line teachers' responses based on core practice standards and rules. In this study, we adopted open coding of grounded theory and decomposed the excerpts to ensure that a sentence belongs to only one concept genus and then used the nodes in NVivo v8.0 software to tag excerpts and conceptualized them. Finally the following 20 teaching practices as shown in Table 1 is obtained.

**Table 1.** Phase I survey results: important teaching practice frequency table

| No. | Teaching practices | Frequency (n = 684) |
|---|---|---|
| 1 | Creating good classroom atmosphere | 125 |
| 2 | Increasing students' participation | 101 |
| 3 | Stimulating students' motivation to learn | 94 |
| 4 | Adjusting teaching based on students' performance | 52 |
| 5 | Orchestrating group activities | 37 |
| 6 | Guiding students to review existing knowledge | 36 |
| 7 | Summarizes contents of the class by concentrating on the main points | 33 |
| 8 | Putting forward questions to inspire students to think | 29 |
| 9 | Creating learning context | 28 |
| 10 | Understand why students answered wrongly | 23 |
| 11 | Offer students timely feedback and comments on students' expression | 22 |
| 12 | Teaching students how to solve problems | 20 |
| 13 | Guiding students to explore | 20 |
| 14 | Realizing teaching objectives required by the curriculum standards | 18 |
| 15 | Building scaffolding for students thinking | 15 |
| 16 | providing students with opportunities of full expressing | 9 |
| 17 | Listening carefully to the student's expression | 9 |
| 18 | Leaving students sufficient time to think after asking questions | 6 |
| 19 | Using information technology appropriately to assist teaching | 5 |
| 20 | Respecting students | 2 |

## 3.2 Analysis of Phase II Survey Results

In the first phase of survey, researchers found that front-line teachers have difficulty in articulating core teaching practices occurred in class because of the lack of corresponding knowledge schema in their cognitive system (Xu et al. 2016). Above teaching practices are not compliance with core practice standard entirely. Therefore, expert teachers are required to further refine and cluster existing practices.

### 3.2.1 Quantitative Data Analysis

Respondents were requested to make professional judgment about the importance of each core practice based on Likert five-level scale. After descriptive statistical analysis of quantitative data, the researchers obtained the results (n = 10) as shown in Table 2.

**Table 2.** Phase II survey results: core practice score statistics table

| No. | Core practices items | M | Mode | SD | Δ/top | Δ/prev |
|---|---|---|---|---|---|---|
| 1 | Realizing teaching objectives required by the curriculum standards | 4.80 | 5 | 0.422 | – | – |
| 2 | Guiding students to review existing knowledge | 4.80 | 5 | 0.422 | 0.00 | 0.00 |
| 3 | Creating learning context | 4.60 | 5 | 0.516 | −0.20 | -0.20 |
| 4 | Increasing students' participation | 4.60 | 5 | 0.516 | −0.20 | 0.00 |
| 5 | Creating good classroom atmosphere | 4.60 | 5 | 0.516 | −0.20 | 0.00 |
| 6 | Building scaffolding for students thinking | 4.50 | 5 | 0.527 | −0.30 | −0.10 |
| 7 | Summarizes contents of the class by concentrating on the main points | 4.50 | 5 | 0.527 | −0.30 | 0.00 |
| 8 | Putting forward questions to inspire students to think | 4.40 | 4 | 0.516 | −0.40 | −0.10 |
| 9 | Understand why students answered wrongly | 4.40 | 4 | 0.516 | −0.40 | 0.00 |
| 10 | Teaching students how to solve problems | 4.40 | 4 | 0.516 | −0.40 | 0.00 |
| 11 | Offer students timely feedback and comments on students' expression | 4.40 | 5 | 0.699 | −0.40 | 0.00 |
| 12 | Orchestrating group activities | 4.40 | 4 | 0.516 | −0.40 | 0.00 |
| 13 | Adjusting teaching based on students' performance | 4.40 | 4 | 0.516 | −0.40 | 0.00 |
| 14 | Listening carefully to the student's expression | 4.40 | 5 | 0.699 | −0.40 | 0.00 |
| 15 | Stimulating students' motivation to learn | 4.40 | 5 | 0.699 | −0.40 | 0.00 |
| 16 | Leaving students sufficient time to think after asking questions | 4.40 | 4 | 0.516 | −0.40 | 0.00 |
| 17 | Guiding students to explore | 4.40 | 4 | 0.516 | −0.40 | 0.00 |
| 18 | Providing students with opportunities of full expressing | 4.30 | 4 | 0.675 | −0.50 | −0.10 |
| 19 | Using information technology appropriately to assist teaching | 4.30 | 4 | 0.632 | −0.50 | 0.00 |
| 20 | Respecting students | 4.20 | 4 | 0.632 | −0.60 | −0.10 |

As shown in the above data, mean $\geq$ 4.20, mode $\geq$ 4, standard deviation < 0.70, the mean of every practice is high. Expert teachers' recognition degree about importance of different experts for each practice in teaching tend to be consistent. But researchers did not directly make choice based on the quantitative data.

### 3.2.2 Qualitative Data Analysis

Expert teachers clustered these practices in line with the teaching practice put forward by front-line teachers, the view is as follows.

(1) There are two bases of teaching: prior knowledge and demand of students and curriculum standard. Curriculum standards, in addition to the three-dimensional goals, emphasize on the core literacy. Teachers should know if misconceptions, difficulties, priorities and questions of students have been solved. Therefore, expert teachers believe that "realizing teaching objectives required by the curriculum standards" and "understanding why students answered wrongly" are crucial teaching practices in class.

(2) Nowadays, there is a shift in student learning goals from acquiring of concept to learning to think, question, learn and solve specific problems. Teaching is required that ask questions, organize inquiries and provide support to students based on the situation as real as possible. The process of problem solving should be similar to exploring process of subject specialist so that students can apply disciplinary-specific ways of thinking in their inquiries. This fully affirmed "creating learning context ", "teaching students how to solve problems" and "guiding students to explore", "building scaffolding for students thinking" and "teaching students how to solve problems" can be reflected in "guiding students to explore", latter practice is more inclusive than previous two.

(3) Learning is a kind of social activity and good result usually comes from special social interaction: teachers and students construct and share knowledge by interacting with each other in shared situational activities. Sharing, discussion, communication and cooperation contribute to developing the disciplinary understanding for students and teaching should create opportunities and possibilities for these particular social interaction. "Orchestrating group activities", "providing students with opportunities of full expressing", "putting forward questions to inspire students to think", "leaving students sufficient time to think after asking questions", "offer students timely feedback and comments on students' expression", "adjusting teaching based on student performance" are parts of effective classroom interaction.

(4) The current integration can be divided into multi-dimensions: the integration between information technology and subject, different disciplines, subject knowledge, students' perspectives. "Guiding students to review existing knowledge", "summarizes contents of the class by concentrating on the main points" and "using information technology appropriately to assist teaching" embody the integration in different degrees. The first two can be clustered into "building connections between different knowledge" because their essence is linking new knowledge and previous.

(5) Core practices are specific, executable and should be distinguished from the purpose of effective teaching. For example, "increasing students' participation" and "stimulating students' motivation to learn" mean providing productive learning situation for students. A variety of teaching practices can achieve this goal, such as "putting forward questions to inspire students to think", "creating good classroom atmosphere" and "guiding students to explore".
(6) Core practices are integrated teaching practices with similar fine-grained levels. Research on fragmented and over-microscopic teaching behaviors has limitations, such as "leaving students sufficient time to think after asking questions" and "providing students with opportunities of full expressing", "listening carefully to the student's expression" and "offer students timely feedback and comments on students' expression" are four divided teaching behaviors, which should be clustered into one teaching practice: "listening to students carefully and responding effectively".
(7) Core practices closely focus on supporting student learning. Practices that away from efficient teaching centers can't be regard as core practices, for instance, "respecting students" is a basic practice, not core. Expert teacher Y mentioned: teachers generally do it, it is basic but not central. Score of this practice is lower than others showed in quantitative data table.

Core practices are well-selected and refined, they reflect the essence of effective instruction and educational equality, not the accumulation of teaching practices. According to quantitative data and experts' viewpoint, core practices results of the second phase are shown in Table 3.

**Table 3.** Phase II survey results: core practice score statistics table

| No. | Core practices |
|---|---|
| 1 | Realizing teaching objectives required by the curriculum standards |
| 2 | Building connections between different knowledge |
| 3 | Creating learning context |
| 4 | Creating good classroom atmosphere |
| 5 | Guiding students to explore |
| 6 | Putting forward questions to inspire students to think |
| 7 | Understand why students answered wrongly |
| 8 | Listening to students carefully and responding effectively |
| 9 | Orchestrating group activities |
| 10 | Adjusting teaching based on students' performance |
| 11 | Using information technology appropriately to assist teaching |

## 3.3 Analysis of Phase III Survey Results

In this survey, researchers modified the questionnaire by changing the ambiguous term "importance" to "core practices standards" (see Table 4) proposed by Grossman et al. (2009a, b). The researchers carefully selected 14 teacher educators, all of whom are subject pedagogical professors, which participated in the training about explaining on defining methods and presentation norms of core practices designed by researchers referring to core practices standards. Afterwards, experts immediately made professional judgment for each practice presented on the evaluation scale. In the same time, experts were required to write down their own views and essential characteristics of each practice. For example, they might find certain practice to be too discrete to construct an integrated practice. Or too general to be considered "core" and explain it. Or, they might provide a brief description to highlight the core nature of one practice. A descriptive statistical analysis on quantitative data (n = 14) is shown in Table 5.

**Table 4.** Core practices standard

| No. | Core practices standard | Code |
|---|---|---|
| 1 | Practices that occur with high frequency in teaching | HF |
| 2 | Practices that novices can enact in classrooms across different curricula or instructional approaches | AE |
| 3 | Practices that that novices can actually begin to master | BM |
| 4 | Practices that allow novices to learn more about students and about teaching | LM |
| 5 | Practices that preserve the integrity and complexity of teaching | IC |
| 6 | Practices that are research-based and have the potential to improve student achievement | RI |

**Table 5.** Phase III survey: Scores of core practices statistical table

| No. | Core practices items | M | Mode | SD | Δ/top | Δ/prev |
|---|---|---|---|---|---|---|
| 1 | Realizing teaching objectives required by the curriculum standards | 4.62 | 4 | 0.655 | – | – |
| 2 | Listening to students carefully and responding effectively | 4.61 | 4 | 0.747 | −0.01 | −0.01 |
| 3 | Putting forward questions to inspire students to think | 4.56 | 5 | 0.786 | −0.06 | −0.05 |
| 4 | Building connections between different knowledge | 4.44 | 4 | 0.808 | −0.18 | −0.12 |
| 5 | Understand why students answered wrongly | 4.43 | 5 | 0.745 | −0.19 | −0.01 |
| 6 | Guiding students to explore | 4.30 | 5 | 0.754 | −0.32 | −0.13 |
| 7 | Creating learning context | 4.25 | 5 | 1.012 | −0.37 | −0.05 |
| 8 | Creating good classroom atmosphere | 4.23 | 5 | 0.914 | −0.39 | −0.02 |
| 9 | Adjusting teaching based on students' performance | 4.21 | 5 | 1.016 | −0.41 | −0.02 |
| 10 | Orchestrating group activities | 4.08 | 5 | 0.903 | −0.54 | −0.13 |
| 11 | Using information technology appropriately to assist teaching | 3.83 | 5 | 0.701 | −0.79 | −0.25 |

As shown in Table 5, the differences in each practice's score in standard dimension is insignificant, which indicating that experts' professional judgment of core practices in all dimensions tend to be agreed. The score of "using information technology appropriately to assist teaching" in all dimensions is lower than other practices. Expert X viewed it:

*Well, not so important, no matter what course…… this is too biased. Novices can actually begin to master…… Novice teacher can, but the old teacher can't….. You can go to school to observe, information technology used by young teachers, it's also very important for novice teachers. Preserve the integrity and complexity of teaching, this is not always. are research-based and have the potential to improve student achievement, study shows that information technology and usual teaching are same, there is no difference. It should be used with caution, not all disciplines are used, not all teachers use. Young teachers can use it, it mainly prompt teaching script and framework.*

Core practices are at meso-level and with similar fine-grained hierarchy. "Creating good classroom atmosphere" is too inclusive to conduct and be trained. Expert Z said:

*First of all, according to our pedagogical teaching method, good is a judgment word. Everyone have different opinion about it. Some people think it is good for students to be quiet. Some say that not only students should be quiet but questions should be asked to make students think quietly. Others hold not only let students think in silence, but tell them way to think... Secondly, this practice can be assumed as a dominant practice, and other practices to achieve practice indirectly. Doing research is slowly toward specific.*

The core practices should be as specific and scientific as possible. Nevertheless, several teacher educators argued that some of core practices are ambiguous and should be further modified in description in order to articulating core practices with clear teacher behaviors and ways of achieving goals. Such as, "understand why students answered wrongly" was revised to" exploring students' thinking", "adjusting teaching based on students' performance" was modified to "making appropriate decisions to adjust teaching". Teaching aims at helping students to form disciplinary thinking in the process of knowledge obtain and fully understand the world in life owing to unique thinking ways of distinct discipline (Gardner 1999). Teaching objectives of curriculum focus on cultivating students' disciplinary thinking and achievement of teaching

**Table 6.** Phase III survey: co-constructed core practices

| No. | Teaching routine genericity | Core practices |
|---|---|---|
| 1 | Lead-in in classroom | Creating learning context |
| 2 | Conversation in classroom | Exploring students' thinking |
| 3 | | Putting forward questions to inspire students to think |
| 4 | | Listening to students carefully and responding effectively |
| 5 | Activity in classroom | Guiding students to explore |
| 6 | | Guiding students discuss |
| 7 | Improvise in classroom | Making appropriate decisions to adjust teaching |
| 8 | Evaluation in classroom | Evaluating students' disciplinary thinking |
| 9 | Summary in classroom | Building connections between different knowledge |

objectives needs to be based on teaching evaluation. In consequence, "realizing teaching objectives required by the curriculum standards" was adjusted to "evaluating students' disciplinary thinking." Experts considered that one of the most representative teaching activities that promote teacher-students and students-students interaction should be selected as core practice. "Orchestrating group activities" was revised to "guiding students discuss". In the end, co-constructed core practices is shown in Table 6.

## 4 Discussion and Conclusion

In this study, we used three rounds of survey to let three types of respondents (front-line teachers, expert teachers and teacher educators) come up with the professional consensus around a set of teaching practices that are efficient and in consonance with core practice standard. The lack of direct interaction between group members prevented the development of factions, the influence of domineering participants, and the distraction of personality clashes. They jointly constructed the theoretical and practical core teaching practices.

Grossman, Compton (2009) argued that core practices should be broken down into smaller grain sizes and described more concretely covering tactics, conventions and key elements of teaching behavior. For example, "exploring students' thinking" can be decomposed into judging student's point of view; thinking about what questions to ask next and how to state it, if you asking student to further explain it, you can asking: "can you explain that what you said?"; predicting student's response; guiding students to think and express their reasoning process clearly, so that teachers can organize teaching based on teachable and myth points. "Making appropriate decisions to adjust teaching" can be broken down into having an insight into needs; distinguishing context; recalling teaching routine and cases; deciding to execute instructional routine or the use cases to explain new situations or use teaching tact (Lu and Xu 2013); predicting thinking (Ohlsson 2011); rehearsing and carrying out decision. Listening is the first step for achieving democratic classroom (Sato 2014). It is not only an auditory behavior in the sense organs, but also an interactive process of communication, feedback and relationship construction involving knowledge, thought and meaning (Song 2016). "Listening to students carefully and responding effectively" can be decomposed into providing emotional support; abandoning the correct answer or fixed thinking; listening to opinions, reasons and even mood, which including audio and silent language; accepting non-standard answers; understanding students and expressing resonance. All of the core practices can be decomposed as above. These practices guide the teaching of teachers 'educators and teachers' learning as part of a larger teaching framework. Learning these practices separately facilitates the analysis and exploration of different parts of teaching. It is important to ensure that the integrity and systematicness of each practice, and the balance between the decomposed practice elements and larger learning objectives and routine.

The results of this study, as well as the analysis and decomposition of core practices, are part of the larger study focused on teaching practice. It is significant that continued verification and further refinement of core practices and field differentiation for future research. Therefore, it is the other research direction that how to implement core practices and what about the effect in the real situation that take into account the reality of students and other complex elements.

## References

Ball, D.L., Forzani, F.M.: The work of teaching and the challenge for teacher education. J. Teach. Educ. **60**(5), 497–511 (2009)

Fogo, B.: Core practices for teaching history: the results of a delphi panel survey. Theory Res. Soc. Educ. **42**(2), 151–196 (2014)

Troyan, F.J., Davin, K.J., Donato, R.: Exploring a practice-based approach to foreign language teacher preparation: a work in progress. Can. Mod. Lang. Rev. **69**(2), 154–180 (2013)

Forzani, F.M.: Understanding "core practices" and "practice-based" teacher education: learning from the past. J. Teach. Educ. **65**(4), 357–368 (2014)

Gardner, H.: The Disciplined Mind: What All Students Should Understand, pp. 14–20. Simon and Schuster, New York (1999)

Grossman, W.J., Borko, H., Liston, D.: Growing talent: promising professional development models and practices. J. Teach. Educ. **60**(3), 07–212 (2009a)

Lu, F., Xu, X.: A case study on teacher teaching decision level modes. Open Educ. Res. **19**(2), 93–101 (2013)

Millican, J.S., Forrester, S.H.: Core practices in music teaching: a delphi expert panel survey. J. Music Teach. Educ. **13**(8) 1–14 (2017)

McDonald, M., Kazemi, E., Kavanagh, S.S.: Core practices and pedagogies of teacher education: a call for a common language and collective activity. J. Teach. Educ. **64**(5), 378–386 (2013)

Lampert, M.: Teaching Problems and the Problem of Teaching. Yale University Press, New Haven (2001)

Sato, M.: Quiet revolution: the classroom changes, the school will change. Education Science Press, Beijing (2014). (translated by Li Jimei)

Kloser, M.: Identifying a core set of science teaching practices: a delphi expert panel approach. J. Res. Sci. Teach. **51**(9), 1185–1217 (2014)

Grossman, P., Hammerness, K., McDonald, M.: Redefining teaching, re-imagining teacher education. Teach. Teach. **15**(2), 273–289 (2009b)

Song, L.: Study on Teaching Listening. China Social Sciences Press, Beijing (2016)

Ohlsson, S.: Deep Learning: How the Mind Overrides Experience. Cambridge University Press, Cambridge (2011)

TeachingWorks: High leverage practices (2013a). http://wwwteachingworks.org/work-of-teaching/high-leverage-practices

Xu, X., He, X., Zhou, X., Zhang, J., Y Qian, Y., Xu, M., Lv, S., Ren, Y.: Project of experts enter classroom to promote professional development of teachers. J. China Educ. Technol. **1**, 95–102 (2016)

Xu, X., Yan, N., Li, S., Lu, D.: Research progress of teacher learning and learning methods. J. Distance Educ. **29**(05), 22–33 (2011)

Franke, M., Grossman, P., Hatch, T., Richert, A., Schultz, K.: Using representations of practice in teacher education. Paper presented at the annual meeting of the American Educational Research Association, San Francisco, CA (2006)

Naigui, L., Taisheng, C.: Professional Development and Changes of Chinese Teachers. Education Science Press (2010)

Grossman, P., Compton, C., Igra, D., Ronfeldt, M., Shahan, E., Williamson, P.: Teaching practice: a cross-professional perspective. Teachers Coll. Rec. **111**(9) (2009)

# Design, Implementation and Evaluation of Blended Learning for the Undergraduate Course "Education and Artificial Intelligence"

Jiyou Jia(✉)

Department of Educational Technology, School of Education, Peking University, Yiheyuanlu 5, Beijing, 100871, China
jjy@pku.edu.cn

**Abstract.** For the ambitious aim toward world-class university, Peking University encourages the blended learning of information and communication technology with classroom teaching for undergraduates. This paper introduces the design and implementation of blended learning approach for the teaching of one undergraduate course "Educational and artificial intelligence". Along with the traditional face-to-face classroom instruction including individual presentation, discussion and debate, the instructor used course management system Moodle to deliver course resources such as lecture notes and supplementary video clips, and to manage many kinds of learning activities like quizzes and assignments. One field trip was also organized to enrich the students' hands-on experience. The students' final score and the overall satisfying result of students' anonymous evaluation held independently and officially by the university demonstrate that the course's goal was somewhat achieved, for example the students' independent thought and innovative spirit were motivated. But how to design blended learning to meet the students' individual demand is still a great challenge.

**Keywords:** Blended learning · Instructional design · Student engagement
Student satisfaction · Undergraduate course

## 1 Introduction

The blended learning combines traditional face-to-face instruction with computer-mediated or online instruction (Bonk and Graham 2006), links traditional classroom teaching to online learning that usually means the learning over the Internet or Intranet (Singh 2003), or combines the effectiveness and socialization opportunities of the classroom with the technologically enhanced active learning possibilities of the online environment, rather than a ratio of delivery modalities (Dziuban et al. 2004). Many meta-analysis studies analyzed dozens, hundreds or even thousands of studies dealing with thousands of subjects, and found that blended learning generally can have a more positive effect on learning performance than traditional instructional approaches (Liao 2007; Tamim et al. 2011; Spanjers et al. 2015).

Peking University, as a leading higher education institution in China, is aiming to rank among the world's best universities in the future. It highly emphasizes the


S. K. S. Cheung et al. (Eds.): ICTE 2018, CCIS 843, pp. 211–222, 2018.
https://doi.org/10.1007/978-981-13-0008-0_20

undergraduate education and encourages the faculty members to blend information and communication technology with traditional classroom instruction. It also encourages faculty members to offer publicly selective courses on interdisciplinary research for all undergraduates to broaden their visions besides their majors.

"Education and Artificial Intelligence" is such a public elective course for undergraduate students in Peking University. Its objective is that the students should acquire the skill of explorative and innovative learning, self-reading, literature searching and scientific research, master one tool of educational data mining, understand the relationship among education, artificial intelligence and educational technology, review the educational technologies through the lens of technical philosophy, and explore the effect or potential of artificial intelligence's application in education.

Ten Juniors and seniors from Peking University were enrolled in this course in the first semester of the academic year from 2017 to 2018, starting in September and ending in December 2017. They came from various colleges and departments: physics, psychology, information management, biology, linguistics, economics and sociology. Three are males, and the others are females. Their common interest is artificial intelligence and its educational application, though their knowledge in education and computer science differs from each other. They all had their own notebooks and smart phones, and could use them in the classroom and in the dormitory for reading, writing and browsing Internet via campus-wide WIFI with their own student ids. In the classroom there is one desktop computer which is connected to Internet through wired local area network and also connected to a LCD TV set with 43-inch screen embedded in the blackboard. The equipment from the students and from the university provided adequate hardware infrastructure for blended learning.

## 2 Syllabus Design

To engage the student's participation in the course activities, formative assessment was adapted for the course's grading. To facilitate the students' learning, latest literatures from international journals and supplementary materials were selected and provided to students. Individual presentation, guided reading in dyads, midterm assignment, discussion and debate, final content quiz and semester thesis were all required learning activities and implemented in the course management system Moodle. Besides classroom and campus instruction, field trip to high-tech company was also organized to enrich the students' hands-on experience and enlarge their vision. In the following Sects. 1 introduce the syllabus design in details.

### 2.1 Grading

The formative evaluation approach was adapted to assess the students' learning behavior and performance during the whole semester. The grading components and their scores are listed in Table 1.

**Table 1.** Course grading components and their scores

| Learning activity | Score (with 100 as full) |
|---|---|
| Presence and discussion | 10 |
| Presentation | 20 |
| Midterm assignment | 20 |
| Content quiz | 20 |
| Thesis | 30 |

## 2.2 Course Management System

The instructor uses Moodle (http://www.moodle.org) V3.1, a world-widely used course management system (CMS), as a platform to design and implement the blended learning. This system can be easily installed and managed. Its interface is adaptive to client equipment from desktop computers, notebooks to tablet computers or smart phones. Through activity completion setting the students' activity participation and resource review can be traced. In this platform one course "Education and Artificial Intelligence" was created. Each student was given one account to browse the course content and take part in the learning activities. Figure 1 shows the homepage of this course in the course management system. The course content was arranged linearly according to the chapters' sequence.

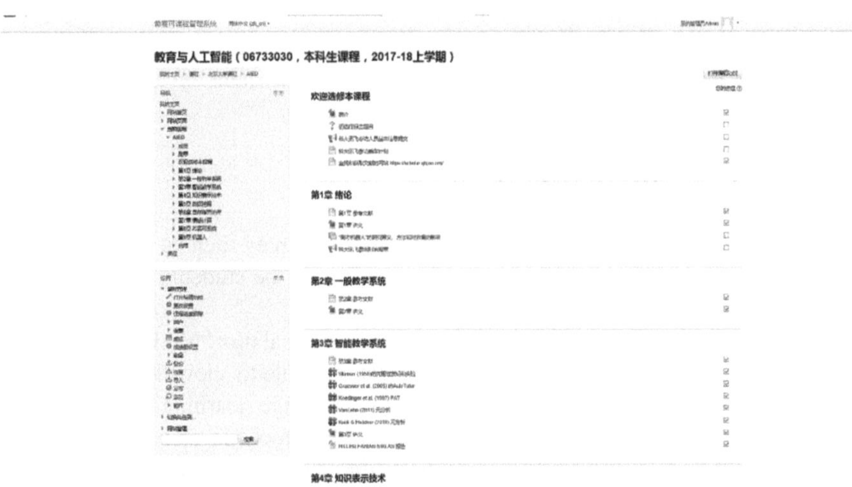


**Fig. 1.** The course homepage on the course management system

## 2.3 Learning Content

Considering remarkable achievements in artificial intelligence in the past few years and its application in education, this course is designed to help students to understand the multilateral relationship among education, educational technology and artificial intelligence, to explore the potential of applying the emerging technology of artificial intelligence in education. The broad range of topics covers most areas in the field of artificial intelligence, including the nature of natural intelligence and artificial intelligence, the education system and its components, knowledge presentation and engineering, educational data mining, natural language processing, affective computing, robotics, intelligent tutoring systems, and an intelligent computer supported language learning system CSIEC developed by the instructor. Nine chapters were included in the course for 16-week duration in one semester.

### 2.4 Literature and Lecture Notes

Because both artificial intelligence and educational technology are emerging and inter disciplinary research fields, it seems impossible to find one appropriate work about education and artificial intelligence as textbook for the students to read. Therefore the instructor searched the corresponding articles published in the past five years in internationally journals listed in SCI (Scientific Citation Index) or SSCI (Social Scientific Citation Index) from Institute for Scientific Information, the USA (http://apps.webofknowledge.com), and selected most best five to six papers according to their citation and content quality as recommended readings for the students. Because all students have their own notebooks computers and smart phones, those readings were not printed, but put onto the course management system as learning resources for the students to download. In the weekly two-hour classroom session, the instructor introduced the course content in the chapter sequence using the corresponding lecture notes. After the class all the lecture notes were uploaded to the course management system for students' review, too.

### 2.5 Supplementary Recourses

In addition to the referred literature, extra learning resources such as links to external websites and video clips were also supplied to facilitate the students' learning and to improve their interest in the course.

For example, the award-winning 1964 American musical film "My Fair Lady" based on George Bernard Shaw's Pygmalion is a perfect example to show the importance of human language and behavioral pedagogy for language learning. Moreover, the humorous dialogue between the leading lady ELIZA Doolittle and other characters before the Ascot Racecourse might inspire the artificial intelligence researcher Weizenbaum to design the first human-computer dialogue program ELIZA (Weizenbaum 1966). However, due to the lengthy running time of this film, c.a. 170 min and the difficulty of the English vocabulary spoken in this film, the undergraduate students might not have enough time to watch the whole film. So the instructor used the video recording and editing software Camtasia to produce three typical clips that are most relevant to the topic of the course "Education and Artificial Intelligence", each of whom lasts just around 10 min. They are "Why Can't the English Learn to Speak?" demonstrating the importance of language and language education, "The Rain in Spain Stays Mainly in the Plain" showing the difficulty of language learning and especially the speech recognition and synthesis, and "The Small Talk" exemplifying the key words matching mechanism of human dialogues. To facilitate the understanding of the students, the subtitles in Chinese were also added to those clips.

The three clips were supplied in the course management system, and the students are required to watch the film clips. Three questions were put onto the forum following this URL: How important are language and language education? What pedagogy did the phonetics professor use to teach Eliza the pronunciation of English words? How did Eliza use the words, phrases and sentences she learns from the professor to manage the dialogue with others? The students were required to post their answers to the forum and to discuss the film during the classroom session.

## 2.6 Discussion and Debate

Discussion and debate were also designed to motivate the students after they read the literatures. The online activity including discussion forum and Wiki were created in the course management system. The students could write their consideration about some topics. However, those activities were optional, but not obligatory.

A debate took place after the students had read the literature about intelligent tutoring system and language technology. The students were divided into two groups, each with five, and argued the pros and cons of the possibility that the student would learn a foreign language with the help of advanced technology but without the teaching of a human teacher in the school. Every member of each group should use the empirical cases given in the literature to support its argumentation and to refute the opposite. This debate continued half one hour, and it inspired the students to read the literature in details and to get familiar with the empirical studies.

## 2.7 Individual Presentation

Every student was required to make a presentation for 20 min or so about one topic selected by himself or herself. The choices were made through a "Vote" activity in the course management system. The student should read the reference corresponding to this chapter before the class and write the presentation with Microsoft PowerPoint based on the reference. The student's slides file was also uploaded to the course management system for others' downloading and review.

## 2.8 Guided Reading in Dyads

Because the chapter "Intelligent Tutoring System" was the most important part in this course, and the references seemed longer and more difficult than others, the students were divided into five dyads. The instructor put forward five questions for each dyad. The two students in each dyad cooperated to read an article and presented it in the classroom in responding to the instructor's questions.

## 2.9 Midterm Assignment

After the concept of data mining and the tools for data mining had been introduced in the classroom at the end of October, the students were required to use Excel, SPSS, WEKA or other data mining software to analyze the log data retrieved from MOOCs (Massive Open Online Course) of Peking University, and to submit the analysis result to the midterm assignment in the course management system. The data set for each student came from different MOOC, and was different from each other. Therefore, every student should analyze the specific data by using the same tools.

Since the background of the students was various, the midterm assignment had obligatory requirement and optional requirement. The students were required to complete the correlation analysis and linear regression charts drawn by using Excel or other tools, and could further complete the clustering analysis by using WEKA, SPSS or other tools.

## 2.10 Learning Content Quiz

In order to examine the students' reading and understanding of all lecture notes and recommended literature, one quiz with ten multiple-choice questions based on the lecture notes was designed and put onto the course management system in the last period of the course. Deliberate scoring mechanism was designed to prevent students from guessing question answers. Only correct answers would be given positive and proportional scores, and false answers would be given proportional but minus scores. However, the minimum score for one question was zero. For example, if there was only one correct answer in one question, and the student submitted more than one answer, the student would not get any score. For those questions with just two correct answers, the student would get one quarter of the full score if he or she submitted one correct answer, but lose one quarter of the full score if he or she submitted one false answer.

The quiz could only be written once and the students should submit the answers within twenty minutes, otherwise the system collected all students' answers automatically. Although every question has definite choices, the order of the choices for every question and the order of the questions in the quiz were shuffled randomly for every attempt of every student. This could make it harder for students to share answers. Once answers were submitted, the score and correct answers were shown to the students.

## 2.11 Field Trip

In order to get to know the latest development of artificial intelligence application in education, i.e. the main topic of this course, one field trip was arranged during the semester. The instructor, the teaching assistant and the students visited one high-tech company located in Hefei city, Anhui Province, IFLYTEK CO., LTD. (http://www.iflytek.com/en/index.html). It is "a national key software enterprise dedicated to the research of intelligent speech and language technologies, development of software and chip products, provision of speech information services, and integration of E-government systems." Speech recognition and synthesis technology is the company's core technology. The speech product is also embedded into educational products to facilitate language learning, for example "Changyan Intelligent Speech Teaching Aid System", "Multilingual Intelligent Speech Evaluation System", "Multilingual Intelligent Speech Evaluation System", "Chinese-learning Portal for Foreigners", and "Education Toys". Moreover, this company also produces digital campus management system and course management system. The speech products occupy more than 70% of market share in the Chinese speech technology market, and the educational products also occupy more and more market shares in China. During one day's visit in this company, the division managers for educational products introduced their achievements and answered questions from the students, guided the students through their research centers, and demonstrated their latest product in the exhibition hall. Through this onsite visit and hands-on experience of smart robots, AI home assistant and other advanced systems, the students were very surprised about this company's excellent accomplishment in speech technology and educational products.

### 2.12 Final Thesis

The student was required to write an article based on the presentation and submit it as an attachment to the assignment "Final paper" activity in the course management system at the end of the semester. The student should use the specified template file to write the article. This article should include the research question, method, findings and conclusion of the referred literature, and have the length of at least three pages.

## 3 Student Performance

All the students took part in the classroom session, individual presentation, guided reading in dyads, discussion and debate. The students edited their presentation slides carefully with the help of some pretty templates. Only one student was absent to the field trip due to schedule conflict with other classes in the university.

All the students submitted their midterm work on time. Only one just completed the obligatory task, and all the others completed both the obligatory and optional tasks. One student's midterm work was selected and revised by the instructor, submitted to a Chinese journal, and will be published by this journal in February 2018.

All the students completed the content quiz online in the course management system. The average score is 12.1 of 20, or 60.5%, and the standard deviation is 4.4. The minimum score is 4, and the maximum is 19. The result seems unsatisfying, as three students' scores were less than half of the full score. The reason for the unsatisfying result may be the strict scoring mechanism of the quiz.

The course theses were submitted to the course platform and graded according to their qualities. The overall quality of the theses was very good. The final course scores were calculated by summarizing all the grading components in January 2018. The mean and standard deviation of the final grades is 90.1% and 5.52%, respectively, corresponding to GPA 3.6/4 and 0.22/4.

The online participation can be analyzed through the progress tracing function in the course management system. For all the nine chapters' lectures notes, eight of ten students (80%) downloaded them on average, with the minimum 1 and the maximum 10. For all the nine chapters' literature readings, 5.3 of ten students (53%) viewed them on average, with the minimum 3 and the maximum 9. The students viewed other supplementary materials including other students' presentation files very seldom, and took part in online discussion and wiki activities seldom, too.

## 4 Independent Student Evaluation

The students are required by the university to submit their answers to the official anonymous online course evaluation survey designed by the Office of Educational Administration. The author did not design extra survey for the students to fill in in order not to burden them. According to the university's course evaluation rule, the student can only see his or her course score just after submitting the survey answer, and the instructor can only see the statistical result of the anonymous survey just after submitting all students' final grades in order to prevent the bi-directional influence between the students' evaluation and the instructor's grading,

Through the university portal, the instructor got the anonymous survey result on January 30, 2018. By January 30, 2018, eight of ten enrolled students had answered the online survey. The survey content and the statistics of students' answers are introduced as the following.

The overall score of the survey answers is 95.02%, and is listed in the top 20% (A+) among all the 3552 courses in the whole university evaluated in the whole year.

The survey contains five parts: satisfaction, recommendation, others, communication, and subject comments.

In the satisfaction part, there are ten questions about students' satisfaction degree to the course. They are labeled as S1 through S10 in this paper for the simplicity.

S1: The course has a clear goal, and emphasizes the students' knowledge system construction and the improvement of their ability.
S2: The course organization is clear, rational, systematic and logic.
S3: The course content is challenging and motivating for students' active learning.
S4: The course examination approach is fair and reasonable.
S5: The course teaching refines my knowledge structure and improves my ability.
S6: The teacher's lecture is lucid and well organized, and illustrates the key points.
S7: The teacher's teaching inspires my enthusiasm for learning and my interest in deep learning.
S8: The teacher encourages my independent thought and pay more attention to the cultivation of my innovative spirit.
S9: The teacher gives timely and helpful feedback to my questions including homework and assessment.
S10: The teacher carries out instruction effectively according to the students' learning situation and teaching arrangement.

In the recommendation part, there are two questions labeled as R1 and R2.

R1: I will recommend this course to my friends.
R2: I will recommend this teacher's courses to my friends.

The answers to those questions in the two parts are 5-points Likert scale choice, ranging from "strongly not agree", "not agree", "uncertain", "agree", to "strongly agree". Different from the calculation method in statistics that assigns the five answers with the value 1 through 5 and then calculate the weighted mean of all respondents' answers, the university's survey result reports the students' number to each choice, mean score and standard deviation in one question. But the mean score and standard deviation are ranged from 0 to 100, and it is not explained how they are calculated. So this paper tags them as university mean and university standard deviation to distinguish them with statistical definition. Meanwhile, this paper assigns the value 1, 2, 3, 4, 5 to "strongly not agree", "not agree", "uncertain", "agree", to "strongly agree", respectively, and calculate the weighted mean. All the survey results for the satisfaction part and recommendation part are listed in Table 2.

**Table 2.** The answer result for satisfaction and recommendation part in the survey

| Satisfaction | Strongly not agree | Not agree | Uncertain | Agree | Strongly agree | University mean | University std. dev. | Mean |
|---|---|---|---|---|---|---|---|---|
| S1 | 0 | 0 | 0 | 2 | 6 | 93.75 | 11.57 | 4.8 |
| S2 | 0 | 0 | 0 | 1 | 7 | 96.88 | 8.84 | 4.9 |
| S3 | 0 | 0 | 0 | 1 | 7 | 96.88 | 8.84 | 4.9 |
| S4 | 0 | 0 | 0 | 1 | 7 | 96.88 | 8.84 | 4.9 |
| S5 | 0 | 0 | 0 | 1 | 7 | 96.88 | 8.84 | 4.9 |
| S6 | 0 | 0 | 1 | 1 | 6 | 90.63 | 18.6 | 4.6 |
| S7 | 0 | 0 | 0 | 2 | 6 | 93.75 | 11.57 | 4.8 |
| S8 | 0 | 0 | 0 | 0 | 8 | 100 | 0 | 5 |
| S9 | 0 | 0 | 1 | 0 | 7 | 93.75 | 17.68 | 4.8 |
| S10 | 0 | 0 | 1 | 1 | 6 | 90.63 | 18.6 | 4.6 |
| Recommendation | Strongly not agree | Not agree | Uncertain | agree | Strongly agree | University mean | University std. dev. | Mean |
| R1 | 0 | 0 | 1 | 1 | 6 | 90.63 | 18.6 | 4.6 |
| R2 | 0 | 0 | 0 | 2 | 6 | 93.5 | 11.57 | 4.8 |

Among those questions, only one received all students' same answer "strongly agree", or the university full score. The question is "S8: The teacher encourages my independent thought and pay more attention to the cultivation of my innovative spirit." This result is satisfying and inspiring to the lecturer, because the instruction approach of this course is explorative and innovative learning, and one aim of this course is that "the students should acquire the skill of self-reading and searching literature and scientific research", as declared in the first period of this class. The course's aim seems to be achieved from the view point of the student's survey answers.

However, the students' answers to three questions are not satisfying. They are "S6: The teacher's lecture is lucid and well organized, and illustrates the key points.", "S9: The teacher gives timely and helpful feedback to my questions including homework and assessment.," and "S10: The teacher carries out instruction effectively according to the students' learning situation and teaching arrangement." The result of S6 shows that some students might not understand the teacher's lecture very well or the teacher should improve the classroom presentation skill. The result of S9 and S10 show that the students should get more individual instruction and help.

In the others part, there are four questions. The first question is "the average time of every week I spent in this course outside the class". One answer is less than one hour, two answers are from 1 to 2 h, three answers are from 2 to 3 h, and two answers are more than 4 h. Compared with the average spare time all undergraduate students of this university spent in one two-hours course, 2.24 h (Office of Educational Administration Peking University 2018), this course looks more time-consuming.

The second question is "how many learning activities are accounted in the final score including final exam, classroom quiz, oral presentation, assignment, mid-term quiz, etc." Three answers are three, two answers are four, and two answers are five or above. Those answers are surprising because the instructor definitely informed all the students in the first and last period of the class that the final score included five parts: usual presence, oral presentation, mid-term assignment, content exam and final thesis. But it seems that only two students knew this assessment rule and the others did not care about it.

The third question is "how about the learning materials the teacher provided me with except the textbook". Three choices are "much less", "proper", and "too more". All the eight answers checked "proper".

The fourth question is "Are the learning materials the teacher provided me with except the textbook helpful for my learning". Three choices are "no", "somewhat", and "very much". One answers checked "somewhat", and the other seven checked "very much".

The only single-choice question in the communication part is "how many times do you communicate with the teacher outside the classroom including office hour, email, short message, etc." Two answers checked zero, one answer checked once, two answers checked twice, one answer checked three times, and two answers checked four times or above.

In the subjective comments part, there are two questions. The first is "your opinion and suggestion to improve the instructional design and organization". There is just one answer to this question: "The teacher is perfect and the lecture is very good!" The second question is "your opinion and suggestion to the teacher's teaching". There are just two positive praises: "The teacher is perfect and the lecture is very good!", and "Thank you teacher! From you I see the earnest attitude of a teacher toward the work."

The overall result of the anonymous evaluation including four parts is satisfying. Besides the student evaluation, one student emailed to the instructor to express her gratitude and thought: "We all devoted ourselves to this elective course, because you have designed so many interesting learning activities to motivate us. You selected so many excellent research papers for our reference. Your excellent introduction in the classroom and clear guidance help us understand the difficult learning content."

## 5 Conclusion and Discussion

Aiming at becoming a world-class university, Peking University encourages the blended learning of information and communication technology with classroom teaching for undergraduates. The author designed and implemented blended learning approach for the teaching of one undergraduate course "Educational and artificial intelligence". Along with traditional face-to-face classroom instruction including individual presentation, discussion and debate, the instructor used course management system Moodle to deliver course resources such as lecture notes and supplementary video clips, and to manage many kinds of learning activities like quizzes and assignments. One field trip was organized to enrich the students' hands-on experience. This blended learning approach was hoped by the author to implement personalized learning adaptive to students' different backgrounds and needs, and to help students acquire the skill of explorative and innovative learning, self-reading, literature searching and scientific research, master one tool of educational data mining, understand the relationship among education, artificial intelligence and educational technology, and explore the effect or potential of artificial intelligence's application in education.

The students' high final score and the overall satisfying result of students' anonymous evaluation held independently and officially by the university demonstrate that the course's aim seems to have been achieved, at least the students' independent thought and innovative spirit were motivated.

Despite the instructor's great effort, the students' learning progress and performance analysis shows that students just participated in the required online activities and onsite activities, and the content quiz performance was not very good. The survey result shows that only two students learned the course's assessment rule in heart and the others did not take care of it seriously. The reason may be that the majority of the students just wanted to get a grade from this selective course through participating in the obligatory learning activities. The instructor, i.e. also the author of this paper, should improve the lecture presentation in the classroom in the future, as some students expressed their discontent in the survey.

The survey result also shows that some students did not perceive enough individual instruction and timely help. One reason may be that the course content was too difficult for them, as one student expressed in the email to the instructor. The difficult content also costed them more extra learning time, as the survey result shows. Though the blended learning was specifically used during this course to facilitate the students' personalized learning, it seemed not effective for all students' personalized learning. How to design the blended learning to meet all students' individual demand to the selective course is still a great challenge.

**Acknowledgement.** This research is supported by Instruction Reform Project 2017 (No. 20173048) from Office of Educational Administration, Peking University. The author thanks all the students who have participated in the course.

## References

Bonk, C.J., Graham, C.R.: Handbook of Blended Learning: Global Perspectives Local Designs, p. 1. Wiley, San Francisco (2006)

Dziuban, C.D., Hartman, J.L., Moskal, P.D.: Blended learning. Educause Center for Applied Research (ECAR) Research Bulletin, **2004**(7) (2004). http://www.educause.edu/ir/library/pdf/ERB0407.pdf

Liao, Y.: Effects of computer-assisted instruction on students' achievement in Taiwan: a meta-analysis. Comput. Educ. **48**, 216–233 (2007)

Spanjers, I.A.E., Konings, K.D., Leppink, J., Verstegen, D.M.L., de Jong, N., Czabanowska, K., van Merrienboer, J.J.G.: The promised land of blended learning: quizzes as a moderator. Educ. Res. Rev. **15**, 59–74 (2015)

Singh, H.: Building effective blended learning programs. Issue Educ. Technol. **43**, 51–54 (2003)

Tamim, R.M., Bernard, R.M., Borokhovski, E., Abrami, P.C., Schmid, R.F.: What forty years of research says about the impact of technology on learning: a second-order meta-analysis and validation study. Rev. Educ. Res. **81**, 4–28 (2011)

Weizenbaum, J.: ELIZA-a computer program for the study of natural language communication between men and machines. Commun. ACM **9**(1), 36–45 (1966)

Office of Educational Administration Peking University: Undergraduate course evaluation result (2018). https://mp.weixin.qq.com/s/7HKhpWBQS-VIndWLom5AUw

# Learning Administration with Technologies

# An Application of NFC Technology on Class Attendance Systems

Sasivimon Sukaphat(✉), Wachirawit Chaipuvaphat, Suphisra Ketsuthi, Sathinee Paisopa, and Sirinoot Teanrungroj

Department of Computer Science, Faculty of Science, Srinakharinwirot University, Bangkok 10110, Thailand
{sasivimon,sc551010321,sc551011022,sc551011020, sirinoot}@g.swu.ac.th

**Abstract.** Currently, the class attendance checking process of Computer Science program in Srinakharinwirot University still performs manually by calling student's name one by one. This process is impractical and such a waste of time especially in a large class. Therefore, we aim to present an alternative way for the class attendance checking by applying the wireless technology in smartphone, NFC, to help the lecturers manage their class at ease. The proposed system consisted of two modules: the NFC module and the web module. The NFC module performs on the mobile site which transfers the student's personal data from the student's smartphone to the lecturer's smartphone by tapping both phones to each other. The web module performs on the server site which contains the class attendance database. Moreover, the web module also provides class attendance application which will be used for some students who do not have NFC supported in their smartphones. All class attendant information can be represented on the web application. The proposed system will help the lecturers to reduce their time spending in class attendance process and this system can be in the other faculties.

**Keywords:** E-learning · Quality assurance · Student engagement
Student satisfaction · Android platform · Class attendance system · NFC

## 1 Introduction

Class attendance checking is the one of Srinakharinwirot University regulation which aims to cultivate students to be a punctual person. In addition, students who attend class on time will get more chances to learn all contents according to the course syllabus. However, the class attendance checking method in Srinakharinwirot University still uses a roll call method which is inconvenient and such a waste of time, especially in big classrooms. It should be better if we can find a technology that helps class attendance checking process more conveniently and more efficiently.

Recently, NFC (Near Field Communication) technology are built in most smartphones for serving demands of usage wireless communication in anywhere and anytime. According to Igoe et al. (2014); Faulkner (2013); Ortiz (2008), NFC emerged from RFID (radio-frequency identification) technology that establishes a communication between


S. K. S. Cheung et al. (Eds.): ICTE 2018, CCIS 843, pp. 225–234, 2018.
https://doi.org/10.1007/978-981-13-0008-0_21

two electronic devices within a short distance (up to 10 cm) which can be setup faster and easier than Bluetooth. As NFC enables two electronic devices to transfer small data to each other in the simplest way, it can be used as a contactless smart card for storing personal information. The NFC contact less smart card can be used in various purposes such a tickets to access transportation gates or an employee card to give someone contact information or even used in attendance system.

As mentioned above, we interested in applying the NFC technology in a smartphone for checking the student's class attendance in Department of Computer Science, Faculty of Science, Srinakharinwirot University. Because most students have their own smartphones which support NFC technology, it is easy for them it uses their smartphones for checking the class attendance without purchasing anything else.

## 2 Related Works

NFC has been announced since 2004 which aims to provide a set of wireless communication in a very short range. Compared with Bluetooth, NFC consumes less power, easier and faster to set up the connections between mobile devices. With the capability of secure data exchanging, NFC has been used in many authentication systems which are described as below:

According to Keene (2012), Samsung introduced a NFC-based employee ID card system, which allows workers at its Suwon offices to check in work using their smartphones. Rather than having to carry an ID card everywhere and more likely to forget or lose it, Samsung workers at Suwon has been able to touch their smartphones to a barrier to enter the building. Samsung said that this method will be cost-saving, since their employees will not have to spend money on replacing the lost cards.

In 2013, Bangkok Mass Transit System (BTS) cooperated with Advanced Info Service Co. Ltd, one of Thailand mobile operator, announced to use a smartphone embedded with NFC to enter or exit through an automatic gate. Customer have to purchase a special SIM card to use with NFC technology-enable handset. Then, they can use their electronic wallet for accessing the transportation gates.

In order to enhance the e-learning system, Bucicoiu and Tapus (2013) proposed a location-based authentication method using NFC which determines the location of the students for keeping track of their activity. This application also uses a photo in order to ensure double authentication. All these features will ensure the student is attending the class and the teacher made note of it in an easier manner. Moreover, Wei et al. (2017), also proposed an interactive learning system embedded with NFC attendance system that helps instructors to conduct their class in a more interactive way.

As mentioned above, NFC technology has been used in many applications that require the identification process. By storing personal data in user smartphone, we can transfer those data via NFC tag to the NFC reader device to identify the user. Therefore, we decide to apply NFC technology in Android platform for using in class attendance system. The essential student's information is stored in their smartphone. When students attend to their class, they have to tap their smartphone to the NFC reader device for keeping their record of their class attendance. The proposed system will help the class checking process faster and easier and can report the student's class attendance information in many ways.

## 3 Implementation

With the benefits of NFC, we have developed SWU class attendance system to enhance the school's class checking method. This system consisted of two modules which are the NFC module and the Web module. The overall of SWU class attendance system architecture is represented in Fig. 1.

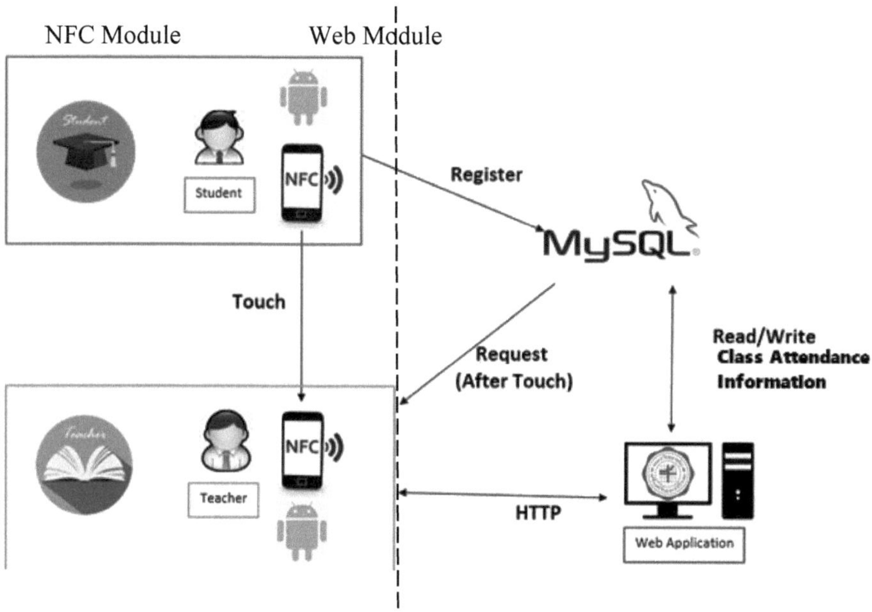


**Fig. 1.** SWU class attendance system architecture.

### 3.1 NFC Module

First of all, the students have to install SWU class attendance application in their smartphones. After logging into our application (Fig. 2(a)), the students must proceed the registration process to our application by submitting their personal information such as ID, name and their class on the registration screen (Fig. 2(b)). An example screen of user information including their class information is shown in the screen (Fig. 2(c)). When the students attend in the class, they have to tap their smartphone to the NFC receiver device. For preliminary experiment we use the instructor's smartphone as a NFC receiver device. The application will display the successful class attendance checking status as shown in Fig. 2(d).

**Fig. 2.** Student application interfaces: (a) the student login screen (b) the registration screen, (c) the student information screen and (d) the successful notification screen after tapping student smartphone to a NFC receiver device.

In the instructor application, after logging into our application (Fig. 3(a)), the instructors are able to view their course list and the student names in the roster files of their courses as shown in Fig. 3(b) and (c) respectively. The instructor smartphone is used as an NFC receiver device in this experiment. After a successful class attendance checking process of each student, the instructor screen will display a successful notification as shown in Fig. 3(d).

**Fig. 3.** Instructor application interfaces: (a) the instructor login screen (b) the instructor's course list screen (c) the roster screen, and (d) the successful notification screen after tapping student smartphone to a NFC receiver device.

In order to allow applications to perform I/O operations over NFC. we have to add a permission in AndroidManifest file (Fig. 4) and use NfcAdapter class to send message between NFC devices. In NfcAdapter class, we call createNdefMessage method to create a message (Fig. 5) and also call createMime method to encode MIME-typed data into an NDEF Record (Fig. 6). Finally, we implement processIntent method to process NFC Data Exchange Format (NDEF) record (Fig. 7).

```
<?xml version="1.0" encoding="utf-8"?>
<manifest xmlns:android="http://schemas.android.com/apk/res/android"
    package="com.example.ize.teacherapp">

    <uses-permission android:name="android.permission.NFC" />
    <uses-feature android:name="android.hardware.nfc" android:required="true" />

    <uses-permission android:name="android.permission.INTERNET" />

    <application
        android:allowBackup="true"
        android:icon="@mipmap/ic_launcher"
        android:label="TeacherApp"
        android:supportsRtl="true"
        android:theme="@style/AppTheme">
        <activity
            android:name=".LoginPage"
            android:screenOrientation="portrait">
            <intent-filter>
                <action android:name="android.intent.action.MAIN" />

                <category android:name="android.intent.category.LAUNCHER" />
```

**Fig. 4.** Adding NFC permission in AndroidManifest file.

```
public NdefMessage createNdefMessage(NfcEvent event) {
    TextView StdId = (TextView) findViewById(R.id.check_stdid);
    String StduId = StdId.getText().toString();
    String text = (StduId);
    NdefMessage msg = new NdefMessage(
            new NdefRecord[]{createMime(
                    "application/vnd.com.example.ize.teacherapp", text.getBytes())

            });
    return msg;
}
```

**Fig. 5.** Calling createNdefMessage method to create a message.

```
public NdefRecord createMime(String mimeType, byte[] payload) {
    byte[] mimeBytes = mimeType.getBytes(Charset.forName("US-ASCII"));
    NdefRecord mimeRecord = new NdefRecord(
            NdefRecord.TNF_MIME_MEDIA, mimeBytes, new byte[0], payload);


    return mimeRecord;

}
```

**Fig. 6.** Calling createMime method to encode MIME-typed data into an NDEF Record.

```
void processIntent(Intent intent) {
    TxtView = (TextView) findViewById(R.id.check_stdid);
    Parcelable[] rawMsgs = intent.getParcelableArrayExtra(
            NfcAdapter.EXTRA_NDEF_MESSAGES);
    // only one message sent during the beam
    NdefMessage msg = (NdefMessage) rawMsgs[0];
    // record 0 contains the MIME type, record 1 is the AAR, if present
    TxtView.setText(new String(msg.getRecords()[0].getPayload()));
}
```

**Fig. 7.** Implementing processIntent method to process NDEF Record.

In addition, the students' smartphones will be turned on vibrate mode automatically after tapping student smartphone to a NFC receiver device. In order to change mobile mode, we have to call AudioManager class to access to android's volume and ringer mode controller. The example code of this process is shown in Fig. 8.

```
AudioManager myAudioManager;

public void vibrateEnable() {
    //set the ring mode to vibrate
    myAudioManager = (AudioManager) getSystemService(Context.AUDIO_SERVICE);
    myAudioManager.setRingerMode(AudioManager.RINGER_MODE_VIBRATE);
    Toast.makeText(CheckPage.this, "Now in Vibrate Mode", Toast.LENGTH_LONG).show();
}
```

**Fig. 8.** The example code to implement the AudioManager class for changing student mobile mode automatically.

## 3.2 Web Module

The web module was used to prepare the course's information for each instructor. First of all, the instructor course's list and the roster file for each course are imported from Srinakharinwirot registration system to the SWU class attendance system (Fig. 9).

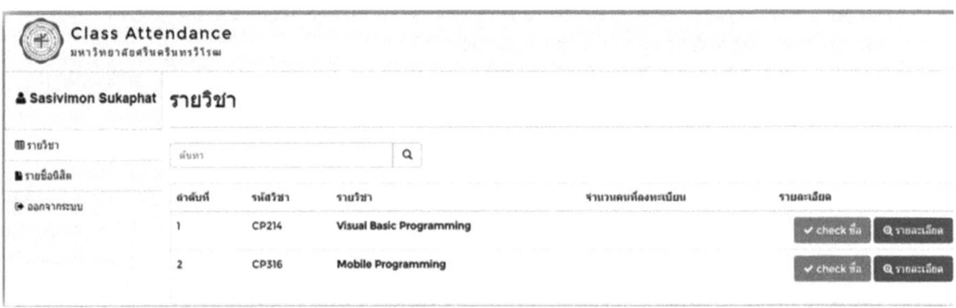


**Fig. 9.** The instructor course's list screen.

Instructors are able to update their roster file such as adding a new student or deleting one that withdrawn from their course, updating the class schedule and also managing the class attendance record of each student manually. Instructors are also able to check the class attendance status of all students and individually (Fig. 10). All of class attendance information can be reported as shown in Fig. 11.

(a)

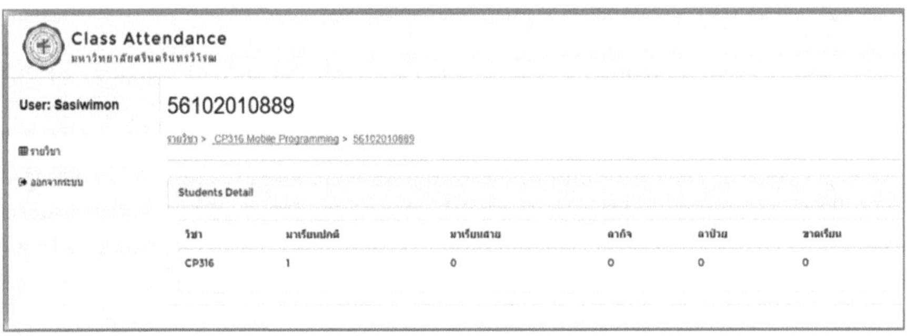


(b)

**Fig. 10.** The example of class attendance reports which show all students attendance status (a) and show individually (b).

| | A | B | C | D | E | F | G | H | I |
|---|---|---|---|---|---|---|---|---|---|
| 1 | สรุปรายการรายงานการเข้าเรียน | | | | | | | | |
| 2 | รหัสวิชา CP316 รายวิชา Mobile Programming | | | | | | | | |
| 3 | ลำดับ | รหัสนิสิต | ชื่อ | section | มาเรียนปกติ | มาเรียนสาย | ลากิจ | ลาป่วย | ขาดเรียน |
| 4 | 1 | 55102010323 | ณัฐพล เชื้อเหลือ | B02 | 1 | 0 | 0 | 0 | 0 |
| 5 | 2 | 56102010889 | Nattajak Rakpongpairoj | B02 | 1 | 0 | 0 | 0 | 0 |
| 6 | 3 | 56102010890 | Taechit Paweeyagoon | B02 | 0 | 0 | 0 | 0 | 0 |
| 7 | 4 | 56102010891 | Tanapat Eeamkajorn | B02 | 0 | 0 | 0 | 0 | 0 |
| 8 | 5 | 56102010893 | Teragoon Sisiwaranggoon | B02 | 0 | 0 | 0 | 0 | 0 |
| 9 | 6 | 56102010894 | Teeraphat Chaipuvaphat | B02 | 0 | 4 | 0 | 0 | 0 |
| 10 | 7 | 56102010895 | Mareerathmongkon | B02 | 2 | 1 | 0 | 1 | 1 |
| 11 | 8 | 56102010896 | นพรัตน์ ศักดิ์สุมลรัตน์ | B02 | 0 | 2 | 0 | 0 | 0 |
| 12 | 9 | 56102010898 | ปริมล ภูมิประโคน | B02 | 0 | 0 | 0 | 0 | 0 |
| 13 | 10 | 56102010899 | นายปัญชร เลิศวิภาดา | B02 | 0 | 0 | 0 | 0 | 0 |
| 14 | 11 | 56102010900 | พงษ์เทพ เดชพล | B02 | 0 | 0 | 0 | 0 | 0 |
| 15 | 12 | 56102010901 | พรพิมพ์ พระนามศรี | B02 | 0 | 0 | 0 | 0 | 0 |
| 16 | 13 | 56102010902 | ภัทรพงศ์ ปีนทอง | B02 | 0 | 0 | 0 | 0 | 0 |
| 17 | 14 | 56102010903 | มลฑกานต์ ปานสาริ | B02 | 0 | 0 | 0 | 0 | 0 |
| 18 | 15 | 56102010904 | มุขรินทร์ ปีนเกตุ | B02 | 0 | 0 | 0 | 0 | 0 |
| 19 | 16 | 56102010905 | รพีพัฒน์ ไชยราบ | B02 | 0 | 0 | 0 | 0 | 0 |
| 20 | 17 | 56102010906 | วรพจน์ เพ็งสว่าง | B02 | 0 | 0 | 0 | 0 | 0 |

**Fig. 11.** The example report of class attendance from one course.

# 4 Experiments Conducted and Discussion

The preliminary experiments were conducted through the second semester of 2016 academic year which performed by 5 subjects of Computer Science Department. The number students who attended our experiment are 78 persons that consists of 10 to 24 persons per course. The roster files of these courses were already prepared in our application. The students must login to the SWU class attendance system before entering their class room. When students entered the class room, they had to tap their smartphone to the instructor smartphone. Each NFC checking process performed less than 1 s with the data transferring rate 421 Kbps. All transferred data which sent from student smartphone to the instructor smartphone are correct and complete and will be further kept in the database server. In order to ensure that smartphone will not interrupt the student while studying, it will be turned in vibrate mode automatically. In case of students who use non-NFC smartphone, the instructor can record their class attendance by using the Web module. Both NFC module and Web module are performed correctly in every function.

In order to evaluate the user's satisfaction, we prepared an e-survey which consists of five categories which are: the performance, the accuracy, the ability to reduce the time for checking class attendance, the simplicity of the system and the necessity to use this system. The results from 28 testers are shown in Table 1.

**Table 1.** The system satisfactory survey results.

| Category | Number of responses | | | | | |
|---|---|---|---|---|---|---|
| | Strongly agree | Agree | Neutral | Disagree | Strongly disagree | Response % |
| Performance | 18 | 6 | 2 | 2 | 0 | 85.71 |
| Accuracy | 19 | 6 | 2 | 1 | 0 | 89.29 |
| Time reducing | 18 | 6 | 2 | 2 | 0 | 85.71 |
| Simplicity | 19 | 6 | 3 | 2 | 0 | 89.29 |
| Necessity | 25 | 1 | 1 | 1 | 0 | 92.86 |
| Average | | | | | | 88.57 |

## 5 Conclusion

This paper presents a prototype class attendance checking application by applying NFC technology in Android smartphone. We develop an application which consists of two main modules: NFC module and web module. The students are able use their smartphone for checking their class attendance by tapping their smartphone to the instructor smartphone. The instructors are able to manage their class information, the student information and also print the report of class attendance information. Our application is able to transfer data with a good speed (421 Kbps). The overall functions are able to perform correctly and completely. In addition, the system satisfactory survey results shown that the average satisfaction is 88.57%.

The SWU class attendance system provides many benefits for the instructor. Not only facilitates in checking class attendance process, our system also informs the instructor if it found the students who tend to have been absent more than the maximum allowance of the class. Moreover the instructors can easily review the students' study progress and provide immediate academic advising if necessary by checking the student academic records in our system.

In the next semester, we plan to extend our system for supporting other mobile platforms by using a small Bluetooth transmitter device, beacon, to identify the students when they attend the class.

## References

Igoe, T., Coleman, D., Jepson, B.: Beginning NFC: Near Field Communication with Arduino, Android, and PhoneGap, 1st edn, p. 12. O'Reilly, Sebastopol (2014)

Faulkner, C.: What is NFC? Everything you need to know (2017). Techradar.com. Accessed 30 Oct 2017

Ortiz, C.E.: An introduction to near-field communication and the contactless communication API (2008). Oracle.com. Accessed 30 Oct 2017

Keene, J.: Samsung scrapping ID cards in favor of NFC-equipped handsets (2012). Theverge.com. Accessed 30 Oct 2017

Bucicoiu, M., Tapus, N.: Easy attendance: location-based authentication for students integrated with Moodle. In: Proceedings of 11th Roedunet International Conference, Siania (2013)
Wei, K.C., Singh, M.M., Osman, H.M.B.: Near field communication interactive learning system (NILES) for blended learning: a pervasive social networking services. In: Proceedings of 2017 Palestinian International Conference on Information and Communication Technology (PICICT), Palestinian (2017)

# Detecting Emotions in Students' Generated Content: An Evaluation of *EmoTect* System

Emmanuel Awuni Kolog(✉)

School of Computing, University of Eastern Finland,
P. O. Box 111, 80101 Joensuu, Finland
emmanuk@uef.fi

**Abstract.** In this paper, an intelligent e-counselling system for automatic detection of emotion in text is evaluated. A support vector machine classifier was used for the development of the e-counselling system, hence we compared the performance of the e-counselling system's classifier with WEKA's Multinomial Naïve-Bayes and J48 decision tree classifiers. While this paper is geared towards ascertaining the efficacy of the various classifiers for classifying emotions in learners' generated text content, this paper also aims to ascertain the performance of the e-counselling system for complementing decision making concerning students in counselling delivery. In building the system, an annotated students' life story corpus was developed and used for the experiment. Therefore, 85% of the total instances of the life stories was used as training data while the remaining 15% was used as test data with sample instances of real-time data from students' textual submission through the e-counselling system. The results of the experiment show that the SVM, implemented in our proposed e-counselling system, is superior over the MNB and J48 classifiers.

**Keywords:** Emotion detection · Text classification · Counselling
Decision making machine learning · Students

## 1 Introduction

Emotions are a conscious experience which can be described as the state of feeling that result in physical and psychological changes. In the arena of counselling, emotion is regarded as one aspect of human behaviour that plays an important role in decision making processes (Jain and Kulkarni 2014). Counsellors are thus expected to devise strategies for understanding the emotional behaviours of their clients. It is well-known that counsellors often rely on the emotional cues of their clients to understand their emotional behaviours (UNESCO 2002). From this perspective, research has shown that counsellors' own state of emotions, in some cases, influence their decision while adjudicating and deciding the emotional state of their clients (Kolog and Montero 2018; Lerner *et al.* 2015).

Although, emotions of students can be expressed in different ways, such as body movement and text, Witten *et al.* (2014) believe that people express much of their emotions in text when they are given the opportunity to write. This considerably


S. K. S. Cheung et al. (Eds.): ICTE 2018, CCIS 843, pp. 235–248, 2018.
https://doi.org/10.1007/978-981-13-0008-0_22

underpins the relevance of recognising emotions in text for decision making. In this view, school counsellors are able to assess the academic performance of their students by linking their change in academic performance to their emotional changes, in order to aid decision making concerning students. Being able to track the emotions of students in text, counsellors and school administrators would be able to prevent suicide, anti-social behaviour, among others as these can be triggered by emotions.

Expression of emotions in text constitutes a semantic component of human communications, which has the tendency to influence one's decision (Kolog *et al.* 2018). Research has shown that a person's state of emotion could influence his or her concentration (Kolakowska *et al.* 2014), task solving (Jung *et al.* 2014) and decision making skills (Kolog *et al.* 2016; Lerner *et al.* 2015). The computational tracking of emotions in text is eminent as it helps to minimise the human influence on decision making process or other related processes. This is particularly important in counselling delivery where emotions are a core component of a communication between counsellors and their clients. Extracting emotions in text is useful as it represents a conduit for understanding the behaviour of humans (Sebe *et al.* 2005).

Given the impact of educational advocacy groups towards campaigning on equal and universal accessibility of education, students' populations have increased exponentially over time (Roser and Ortiz-Opina *et al.* 2017). Therefore, manually tracking and taking decisions of large number of students regarding their emotional behaviour from their textual submissions has become difficult and as well a costly process (Gandomi and Haider 2015; Mohammed 2015). In this era of digital revolution, it is not surprising that people, especially counsellors, are often reluctant to read large volume of students' textual submissions regarding counselling delivery (Kolog *et al.* 2016: Igbokwe *et al.* 2012). These difficulties highlight the need for computational tracking of emotions and this is useful for ensuring efficiency, consistency and effectiveness in text-based emotion analysis.

Despite the fact that emotions can be expressed in text, there is no doubt that text-based media cannot mediate body language and tone of voices fully (Hrastinski, 2006). This represents one of the limitations associated with text-based emotion detection. In the educational setting, nowadays, students prefer to seek counselling anonymously through text (King *et al.* 2006; Kolog 2017a). It is therefore worth noting that students who prefer anonymous counselling do so because of the lack of trust they have in their counsellors (Kolog *et al.* 2015; Glasheen *et al.* 2013; Inman *et al.* 2009).

In this paper, an e-counselling system- hereafter-called- ***EmoTect***- for detection of emotions in text is evaluated. The system was developed using a machine learning support vector machine (SVM). Coupled with the *EmoTect*'s SVM classifier, WEKA's Multinomial Naïve-Bayes (MNB) and J48 decision tree classifiers are evaluated and their performances compared. WEKA is commonly used machine learning software developed by the University of Waikato (Witten *et al.* 2014). While this paper is geared towards ascertaining the performance of the various classifiers in recognising emotions of students in their life stories and real-time textual submissions, this paper aims to ascertain the performance of the EmoTect classifier for complementing decision making in counseling delivery.

## 2 Related Works

Text classifiers, in supervised learning, are algorithms that perform the classification when unseen data is fed into them, and this is based on a training data. There are several machine learning classifiers that have been used widely. Research has shown that the most efficient classifiers for text classification are the support vector machine (SVM), Naïve-Bayes, decision tree and Neural networks. It is for this reason that support vector machine, multinomial Naïve-Bayes and J48 decision tree classifiers are used in this study. The method for extracting feature words, during pre-processing of text, for the classifier to learn to create a model is also an important component for the level of predictive accuracy of text classifiers. In the subsequent paragraphs, this researcher discusses some related works in the area.

Crowston *et al.* (2010) investigated the performance of human-developed natural language processing rules to those inferred with machine learning (ML) technique for coding qualitative data. The study investigated which among the techniques is effective for researchers when coding qualitative data. During the experiment, Crowston *et al.* (2010) used messages from human discourse platforms, such as chats and blogposts. First, Crowston *et al.* (2010) employed two PhD students to manually code the data with predefined themes. Reliability kappa score of 80% after the manual coding was obtained, which prompted the researchers to use the data for training their machine learning classifier. Unlike our approach in this study, 75% of the total data was used for training a ML classifier while the remaining 25% was used for testing of the classifier. On the other hand, the researchers developed and applied human-developed NLP rules to detect and classify the data according to the themes. The results suggest that NLP with ML can be effective in qualitative coding of data than that of the Human-developed rules. Crowston *et al.* (2010) therefore recommended for researchers to code qualitative data with ML techniques instead of manually coding of qualitative data, especially when the data is very large.

An approach for detecting emotions in text was proposed by Obdal and Wang (2014). Obdal and Wang (2014) contextualised their approach for detecting emotions in Chinese language. Their proposed model is based on a supervised machine learning technique. The proposed model is a segment-based fine grained emotion detection. The model applies to the hierarchical structure of sentence, such as dependency relationship. In their model, the emotion label of each dependency sub-tree of a subjective sentence or short text is represented by a hidden variable. The values of the hidden variables are then calculated based on the interactions between variables whose nodes have head-modifier relation in the dependency tree. Obdal and Wang (2014) evaluated their model with datasets from news content, fairly tales, and blogposts. The researchers compared the results from their experiment to some existing approaches. According to the Obdal and Wang (2014), the experimental results from their proposed segment-based model demonstrated some levels of effectiveness.

Suttles and Ide (2013) have experimented the classification of emotions in tweets. The researchers adopted Plutchik's eight basic emotion categories but reformulated the emotion categories into four bi-polar emotions which is based on the Plutchik's wheel of emotions (Plutchik 1980). The rationale for the bi-polar approach was to allow the researchers to treat a multi-class problem of emotions as a binary problem. During the pre-processing of their tweets, the researchers considered and labelled the '*emoticons*' and '*emoji's*' in the tweets with the emotion categories. This is because the researchers believe that 'emoticons' and 'emojis' carry information, which are useful and could significantly contribute to the results of their experiment. Part of the tweets they collected were used as training data while the other part was used as testing data. After experimenting, Suttles and Ide (2013) found that their approach can be used to determine reliable text classifiers.

Balabantaray *et al.* (2012) explored how a machine learning technique could be used to detect emotions in microblogging sites. This is because the researchers believed that microblogging sites are user-generated sites that contain much emotions and attitudinal contents. In this light, the authors performed emotion detection experiments on a collected twitter. Supervised machine learning technique was used. The collected tweets were manually annotated by five trained annotators according to some predefined emotion categories. The authors were more concerned with the annotation process. Therefore, they found the annotators to have agreed strongly for identifying instances of *happiness* and *anger* in the text corpus (tweets). Upon using a multi-class SVM classifier to classify emotions in the tweets, the study found 73.4% accuracy.

## 3 *EmoTect*: Implementation Overview

As stated earlier in this work, EmoTect is a web-based machine learning classification system that has been developed purposely to complement the work of counsellors. The overview of the EmoTect implementation is elaborated in this section. Also, the section presents the role of EmoTect in counselling delivery. Figure 1 is the process diagram of EmoTect in counselling delivery. The figure is elaborated in the subsequent sections.

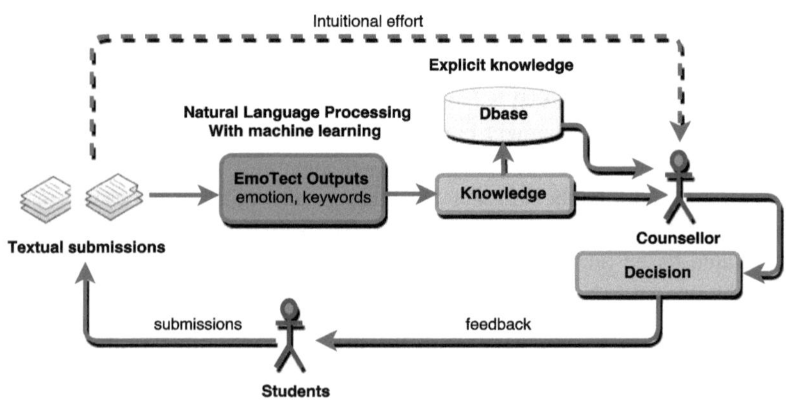


**Fig. 1.** Process diagram for EmoTect in counselling delivery

### 3.1 EmoTect Development

The EmoTect system was developed by considering Peffers *et al.* (2006) design science research (DSR) framework (Kolog 2017a). With this, selected counsellors were intermittently involved in the development of the EmoTect system, particularly in the aspect of the requirement elicitation and the evaluation phases. The various stages of the Peffers *et al.* (2006) framework were broadly categorised into three parts that work in iteration and sequential. These parts are the *requirement elicitation, implementation* and *evaluation (*Kolog 2017a). The EmoTect system was built from implementing a support vector machine learning classifier called *sequential minimum optimisation* (SMO). Much of the developmental process of the EmoTect is covered in Kolog (2017a).

Figure 2 illustrates the context view of EmoTect showing the various processes involved in the data processing. The EmoTect system has two components: *contact counsellor* and *emotion detection.* The "*contact counsellor*" component is the

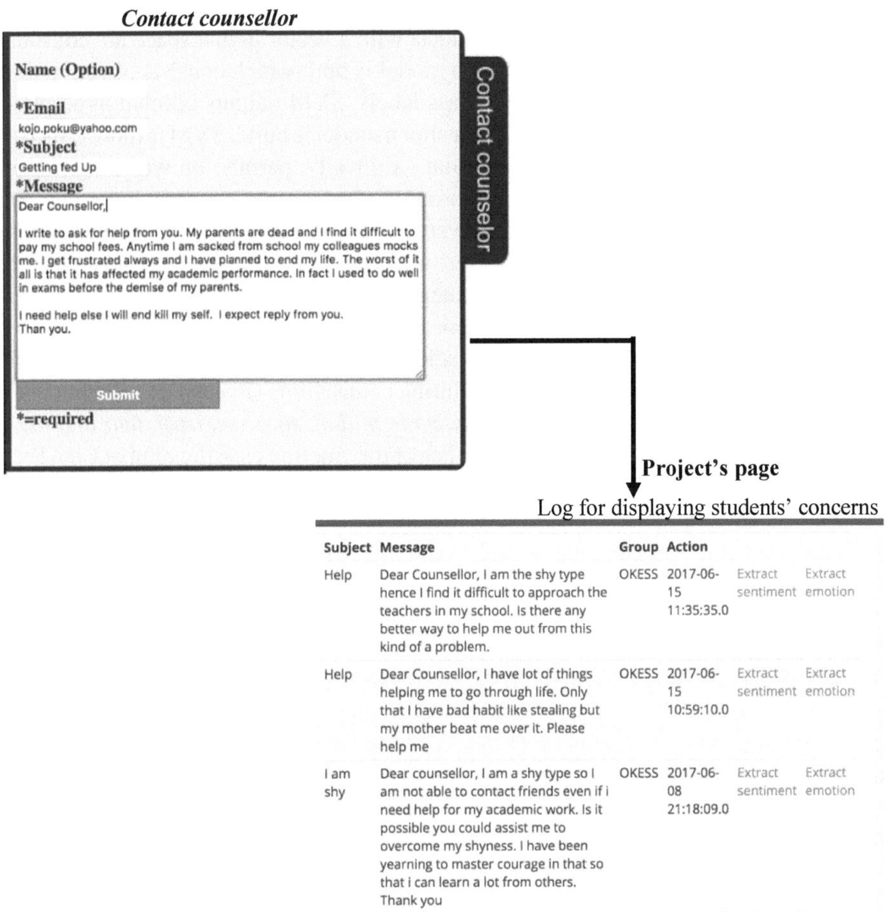


**Fig. 2.** Contact counsellor process from users' page to the project's page

presentation layer that provides opportunity for students to contact their counsellors by text. The textual content of the students' submission is then passed onto the *emotion detection* component for the automatic classification of emotions according to the predefined emotion categories (Plutchik's basic emotions). The result after classifying the emotion is presented in a visual form (see Fig. 5). The "*contact counsellor*" form shown as part of Fig. 2 is expected to appear on users' webpage for students to contact their counsellors. To do this, a user is expected to visit our webpage[1], register, create a database in the system and then generate a JavaScript code to embed in their webpage. This will then appear as a widget form on the users' page. It is from here that the students' submissions are sent to the emotion detection part for processing and visualisation.

A developed *life story* corpus, which is a collection of students' emotional antecedents were collected, annotated and used to train the SVM classifier in this study. Support vector machine is a supervised machine learning algorithm that can be used for both classification and regression problems. The algorithm is discriminative in a sense that it is defined by constructing a hyperplane or a set of hyperplane in a high dimensional space (Hashem and Mabrouk 2014). The hyperplane in the higher-dimensional space is defined as the set of points whose dot products with a vector in that space are constant. When training data is presented to SVM, a model is built which consists of data points chosen from input data space and their class labels. SVM outputs optimal hyperplane which classifies unseen or unclassified data after a model is build. SVM is more effective if more training data are used as training data. Ethically, permission was sought from the students and the school management through informed consent form before the life stories were collected. Also, counsellors were assured of the data protection and those who were unwilling to share the stories were allowed to opt out. Plutchik's (1980) eight basic emotions were used as the emotion categories for the EmoTect classification. This is because Plutchik's basic emotions were confirmed in our previous study, as we conducted a focus group discussion with selected counsellors to understand the basic emotions they often extract from students during counselling. (Kolog 2017a). Plutchik's basic emotions are *anger, disgust, sadness, anticipation, surprise, trust, fear and joy.*

Figure 4 illustrates a visualisation interface of the emotion classification of EmoTect. EmoTect emotion classification undergoes two phases: *training* and *prediction* phases (see Fig. 3). In addition to the collected life stories (LSC), real-time data (RTD) was collected from the system after it had been used by students for counselling. The combined data (LSC and RTD) were labelled with the Plutchik's emotions by selected counsellors. The stories were developed into a corpus– *life story corpus-* which was used in the training of the classifier. To note is that the classifier is freely available for research purpose. Before training the classifier, the stories were pre-processed at different stages, from tokenizing the text, applying Part-of-speech tagging and lemmatising the data for feature extraction before feeding into the SVM classifier. Feature words were then fed into the classifier to create a model for prediction of unseen data.

The second phase is the *prediction*. The prediction phase starts from the sources of the input text, such as the "contact counsellor" form and email sources. This is the stage where users get to interact with the system. Just like the training phase, the input data

[1] www.nlp4counselling.com.

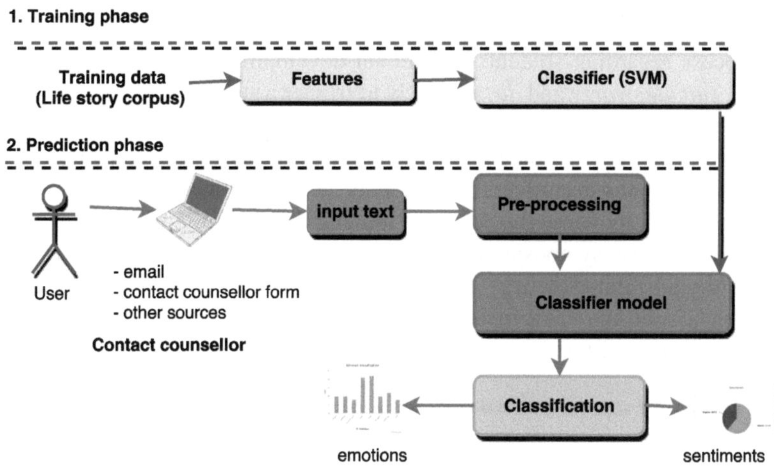


**Fig. 3.** EmoTect's classification process

goes through the same pre-processing stages to extract feature words. The feature words are then fed into the classifier model that was created after the training. The classifier model then predicts the unseen text from users. Detailed work regarding the implementation of EmoTect is presented in Kolog (2017a).

## 3.2 Significance of EmoTect in Counselling

Given the advance in technology, counselling is no longer limited to face-to-face communication, where students have to meet counsellors in person. Some existing ICT tools have shifted the paradigm; students can now receive counselling online. Diverse technologies are available to assist counselling delivery. For instance, artificial intelligence technologies have considerably revolutionised counselling delivery where intelligent and expert systems are able to provide counselling to students without the human intervention. Often, students who are geographically isolated and urgently needing counselling can turn to online media platforms for such services. As explained in Sect. 3.1, the emotion detection component of EmoTect is hosted on our webpage while the "*contact counsellor*" widget form is meant to appear on the webpages of the users.

Apart from the input from the "*contact counsellor*" form, external sources, such as email can be copied and paste into the system for prediction (see Fig. 4). Also, as seen in Fig. 3, text files can be uploaded directly into the system. The textual content of students' submission is then passed on to the emotion detection part for the automatic classification of emotions. The extracted emotions from students' textual submissions are stored for future reference. The intent of implementing this component is to give counsellors, and perhaps school administrators, the opportunity to monitor the emotional changes of their students over a selectable period as illustrated in Fig. 5. Counsellors can use the emotional records of students to match with the performance of their students, thereby making decisions regarding any academic changes or setbacks. The essence of the emotion keywords is to give counsellors a reason to be critical in their decision-making process regarding students' emotional development. For instance, keywords such as *kill, suicide, worry* and *die* are likely to trigger a suspicion that makes it worthwhile for counsellors to consider reviewing the students' submissions.

Counsellors, on knowing the mood or emotional states of their students, are able to make general decisions that affect their students' academic development. For instance, if the state of anger shown in the visualisation graph in Fig. 5 is high, counsellors can take a step to organise symposia on anger management or any related topics for their students. Although, EmoTect was developed based on data collected from schools in Ghana, it can be used anywhere on the globe for the purpose of complementing decision making during counselling.

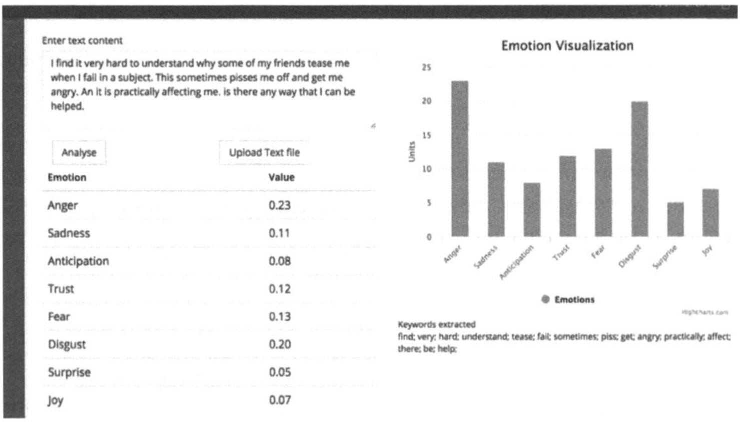


**Fig. 4.** Emotion detection interface

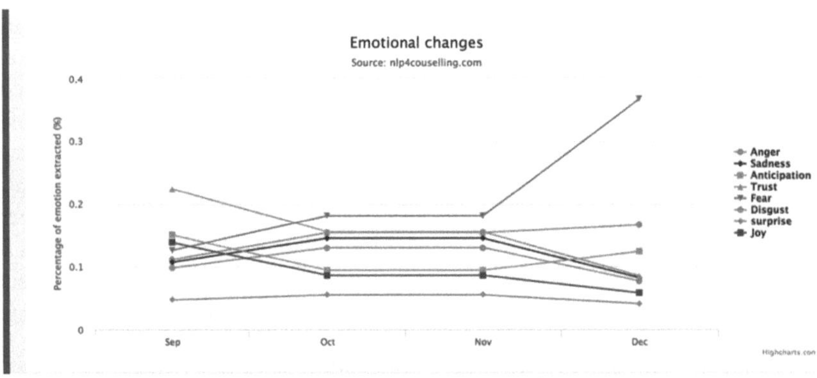


**Fig. 5.** Emotional changes over a selectable period

# 4 Experimental Setup

As part of evaluating EmoTect in this study, this section presents the experimental part of this paper. It reflects on the collection of the text corpus and the annotation strategies used. Also, the classification process is outlined in this section as well.

## 4.1 Corpus and Annotation

Life stories of students were collected through questionnaires (Kolog *et al.* 2014). Students were asked to write about their life stories subjectively. Life story of students, in this study, is defined as students' emotional antecedents that influence their academic development. With this definition, students were made to understand the kinds of stories needed for this study. Lugmayr *et al.* (2016) believe that students are able to express themselves better when they are given opportunity to write about their life stories in text. In addition to the collected life stories (LSC), the system was allowed for use by the counsellors for a period of time. During the contextual evaluation of the system (Kolog 2017a), selected counsellors were allowed to use for a period. After that, sample real-time data (RTD) during the real use of the system was used as part of the total dataset used for the experiment.

The data was first pre-processed for easy annotation. The rationale for the pre-processing was to make the data more suitable for the counsellors to annotate with the emotions categories (Plutchik emotions). In the end, the data were then given out to three selected school counsellors, who have a lot of experience in counselling, to annotate with the emotions. Before the annotation, the annotators were given training on how the annotation exercise should be carried out. After the annotation exercise, the disagreements in the annotated instances of the stories were re-evaluated by the researchers in collaboration with all the three counsellors. Some of the disagreements were later on agreed on consensus. The rationale of this approach was to get a good agreement score for training the classifiers. In the end, a kappa score of 70.5% was obtained, which is a suitable score for training the classifier (Landis and Kouch, 1977).

## 4.2 Classification

To use WEKA for the classification task, the data had to be converted into Attribute-Relation File Format (ARFF)[2]. ARFF file is an ASCII text file that describes a list of instances sharing a set of attributes. ARFF files were developed by the machine learning group at the department of Computer science of the University of Waikato, meant to be used with WEKA machine learning software. Classification algorithms in WEKA can be applied directly to either a dataset or call to a project.

Supervised machine learning technique was used for the classification process in this paper. Just like EmoTect implementation, 15% representing 330 instances (documents) of the total instances of the *life story* corpus (2, 200) was used as §the test data. Additionally, 120 instances of a real-time data were collected from the EmoTect system after

[2] http://www.cs.waikato.ac.nz/ml/weka/arff.html.

it had been used for a period of time with students. Table 1 shows the various instances data that was used in the experiment. Besides EmoTect, as described in Sect. 3, the training data, which is the remaining 85% of the total data, was used to train the various classifiers implemented in WEKA- MNB and J48.

**Table 1.** Test data according to the life stories (LSC) and the real-time data (RTD)

| Dataset | # Test instances |
|---|---|
| LSC | 330 |
| RTD | 120 |
| **LSC + RTD** | **450** |

## 5 Results and Discussion

Coarse-grained evaluation measure was used to determine the performance of the EmoTect's support vector machine, WEKA's Multinomial Naïve-Bayes and J48 decision tree classifiers for detecting emotions in the learner generated data (i.e. LSC + RTD). By this approach, this researcher computed for the *precision, recall* and *f-measure* of each of the individual emotion categories, and as well the overall weighted average. The proportion of the labelled instances of the *gold standard* (test data) that were identified and extracted by the classifiers is referred to as the *recall*. The fraction of the automatically extracted data that is found to be labelled correctly as the gold standard by the classifiers is termed *precision*. The *F-measure*, also termed F-score, is the harmonic mean (average) of the recall and precision measures.

In Table 2, WEKA's Multinomial Naïve-Bayes (MNB) classifier performed poorly for classifying *anger* and *disgust* when taking into account the score of the f-measure. However, the MNB classifier preformed well beyond the acceptable threshold (>70%) in the remaining individual emotion categories. Thus, *Joy* and *surprise* yielded the highest f-measure of 80%. The implication is that the harmonic mean of the recall and precision for the MNB is 80%. Overall, only 70% of the proportion of the human labelled test data-*gold standard*- was actually identified by the WEKA's MNB classifier while

**Table 2.** Evaluation results from WEKA'S MNB classifier

| Dataset | Emotion | Precision (%) | Recall (%) | F-measure (%) |
|---|---|---|---|---|
| LSC + RTD | Anger | 54 | 69 | 57 |
| | Anticipation | 67 | 65 | 66 |
| | Disgust | 58 | 50 | 54 |
| | Fear | 75 | 76 | 74 |
| | Joy | 86 | 74 | 80 |
| | Sadness | 79 | 71 | 75 |
| | Surprise | 70 | 90 | 80 |
| | Trust | 68 | 78 | 73 |
| **Weighted Avg.** | | **69** | **70** | **65** |

69% of the identified emotions categories were correctly predicted by the classifier as the *gold standard*. This implies a low performance of the WEKA's MNB classifier for classifying emotions in the students' generated data which was used in this study.

In Table 3, WEKA'S J48 decision tree performed averagely for predicting *fear, anticipation,* and *disgust* (50% < J48 < 60%) when considering the f-measure score. The remaining emotion categories that yielded a score above the 70% are satisfactory in terms of the predictions against the *gold standard*. From Table 3, the overall performance of the J48 decision tree classifier is 63% recall, 66% precision and 66% f-measure. In this light, the overall performance of the J48 decision tree is slightly below the acceptable threshold and the performance is considered mediocre. This implies that 63% of the test data was correctly identified as the labelled data from the *gold standard* while 66% of the identified data was correct as the gold standard.

**Table 3.** Evaluation results of WEKA's J48 decision tree

| Dataset | Emotion | Precision (%) | Recall (%) | F-measure (%) |
|---|---|---|---|---|
| LSC + RTD | Anger | 62 | 77 | 70 |
| | Anticipation | 58 | 60 | 59 |
| | Disgust | 55 | 50 | 53 |
| | Fear | 63 | 55 | 58 |
| | Joy | 72 | 68 | 70 |
| | Sadness | 71 | 82 | 75 |
| | Surprise | 80 | 63 | 71 |
| | Trust | 70 | 54 | 62 |
| **Weighted Avg.** | | **66** | **63** | **66** |

From Table 4, the performance of the EmoTect's SVM with respect to the individual's emotion categories was also ascertained. Except for the *trust* and *joy* categories whose f-measure scores were slightly below the threshold of the 70%, the rest of the emotion categories were satisfactorily predicted, of which their f-measures are more than the threshold of the 70%. However, the overall performance of the EmoTect's SVM yielded 75% precision, 70% recall and 73% f-measure. This implies that, the performance of the EmoTect's SVM classifier was superior over the WEKA's MNB and the J48 decision tree. What this means is that 70% of the test data was correctly identified as the gold standard data while 75% of the identified data (compared with the test data) was correct when comparing with the gold standard data. The harmonic mean (average) of the recall and precision is 73%. It is therefore clear that EmoTect, our proposed system, produced the best performance in terms of the detection of emotions in the learners generated content as against the MNB and the J48 decision tree implemented in WEKA.

As reported in the earlier paragraphs of this section, the performance of each of the classifiers varied but slightly. By comparing the classifiers, the overall performance of the EmoTect's SVM was found to be superior over the WEKA's J48 and the MNB classifiers. For having established the performance of the various classifiers in terms of the detection of emotions in text, there is the need to look into what might have accounted for these performances. One of the key areas to look at is the data which was used in the

**Table 4.** Evaluation results from the SVM implemented in EmoTect

| Dataset | Emotion | Precision (%) | Recall (%) | F-measure (%) |
|---|---|---|---|---|
| LSC + RTD | Anger | 79 | 67 | 73 |
| | Anticipation | 80 | 65 | 73 |
| | Disgust | 70 | 72 | 71 |
| | Fear | 80 | 70 | 75 |
| | Joy | 67 | 68 | 68 |
| | Sadness | 74 | 72 | 73 |
| | Surprise | 80 | 71 | 76 |
| | Trust | 66 | 73 | 69 |
| **Weighted Avg.** | | **75** | **70** | **73** |

experiment. The life stories were collected from students in three senior high schools of Ghana where English language is not the native language. Based on this, some challenges associated with the use of emotion words to describe or fit into a particular situation was observed. Although, the British English is the official language of instruction in schools, students, at that level of their studies struggled to use appropriate emotions words to describe situations. For instance, if student could write "*I wil kel masef*" instead of "*I will kill myself*", it became difficult for the annotators to figure out what the student meant. In the same vein, EmoTect algorithm picks the features as it is and trains the classifier with it. This, we assumed might have contributed to the performance of the various classifiers.

In addition, some of the students understood their life stories as life challenges, so we deduced that most of the extracted features were negative rather than positive. From close observation, this researcher believes that to achieve higher accuracy, more emotionally-charged data is required. For this reason, this researcher will collect more data to train the system as it is still being used by school counsellors. Despite the aforementioned challenges in the data content, we conclude that a natural language processing with machine learning techniques can be an effective tool for tracking emotions in text if they are implemented efficiently.

In counselling, emotion is thought to represent useful linguistic information that contributes to human communication. As revealed, the performance of the EmoTect system, comparing with WEKA classifiers and with human way of analysing emotions in text, is suitable for tracking emotions in text thereby complementing the work of school counsellors in understanding the emotional behaviours of their students. These findings are consistent with our previous study where the EmoTect system was evaluated with end-users in their settings (Kolog 2017a). From that study, counsellors were enthused about the capabilities and the aesthetic view of the EmoTect system and further recommended for improvement. Subsequently and before this study, the system was afterwards improved in terms of the efficacy of the output.

## 6 Conclusion

In this paper, we have demonstrated how a supervised machine learning technique could be used to classify emotions in students' textual submissions for counselling. This was investigated through our intelligent e-counselling system for emotion detection in text. The demonstration was conducted through an experiment where the EmoTect's classifier (SVM) was compared with WEKA's Multinomial naïve-Bayes and J48 decision tree classifiers. Since EmoTect is a system to complement the work of counsellors in their decision making of students, the rationale of this study is to determine the efficacy and the performance of the EmoTect classification algorithm. Overall, EmoTect's SVM performed slightly better than the WEKA's J48 and MNB classifiers in terms of the classification of emotions in students' generated content. This researcher further looked into the reason that might have accounted for the performance of the classifier. Based on the findings, this researcher concludes that more emotionally charged students' life stories are required to increase the quantity of the training data, in order to improve its accuracy of the emotion detection component of the e-counselling system-EmoTect.

## References


Balabantaray, R.C., Mohammad, M., Sharma, N.: Multi-class twitter emotion classification: a new approach. Int. J. Appl. Inf. Syst. **4**(1), 48–53 (2012)

Crowston, K., Liu, X., Allen, E.E.: Machine learning and rule-based automated coding of qualitative data. Proc. Am. Soc. Inf. Sci. Technol. **47**, 1–2 (2010)

Gandomi, A., Haider, M.: Beyond the hype: big data concepts, methods, and analytics. Int. J. Inf. Manag. **35**(2), 137–144 (2015)

Glasheen, K., Campbell, M., Shochet, I.: Opportunities and challenges: school guidance counsellors' perceptions of counselling students online. Aust. J. Guid. Couns. **23**, 222–235 (2013)

Hashem, E., Mabrouk, M.: A study of support vector machine algorithm for liver disease diagnosis. Am. J. Intell. Syst. **4**(1), 9–14 (2014)

Hrastinski, S.: Introducing an informal synchronous medium in a distance learning course: how is participation affected? Internet High. Educ. **9**(2), 117–131 (2006)

Igbokwe, J.C., Obidike, N.A., Ezeji, E.C.: Influence of electronic media on reading ability of school children (2012)

Inman, A., Ngoubene-Atioky, A., Ladany, N., Mack, T.: School counselors in international school: critical issues and challenges. Int. J. Adv. Couns. **31**, 80–99 (2009)

Jain, M.C., Kulkarni, V.Y.: TexEmo: conveying emotion from text-the study. Int. J. Comput. Appl. **86**(4), 43–49 (2014)

Jung, N., Wranke, C., Hamburger, K., Knauff, M.: How emotions affect logical reasoning: evidence from experiments with mood-manipulated participants, spider phobics, and people with exam anxiety. Front. Psychol. **5**, 570 (2014)

King, R., Bambling, M., Reid, W., Thomas, I.: Telephone and online counselling for young people: a naturalistic comparison of session outcome, session impact and therapeutic alliance. Couns. Psychother. Res. **6**(3), 175–181 (2006)

Kołakowska, A., Landowska, A., Szwoch, M., Szwoch, W., Wróbel, M.R.: Emotion recognition and its applications. In: Hippe, Z.S., Kulikowski, J.L., Mroczek, T., Wtorek, J. (eds.) Human-Computer Systems Interaction: Backgrounds and Applications 3. AISC, vol. 300, pp. 51–62. Springer, Cham (2014). https://doi.org/10.1007/978-3-319-08491-6_5

Kolog, E.A.: Contextuallising the application of human language technologies for counselling. Ph.D. thesis, University of Eastern Finland (2017a)

Kolog, E.A., Montero, C.S.: Towards automated e-counselling system based on counsellors' emotion perception. Educ. Inf. Technol. **23**(2), 911–933 (2018)

Kolog, E.A., Montero, C.S., Toivonen, T.: Using machine learning for sentiment and social influence analysis in text. In: Rocha, A., Guarda, T. (eds.) Proceedings of the International Conference on Information Technology & Systems (ICITS 2018). AISC, vol. 721, pp. 453–463. Springer, Cham (2018). https://doi.org/10.1007/978-3-319-73450-7_43

Kolog, E.A., Sutinen, E.,Vanhalakka-Ruoho, M.: E-counselling implementation: students' life stories and counselling technologies in perspective. Int. J. Educ. Dev. Using Inf. Commun. Technol. **10**(3), 32 (2014)

Kolog, E.A., Sutinen, E., Vanhalakka-Ruoho, M., Sohunen, J., Anohah, E.: Using unified theory of acceptance and use of technology model to predict students' behavioral intention to adopt and use e - counseling in Ghana. Int. J. Mod. Educ. Comput. Sci. **7**(11), 1–11 (2015)

Kolog, E.A., Montero, S.C., Sutinen, E.: Annotation agreement of emotions in text: the influence of counselors' emotional state on their emotion perception. In: Proceeding of International Conference on Advanced Learning Technologies (ICALT), pp. 357–359. IEEE (2016)

Landis, J., Kouch, G.: The measurement of observer agreement for categorical data. Biometrics **33**(1), 159–174 (1977)

Lerner, J., Li, Y., Valdesolo, P., Kassam, K.S.: Emotion and decision making. Annu. Rev. Psychol. **66**, 799–823 (2015)

Lugmayr, A., Sutinen, E., Suhonen, J., Sedano, C., Hlavacs, H., Montero, C.: Serious storytelling – a first definition and review. Multimed. Tools Appl. **76**, 1–27 (2016)

Mohammad, S.M.: Sentiment analysis: detecting valence, emotions, and other affectual states from text. In: Emotion measurement, pp. 201–238 (2015)

Odbal, S., Wang, Z.: Segment-based fine-grained emotion detection for chinese text. In: CLP, p. 52 (2014)

Peffers, K., Tuunanen, T., Gengler, C.E., Rossi, M., Hui, W., Virtanen, V., Bragge, J.: The design science research process: a model for producing and presenting information systems research. In: Proceedings of the First International Conference on Design Science Research in Information Systems and Technology, pp. 83–106 (2006)

Plutchik, R.: Emotion: Theory, Research, and Experience: Theories of Emotion, vol. 1, p. 399. Academic Press, New York (1980)

Roser, M., Ortiz-Ospina, E.: Global Rise of Education (2017). From WorldInData.org: https://ourworldindata.org/global-rise-of-education. Retrieved 5 July 2017

Sebe, N., Cohen, I., Gevers, T., Huang, T.S.: Multimodal approaches for emotion recognition: a survey. In: Proceedings of SPIE, vol. 5670, pp. 56–67 (2005)

Suttles, J., Ide, N.: Distant supervision for emotion classification with discrete binary values. In: Gelbukh, A. (ed.) Computational Linguistics and Intelligent Text Processing (CICLing 2013). LNCS, vol. 7817, pp. 121–136. Springer, Heidelberg (2013). https://doi.org/10.1007/978-3-642-37256-8_11

UNESCO: Technical and vocational education and training in the 21st century: New roles and challenges for guidance and counselling (2002)

Witten, I.H., Frank, E., Hall, M.A., Pal, C.J.: Data mining: practical machine learning tools and techniques (2014)

# The Acceptance of Using Open-Source Learning Platform (Moodle) for Learning in Hong Kong's Higher Education

Ching-Hong Luk[1(✉)], Kwan-Keung Ng[2(✉)], and Wai-Ming Lam[1(✉)]

[1] School of Business and Hospitality Management, Caritas Institute of Higher Education, Tseung Kwan O, New Territories, Hong Kong, China
{eluk,plam}@cihe.edu.hk
[2] University of Sunderland, Central, Hong Kong, China
steven.ng@sunderland.edu.hk

**Abstract.** Using online learning platforms for teaching and learning is common in this generation and development is driving innovation. The advances of information technology have significantly changed ways of teaching and learning in higher education. Online learning platforms take many forms depending on a particular application. In addition to Blackboard, Moodle is one of the most popular online learning platforms nowadays worldwide. Moodle is a learning platform designed to provide educators, administrators and learners with a single robust, secure and integrated system to create personalized learning environments. In addition, the acceptance of the students to the online learning platform will affect the higher education information and the construction of modernization of education in a certain extent. A number of studies have indicated that the successful pedagogical use of technology depends on students' attitudes and acceptance towards technology. Therefore, the prediction of students' attitude and acceptance towards online learning platform is crucial for the teaching and learning quality in education. This study is to investigate the acceptance of using online learning platform, i.e. Moodle by using the augmented version of TAM model (A-TAM) to investigate their behavioral intention and use behavior of Moodle for their learning, as Moodle is one of the most common online learning platform in Hong Kong and there are a significant proportion of Institutes adopting Moodle in Hong Kong higher education. In other words, this study investigates how perceived usefulness, perceived ease of use, attitude towards behavior and subjective norm affect behavioral intention so as to actual behavior of using Moodle in Hong Kong higher education.

**Keywords:** A-TAM · Online learning platform · Open-source Learning management system · Moodle · Higher education

## 1 Introduction

Information technology (IT) in education is still a main concern. There are lots of studies in the information technology adoption and acceptance by using Unified Theory of


S. K. S. Cheung et al. (Eds.): ICTE 2018, CCIS 843, pp. 249–257, 2018.
https://doi.org/10.1007/978-981-13-0008-0_23

Acceptance and Use of Technology (UTAUT) or Technology Acceptance Model (TAM) models (Escobar-Rodriguez and Monge-Lozano 2012; Cornell et al. 2011; Dasgupta et al. 2002). IT facilitates teaching and learning process, besides the availability of online courses, it also supports and assists student learning (Martin and Serrano 2009; Romero et al. 2008). As most of the higher education institutions are using web-based instruction system for teaching, the development of e-learning is getting rapid. Advances in technology have enabled new forms of information processing and created new structures, which will complement universities and transform them. Therefore, virtual classrooms become very common when new technologies are included in the University context. This is currently bringing together the possibilities of teaching-learning based upon a communication system using computers (Ciudad 2010).

The ways teachers and students learn have been changed by E-learning platforms (Fillion et al. 2007). This change enables students to manage their learning process, while the teacher's role is orchestrating and guiding students their education (Ciudad 2010). Therefore, nowadays, university teachers need to have modifications in the subjects and methodology involved in teaching and learning. Students have to actively collaborate in learning, participating and collaborating with their teachers (Clausen 2005; Reichert and Tauch 2003). In recent years, e-learning platforms are becoming common and there is a number of these e-learning platforms. Some require paying for access to the software, while in others this is not required. One of the most commonly used e-learning platforms is the Moodle platform, it offers different kinds of services, such as chat, discussion forums, questionnaires, etc. it is easy to use and simple for teachers to change or increase its contents. Students can gradually connect to the information as the course progresses (Bergeren et al. 2005; Rice 2006).

Since a number of studies used UTAUT and TAM models to investigate the acceptance of using technology in various fields, including higher education, this study is going to use augmented version of TAM (A-TAM) model, which eliminates the limitations of TAM to measure the social and other control factors affecting the students' acceptance of using technology in higher education. The continuous evolution of TAM results in the inclusion of additional constructs related to the social influence (Venkatesh and Davis 2000). A-TAM gives a higher priority to the social factors, e.g. social norm especially in IT (Compeau and Higgins 1991; Mathieson 1991; Moore and Benbasat 1991). In this study, the result shows that the seven hypotheses are supported. In other words, perceived usefulness, perceived ease of use, attitude towards behavior and subjective norm affect behavioral intention so as to actual behavior of using Moodle in Hong Kong higher education.

## 2 Literature Review

### 2.1 Benefits of Open Source Learning Management System (LMS)

A Learning Management System (LMS) is a software package enabling managing and delivering learning content and resources to students. Most LMS systems are using web-based platform to facilitate access to learning content and administration at anytime and anywhere. Most of the LMS applications allow student registration, the tracking and delivery of e-learning courses and content. They may also facilitate the management of instructor-led training classes. In addition, the LMS allows learner self-service, facilitating self-enrolment, and access to courses. Generally, LMS can be categorized into two categories, namely Open Source LMS and proprietary LMS. OSS refers to software developed, tested or improved through public collaboration and distributed with the idea that it must be shared with others, ensuring open future collaboration (Feller and Fitzgerald 2000). The advantages of OSS include that it is free and it can be adapted and extended to meet individuals' needs. The advantage to educational institutes is that what they can gain from OSS is to profile e-learning according to a clear vision of the educational methods one plans to apply.

Open Source has facilitated a strong new way to generate knowledge and economic value. It is at usually little or no cost and available to anyone. It also offers users the choice to learn from, probe, modify, and customize the software, harnessing the power of many small contributions from a large network of individuals, to suit their needs. On the other hand, they are affordable software for individuals, enterprise and government, universal access through mass software rollout without costly licensing implication, ability to customize software to local languages and cultures, lowered barriers to entry for software businesses and participation in global network of software development (Machado and Thompson 2004). All these explain the reason why there is an increasing number of institutes using Open Source LMS in their programmes.

## 2.2 The Use of Learning Management Systems (LMs) in Learning Environments

Recently, there is a growing introduction of LMSs in various levels of schooling. Most university students nowadays have their own laptop computers with Internet connection and there is an increasing number of students have used an LMS in school. In spite of the increase in LMS adoption in schools and universities, discussion has been expressed to whether LMSs are being used as effective learning tools or merely as electronic document repositories (Badge et al. 2005; Hall 2006). The successful implementations of LMSs depend on providing training and support for instructors, the level of student active engagement and student and instructor satisfaction with the LMS used (Hall 2006). Therefore, the user perspective is critical to examine the implementation of LMSs and to evaluate their success.

Francis and Raftery (2005) distinguish among three e-learning modes of engagement, depending on depth in LMS usage and growing levels of complexity. The first mode is defined as baseline course administration and learner support and it illustrates situations where an LMS is used only to carry out course administration, distribute course information and most learning activities occur in traditional classroom settings. The second mode is blended learning with crucial enhancements to learning and teaching processes. This particular mode facilitates combining face-to-face classes with a more widespread use of features such as communication tools, enhancing interaction between tutor and students or among students; collaboration tools that help students in group works and allow for the sharing of learning resources; assessment tools, including the completion of quiz tests, submission of graded assignments, and the provision of feedback on work submitted as well as the inclusion of learning content that allows each student to independently continue their learning at their own pace and specific interest. The third mode is talking about a fully-fledged online course or module where most learning will take place using the LMS, with extensive use of the tools described above and only marginal face-to-face interaction.

### 2.3 Moodle

Moodle is a Learning Management System (LMS) as well as a course management system. Educators can use this free web application to create effective online sites. It allows very large deployments and a large number of students. Nowadays, there are many institutions using it as their platform to conduct fully online courses, while some use it simply to augment face-to-face courses, classified as blended learning. Many Moodle users use the many activity modules, such as discussion forums, databases and so on to build richly collaborative communities of learning around their subject matter. Others prefer to use it to access learning using assignments or quizzes and deliver content to students (Moodle 2017).

## 3 Methodology

This study used augmented version of TAM (A-TAM) model (Taylor and Todd 1995) to investigate the relationships between the constructs of perceived usefulness, perceived ease of use, attitude towards behaviour, subjective norm, behaviour intention and actual behaviour in higher education context. The construct of perceived behavioural control was not adopted in this study as Sawang et al. (2014) suggested a non-significant effect of perceived behavioural control on intention. In addition, this construct was mainly adopted in the Theory of Planned Behaviour (TPB) (Ajzen 1991). Meanwhile, this construct was defined as "the perceived ease or difficulty of performing the behaviour and assumed to reflect past experience as well as anticipated impediments and obstacles" (Doll and Ajzen 1992), which was already included in the construct of "perceived ease of use" in our A-TAM model. Therefore, A-TAM model is a hybrid model of TAM and TPB (Taylor and Todd 1995).

There are SEVEN research hypotheses which are listed as follows (as shown in Fig. 1):

H1: Students' PEU has a significant influence on students' PU for using Moodle.
H2: Students' PU has a significant influence on students' ATB for using Moodle.
H3: Students' PEU has a significant influence on students' ATB for using Moodle.
H4: Students' PU has a significant influence on students' BI for using Moodle.
H5: Students' ATB has a significant influence on students' BI for using Moodle.
H6: Students' SN has a significant influence on students' BI for using Moodle.
H7: Students' BI has a significant influence on students' AB for using Moodle

A 5-point Likert-type scale was used in the questionnaires; total 132 questionnaires were collected from Caritas Institute of Higher Education and Caritas Bianchi College of Careers, and 4 questionnaires were unusable due to incomplete responses; as a result, there were 129 valid data input via Partial Least Squares regression (PLS) software.

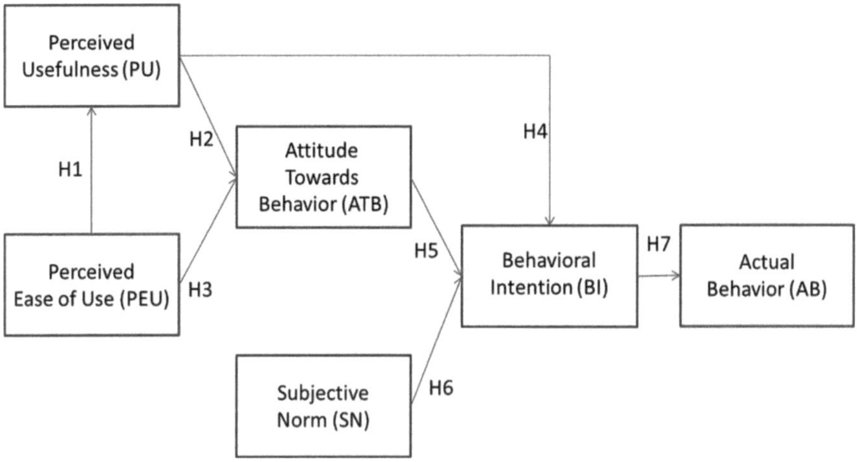


**Fig. 1.** Research model on the acceptance of using open-source learning platform (Moodle) for learning in Hong Kong's Higher Education

# 4 Research Findings

In these 129 valid responses, the gender percentage is quite even, i.e. 64 are male students and 65 are female; besides, 68 are local students and 61 are non-local students. Besides, Perceived Usefulness (PU), Perceived Ease of Use (PEU), Attitude Towards Behaviour (ATB), Subjective Norm (SN), Behavioural Intention (BI), and Actual Behaviour (AB) have received quite similar mean scores from 3.52 to 3.69; however, in the questions of SN2 "*Other students think that it is good to use Moodle*" and AB2 "*I actively participated and interact with others in Moodle in the last semester*" have received the lowest mean scores 3.46 and 3.44 respectively among these questions as shown in Table 1.

**Table 1.** Summary of students' responses on using Moodle (Mean and Standard Deviation [S.D.])

| | **PU** | PU1 | PU2 | PU3 | PU4 | PU5 | **ATB** | ATB1 | ATB2 | ATB3 | **SN** | SN1 | SN2 | SN3 | SN4 |
|---|---|---|---|---|---|---|---|---|---|---|---|---|---|---|---|
| **MEAN** | **3.64** | 3.71 | 3.58 | 3.70 | 3.62 | 3.57 | **3.59** | 3.59 | 3.72 | 3.47 | **3.56** | 3.49 | 3.46 | 3.67 | 3.64 |
| **S.D.** | **0.97** | 0.96 | 1.01 | 0.96 | 0.95 | 0.98 | **1.01** | 0.96 | 1.04 | 1.02 | **0.95** | 0.98 | 0.93 | 0.96 | 0.94 |
| | **PEU** | PEU1 | PEU2 | PEU3 | PEU4 | PEU5 | **BI** | BI1 | BI2 | BI3 | **AB** | AB1 | AB2 | AB3 | |
| **MEAN** | **3.69** | 3.73 | 3.71 | 3.67 | 3.58 | 3.74 | **3.67** | 3.61 | 3.78 | 3.61 | **3.52** | 3.63 | 3.44 | 3.50 | |
| **S.D.** | **0.97** | 0.93 | 1.01 | 0.96 | 0.92 | 1.02 | **1.02** | 1.00 | 1.05 | 1.02 | **1.02** | 1.05 | 1.05 | 0.98 | |

Regarding the reliability and validity test results are shown in Table 2, the score of AVE (Average Variance Extracted) and Cronbach's Alpha are higher than 0.5 and 0.7 respectively in both analyses; therefore, the captioned results indicate the construction of the questionnaires and responses are reliable and acceptable as shown in Table 2. Regarding the correlation analysis, the correlation values among these six constructs are reported in Table 3:

**Table 2.** Cornbach's alpha and the AVE (Average Variance Extracted) analysis of using Moodle

| | AVE | Composite reliability | R square | Cronbach's alpha | Communality | Redundancy |
|---|---|---|---|---|---|---|
| PU | 0.825767 | 0.959507 | 0.712273 | 0.947274 | 0.825767 | 0.586222 |
| PEU | 0.759112 | 0.940259 | | 0.920357 | 0.759112 | |
| ATB | 0.826240 | 0.934465 | 0.820836 | 0.894633 | 0.826240 | 0.227841 |
| SN | 0.754257 | 0.924664 | | 0.891307 | 0.754257 | |
| BI | 0.861392 | 0.949088 | 0.800876 | 0.919487 | 0.861392 | 0.166840 |
| AB | 0.795550 | 0.921094 | 0.740538 | 0.871984 | 0.795550 | 0.582950 |

**Table 3.** Latent variable correlations analysis of students' behaviour intention for using Moodle

| | PU | PEU | ATB | SN | BI | AB |
|---|---|---|---|---|---|---|
| PU | 1 | | | | | |
| PEU | 0.843963 | 1 | | | | |
| ATB | 0.814911 | 0.900129 | 1 | | | |
| SN | 0.830488 | 0.862679 | 0.851388 | 1 | | |
| BI | 0.798817 | 0.860816 | 0.851761 | 0.864648 | 1 | |
| AB | 0.825764 | 0.879601 | 0.880938 | 0.861783 | 0.860545 | 1 |

Regarding the coefficients to all six constructs, i.e. PU, PEU, ATB, SN to Behavioural Intention (BI) and BI to Actual Behaviour (AB), are all over 0.7, please refer to the Partial Least Squares Structural Equation Modelling (PLS-SEM) as shown in Fig. 2:

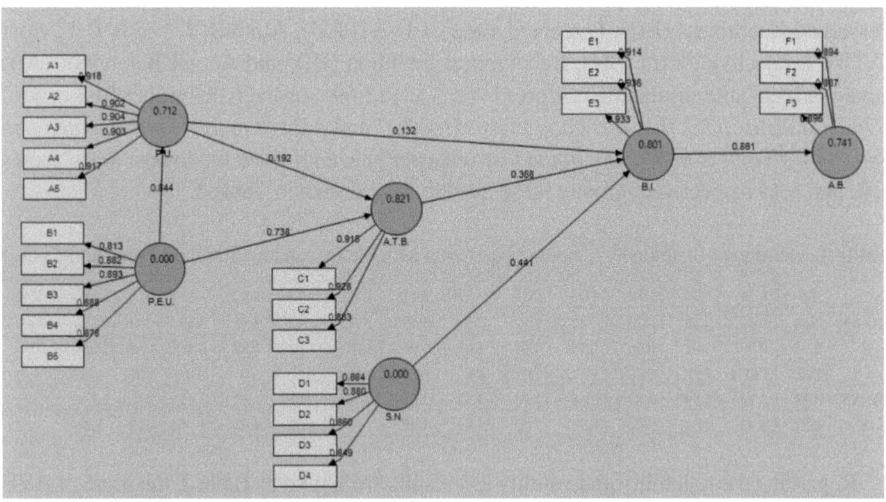


**Fig. 2.** PLS-SEM path analysis of the acceptance of using open-source learning platform (Moodle) for learning in Hong Kong's Higher Education.

Furthermore, a bootstrapping analysis via SmartPLS programme from 129 responses to 5000 samples has been run in order to assess the significance of the path coefficients among these six constructs are listed in Table 4:

**Table 4.** Research test results of students' behaviour intention for using Moodle (Beta value & T-statistics)

| FACTOR → BI (Behavioural Intention) | Beta value | T-statistics |
|---|---|---|
| H1: Perceived Ease of Use (PEU) → Perceived Usefulness (PU) | 0.844 | 22.784870 |
| H2: Perceived Usefulness (PU) → Attitude Towards Behaviour (ATB) | 0.192 | 2.374385 |
| H3: Perceived Ease of Use (PEU) → Attitude Towards Behaviour (ATB) | 0.738 | 9.663791 |
| H4: Perceived Usefulness (PU) → Behavioural Intention (BI) | 0.132 | 1.345661 |
| H5: Attitude Towards Behaviour (ATB) → Behavioural Intention (BI) | 0.368 | 3.490206 |
| H6: Subjective Norm (SN) → Behavioural Intention (BI) | 0.441 | 4.556960 |
| H7: Behavioural Intention (BI) → Actual Behaviour (AB) | 0.861 | 32.473308 |

According to the Beta Value and T-Statistics listed on the above table, seven hypotheses are supported by the research results of both analyses. Perceived East of Use (PEU) has a strong influence on Perceived Usefulness (PU) on Moodle, Perceived East of Use (PEU) also has strong impact on Attitude Towards Behaviour (ATB); besides, Attitude Towards Behaviour (ATB) and Subjective Norm (SN) have demonstrated significant influences on college students' Behavioural Intention (BI) toward using Moodle. As a result, Behavioural Intention (BI) also demonstrates a strong influence on students' Actual Behaviour (AB) as well.

## 5 Limitation and Further Research

Since this is a preliminary research on finding students' behavioural intention and actual behaviour on using Moodle for their studies, the sample size is limited. In addition, most of the respondents are studying in business and hospitality management and come from two institutes. It is recommended that further research would be conducted in a wider based, and respondents should be invited from other schools/departments, and other higher education institutes as well. Moreover, researchers also recommend that other open source learning platforms should also be investigated which platform would mostly influence students' learning behavioural intention.

## 6 Conclusion

This study is to investigate the acceptance of using online learning platform, i.e. Moodle by using the augmented version of TAM model (A-TAM) to investigate their behavioural intention and using behaviour of Moodle. The result shows that all six constructs, namely Perceived Usefulness (PU), Perceived Ease of Use (PEU), Attitude Towards Behaviour (ATB), Subjective Norm (SN), Behavioural Intention (BI), and Actual Behaviour (AB) received similar above average mean scores from 3.52 to 3.69. In addition, the analyses show that PEU has a significant influence on PU and ATB; PU has a significant influence on ATB and BI; ATB has a significant influence on BI; SN has a significant influence on BI; and finally, BI has a significant influence on AB.

In other words, Perceived Usefulness, Perceived Ease of Use, Attitude Towards Behaviour and Subjective Norm affect Behavioural Intention so as to Actual Behaviour of using Moodle in Hong Kong higher education.

However, in order to improve the generalization of the study, future study should be extended to students in other disciplines and various types of open source learning platforms can be examined.

## References


Ajzen, I.: The theory of planned behavior. Organ. Behav. Hum. Decis. Process. **50**, 179–211 (1991)

Badge, J.L., Cann, A.J., Scott, J.: e-Learning versus e-teaching: seeing the pedagogic wood for the technological trees. Biosci. Educ. **5**, 1–11 (2005). http://www.bioscience.heacademy.ac.uk/journal/vol5/beej-5-6.pdf

Bergeren, A., Burgos, D., Fontana, J.M., Hinkelman, D., Hung, V., Hursh, A.: Practical and pedagogical issues for teacher adoption of IMS learning design standards in Moodle LMS. Journal of Interactive Media in Education, 2 (2005)

Ciudad, A.: Teaching innovation and use of the ICT in the teaching-learning process within the new framework of the EHEA, by jeans of Moodle platform. Am. J. Bus. Educ. **3**(13), 13–19 (2010)

Clausen, T.: Undergraduate engineering education challenged by de Bologna declaration. IEEE Trans. Educ. **48**(2), 213–315 (2005)

Compeau, D.R., Higgins, C.A.: A social cognitive theory perspective on individual reactions to computing technology. In: Proceedings of The Twelfth International Conference on Information Systems, University of Minnesota, pp. 187–198 (1991)

Cornell, R.M., Eining, M.M., Hu, P.J.: The effects of process accountability on individuals' use of a familiar technology. J. Inf. Syst. **25**(1), 109–128 (2011)

Dasgupta, S., Granger, M., McGarry, N.: User acceptance of r-collaboration technology: an extension of the technology acceptance model. Group Decis. Negot. **11**, 87–100 (2002)

Doll, J., Ajzen, I.: Accessibility and stability of predictors in the theory of planned behavior. J. Pers. Soc. Psychol. **63**(5), 754–765 (1992)

Escobar-Rodriguez, T., Monge-Lozano, P.: The acceptance of Moodle technology by business administration students. Comput. Educ. **58**(2012), 1085–1093 (2012)

Feller, J., Fitzerald, B.: A framework analysis of the open source software development paradigm. University College Cork, Ireland (2000). http://www.josephfeller.com/publications/ICIS2000.pdf

Fillion, G., Limayem, M., Laferrière, T., Mantha, R.: Integrating ICT into higher education: a study of onsite vs online students' perceptions. Acad. Educ. Leadersh. J. **11**(2), 45–72 (2007)
Francis, R., Raftery, J.: Blended learning landscapes. Brookes eJ. Learn. Teach. **1**(3), 1–5 (2005)
Hall, C.: Lighting a fire or filling a pail? Users' perceptions of a virtual learning environment. Survey Report, University of Swansea (2006). http://learninglab.swan.ac.uk/Downloads/User_Survey_Report%201.1.pdf
Machado, C., Thompson, K.: The adoption of open sources within higher education in Europe and a dissemination case study (2004). http://tojde.anadolu.edu.tr/tojde17/articles/carlos.htm
Martin, T., Serrano, A.: The role of new technologies in the learning process: Moodle as a teaching tool in physics. Comput. Educ. **52**, 35–44 (2009)
Mathieson, K.: Predicting user intentions: comparing the technology acceptance model with the theory of planned behavior. Inf. Syst. Res. **2**, 173–191 (1991)
Moodle (2017). https://docs.moodle.org/33/en/Aboute_Moodle. Accessed 16 Oct 2017
Moore, G.C., Benbasat, I.: Development of an instrument to measure the perceptions of adopting an information technology innovation. Inf. Syst. Res. **2**, 192–222 (1991)
Reichert, S., Tauch, C.: Trends in learning structures in European higher education. In: EUA Graz Convention (2003)
Rice, W.H.: Moodle E-learning Course Development: A Complete Guide Successful Learning Using Moodle. Packt Publishing, USA (2006)
Romero, C., Ventura, S., García, E.: Data mining in course management systems: Moodle case study and tutorial. Comput. Educ. **51**, 368–384 (2008)
Sawang, S., Sun, Y., Salim, S.A.: It's not only what I think but what they think! The moderating effect of social norms. Comput. Educ. **76**, 182–189 (2014)
Taylor, S., Todd, P.: Assessing IT usage: the role of prior experience. MIS Q. 561–570 (1995)
Venkatesh, V., Davis, F.D.: A theoretical extension of the technology acceptance model: four longitudinal field studies. Manag. Sci. **46**(2), 186–204 (2000)

# The E-learning Trends for Continuing Professional Development in the Accountancy Profession in Hong Kong

Billy Tak-Ming Wong[1(✉)], Kam Cheong Li[1], Beryl Yuen-Yee Wong[1], and Joseph Shiu-Wing Yau[2]

[1] The Open University of Hong Kong, Kowloon, Hong Kong, China
{tamiwong,kcli,byywong}@ouhk.edu.hk
[2] Centennial College, Pok Fu Lam, Hong Kong, China
joseph.yau@centennialcollege.hku.hk

**Abstract.** Continuing professional development (CPD) refers to the ongoing learning and development in order to keep abreast of the advances and changes in a profession and perform competently. For accountancy professionals, CPD is needed throughout their careers. To cater for their needs in Hong Kong in terms of flexibility in time and place, the e-learning mode has become popular and is the future trend in CPD. This paper reviews the modes of delivery of CPD programmes for the accountancy profession in Hong Kong. It examines the programmes which have adopted diverse ways to support accountants to maintain and enhance their technical knowledge and professional skills. This article analyses the features of e-learning for the CPD programmes. They offer benefits for the participants such as self-controlled learning, self-assessment of understanding, and social learning with the online community of peers and colleagues. However, the e-learning channels may have limitations in supporting high-level training. Based on the results of this study, the future trends in CPD for the accountancy profession are discussed in relation to the potential of the latest advances in technology-enhanced learning.

**Keywords:** Continuing Professional Development (CPD) · Accountancy profession · E-learning

## 1 Continuing Professional Development for the Accountancy Profession in Hong Kong

Continuing professional development (CPD) is the learning and development that professional accountants need to carry out throughout their careers to keep abreast of advancements and changes in the profession, and to perform their role competently [1]. It is a compulsory requirement for the accountancy profession in Hong Kong. As required by the Hong Kong Institute of Certified Public Accountants (HKICPA), every professional accountant has to complete at least 40 CPD hours per year, within which 20 h should be verifiable training, such as attending the professional seminars offered by recognised professional accountancy bodies. In developing and offering CPD


S. K. S. Cheung et al. (Eds.): ICTE 2018, CCIS 843, pp. 258–266, 2018.
https://doi.org/10.1007/978-981-13-0008-0_24

activities, the professional accountancy bodies are required to comply with the International Accounting Education Standards Board (IAESB) governed by the International Federation of Accountants (IFA), which develops the International Education Standards as the authoritative framework providing guidance for the CPD [2]. It has been widely contended that the CPD for accountants promotes the formation of high-quality corporate reporting [3–5].

Since it is common that the professional accountants have to work overtime and overseas inside and outside their workplace, many of them in Hong Kong have difficulty in attending the CPD activities in a classroom setting. To help members to fulfil the CPD requirement, the HKICPA and other local professional accountancy bodies in Hong Kong have recognised e-learning as an acceptable mode of CPD training. Furthermore, they have been offering their self-produced programmes or collaborating with the local academic institutions to providing formal CPD education and training opportunities in the e-learning mode.

This paper aims to offer an overview of the developments of CPD for the accountancy profession in Hong Kong. It presents the findings of a survey showing the features of CPD programmes, based on which their future trends towards the e-learning mode are discussed.

## 2 E-learning in Accounting CPD

Supported by the technological advances, e-learning has been gradually adopted as a popular delivery mode of accountancy CPD. As identified by Ross and Anderson [6], popular delivery modes of CPD in accounting range from face-to-face seminars and webinars to face-to-face courses, online courses and computerised education. Visual media, interactive software, quizzes, simulation games and collaborative learning have also been promoted in the accounting field [7, 8]. Distance-learning programmes with multimedia materials and bulletin boards have also been used [9].

The benefits of e-learning for accountancy professionals have been studied and reported. For example, Dimitrios et al. [7] found that online collaborative learning got students involved in study and helped them to gain an in-depth understanding. Sandras and Walsh [10] also reported that a web-based delivery system, together with an online discussion group, effectively improved students' knowledge and skills. Basioudis and de Lange [9] stated that the interactive feature of e-learning, such as online chat, can stimulate active participation, mental effort and mutual learning, and that students are motivated to learn independently in the online environment.

While technology has been shown to benefit accounting education, there are also challenges and limitations which may hamper its effectiveness. Online professional learning may be underutilized because of insufficient technology infrastructure and ineffective application [9, 11, 12]. The online interactive elements that have been applied in CPD — such as online discussion groups and interactive videoconferencing — may be less effective than expected because of badly designed online modules, where interaction with peers or instructors can be totally lost [11, 13]. Also, Dimitrios et al. [7] expressed concern about the excessive use of computer programs for teaching as they possibly imply a "coded" way of acquisition rather than a deep understanding of the accounting subject, resulting in "mechanistic" or superficial knowledge. Thus, careful planning is required for electronic and blended learning modes to ensure that online and/or face-to-face components reflect the learning outcomes and are able to meet the learning needs of the professionals [13].

To cope with the needs of accounting professionals, Ross and Anderson [6] and Hare [11] proposed the factors which influence accounting professionals in choosing CPD events, among which accessibility was a major one. Glogowska et al. [13] showed that an advantage of online delivery is that temporal and spatial obstacles are minimised so that practitioners are more encouraged to take part in CPD activities. Also, de Lange et al. [8] presented their findings on the effectiveness of CPD resources among accountants in the Asia-Pacific region, covering the accountants' attitudes and the types, modes and selection of CPD activities. These findings show that both professional accounting bodies and practitioners have become more inclined to adopt e-learning due to its flexibility.

Despite e-learning having been emphasised as a promising means for accounting CPD and its benefits being recognised, the overall adoption of e-learning in accounting CPD in Hong Kong has not been comprehensively studied. This paper addresses this issue through a survey of local accounting CPD programmes.

# 3 Survey of Accounting CPD Programmes in Hong Kong

## 3.1 Method

A survey was conducted to examine the accounting CPD programmes offered by local professional bodies, as well as higher education institutions. The CPD programmes were surveyed from the official websites of these professional bodies and institutions, and relevant information was collected. The survey was conducted in September 2017, with a total of 71 programmes. Eight categories of information were collected, including: (1) medium of delivery; (2) delivery mode; (3) type of learning resource; (4) institutions; (5) CPD hours; (6) ways of keeping CPD evidence; (7) mode of payment; and (8) enrolment. The webpages of some programmes did not provide certain categories of information, such as the way to keep CPD evidence. In addition, a programme may provide more than one type of learning resources, such as online courses and reading materials.

## 3.2 Results

**Medium of Delivery**

Figure 1 reports the medium of delivery for the CPD programmes. The internet is the major medium of delivery, with 62% of the programmes delivered online, whereas only 38% were face-to-face.

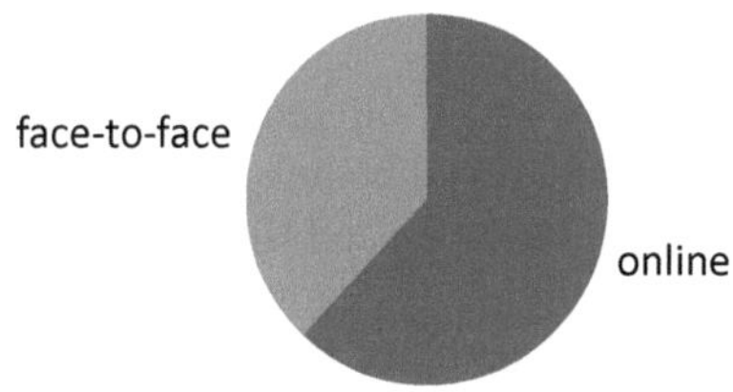


**Fig. 1.** Medium of delivery

**Delivery Mode**

Figure 2 presents the mode of delivery, with some of the CPD programmes involving more than one means of learning. For example, online courses may also cover online quizzes, interactive group sessions and online reading. Seminars were a major mode of delivery, among which 29 were live webinars and seven were recorded webinars. Some seminars were held face-to-face, alongside other kinds of events.

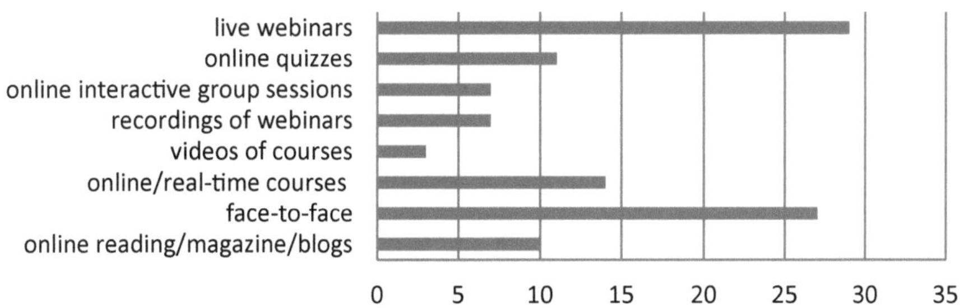


**Fig. 2.** Mode of delivery

**Type of Learning Resources**

Figure 3 shows the different types of learning resources. Apart from attending seminars, taking courses was a common form of accounting CPD. Technology is playing an essential role in offering e-resources, electronic books and articles. On the other hand, workshops, forums and conferences, usually conducted face-to-face, were still in use.

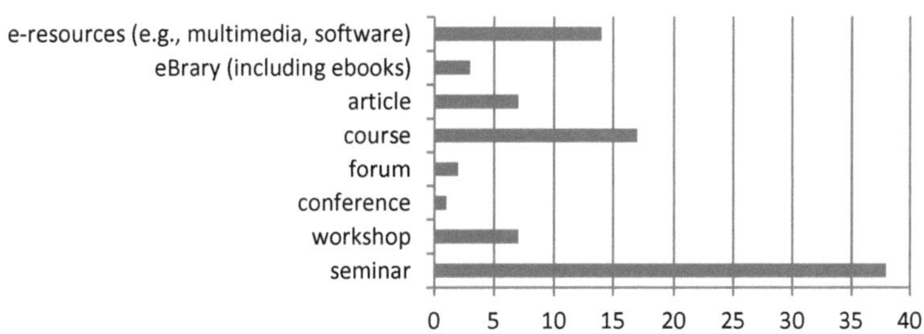


**Fig. 3.** Type of learning resources

**Institutions**

Figure 4 presents the institutions which offered the CPD programmes. Most of the programmes were offered by professional bodies such as the Association of Chartered Certified Accountants (ACCA) Hong Kong and Hong Kong Institute of Certified Public Accountants (HKICPA). Local higher education institutions mainly (co-) organise single events, except the Open University of Hong Kong and City University of Hong Kong which also provided specialised courses.

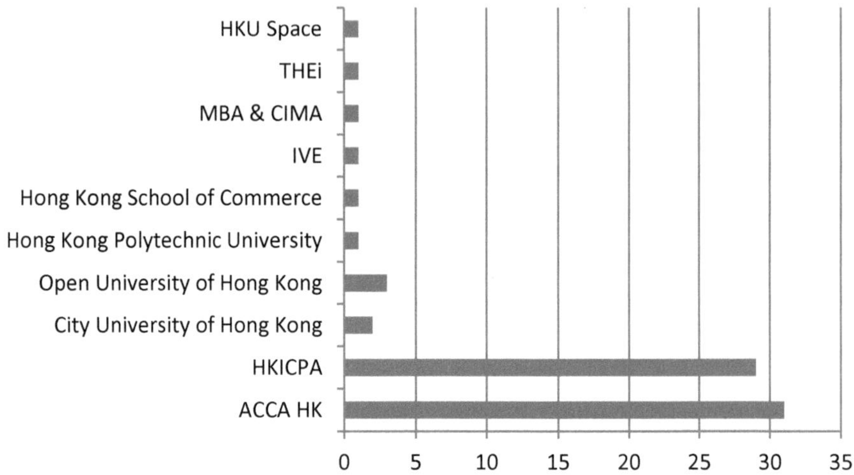


**Fig. 4.** Name of institution (CIMA: Chartered Institute of Management Accountant. IVY: Institute of Vocational Education. MBA: Manchester Business School. THEi: Technological and Higher Education Institute of Hong Kong.)

**CPD Hours**

Figure 5 shows the ways that CPD hours are recognised. A majority of programmes, such as online courses or activities, preassigned a specific number of CPD hours for participants, who are expected to spend the hours on the e-learning platform to complete the programmes. On the other hand, face-to-face activities, such as seminars or workshops, counted the actual attendance time of participants.

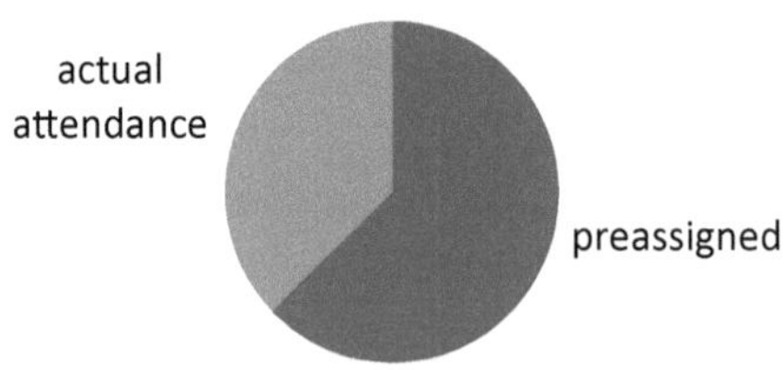


**Fig. 5.** CPD hours

**Ways of Keeping CPD Evidence**

Figure 6 presents the ways of keeping CPD evidence that is required for participants for audit purposes. Online events naturally keep electronic evidence on the e-learning platform. For face-to-face events, hardcopy certificates were usually distributed to participants after the events.

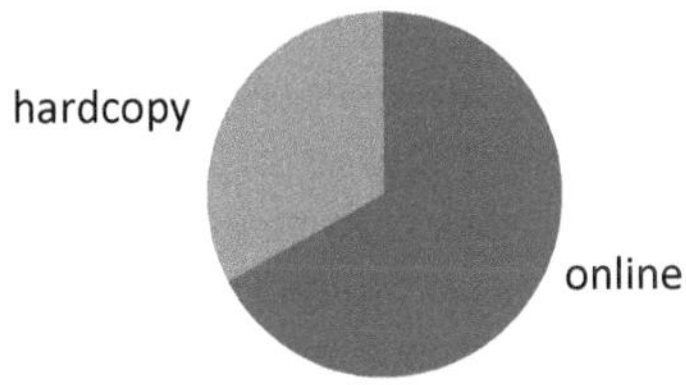


**Fig. 6.** Ways of keeping CPD evidence

**Mode of Payment**

Figure 7 outlines the mode of payment. Over half of the CPD activities are paid for (e.g. a fee for each CPD hour offered by HKICPA), whereas the others are free of charge for members of professional bodies.

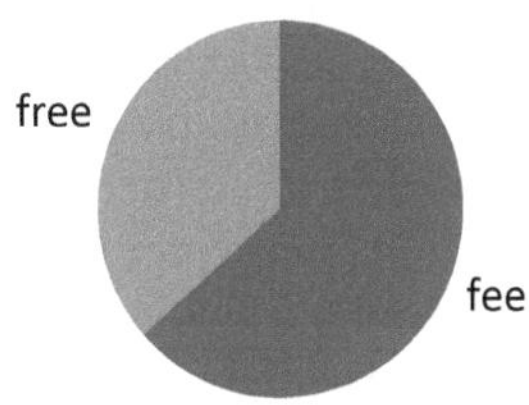


**Fig. 7.** Mode of payment

**Enrolment**

Figure 8 presents the application procedure. Most of the events, regardless of whether they were delivered in the face-to-face or online mode, offered online enrolment. However, some face-to-face activities required enrolment by mail or in person; and a few of them had a specific deadline for applications.

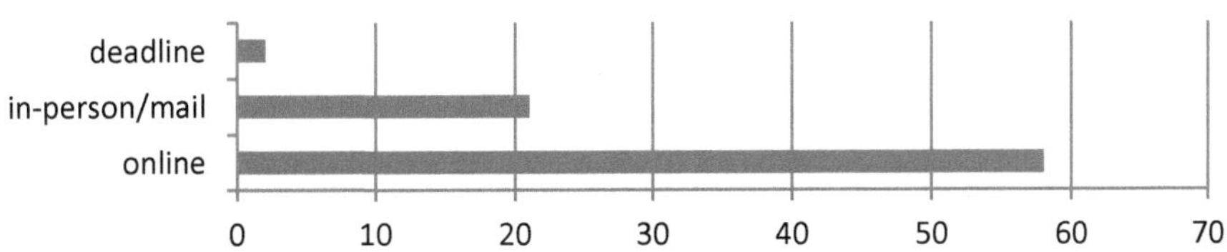


**Fig. 8.** Enrolment

# 4 The Future of CPD of the Accountancy Profession

Technology is recognised as an enabler in accounting CPD. In the ACCA survey conducted in 2016 which covered a broad range of stakeholders in accountancy, 57% of the respondents agreed that many entry level roles in the accountancy profession will be replaced by technology; and 84% believed that accounting and finance professionals can focus on higher value-added activity with the aid of technology [14, 15]. In addition, reflecting the growing expectations of employers, clients, regulators and other stakeholders for professional accountants, the results also suggested that CPD through various technological means, or e-learning, has become essential in order to equip accountants to face the opportunities and challenges brought by technological advances.

E-learning has become a powerful and influential trend for CPD in the accounting profession. It is recognised that technology will continue to play a determining role in CPD for accountants, though it may not entirely replace conventional teaching methods. Dimitrios et al. [7] suggested that information and communication technologies should be integrated only when they can adapt to students' abilities and ambitions, while making the learning process more effective and interesting. Likewise, Rothwell and Herbert [16] commented that the accountancy profession must realise the importance of CPD for maintaining its credibility. Future CPD has to be less supply-led and more demand-driven, and should take account of individual needs, development goals and priorities.

In addition, Ross and Anderson [6] mentioned that accessibility is a recurring indicator for choosing CPD activities as accounting practitioners rank the factors of cost and location high in their decisions on participation. Therefore, mobile technology is a viable way to support accessible CPD for learners from different regions. The provision of distance, online and on-demand learning activities can assist accountants in attaining their work/life scheduling needs. As the next generation is likely to possess an increasing comfort level with technology and mobile applications, Ross and Anderson [6] forecast that newly qualified accountants may prefer online and distance modalities, and thus more and more CPD providers will offer a wide range of programmes in all modalities. They elaborate that there is potential for the application of mobile technology in live webinars, recorded seminars, and recorded conferences, as well as self-paced computer-aided education. Despite the fact that there are still few courses and programmes fully compatible with mobile devices, the number is going to rise as relevant technologies and users develop.

# 5 Conclusions

The findings of this study supplement the literature on CPD modalities for accounting professionals. The medium for delivering CPD resources is inclining towards online rather than conventional face-to-face approaches. Nonetheless, though the number of accounting CPD events conducted in the virtual world exceeds that of activities with physical attendance, face-to-face events still comprise a large proportion and are yet to be replaced [7].

Regarding the mode of delivery, the results of this study have similarities to, but also differences from, the previous literature. As indicated by Dimitrios et al. [7], there is a great variety of delivery modes and materials ranging from face-to-face meetings and live webinars to online quizzes and interactive groups. However, the observations from studies such as Glogowska et al. [13] that suggest blended learning modes were not supported by the results of this study. All of the face-to-face occasions in this survey did not involve any supplementary resources or activities online.

The diverse types of learning resources show a trend towards e-learning — not only did the number of webinars outnumbers that of seminars, but e-resources have also emerged as one of the main types of learning [8]. Furthermore, it is worth noting that over half of the accounting CPD programmes facilitate online records and enrolment, which is another sign that CPD in the accountancy profession is heading towards e-learning.

Overall, this paper has presented the major patterns of local CPD practices in the accounting profession. It provides insights into recent delivery modes and teaching materials, and reveals potential areas for further development and exploration. While online tools and practices can hardly replace traditional methods, e-learning can enhance the effectiveness of teaching. In spite of some drawbacks, e-learning is also a prevailing trend as it is convenient and encourages active participation.

Looking ahead, this study suggests further work in investigating this dynamic profession and its new patterns of CPD practices. In light of relevant literature and data, we should keep an eye on the potential future developments in Hong Kong accounting CPD. Further research on the evaluation of human and infrastructure support should be conducted.

**Acknowledgement.** The work described in this paper was partially supported by a grant from the Research Grants Council of the Hong Kong Special Administrative Region, China (UGC/IDS16/15).

## References

1. Association of International Accountants. http://www.aiaworldwide.com/hong-kong. Accessed 31 Jan 2018
2. Lange, P., Jackling, B., Suwardy, T.: Continuing professional development in the accounting profession: practices and perceptions from the Asia pacific region. Acc. Educ. **24**(1), 41–56 (2015)
3. Kaspina, R.: Continuing professional development of accounting and auditing: Russian experience and challenges. Procedia – Soc. Behav. Sci. **191**, 550–553 (2015)
4. Mendoza, R.: Continuing professional development in public accountancy practice: the Philippine experience. South East Asia J. Contemp. Bus. Econ. Law **2**(1) (2013). https://ssrn.com/abstract=2516865
5. Wahab, M., Yusof, M.: Accountants' structured continuing professional education learning programs in Malaysia. Int. J. Humanit. Soc. Sci. **3**(2), 125–129 (2013)
6. Ross, K., Anderson, T.: Deciding what kind of course to take: factors that influence modality selection in accounting continuing professional development. Knowl. Manag. E-Learn. **5**(2), 137–152 (2013)

7. Dimitrios, B., Labros, S., Nikolaos, K., Maria, K., Athanasios, K.: Traditional teaching methods vs. teaching through the application of information and communication technologies in the accounting field: Quo vadis? Eur. Sci. J. **9**(28), 73–101 (2013)
8. de Lange, P., Jackling, B., Suwardy, T.: Access to CPD opportunities and resources to assist professional accountants to meet their commitment to life long learning: evidence from the Asia Pacific region (2011). http://files.iaaer.org/research/de_Lange_Final_Report.pdf?1406817147
9. Basioudis, G., de Lange, P.A.: An assessment of the learning benefits of using a web-based learning environment when teaching accounting. Adv. Account. **25**, 13–19 (2009)
10. Sandars, J., Walsh, K.: E-learning for general practitioners: lessons from the recent literature. Work Based Learn. Prim. Care **2**(4), 305–314 (2004)
11. Hare, E.E.: E-learning for psychiatrists. Psychiatri. Bull. **33**, 81–83 (2009)
12. Kashora, T., van der Poll, H.M., van der Poll, J.A.: E-learning and technologies for open distance learning in management accounting. Afr. Educ. Rev. **13**(1), 1–19 (2016)
13. Glogowska, M., Young, P., Lockyer, L., Moule, P.: How 'blended' is blended learning?: students' perceptions of issues around the integration of online and face-to-face learning in a continuing professional development (CPD) health care context. Nurse Educ. Today **31**, 887–891 (2011)
14. ACCA survey: Accountancy Futures. 13rd edn. ACCA (HK) (2016). http://insights.accaglobal.com/2016/10/24/af13_welcome/pugpig_index.html
15. Li, J.: New technologies key for Hong Kong CFOs in 2017, survey finds. South China Morning Post (2017). http://www.scmp.com/business/banking-finance/article/2075150/new-technologies-key-hong-kong-cfos-2017-survey-finds
16. Rothwell, A., Herbert, I.: Accounting professionals and CPD: attitudes and engagement — some survey evidence. Res. Post-Compuls. Educ. **12**(1), 121–138 (2007)

# Status of Learning Analytics in Asia: Perspectives of Higher Education Stakeholders

Kam Cheong LI[1], Carmen Jiawen YE[2], and Billy Tak-Ming WONG[1(✉)]

[1] The Open University of Hong Kong, Ho Man Tin, Hong Kong
{kcli,tamiwong}@ouhk.edu.hk
[2] Caritas Institute of Higher Education, Tseung Kwan O, Hong Kong
cye@cihe.edu.hk

**Abstract.** Despite the growing popularity of learning analytics in higher education, its development status in Asia was barely studied. This paper reports a study on the development of learning analytics in higher education in Asia. Semi-structured interviews were conducted with eight senior managers or senior academics from various tertiary institutions in Asia. The participants were asked about their institutions' position on learning analytics, the progress in its implementation, factors leading to effective implementation, and challenges encountered, if any. The results showed that in those institutions where learning analytics has been implemented, it aimed mainly at enhancing student retention, pedagogy and student learning experience. Its effective implementation relies on support from senior management, and taking students' views into account in decision-making. The participants' institutions encountered difficulties due to teachers' and students' concerns, such as the increased workload and data privacy, as well as technical issues in data collection, processing and analysis. In short, though starting late in Asia, learning analytics has been gradually gaining attention and is being implemented. The future directions of research and practices in learning analytics are also discussed.

**Keywords:** Learning analytics · Higher education · Tertiary institutions · Asia

## 1 Introduction

Learning analytics (LA) refers to "the measurement, collection, analysis, and reporting of data about learners and their contexts, for the purposes of understanding and optimizing learning and the environments in which it occurs" [1] (p. 1382). Its implementation covers various levels—from the micro- and meso-levels, which target respectively individual learners and the institution as a whole, to the macro-level which focuses on a cross-institutional perspective [2]. By bringing together the advances in technological, pedagogical and social development, LA has been regarded as having high potential for enhancing learning and addressing the diverse needs of the stakeholders in higher education institutions [3].

LA has had an impact on changing educational practices and improving learning experiences. For example, in reviewing the case studies on the implementation of LA


S. K. S. Cheung et al. (Eds.): ICTE 2018, CCIS 843, pp. 267–275, 2018.
https://doi.org/10.1007/978-981-13-0008-0_25

between 2008 and 2013, Avella, Kebritchi, Nunn, and Kanai [4] found that LA was beneficial to students' learning behaviours and outcomes, instructors' performance, curriculum development, personalised learning, and research in the field. Also, Sclater, Peasgood and Mullan [5] revealed that LA enables higher education institutions to enhance teaching quality and improve student retention, and helps students to take control of their own learning.

Despite the growing popularity of LA in higher education, its development in Asia is relatively slow. The existing work has been mostly done in the USA, Australia, and the UK [5]. From a survey of academics' views on the adoption of LA, Drachsler and Greller [6] found that the responses from Romance and Latin American countries were rather limited when compared with those from Anglo-Saxon countries. There was even a lack of response from Russia, China and India. One possibility is a general lack of awareness of LA in these countries. According to a survey targeting instructors in higher education institutions in China, Xiong and Zhang [7] found that more than half of the respondents regarded LA as their most unfamiliar teaching technology. In analysing the authorship of the Third Conference on Learning Analytics and Knowledge, Ochoa, Suthers, Verbert and Duval [8] revealed that, while Europe and North America contributed a total of 134 authors, there was only one from Asia. The notably lower proportion of Asian researchers in this field may have also constrained the development of LA in the region.

This paper seeks to unveil the development of LA in higher education institutions in Asia and explore the future directions in the field. It presents findings from interviewing academics and senior managers from various higher education institutions in China, Japan, India, the Philippines and Malaysia. They shared their views on and experience of LA, covering their institutions' position, the progress in implementation, factors contributing to the effective implementation, and challenges encountered.

## 2 Literature Review

Despite a few papers illustrating LA's overall development across the globe, the existing literature has yet to provide a thorough coverage of the situation in Asia. For example, Sclater et al. [5] examined the case studies from the USA, the UK and Australia. From the LACE Evidence Hub [9], which collects and summarises the features of LA cases, these three counties together contributed more than half of the cases in its latest collection.[1] Other literature reviews of LA also have not put regional speciality as a focus. For instance, Arroway, Morgan, O'Keefe and Yanosky [10] covered in general the driving factors, uses, institutional readiness, and strategies to guide LA implementation. Also, Leitner, Khalil and Ebner [11] analysed more than a hundred papers on LA and identified the research strands, LA techniques, limitations of research studies, and stakeholders.

In contrast, the related literature mainly presents the situation or reports particular projects in some Asian countries. The following summarised examples of the literature for several of these countries.

[1] As of 24 November 2017.

## 2.1 China

In China, the literature focuses more on the conceptual aspect. Gao and Fu [12] reported a systematic review of the LA literature in China between 2012 and 2014, and showed that they were mostly concerned with the value of analytical data, the importance of LA in constructing a smart learning environment, and the research and application of LA in the West. Jiang, Zhao, Li and Li [13] conducted a detailed analysis of LA dashboard applications to examine their potential benefits and limitations. Meng et al. [14] categorised different LA tools and compared their functionalities, providing a guideline on the selection of learning tools in learning and teaching. Also, Xiong and Zhang [7] collected instructors' views on LA and identified the major obstacles that restrained its implementation in Chinese higher education, viz. limited sources of data due to the insufficient popularity of e-learning, the difficulty of developing an analytical model, and the limited level of instructors' digital literacy.

There is a limited number of case studies presenting the practices of LA in China. For example, Zhang et al. [15] collected and analysed students' data in a college, such as library records, Internet access, and course performance, in order to improve the effectiveness of a programme. Ma et al. [16] assessed the role of instructors for students' engagement in an online learning environment by tracking the weblog data related to the activities of instructors and students in a university.

## 2.2 South Korea

In South Korea, Jo [17] developed a dashboard, called the "Learning Analytics for Prediction and Action" (LAPA), which was implemented in a private university with the aims of visualising students' online learning behaviours, and promoting their development of a smart and personalised learning style. Jo also identified the difficulties of interpreting the visualised LA data, and recognised the importance of LA in providing personalised and timely educational opportunities and feedback to learners on their needs and ability. In addition, Jo et al. [18] suggested more LA components for tracking the weblog data, and discovered factors which were significant in predicting students' performance, such as the login frequency and regularity of the learning interval in a learning management system (LMS).

## 2.3 Japan

In Japan, new LA tools and approaches have been proposed for enhancing learning experience. Ogata et al. [19] proposed a system called "System for Capturing and Reusing of Learning Log" (SCROLL), which aimed to help learners to record, recall, and organise their learning logs. Ogata et al. stressed that the system can be further extended to analyse learning content by accumulating data in learning logs, so as to find learning patterns and supply appropriate learning materials in accordance with learners' habits. Sorour, Goda and Mine [20] collected comment data from a course in the Kyushu Institute of Information Science and applied text mining techniques in order to predict the grades of students. By applying latent semantic analysis, they found that students' comment data was influential in predicting their grade. Ogata et al. [21] implemented LA based on e-book data in Kyushu University. They tracked and analysed educational big data from the LMS, the e-portfolio system and the e-book system, and found that the time students spent on reading or viewing e-books had a positive effect on their study results.

### 2.4 India

In the literature focusing on India, Pratheesh and Devi [22] analysed a collection of students' opinions and argued for the importance of adopting LA in software engineering education. They discovered that most students preferred a technology-based collaborative learning environment, in which LA would be helpful in detecting learners' learning styles and preparing learning materials that suited them. Also, Boulanger et al. [23] carried out an experimental study in the Anna University in India, implementing an LA system called "Smart Causal Analytics on Learning", which aimed at "collecting learning traces from any learning domain and analysing those learning traces to extract the underlying competency levels in the same learning domain" (p. 291). They found that the classes which adopted this system generally outperformed the others.

### 2.5 Summary

Overall, the literature regarding LA in Asia has been limited. Case studies reporting practices of LA cover only certain countries, such as South Korea and Japan, and most of them were only at an initial stage. Although this literature review only provides a glimpse of the adoption of LA in individual countries, there is a scarcity of studies showing the situation of LA in Asia, such as the progress, the goals, the success factors and challenges. This study aims to address this limitation by collecting the views and experience of academics and managers in higher education institutions in Asia on the implementation of LA in their respective institutions.

## 3 Methodology

### 3.1 Participants

A total of eight senior academics and managers were invited to participate in semi-structured interviews. They came from higher education institutions in a total of five Asian countries—China, India, Japan, Malaysia and the Philippines. They were all Professors or unit heads in their institutions.

### 3.2 Semi-Structured Interviews

The semi-structured interviews were conducted in July 2017, which took about 5 to 20 min. Below are the key interview questions. The researcher also asked other follow-up questions according to the interviewees' responses.

*Interview questions*

1. Have you heard of learning analytics?
2. Is your institution developing learning analytics?
3. How long has your institution been developing learning analytics?
4. What are the goals of your institution for developing learning analytics? What is expected to be gain from the learning analytics?
5. What is the progress in the development of learning analytics in your institution?
6. What obstacles, if any, have your institution encounter during the development?
7. What are the future plans on the development of learning analytics in your institution?
8. What do you think of learning analytics?

## 4 Results and Discussion

The results showed that all the participants had heard of LA. Six of them reported that their institutions were developing LA. Most of the other institutions were at the early stage of the development, e.g. less than five years; and some of them are still in the process of planning. In this section, the findings were categorised into the following themes and discussed along with the results of the past research.

1. The development of learning analytics in higher education institutions mainly aims to enhance student retention, better pedagogy, and improve student learning experiences.

The institutions aimed to develop LA to achieve various goals. During the interviews, goals at different levels were mentioned by the participants. At the institutional level, most of the institutions aimed to maximise the student attendance, improve student-teacher interaction, and enhance retention with the use of LA. This finding is consistent with the research done in the UK and US, which shows that one of the drivers for universities implementing LA is to use it as a presdictive tool to identify students at risk of attrition so as to increase their continuation on the programme [10]. One participant mentioned that his university applied LA in order to discover trends and problems in education that could not be identified by using conventional means. This reflected a positive attitude from the university's senior management towards investment in LA.

At the teacher level, the participants replied that the application of LA in higher education would offer insights for teachers to improve their teaching. Specifically, it was expected that LA would help to achieve the goal of facilitating policy-making to improve pedagogy, meet the teachers' needs, monitor students' learning progress, and gather student feedback.

At the student level, most participants expected that the use of LA would improve students' learning experiences, making learning and teaching more meaningful.

To sum up, the development of LA was considered to fulfil goals in the areas of university administration, pedagogy, and students' learning experiences and performance. The most important driver for the senior management for implementing LA was to enhance student retention; and to improve the pedagogy and students' learning experiences and performance were the main goals of academics.

2. The implementation of learning analytics in higher education institutions needs to listen to students' voices.

Three participants mentioned that a small working group had been formed for the implementation of, or a pilot study on, LA in their institutions. One of the institutions even provided funds for the preliminary research on this topic. As for the progress, five institutions were planning to collect or had been collecting student data for the LA projects. The main sources of data included student demographic information, the LMS login data, information on enrolment and retention, course performance (e.g. attendance rates, assignments, and exam pass rates), and course evaluation.

3. The difficulties of implementing learning analytics in higher education institutions consist of concerns from teachers and students and technical issues of learning analytics.

The participants identified several difficulties in implementing LA in their institutions. In some institutions, the academics hate changes and so it was difficult to get them on board. In addition, they were not happy that some information is shared with students through student dashboard, which may increase their workload. Similar concerns have been found in other studies. For example, Howell et al. [24] found that academics were uncertain about the responsibility they should bear after releasing the findings of LA to students. The follow-up efforts to help the students deal with the negative reports based on LA analyses may have had a significant impact on their workload. To solve this problem, clear responsibility, instructions, and procedures should be provided to the teachers to facilitate their follow-up with the students. It is preferable that an intervention unit to offer necessary and timely assistance and consultancy to students be set up to reduce the workload of the teaching staff. One of the participants mentioned this mechanism in her university which has been functioning effectively and has provided considerable help to students in need.

The participants mentioned that some of the students do not like the idea that the university can track their digital footprints and they are concerned about the issue of data protection and privacy. However, most of the participants indicated that their students were informed that their personal data and data generated from their study in the university would be collected and used for analysis and report purposes once they were admitted to a programme. The practices of the interviewees' institutions showed that there may not be an option for students to opt out of data collection for LA. The need for informed consent and the option of opting out should be provided in the universities in the planning of LA [25].

In some of the institutions, LA is a new field to be explored. Some participants found it difficult and time-consuming to consolidate data from different sources and make an integral use of them. In particular, one mentioned that sometimes there is no clue to identify the useful and important data in the huge dataset. These comments revealed that the data collection for LA needs cooperation from different departments and units within the university, where support and coordination from senior management is considered of great importance. Hiring data analytics specialists to form a specific working group for learning analytics would be a solution to managing the collected data in an efficient way.

4. The senior managers interviewed from most of the institutions provided sufficient support for the development of learning analytics.

Most of the participants expressed that the senior management at their universities have a positive view of LA. Some of them provided administrative support to coordinate the data collection for the LA projects, while others offered research funds for a pilot study on LA. However, in one university in Japan, the participant said that the senior management was sceptical about the effectiveness of LA and did not provide any support for it.

5. Most of the participants possessed a positive attitude towards learning analytics and consider it as an effective tool for higher education.

The participants expressed that research and the application of LA should become one of the foci in tertiary education. More useful predictive models should be discovered and the findings should be used not only for monitoring students, but more importantly for intervention when students at risk are identified. It is hoped that it can help to personalise the students' learning process and improve their learning experiences and performance.

## 5 Conclusions

The present study reveals the trends of LA in Asia, which are not adequately addressed in the previous research. It contributes to showing that tertiary institutions in Asia, though starting late, have gradually become aware of the usefulness and importance of LA. In the interviews, two of the eight participants reported that their universities have been using LA for policy-making and student retention. Four of the participants' institutions have been conducting preliminary research on LA and plan to make use of it in the near future. The other two participants reported that their universities were not in favour of LA or even doubted its effectiveness, and therefore, no support was received from the senior management for its implementation.

In the interviews, no participant mentioned the views of students. It has been pointed out that students' views have been missing for a long time in the decision-making on LA and attention should be paid to engaging them in such a process [26]. The students should be empowered and enabled to become one of the designers of their own learning experiences so that they can gain control over their own learning. For developing LA in Asian universities, it is therefore recommended that students' perspectives should be taken into account in decision-making.

The follow-up intervention based on the results of LA may not be welcomed by students. The students at risk may not want to be identified, as the negative feedback from LA may damage their psychological well-being by labelling them and lowering their self-esteem [24]. Therefore, how to deal properly with the students' data and provide feedback to them needs a more considerate and informed approach.

Despite the relatively small sample size, the findings of the present study suggest that the development of LA has been slow but is gradually progressing in Asia, and the tertiary institutions in Asia are generally positive towards it. The challenges for the institutions, as raised by the participants in this study, have also been reported and addressed in the relevant literature. It can be expected that LA will gain a more important position on the agenda of higher education development in the continent.

**Acknowledgement.** The work described in this paper was partially supported by a grant from the Research Grants Council of the Hong Kong Special Administrative Region, China (UGC/IDS16/15).

## References

1. Siemens, G.: Learning analytics: the emergence of a discipline. Am. Behav. Sci. **57**(10), 1380–1400 (2013)
2. Shum, B.S.: Learning analytics. UNESCO policy brief (2012). http://iite.unesco.org/pics/publications/en/files/3214711.pdf
3. Siemens, G.: Learning analytics: envisioning a research discipline and a domain of practice. In: Proceedings of the 2nd International Conference on Learning Analytics and Knowledge, Vancouver, Canada, pp. 4–8 (2012)
4. Avella, J.T., Kebritchi, M., Nunn, S. G., Kanai, T.: Learning analytics methods, benefits, and challenges in higher education: A systematic literature review. Online Learn. **20**(2) (2016). http://olj.onlinelearningconsortium.org/index.php/olj/article/view/790/201
5. Sclater, N., Peasgood, A., Mullan, J.: Learning analytics in higher education. A review of UK and international practice. Full report. JISC, **4**(22.04) (2016)
6. Drachsler, H., Greller, W.: The pulse of learning analytics understandings and expectations from the stakeholders. In: Proceedings of the 2nd International Conference on Learning Analytics and Knowledge, pp. 120–129, Vancouver, Canada (2012)
7. Xiong, Q.E., Zhang, X.H.: The strategies of learning analytics in the practice of teaching innovation in higher education. Mod. Distance Educ. **5**, 56–61 (2015). (in Chinese)
8. Ochoa, X., Suthers, D., Verbert, K., Duval, E.: Analysis and reflections on the third learning analytics and knowledge conference (LAK 2013). J. Learn. Anal. **1**(2), 5–22 (2014)
9. LACE: LACE Evidence Hub. http://evidence.laceproject.eu/. Accessed 19 Jan 2018
10. Arroway, P., Morgan, G., O'Keefe, M., Yanosky, R.: Learning analytics in higher education. Research report. Louisville, CO: ECAR, EDUCAUSE (2016)
11. Leitner, P., Khalil, M., Ebner, M.: Learning Analytics in Higher Education—A Literature Review. In: Peña-Ayala, A. (ed.) Learning Analytics: Fundaments, Applications, and Trends. SSDC, vol. 94, pp. 1–23. Springer, Cham (2017). https://doi.org/10.1007/978-3-319-52977-6_1
12. Gao, Y., Fu, G.S.: Review of studies on learning analysis in education in China. China Med. Educ. Technol. **30**(1), 23–26 (2016)
13. Jiang, Q., Zhao, W., Li, Y.F., Li, S.: Research on learning analytics dashboard based on big data. China Educ. Technol. **1**, 113–119 (2017)
14. Meng, L.L., Gu, X.Q., Li, Z.: The comparison of learning analytics tools. Educ. Res. **20**(4), 66–75 (2014)
15. Zhang, Y.H., Wang, F.Q., Han, Q.F., Lv, J.: Research on evaluation model for political and daily performance of students based on big data. Fujian Comput. **9**, 124–127 (2015)

16. Ma, J., Han, X., Yang, J., Cheng, J.: Examining the necessary condition for engagement in an online learning environment based on learning analytics approach: the role of the instructor. Internet High. Educ. **24**, 26–34 (2014)
17. Jo, I.: On the LAPA (Learning Analytics for Prediction & Action) model suggested. Future Research Seminar. Korea Society of Knowledge Management (2012)
18. Jo, I.-H., Yu, T., Lee, H., Kim, Y.: Relations between student online learning behavior and academic achievement in higher education: a learning analytics approach. In: Chen, G., Kumar, V., Kinshuk, {.}., Huang, R., Kong, S.C. (eds.) Emerging Issues in Smart Learning. LNET, pp. 275–287. Springer, Heidelberg (2015). https://doi.org/10.1007/978-3-662-44188-6_38
19. Ogata, H., Houb, B., Li, M., Uosakic, N., Mouri, K., Liu, S.: Ubiquitous learning project using life-logging technology in Japan. Educ. Technol. Soc. **27**(2), 85–100 (2014)
20. Sorour, S.E., Goda, K., Mine, T.: Correlation of topic model and student grades using comment data mining. In: Proceeding of the 46th ACM Technical Symposium on Computer Science Education, Kansas City, USA, pp. 441–446 (2015)
21. Ogata, H., Yin, C., Oi, M., Okubo, F., Shimada, A., Kojima, K., Yamada, M.: E-book based learning analytics in university education. In: Proceeding of the 23rd International Conference on Computers in Education, Asia Pacific Society for Computers in Education, China, pp. 401–406 (2015)
22. Pratheesh, N., Devi, T.: Necessity of learning analytics in software engineering education. J Eng. Sci. Technol. **10**(3), 269–281 (2015)
23. Boulanger, D., Seanosky, J., Kumar, V., Kinshuk, Panneerselvam, K., Somasundaram, T.S.: Smart learning analytics. In: Chen, G., Kumar, V., Kinshuk, Huang, R., Kong, S.C. (eds.) Emerging issues in Smart Learning. Lecture Notes in Educational Technology, pp. 289–296. Springer, Berlin (2015). https://doi.org/10.1007/978-3-662-44188-6_39
24. Howell, J.A., Roberts, L.D., Seaman, K., Gibson, D.C.: Are we on our way to becoming a "Helicopter University"? Academics' views on learning analytics. Technol. Knowl. Learn. **23**, 1–20 (2017). https://link.springer.com/article/10.1007/s10758-017-9329-9
25. Slade, S., Prinsloo, P.: Student perspectives on the use of their data: Between intrusion, surveillance and care. European J. Open Distance E-learn. **18**(1) (2015). http://www.eurodl.org/index.php?p=special&sp=articles&inum=6&abstract=672&article=679
26. Roberts, L.D., Howell, J.A., Seaman, K., Gibson, D.C.: Student attitudes toward learning analytics in higher education: "the fitbit version of the learning world". Frontiers in Psychology **7** (2016). https://www.frontiersin.org/articles/10.3389/fpsyg.2016.01959/full

Check for updates

# An Exploration on the Regional Sharing Mechanism for High-Quality Online Teaching Resources of Colleges and Universities in the Internet Era

Xiao-yan Su[1(✉)], Cong-dong Li[1], and Ivan Ka-wai Lai[2]

[1] International Business School, Jinan University, Zhuhai 519070, China
{tsuxyan,licd}@jnu.edu.cn

[2] Faculty of International Tourism and Management, City University of Macau, Taipa, Macau, China
ivanlai@cityu.mo

**Abstract.** With the "Internet +" strategy, more and more high quality online teaching resources are constantly developed to solve the issue of imbalance in high-quality teaching resources among universities. However, the lack of resource sharing mechanism seriously restricts the effectiveness of the resource sharing. Based on an analysis of the status quo of high quality online teaching resources sharing, this paper proposes five types of resource sharing mechanism, which include the coordination mechanism, motivation mechanism, investment mechanism, payment mechanism and evaluation mechanism.

**Keywords:** Online teaching resources · Regional sharing mechanism · MOOC

## 1 Introduction

In recent years, higher education in China has transformed from elite education to mass education. During this process, the gross enrollment rate of college and university students continues to increase. But in the meanwhile, the contradiction between students' unlimited demand for higher education resources, especially high-quality teaching resources, and limited supply of high-quality teaching resources is becoming increasingly conspicuous. Affected by the development laws of high-quality resources and driven by the self-interest of colleges and universities, the distribution of high-quality teaching resources at colleges and universities is unbalanced and the flow of such resources is strictly limited. The shortage of high-quality teaching resources has been a long-term problem of higher education (Zhou 2006). How to break down the barrier of interest and establish a regional sharing mechanism for high-quality teaching resources at colleges and universities has become one of the important problems that need to be solved in the reform and development of higher education at the present stage.

High-quality teaching resources of colleges and universities refer to excellent courses, top-quality teaching materials, famous teachers, teaching teams, famous majors, key laboratories, etc. with certain features or advantages accumulated by


S. K. S. Cheung et al. (Eds.): ICTE 2018, CCIS 843, pp. 276–284, 2018.
https://doi.org/10.1007/978-981-13-0008-0_26

colleges and universities after many years. Driven by the rapid development of modern educational techniques, many colleges and universities have developed and accumulated a certain number of high-quality online teaching resources by their own teaching staff and brand advantages, which are digital, networked and visualized high-quality teaching resources including courseware, videos, pictures, audio materials, animations and other curriculum resources (Zhou et al. 2013). Due to the scarcity and valuableness of high-quality online teaching resources, the above teaching resources have become objectives pursued by colleges and universities. As the strategic concept of "Internet +" is proposed, more and more online teaching resources will be further developed and utilized in the future. If government authorities as well as relevant colleges and universities help promote the regional sharing of high-quality online teaching resources, then on the one hand, the problem of insufficient supply of high-quality teaching resources of colleges and universities will be eased. And on the other hand, sustainable and Pareto development of high-quality online teaching resources will also be achieved. As a result, students will be able to enjoy the best teaching resources and various colleges and universities will achieve resource intensive development. Thus, it can be seen that the implementation of regional sharing of high-quality online teaching resources at colleges and universities is of a very important practical implication.

## 2 Exploration Course for the Regional Sharing of High-Quality Online Teaching Resources of Colleges and Universities

So far, the exploration course for the regional sharing of high-quality online teaching resources of colleges and universities in mainland China can be divided into three stages:

The first stage started from the 1990 s and mainly involved with large cities where many colleges and universities are located, such as Guangzhou, Beijing, Shanghai, Wuhan and so on. For example, Guangzhou Campus of Jinan University, together with other five universities in the Shipai district (including South China University of Technology, Guangdong University of Technology, South China Normal University, South China Agricultural University and Guangdong Polytechnic Normal University), developed the new pattern of innovative talents training via multi- university cooperation by making full use of various university advantages on the basis of "resource sharing, complementary advantages, division of responsibilities and mutual benefit". From the academic year 1999 to 2002, 3,285 students from other five universities took elective courses in Jinan University, and 2,436 students of Jinan University took elective courses in other universities. On this basis, six universities in Shipai district further signed the "Agreement for Joint Course Selection among Six Universities in Shipai Area of Guangzhou" and "Cross-university Cooperative Teaching Agreement for Minoring a Second Major among Six Universities" (Six Universities in the Shipai Area 2002), which provided system guarantee for the regional sharing of teaching resources. To provide convenience for students' selecting courses and minoring second majors in different universities, free traffic buses traveling to and fro between six universities were provided, which greatly promoted the regional sharing of teaching resources.

The second stage started from the beginning of this century and mainly involved with newly built higher education zones or university towns in various regions, which took “teaching association”, “teaching community”, etc. as main organizational forms. Colleges and universities within a certain region shared teaching resources in an organized way. Relying on the favorable geographic location, both the scale and depth of teaching resources sharing among universities in the university town surpassed the first stage. According to incomplete statistics, over 50 higher education zones or university towns were newly built throughout the country during this period, including those with a relatively large scale such as Guangzhou Higher Education Mega Center, Teaching Community in Beijing Xueyuan Road, Hangzhou Xiasha University Town, Shanghai Songjiang University Town, Chongqing College Town, etc. At the beginning of the Teaching Community in Beijing Xueyuan Road, only 3 public elective courses were offered to 500 students. At present, altogether 80 to 90 public elective courses are offered to about 12,000 students per year. For more than a decade, the “Teaching Community” has successfully set up more than 170 curriculums and offered 1,200 courses to over 100,000 students in such fields as literature, art, sports, medicine, natural science, social science, etc. The proportion of students’ elective course credits account for 40% of all elective courses, and 8% of the total credits. Cross-university course selection not only optimizes students’ knowledge structure and broadens their horizons, but also breaks the tradition of cultivating talents by a single college or university and creates the cooperation mode of multi-university talent training and sharing high-quality teaching resources.

The third stage witnesses the rapid development of modern online educational resources. By virtue of the development of modern educational information and multimedia technologies, some colleges and universities have invested and developed a number of online high-quality teaching resources. In 2003, the Ministry of Education launched the teaching quality and top-quality curriculum construction projects by implementing teaching reform in colleges and universities (Ministry of Education, 2003). The project requires that “teaching syllabuses, teaching plans, exercises, network coursewares, teaching videos, etc.” related to top-quality curriculums of colleges and universities should be uploaded to the Internet for free access and sharing. The construction of national top-quality curriculums is required to “lay emphasis on network resources construction, cover all disciplines, promote network teaching and digital learning, and share high-quality teaching resources”. The top-quality curriculum project has played a positive role in promoting the sharing of online teaching resources. With the vigorous development of online education, the Ministry of Education launched the establishment of a high-quality teaching resources sharing system in 2012. In addition, the Ministry of Education further specifies the key points of work in 2015 that it is necessary to “**perfect the national education resources cloud service system, continue to push the development and application of high-quality digital educational resources, explore the application driven mechanism for online open courses, and strengthen the construction, use and management of ‘MOOC**’. Featuring abundant resources, a large amount of information, convenient and fast delivery, free from time and space constraints, etc., online teaching resources enable learners to study 7 × 24 at any time with the help of existing computer network and mobile communication technologies

(He 2014). Therefore, the current scope and degree of regional sharing of teaching resources will greatly surpass those in the traditional model.

The online teaching resources could create necessary conditions for the regional sharing of high-quality teaching resources by breaking time-space distance limits. However, due to objective factors such as varied teaching skills of different universities, constraints in inter-university sharing agreements, cross-university student management, etc. and subjective factors such as insufficient teachers' motivation, unbalanced income of universities, etc., the development of most high-quality online teaching resources remains slow in practice. Apart from sharing national top-quality curriculums and other teaching resources required to be open to the public for free, most high-quality teaching resources are still shared and used only on campus. According to statistics, 128,972 online teaching courses are offered by colleges and universities nationwide in 2009, but only about 5% of such courses are available for sharing. The degree of sharing inter-university high-quality online teaching resources is far lower than expected.

# 3 Status Quo of High-Quality Online Teaching Resources Sharing

The realization of regional sharing is able to break the traditional pattern of closed talents training at colleges and universities, achieve cooperation among various universities, innovate the talent training mode, enhance the reputation of teachers and universities and reach a win-win situation (among universities, teachers and students). However, in reality, the regional sharing of high-quality teaching resources in various regions does not achieve satisfactory results.

## 3.1 Status Quo of the Regional Sharing of High-Quality Online Teaching Resources

**(1) Number of resources is limited**

At present, most teaching resources shared among colleges and universities are limited to curriculum resources. The sharing of other teaching resources such as books, reference materials, teachers, etc. are relatively infrequent. With respect to the sharing of courses, currently available courses cannot meet students' demands and most of them are offered in the traditional curriculum mode. New online teaching resources, such as micro-class, flipped classroom, MOOC and other forms, etc. are relatively rare (Wang 2014). The following takes inter-university elective courses of 10 colleges and universities in Guangzhou Higher Education Mega Center as an example. In 2014 to 2015, 14 and 12 courses were offered respectively in the first and second semester, and less than 2 courses were offered on average in each semester. The extremely limited number of courses offered and students admissible were not enough to satisfy inter-university course selection demands of more than 30,000 students in the college town.

**(2) Structure of resources is unreasonable**

Seeing from courses offered by colleges and universities currently, cross-university elective courses are mainly limited to humanistic quality elective courses. Professional courses in urgent need by students are very limited, which are not enough to satisfy students' demands to improve their professional knowledge. According to statistics of the Teaching Community in Beijing Xueyuan Road, cross-university elective courses are mainly involved with art, fitness, leisure, etc., followed by literature and art courses (21%), and then sports (14%), computer (12%) and medicine (7%). Popular courses on economic management in urgent need by students are less than 7% in total courses. Seeing from the course setting of universities in Guangzhou Higher Education Mega Center from the academic year 2014 to 2015, over 90% of courses are general elective courses, and less than 8% are professional courses (Zheng and Shao 2010).

**(3) Number of teachers is few**
It can also be seen from the above course setting of universities in Guangzhou Higher Education Mega Center that about 10 to 15 teachers are assigned by 10 colleges and universities in each semester. Compared with the total number of over 4,000 teachers, very few teachers are involved in cross-university course selection, which is less than 0.3% of the total number. In addition, about one-third of teachers who participate in the sharing of curriculum resources are young teachers and the proportion of famous teachers is much lower.

**(4) Sharing scope of resources is small**
From the sharing scope of online teaching resources of existing universities, such resources are only available to students nearby these colleges and universities, not including students from distant colleges, universities and local communities. As a result, the influence scope of high-quality online resources is rather limited. Along with the development of modern information technology, how to improve the sharing degree and scope of high-quality online teaching resources under the background of modern educational technologies has become a practical problem that needs to be resolved immediately.

## 3.2 Cause Analysis

The fundamental cause of problems existing in the sharing of above-mentioned high-quality teaching resources at colleges and universities lies in unreasonable design of the regional sharing mechanism, which results in insufficient motivation to teachers and universities, lack of supervision and coordination and so on. To be specific:

**(1) The motivation mechanism is insufficient**
The limited number of courses and teachers involved in online teaching resources sharing mainly results from insufficient motivation. Teachers and colleges are not motivated to offer cross-university courses. From the point of course-offering, the offering of cross-university elective courses will benefit other universities and students. Following the principle of "whoever benefits from such courses is responsible for payment", beneficiary universities and students should pay to universities and teachers who offer courses. But in fact, students' elective courses in some university towns are completely free of charge or collect very little charges, and teachers' class fees are still

paid by the course-offering university. Some local governments subsidize the universities and teachers to participate in the sharing of resources. For example, the Department of Education of Zhejiang Province gives universities in Hangzhou Xiasha University Town offering inter-university elective courses with a subsidy of 30 Yuan/period for each course. However, the subsidy is not enough to cover teachers' period allowance, course management expenses and other expenditures. As a result, the universities and teachers are not motivated to participate in offering cross-university elective courses.

**(2) The investment mechanism design is unsatisfactory**

Both the real-time data updating of online teaching resources and timely offline interaction with students require the investment of appropriate human, financial and material resources. In addition, in the process of implementing regional sharing of online teaching resources, multiple subjects are needed to participate in the development, coordination and management of high-quality teaching resources. Therefore, stable and reliable investment mechanism design is necessary to ensure the continuous development of online high-quality teaching resources. Currently, the lack of human, financial and material investment in the development, design, maintenance and management of high-quality teaching resources and platforms greatly reduces the motivation of colleges or universities and teachers.

**(3) The payment mechanism design is unreasonable**

For universities or students who use high-quality online teaching resources, the payment of costs is a guarantee for the virtuous circle of development of high-quality teaching resources. At present, some universities in university towns or higher education zones implement different charging systems on cross-university course selection according to the nature of specific courses, among which quality education courses are free of charge, and professional courses are charged appropriately according to the nature of level, credit, subject and other characteristics of specific colleges or universities. However, with the increase in online teaching courses, there will be more and more students from outside the university or other areas. How to make payment reasonable? Shall the payment be made by means of tuition or certification fee? If the payment cannot be effectively settled among universities, will students be required to pay for cross-university elective courses apart from paying the tuition at their own universities? If this form of payment is unreasonable or repeated, it is bound to affect students' enthusiasm to participate in cross-university elective courses.

**(4) The evaluation mechanism is insufficient**

The growth and development of high-quality courses cannot do without active feedback from students. However, as very limited cross-university elective courses are available for the students, no effective evaluation mechanism is set up to select the superior and eliminate the inferior online teaching resources to better meet students' demands.

**(5) The coordination mechanism is deficient**

Offering cross-university courses needs to coordinate between different universities, teachers, students and other subjects concerning time and place arrangements and many other issues, which has great difficulty in coordination. Lacking of an effective coordination mechanism may result in "conflict" courses and unsuccessful course offering. More importantly, if colleges or universities cannot solve mutual recognition of credit, cost settlement and other key issues, it will directly affect the regional sharing of high-quality online resources.

# 4 Designing the Regional Sharing Mechanism of High-Quality Online Teaching Resources

More students, teachers, universities and other subjects can benefit from abundant high-quality online teaching resources only when such resources are used effectively. Therefore, it is very important to design a reasonable teaching resources sharing mechanism to achieve win-win cooperation among colleges and universities.

## 4.1 Coordination Mechanism

Coordination mechanism refers to making coordinated arrangements about activities of the government, universities, teachers, teaching assistants, students and other subjects in the process of curriculum development, construction, use and maintenance, which requires various subjects to understand their respective divisions of work, duties clearly and cooperate with one another. Firstly, the education administrative department shall establish formal systems for mutual recognition of credit, tuition payment and settlement, certificate issuance, remuneration arrangement, teaching resources platform design among universities. In October 2014, the Department of Education of Guangdong Province issued the *Opinions on Credit System Management Implemented by Regular Institutions of Higher Education*, which clearly put forward that colleges and universities should set up the system for students' taking elective courses in other universities, and encourage students to take elective courses in other universities or based on the Internet learning platform. Elective courses taking in other universities can replace students' required courses or elective courses of their own university, which provides a system guarantee for the mutual recognition of credit. Secondly, all university presidents shall set up a Coordinated Management Committee to regularly discuss the overall planning of online teaching resources, number of classes, structural design, teacher arrangements and other issues. The Coordinated Management Committee shall have a teaching affairs department to organize and arrange courses to be offered by various universities, and coordinate time and place issues related to teachers, students and courses. Thirdly, the teachers team is responsible for organizing and designing online resources, giving lessons, answering students' questions offline, and giving students the final performance evaluation. Fourthly, the teaching affairs department is responsible for coordinating the curriculum setting of teachers.

## 4.2 Motivation Mechanism

Whether it is traditional teaching resources or online teaching resources, the motivation mechanism is key to promote the sharing of resources. For universities or teachers who offer resources, their knowledge should bring corresponding economic benefits. Qualification admittance, nature of course, number of students, qualification of teachers, curriculum evaluation and other indicators shall be established to correlate with the course remuneration system, so as to fully mobilize the enthusiasm of colleges or universities and teachers to participate in teaching resources sharing.

## 4.3 Investment Mechanism

The local government and universities shall establish a stable investment mechanism for the development and use of online high-quality teaching resources, including personnel investment, fund investment and platform investment. Firstly, as for personnel investment, the construction, maintenance, updating and interaction of online teaching resources library require teachers and team members to invest a lot of time and effort. The sustainable development of high-quality online teaching resources cannot do without corresponding staff support. Secondly, as for fund investment, the government shall continue to increase information investment in colleges and universities to ensure the development of online teaching resources, truly realize full coverage of the campus wireless network and provide convenience for users of network teaching resources. In November 2014, the Ministry of Education and other five administrative departments jointly issued the Implementation Scheme for Building An Effective Mechanism Utilizing Information-based Means to Expand the Coverage of High-quality Educational Resources, which proposed that by the end of 2015, all types of schools at all levels should achieve full coverage of the "Internet", among which the broadband access ratio should be more than 50%, and the development and application of high-quality teaching resources are listed as primary tasks of educational informationization. The Ten-year Development Planning for Educational Informationization (2011-2020) proposed that governments at all levels should distribute educational informationization funds in the proportion of not less than 8% of educational appropriations. Thirdly, as for platform investment, not only legal and policy platforms supporting the regional sharing of online teaching resources should be set up, but also corresponding organizational platforms, management platforms, settlement platforms, offline support and management platforms, etc. should be established.

## 4.4 Payment Mechanism

At present, most online teaching resources platforms are open to the public free of charge by relying on government grants, college or university funds and corporate support. Such operation pattern cannot last long. With the development of online teaching resources and the rise of online education market, resource users, including colleges and universities, college students and social workers, must pay to course-offering colleges and universities to obtain online teaching resources. Whether such payment is settled by means of tuition fee or certification fee, such issues as the design of payment or settlement platform, the amount of payment, etc. need to be considered comprehensively.

### 4.5 Evaluation Mechanism

As functions of the online teaching resources management platform continue to be enriched, its evaluation mechanism needs to be perfected as well. A reasonable evaluation mechanism, on the one hand, will give positive feedback to the resource supplier, so that the design of teaching resources can be better matched with users' demands and benefit both teachers and students. On the other hand, it can select the superior and eliminate the inferior online teaching resources, so as to improve the quality of online teaching resources. The evaluation of online teaching resources should consider basic features of network technology. Considering online teaching content, online teaching process and user interface interaction, etc., scientific and comprehensive evaluation indicators should be designed to avoid evaluation result deviations based on a single indicator.

**Acknowledgments.** The authors acknowledge supports received from (i) Project of Higher Education Teaching Research and Reform of Guangdong, China (No. GDJG20141027), (ii) Project of Education and Teaching Achievement Award the Innovation Funds of Guangdong, China (No. 55610148), and (iii) The Innovation Funds of Guangdong, China (No. 2014GXJK008).

## References

Six Universities in the Shipai Area. In: Self-Evaluation on the National College Students' Cultural Quality Education Base (2002)

Zheng, C.L., Shao, H.Y.: Research on the teaching resource sharing at college and university. Res. High. Eng. Educ. **3**, 97–102 (2010)

Zhou, Y., Chen, H., Zhang, Y.L.: On share-type quality teaching resources construction in tertiary institutions: an example of development of MOE state quality opec courses. High. Educ. Sanjiang **4**, 1–6 (2013)

Wang, Y.B.: The soul of MOOCs and its enlightenment and resources. J. High. Educ. **35**(1), 57–60 (2014)

He, K.H.: Research on the effects of information technology on education. J. Educ. Inf. Technol. **1**, 3–8 (2014)

Zhou, J.: Teaching evaluation is the key method to improve education quality. In: Presented at the Conference of Experience Sharing of Undergraduate Teaching (2006)

Ministry of Education of P.R.C. Key Points of Work in 2015

Ministry of Education of P.R.C.: Implementation Scheme for Building an Effective Mechanism Utilizing Information-Based Means to Expand The Coverage of High-Quality Educational Resources (2014)

Department of Education of Guangdong Province: Opinions on Credit System Management Implemented By Regular Institutions of Higher Education (2014)

Website of Teaching Community in Beijing Xueyuan Road. http://www.xueyuanlu.cn/

Course Electing Management System of Guangzhou Higher Education Mega. http://unitown.scnu.edu.cn/default.aspx?pid=2

# Analysis of Learner Timeout Behavior in Online Tests of a Bigdata Set Based on the OLAI Concept

Huixiao Le(✉) and Jiyou Jia

Department of Educational Technology, Graduate School of Education, Peking University, 5th Yiheyuan Road, Hai Dian, Beijing 100871, China
{lehuixiao,jjy}@pku.edu.cn

**Abstract.** Based on a dataset of more than 7.4 million records of learners' online tests activity in an online platform, and the concept of Online Learning Activity Index (OLAI) proposed by Jia and Yu (2017a and b), this paper analyzes the learners' timeout behaviors in online tests. Descriptive statistics and correlation analysis are conducted to find the general pattern and characteristics underneath the cases, for example, whether the amount of questions in a test influences learners' timeout behaviors. Taking OLAI and its three dimensions as the features, it's hard to find any significant distinction between the LTBs (Learner with Timeout Behaviors), and LNTBs (Learner with No Timeout Behaviors). However, learners may be more likely to cease answering questions when facing a test with a large number of questions. The findings' implication for online learning system design is discussed and further work is suggested.

**Keywords:** Online learning · Online learning activity index · OLAI
Learning analytics · Timeout behaviors

## 1 Introduction

### 1.1 Background

"Lexue 100" (Happy Learning for 100 Points, http://www.lexue100.com) is a web-based interactive learning system for school mathematics. A large number of corresponding quizzes are designed for the different versions of mathematics textbooks that are used in different provinces and metropolises in China. Each quiz is composed of a series of gap-filling or single-choice questions. So the question's standard answer is predefined and can be compared with the user's trial answer. The quiz score and feedback are instantly provided to the user, as soon as he or she submits the trial answers. Answering quizzes is the main learning activity in this system. Users are allowed to pass only if every answers they give get right response, meaning that if the first try is wrong, they will have to try again until the answer hits the point.

Mining learning activity data of some learners on this platform, figures like Fig. 1 are often met when histogram of learners' time consumption to complete a specific test


S. K. S. Cheung et al. (Eds.): ICTE 2018, CCIS 843, pp. 285–294, 2018.
https://doi.org/10.1007/978-981-13-0008-0_27

on the platform are checked. In these histograms, there is an apparent peak at 3600 s on the time axis.

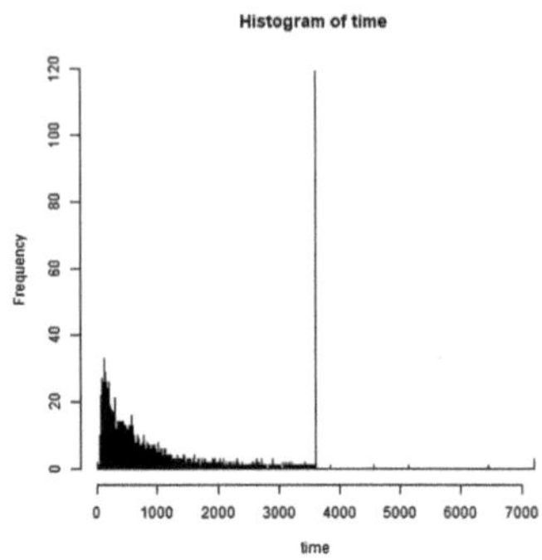


**Fig. 1.** Time frequency histogram of learners' time consumption to complete a test

When a learner does a test, his time consumption to complete the test will be recorded. If the time reaches an hour and the leaner has yet not submitted the answers, the session between the client and server will expire, and a value of 3600 will be recorded as his time consumption of doing this test.

In this research, Timeout Behavior is defined as the behavior exhibited by a learner who failed to submit the answers before the time limitation of the test runs out. Such a learner is named as Learner with Timeout Behaviors (LTB), while the opposite (those who always manage to finish test in time) is named Learner with No Timeout Behaviors (LNTB). The reasons for the generation of a Timeout Behavior can be varied, such as equipment failure by doing tests, the learner ceases to do the test deliberately, and so on.

### 1.2 Research Questions

This research is focused on the following two questions:

1. What are the characteristics of LTBs and LNTBs? Do they have some featured distinctions?
2. Does the amount of questions in a test will influence learners' Timeout Behaviors?

For the first problem, it's an attempt trying to discover the pattern or distinction between LTBs and LNTBs, which would be an interesting topic in the field of Learning Sciences. To answer the first problems, emphasis should be laid on employing an indicator which could represent learners' records of completing a test. Furthermore, comparisons between LTBs and LNTBs should be done.

For the second problem, the answer could offer not only the relationships between learners' Timeout Behaviors when doing a test and the amount of questions of the test, but also suggestions to optimize a test, by setting a decent amount of questions in a test so as to reduce the happening of Timeout Behaviors.

## 2 Relevant Studies

According to Jia and Yu (2017a), Analysis of online learning activities of has become an emerging field of research. Some scholars discussed the significance, necessities, and technical solutions of Learning Analysis such as Gu and Zhang (2011), Zheng and Yang (2016).

Wei (2011) applied conventional statistic methods combined with data visualization, clustering analysis and social network analysis to the analysis of data on a Moodle platform, and revealed the overall situation of interaction between the instructors and learners in online courses meanwhile discovered the learners' preference of visiting some modules and time to log in. Jia et al. (2014) conducted detailed analysis to data generated from MOOCs of Peking University, trying to find out the impact of a learner's online learning activities on his scholastic attainments on a course's level. Results of correlation analysis showed a strong positive relation between a learner's grades of daily quizzes together with his liveness in participating learning activities and scholastic attainments.

Jia and Yu (2017a) developed Learning Activity Index (LAI) and Online Learning Activity Index (OLAI) to evaluate how well a student completes an activity in terms of speed, quality and quantity. It showed that scores were strongly and positively correlated with OLAI, and OLAI can predict learning achievements in a satisfactory manner. Moreover, Jia and Yu (2017b) designed the personalized instructional strategies adaptive to the learner's OLAI and all the OLAI of the learning group members.

### 2.1 OLAI

According to discussions in Sect. 1.2, this research adopts OLAIMMA as the indicator to represent the learners' performance when completing an online test. "OLAI is used to demonstrate how well an online learning activity is going on". The value of OLAI is the sum of its three dimensions – "Speed", "Quality" and "Quantity".

Whenever a learner completes a test (including the situation when time runs out), the server will insert a new record including the time used to complete the test (usetime), the difference between a usetime and a standard time given by the system (difference), and a list that contains his every input into the input boxes (result). By parsing the result list, the amount of questions in a test (question_number), the attempts he made to answer a question (tries), times of his giving wrong answers (wrongs) and times of his guessing to cope with some questions (guesses) can be got. Listed are the formulas which describe how "Speed", "Quality" and "Quantity" can be calculated:

$$\text{Speed} = \text{difference}/(\text{usetime} + \text{difference}) \tag{1}$$

$$\text{Quality} = (\text{question\_number} - \text{guesses})/(\text{question\_number} + \text{tries}) \tag{2}$$

$$\text{Quality} = \text{question\_number}/\text{standard\_number} \tag{3}$$

$$\text{OLAI} = \text{Speed} + \text{Quality} + \text{Quantity} \tag{4}$$

OLAIMMA (OLAI Mean of All Activities) can reflect the general performance of a learner in a certain period of time. Analogously, it also has three dimensions: "Speed", "Quality" and "Quantity". Using OLAIMMA and its three dimensions, a relatively thorough indicator to describe a learners' general learning behavior is obtained.

# 3 Learners as Research Subject

For all the learners involved in the dataset, take all the records as the time extent, calculate each's OLAIMMA and a feature vector α with 4 dimensions is obtained, representing a learner's general performance in terms of "Speed", "Quality" and "Quantity".

$$\alpha = (\text{Speed}, \text{Quality}, \text{Quantity}, \text{OLAIMMA}) \tag{5}$$

Screen all the 98,720 learners involved, remove those learners who have less than 5 records involved in the dataset, and pick those who has at least one record in which the time used reaches 3,600, 9,255 learners are found to be LTBs, accounted for 13.7% of the population, while the rest of the learners are LNTBs (57,992 learners).

Using $r_c$ to reflect the tendency of a learner to have Timeout Behaviors, $r_c$ can be defined as follows. In formula 6, ct is the total counts of a learner's records in which the time used reaches 3600, c is total counts of the learner's records in the dataset.

$$r_c = c_t/c \tag{6}$$

## 3.1 Descriptive Statistics

Figure 2 is the histogram of LTBs, with $r_c$ being the x-axis and count be the y-axis.

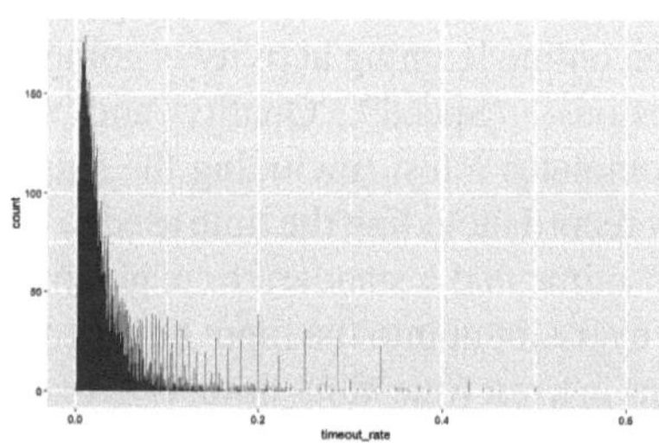


**Fig. 2.** rc-count histogram of LTBs

The maximum $r_c$ in LTBs is 0.61while the minimal is 0.00029. The mean and variance of $r_c$ is 0.04 and 0.0027. A more detailed description of LTBs is given in Table 1.

We compare LTBs and LNTBs in the perspective of "Speed", "Quality" and "Quantity", and make histograms of these two groups:

Figure 3 shows a figure consists of four histograms, in all the four histograms, red portion represents the LNTBs and green portion represents LTBs. The upper left one reveals the relation between "Speed" and count, meanwhile the x-axis of the upper right

**Table 1.** rc value, count and proportion in LTBs

| $r_c$ value | Count | Proportion in LTBs |
|---|---|---|
| [0,0.03) | 5,637 | 60.90% |
| [0.03,0.06) | 1,926 | 20.81% |
| [0.06,0.1) | 886 | 9.57% |
| [0.1,0.3) | 743 | 8.03% |
| [0.3,0.61) | 62 | 0.067% |

one is "Quality", "Quantity" for the lower left one and "OLAIMMA" for the lower right one. A more detailed comparison is given in Table 2.

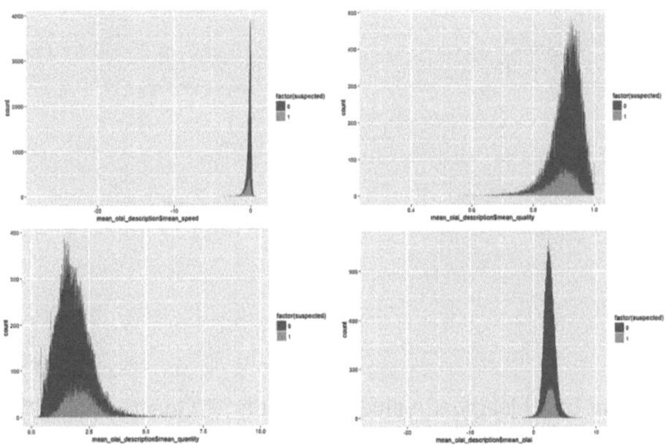

**Fig. 3.** Comparison of between LTBs and LNTBs, taking different dimensions of α as x-axis

**Table 2.** Detailed comparison of LTBs and LNTBs in four dimensions of α

| Dimension | Group | Mean | Variance | Maximum | Minimal |
|---|---|---|---|---|---|
| "Speed" | LTBs | −0.52 | 0.63 | 0.58 | −27.77 |
| | LNTBs | −0.22 | 0.17 | 0.84 | −25.45 |
| "Quality" | LTBs | 0.89 | 0.002 | 0.99 | 0.55 |
| | LNTBs | 0.91 | 0.002 | 1 | 0.27 |
| "Quantity" | LTBs | 2.11 | 0.42 | 9.87 | 0.34 |
| | LNTBs | 1.82 | 0.57 | 8.78 | 0.09 |
| OLAIMM A | LTBs | 2.48 | 1.13 | 10.03 | −25.60 |
| | LNTBs | 2.52 | 0.83 | 9.44 | −24.10 |

From the perspective of "Speed", LTBs and LNTBs are in right-skewed distribution, the mean "Speed" value of LNTBs is greater than LTBS, with a less variance. From the perspective of "Quality", the mean and variance of "Quality" value are nearly equal. From the perspective of "Quantity", the mean "Quantity" value of LTBS is greater than that of LNTBs while the variance is less LNTBs. From a more general point of view –

OLAIMMA, LTBs' mean value of OLAIMMA is greater than LNTBs and the variance is less.

Furthermore, for a specific learner, α can describe his or her general behaviors when doing online tests. Take two dimensions from "Speed", "Quality" and "Quantity" as the two axises of the scatter diagram each time and plot all the learners' value. Figure 4 is obtained.

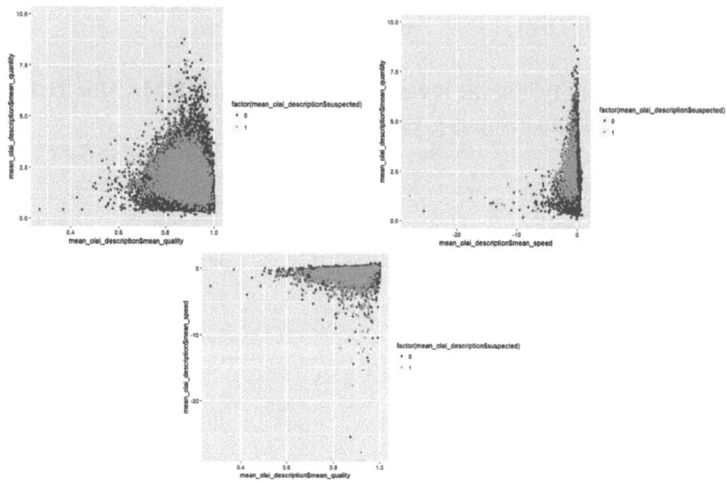

**Fig. 4.** Scatter diagrams of all learners' value of "Quality", "Quantity" and "Speed", taking two dimensions once as two axis. (Color figure online)

In Fig. 4, the red dots represent LNTBs and the green dots represent LTBs. The upper left one takes quality-quantity (x − y) as two axes, the upper right one takes speed-quantity and the lower one takes quality-speed.

### 3.2 Correlation Analysis

Taking $r_c$ and quality, $r_c$ and quantity, $r_c$ and speed, $r_c$ and OLAIMMA in the whole population (bind LTBs and LNTBs together) as the parameters of Pearson correlation analysis, the result is given in Table 3.

**Table 3.** Pearson correlation coefficient of $r_c$ with each of the dimensions in α

| | $r_c$ - quality | $r_c$ - quantity | $r_c$ - speed | $r_c$ - OLAIMMA |
|---|---|---|---|---|
| Pearson correlation coefficient | −0.17 | 0.17 | −0.32 | −0.044 |

The result shows that $r_c$ has weak negative correlation to "Quality", weak positive correlation to "Quantity" and moderate negative correlation to "Speed". Meanwhile, $r_c$ is uncorrelated to OLAIMMA.

### 3.3 Discussion

From the result of analysis above this issues deserve a prominent place in this section: It's hard to find a significant distinction between LNTBs and LTBs under the circumstance that $\alpha$ is used to represent the features of a learner's general behavior when doing online tests. Actually, the "Speed" value is directly related to Timeout Behaviors. Obviously formula 1 implies that if someone has Timeout Behaviors, his "Speed" value of OLAI will be significantly influenced and be set to a minimal value of all the learners who do the same test.

The "Quality" value shows a weak negative correlation with $r_c$, there could be two possible explanations for this: 1. The LNTBs are more likely to be more skilled in handling the test, which implies that they may have a better acquirement of knowledge. 2. Timeout Behaviors implies that the test is ended with several questions not answered. In this way, they will get a worse "Quality". Nevertheless, which may be the real reason (or both could be) of the negative correlation between "Quality" value and rc remains a problem.

The "Quantity" value shows a positive correlation with $r_c$, and the reason for this could be that all the learners are obligated to do the tests - if failed, another chance will be given until he passes the test. So once a record shows a Timeout Behavior, it also indicates that this time, the learner should have the test again, which also means that he will do more questions, accounting for a higher value of "Quantity". However, if this should be the only reason or there should be some other reasons for the positive correlation remains to be discovered.

OLAIMMA is the sum of the three values mentioned above, so it's not so surprising that it should indicate no significant differences between the LNTBs and LTBs.

## 4 Tests as Research Subject

According to Sect. 1.2, another research problem is to find out if the amount of questions in a test will influence learners' tendency to have Timeout Behaviors when doing the test.

Of all the 7.4 million records in the dataset, there are 26,555 tests with more than 20 counts (at least 20 learners have completed that test). Among those 26,555 tests, there are 8,983 TTBs, accounts for 33.9% of the population. $r_t$ is the indicator which reflects the proportion of leaners who fail to complete the test before time runs out.

$$r_t = c_1/r_t \tag{7}$$

In formula 7, $c_l$ is the count of the records of a test in which the time used exceeds 3600 s and c is the total count of the records of the test in the dataset.

### 4.1 Descriptive Statistics

For every test in TTBs, the mean value of $r_t$ is 0.025 and the variance is 0.0013. The value falls into 0.000119 to 0.43, among which the proportion of $r_t$ less than 0.1 accounts for 96.3% of TTBs.

A histogram is made to compare the TTBs and TNTBs (Fig. 5). In Fig. 5, the red portion is TNTBs and the green portion is TTBs. The x-axis is the amount of the questions in a test and the y-axis is the count.

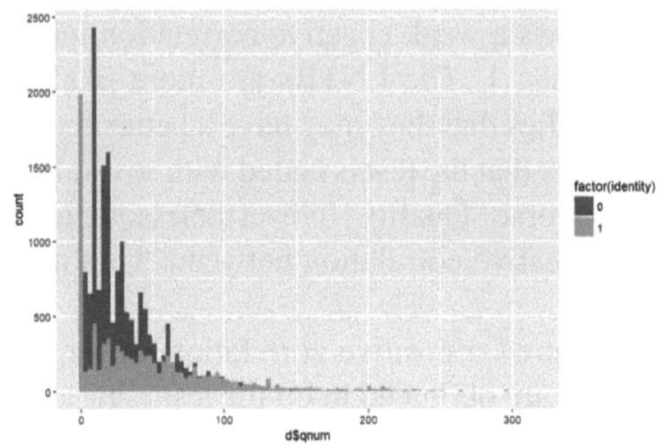


**Fig. 5.** Histogram of amount of questions in a test, comparing TTBs and TNTBs (Color figure online)

For all the tests in TNTBs, the mean value of the amount of questions in the test is 32.66 and the variance is 1,067.04. While for TTBs, the mean value reaches 45.96 and the variance is 2,466.79. Taking the question amount in a test as the x-axis and $r_t$ as the y-axis, the scatter diagram is shown as Fig. 6.

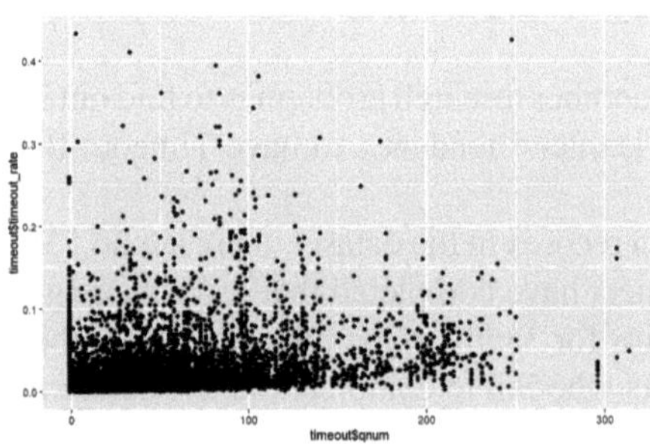


**Fig. 6.** Scatter diagram of TTBs

Taking the mean values of all the tests with a same amount of questions' $r_t$s as the y-axis, the scatter diagram is drawn as Fig. 7.

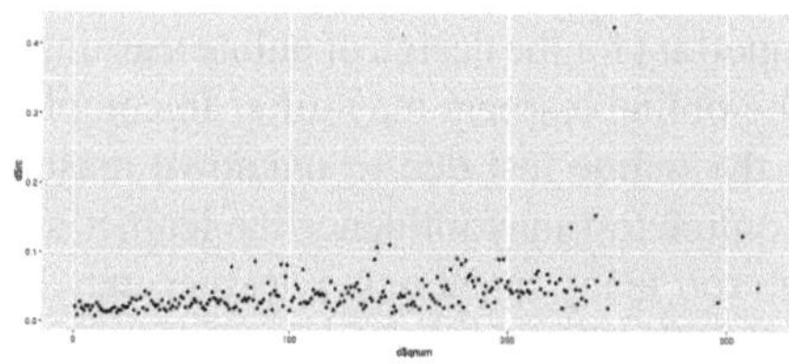

**Fig. 7.** Scatter diagram of TTBs, taking the mean values of all the tests with a same amount of questions' $r_t$s as the y-axis

The scatter diagram shows a great tendency that the $r_t$ will increase with the increasing of the questions in a test. The pearson correlation between the mean $r_t$ and the amount of questions in a test reaches 0.435.

Simple linear regression analysis is conducted and the result is:

$$y = 0.015x + 0.0002 \tag{8}$$

In formula 8, x and y corresponds to the variable of x-axis and y-axis in Fig. 7. Y is the mean $r_t$ values of all the tests with the same amount of questions and x is the amount of questions in a test. R-square of this linear regression is 0.18, which is not so optimal.

### 4.2 Correlation Analysis

Taking the question amount in a test and $r_t$ as two parameters, the Pearson correlation coefficient between the two factors is 0.233, which indicates that the question amount and $r_t$ has weak positive correlation.

### 4.3 Discussion

Result shows that the amount of questions in a test has a positive correlation to $r_t$, meanwhile the correlation between the mean $r_t$ and the amount of question is mediumly considerable. That means that learners may be more likely to cease or give up answering questions when facing a test with a larger number of questions.

## 5 Conclusion and Further Study

This research mines data from a mathematics online learning system and tries to answer the two questions: what are the characteristics of those online learners with timeout behaviors in online tests? Will the amount of questions in a test influence learners' timeout behaviors? Online Learning Activity Index (OLAI) is applied as the indicator to represent the characteristics of online tests. Through descriptive statistics and correlation analysis, the research comes up with two main findings. It's hard to find any significant distinction between the LTBs (Learner with Timeout Behaviors), and LNTBs (Learner with No Timeout Behaviors). However, learners may be more likely to cease answering questions when facing a test with a large number of questions.

Those findings are important for the design of online learning systems, and especially online tests. Although the online learners may differ in completing online tests, every one of them might quit the online test due to unknown reasons and become a LTB. Therefore the design of online test may influence the learner's behavior greatly. When doing an online test with too many questions, a learner may be frustrated or lose the patience to complete the test. So some mechanism to encourage and motivate the learner to go on completing the long test is required during the test, just as the strategies we proposed in previous studies (Jia and Yu 2017). An alternative approach is designing the test with not too many questions to relieve the learner's burden.

In the future we will try to explore the characteristics of learner groups classified by other identities, for example, to investigate the behavior difference between males versus females, senior students versus junior students, and from different provinces. We will also try to study the influence of different questions on learners' behavior. For example, how will the questions of difference difficulties impact learner's behavior? What are the characteristics of learner's learning behavior when doing different types of questions, such as blank filling, single or mulitiple choices and so on. It could be valuable if interesting findings were drawn from such studies, not merely because these can provide new research perspectives and evidence to the field of learning science, but also that these findings can support making a better design of online tests for different learners.

**Acknowledgement.** This research is supported by the project, "Lexue 100, Smart Education", of Beijing Lexue 100 Online Education Co., Ltd. The authors thank also all the teachers and students who have participated in the program.

## References

Gu, X., Zhang, J.: Learning analytics: the emerging data technology. J. Distance Educ. **30**(1), 18–25 (2011)

Jia, J., Miao, J., Wang, Q.: Analysis of learning behavior and effectiveness based on big data – taking six MOOC course as example. Ind. Inf. Educ. Technol. **09**, 23–29 (2014)

Jia, J., Yu, Y.: Analyzing learning activity index and online learning activity index. Distance Educ. China. **4**, 15–22 (2017a)

Jia, J., Yu, Y.: Online Learning Activity Index (OLAI) and its application for adaptive learning. In: Cheung, S.K.S., Kwok, L.F., Ma, W.W.K., Lee, L.K., Yang, H. (eds.) ICBL 2017. LNCS, vol. 10309, pp. 213–224. Springer, Cham (2017b). https://doi.org/10.1007/978-3-319-59360-9_19

Wei, S.: Research on data mining on Moodle platform - taking analyzing of an online course procedure as an example. Distance Educ. China. **01**, 24–30 (2011)

Zheng, X., Yang, J.: The learning analytics in higher education: progress, challenges and future directions. China Educ. Technol. **02**, 2–7 (2016)

# Author Index

MIX
Papier aus verantwortungsvollen Quellen
Paper from responsible sources
FSC® C105338

If you have any concerns about our products,
you can contact us on
**ProductSafety@springernature.com**

In case Publisher is established outside the EU,
the EU authorized representative is:
**Springer Nature Customer Service Center GmbH**
**Europaplatz 3, 69115 Heidelberg, Germany**

Printed by Libri Plureos GmbH
in Hamburg, Germany